Localism and the Ancient Greek City-State

Localism and the Ancient Greek City-State

HANS BECK

The University of Chicago Press
Chicago and London

The University of Chicago Press, Chicago 60637
The University of Chicago Press, Ltd., London
© 2020 by The University of Chicago
All rights reserved. No part of this book may be used or reproduced in any manner whatsoever without written permission, except in the case of brief quotations in critical articles and reviews. For more information, contact the University of Chicago Press, 1427 E. 60th St., Chicago, IL 60637.
Published 2020

29 28 27 26 25 24 23 22 21 20   1 2 3 4 5

ISBN-13: 978-0-226-71134-8 (cloth)
ISBN-13: 978-0-226-71148-5 (paper)
ISBN-13: 978-0-226-71151-5 (e-book)
DOI: https://doi.org/10.7208/chicago/9780226711515.001.0001

Library of Congress Cataloging-in-Publication Data

Names: Beck, Hans, 1969– author.
Title: Localism and the ancient Greek city-state / Hans Beck.
Description: Chicago : University of Chicago Press, 2020. | Includes bibliographical references and index.
Identifiers: LCCN 2019052261 | ISBN 9780226711348 (cloth) | ISBN 9780226711485 (paperback) | ISBN 9780226711515 (ebook)
Subjects: LSCH: City-states—Greece—History. | Local government—Greece—History.
Classification: LCC JC73 .B43 2020 | DDC 938—dc23
LC record available at https://lccn.loc.gov/2019052261

*To my dad
champion of the local
and to my boys
who navigate the global so easily*

Contents

Map viii
List of Illustrations ix
Preface xi

1 Localism and the Local in Ancient Greece 1
2 Attachment to the Land 43
3 Senses and Sensation 75
4 The Gods in Place 121
5 Big Politics, through the Local Lens 161
6 Toward a Local History of Ancient Greece 207

Acknowledgments 213
Notes 215
References 237
Index 261

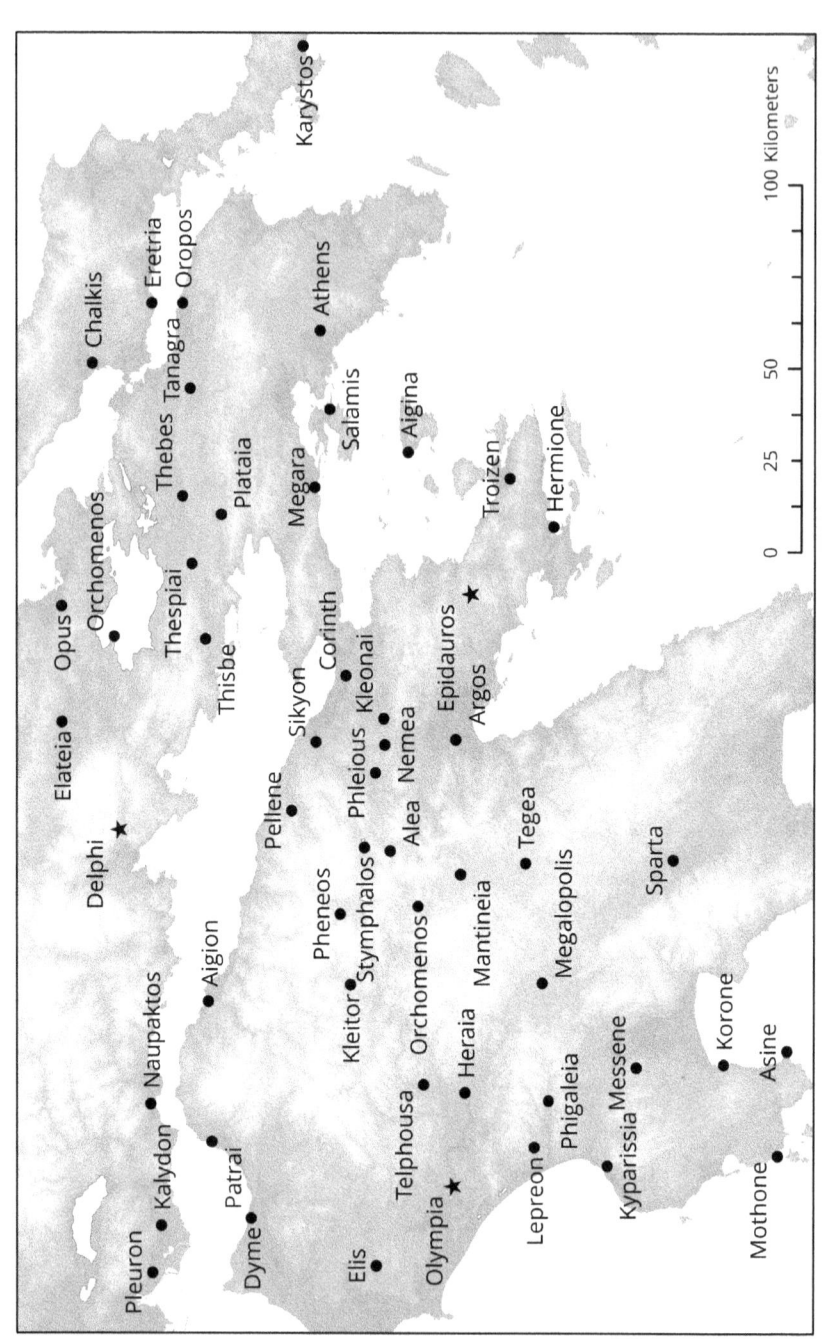

Map of Central and Southern Greece with city-states of a 200+ km² territory.

Illustrations

Map of Central and Southern Greece with city-states of a 200+ km² territory   viii
Fig. 1.1.   View across the plain of Phlious   13
Fig. 1.2.   Phliasian coinage, drachm and hemidrachm (late 5th century BCE)   16
Fig. 1.3.   "Knitting Knowledge: What the Hands Remember"   27
Fig. 1.4.   "Salt, Dry, Bottle, Can: On Preserving More than Protein"   28
Fig. 1.5.   Outline of local accumulation, real and imagined   31
Fig. 1.6.   Connectivity compass   38
Fig. 2.1.   Lakonian black-figure cup: Kadmos and the dragon   57
Fig. 2.2.   Borderlands of the Megarid, Attica, and Southern Boiotia   66
Fig. 2.3.   Calyx-krater: apotheosis of Herakles and nymphs   70
Fig. 3.1.   Didrachm from Selinus (late 6th century BCE)   82
Fig. 3.2.   Theban stater (early 4th century BCE)   93
Fig. 3.3.   Tanagra figurine (late 4th century BCE)   100
Fig. 3.4.   Distribution of coins in the stands of the stadium at Nemea   110
Fig. 4.1.   The storied world of Skillous and surroundings   135
Fig. 4.2.   Sacrifice to the nymphs from the cave at Pitsa   141
Fig. 4.3.   Map detailing the geography of the new cult law from Arkadia   159
Fig. 5.1.   Black-figure bowl: Procession to Athena Itonia in Boiotia (mid-6th century BCE)   200

Preface

The tidal wave of studies on connectivity and network exchanges in the ancient Mediterranean world has amounted to nothing but a true paradigm shift in classical studies. Albert-László Barabási's (2002) verdict that everything is connected to everything else, and that the connection matters, has fully arrived in our field. Along the way, scholars have established a potent theoretical framework that makes the tenets of globalization meaningful to the study of Greek and Roman antiquity. In both cases and, to be sure, under different premises, the exploration of sociocultural and economic exchanges in the Mediterranean, grounded in the distinctiveness of time, place, and culture, effected a knowledge advancement that is as extensive as it is exciting. A book on localism in ancient Greece might therefore appear against the spirit of the day.

Appearances can be deceptive. Globalization scholars recognize the importance of the local as a world where the strands of connectedness translate into real-life constellations, with all triggers and adaptations across the global/local binary. This is how, and why, the terms *glocal* and *glocalization* have entered the debate. In similar vein, the notion of "globalization from below" seeks to accentuate a bottom-up perspective on the process. Yet while the former part of the contraction *glocal* has received tremendous attention in scholarship, the latter continues to be neglected. Postcolonial theory has provided a forum for the development of ideas about the intrinsic value of local culture and "globalectics" (Ngũgĩ wa Thiong'o 2012). A full-fledged debate, however, remains out of sight. The most common view is to assign to the local the capacity to formulate counterstrategies and defend distinctiveness and individuality against the advancement of globalization—an intellectual figure that itself betrays an implicit primacy of the global over the local. The present book can and should be read as a complement to ongoing conversations about connectedness and globalization, and the forces they wield over humans across time. Indeed, as a sociocultural phenomenon with its own historical depth, the globalization paradigm requires that the local enter the scholarly dialogue as a quantity in its own right. The claim that is raised here is therefore straightforward, if not simple: that we should take the local seriously.

Microhistory, so prominent in the human sciences since the 1990s, makes an important contribution to this endeavor. The study of small constellations, often based on bodies of local documents from a narrow time period, offers valuable insights into the local horizon. In the study of the ancient Greek world, where such sources are of a limited availability, microhistory and local history are thus often considered the same. The trend to study larger questions through small places—cities, microregions, etc.—has become extremely influential, as it directs the focus of the investigation to city-states with only an average or low "fame score" (Josiah Ober). In doing so, local history beautifully captures the rich diversity of ancient Greek culture. But the writing of local history and the study of localism are two different exercises. The quest for the governing force of the local entails more than the narration of history in a discrete local context. Rather, it seeks to break into discourse environments that are not only confined in place but relate to it; that prioritize place, real and symbolic, as a source of inspiration and meaning; and, in turn, that receive orientation from the local horizon in changing circumstances that occur in the world writ large.

Classical Greece is particularly well-suited for this type of inquiry. Combining numerous city-states, each one energized by a vivid ideology of self-governance and independence, and shaped by a natural environment that is both dense and diverse in terms of climate, soils, and resources, Greek culture was geared toward local distinctiveness. As their world grew larger, from the Archaic period to the Hellenistic period, the Hellenes were exposed to ever-new degrees of connectedness. In the aftermath of the Persian Wars, and partly in response to them, Aegean Greece witnessed a dazzling increase in the interaction between communities. The driving themes of their interstate affairs inspired the Greeks to intensify their engagement in areas previously out of reach—the rapid rise of spheres of interest beyond the regional horizon of the polis and the establishment of a Panhellenic protocol of political practices and policies to govern their exchange were but two such themes. Survey archaeology has disclosed a substantial growth of settlements and population figures throughout mainland Greece in the period. In some places, the corresponding numbers reached an all-time peak. The demographic development was paralleled by new heights of economic productivity and trade.

PREFACE   xiii

Participation in interstate affairs and thriving cultural exchange further increased the volume of travel on land. At sea, technical innovation in shipbuilding and advanced nautical skills allowed communities to interact with each other faster than ever; on average, it would take less than a week to reach the most remote destinations in the Mediterranean world. All this is to say that Classical Greece was a tight, high-powered, interstate environment, one in which countless locally bound city-states grappled with the challenge to position themselves in a swiftly expanding universe of change.

I have spent much of my life thus far in Bavaria and Quebec, societies that are renowned for their marked localism. Whether I think of this as a blessing or a curse is difficult to tell. The choice depends on sentiments and convictions that are not only deep and wide, but, at times, contradictory. I would suspect that the embodied experience from daily interactions further informs the assessment, although I ought to acknowledge quickly that such encounters can be highly coincidental, sometimes random. In other words, there is a wide gulf between more general views of the world and the quotidian experience. In Bavaria, it is difficult to ignore, let alone escape from, the omnipresent articulation of bursting self-confidence in what is considered the supreme value of the Bavarian way of life; whereas in Quebec, the opposite, a lack of societal self-confidence, is not uncommon. A standard reaction to critical assertions about Quebec society is to fence them off as acts of Quebec-bashing and, hence, dismiss them as disingenuous to begin with.

From a scholarly point of view, what can be drawn from both examples is that parochial attitudes translate into a broad spectrum of communal beliefs. At the same time, they are united by the self-evident importance they bear for those who nourish them. They are real to society, true. If, as I believe, the accelerated process of globalization will also see an intensification of localism—for some, the rise of a neo-localism movement is approaching promptly—it will become even more critical for us to hear and to understand the local voice. In this sense, too, this study on ancient Greece is part of a wider conversation about one of the pressing challenges of the day.

1

Localism and the Local in Ancient Greece

Language is a curious thing. Take the harmless word *local*. In its most common usage, *local* appears in an attributive sense, as in local cuisines, local elites, or local weather. The word has hidden connotations of tininess. *Local* insinuates confinement in place and relevance; effectively, it suggests an implicit relation to something of greater exposure. This is even clearer with the noun, when the plural *locals* is used in a patronizing sense, referring to people with a limited understanding of prevailing complexities and a worldview that is characterized as parochial—another harmless word. All the while, *local* also triggers a different intervention. As early as 1983, the acclaimed film *Local Hero* captured the desire for deceleration and secludedness in times of rapid change. In the movie, both are found in fictional Ferness, a village along the remote shores of Scotland's North Atlantic coast. As the plot unfolds, Ferness becomes emblematic of a plain, authentic lifestyle. Although variously connected with the outside world by land and sea, the magnetic force of place ties the lead characters to the local horizon: its natural environment, social practices, and patterns of reasoning. The small town gradually reveals itself as *Gegenwelt* to global networks and faceless corporations, yet this innate quality of the local is understood only if and when translated into an embodied experience.

The movie played at a time when an all-new era of connectivity was only just beginning to loom on the horizon. As globalization turned from fiction to reality, the local became the live wire that grounded its critics, providing them with a robust alternative to the advancement of global capitalism. Prioritization of local governance, culture, and production soon inspired a towering wave of localism. Today, advocacy for the local might often be a commercial cliché or a slogan in support of frontline politics. But it can also be a potent response to the seismic shifts of globalization.

The charged semantics of the term *local* bear heavily on conversations about one of the most basic traits of ancient Greek history and culture: that is, that the city-states of Aegean Greece were through and through local formations. The typical Greek polis was a notoriously small enterprise, with a limited territory and a modest population size. Scholars estimate an average figure of less than ten thousand inhabitants, which puts the casual city-state in the range of a face-to-face society. Everything happened in a small environment. From storytelling to learned discourses in philosophy, from the creation of material styles to self-subsistent economic activities, and from the conduct of politics to the exercise of religion: the local world was the place where relevant conversations took place and related practices played out. It was a stage that was as real as it was inspirational, a rich source of meaning and orientation to all. This is of course not to deny the obvious, that ancient Greece, from the Archaic period on, was a world on its feet. A high degree of mobility and economic entanglement, powered by the adventurous spirit of heroic travelers and their desire for distant shores, induced all sorts of fluid connections near and far that energized Hellenic culture. But there was a notorious flipside, a subtle dialectic that tied those global exchanges to, and grounded them in, the local horizon.[1]

This book takes stock of the local part of the dialectic. The local, or epichoric, horizon of ancient Greece is both the subject and the scope of our investigation. Rather than projecting reductionist images of social slow motion or seclusion, the local lens captures a world of immediacy. As we shall see, the local was not merely subject to the call for self-governance (*autonomia*), articulated by a body of citizens whose political status was typically connected with landholding. Reference to the corresponding social ambience of a farmer's life, itself frequently associated with the tenets of a primitivist economy, doesn't suffice either to unravel the threads of local attachment. Instead, the local was fueled by charged ideas of belonging and intricate ways of knowing; it was an outlet of cultural creativity and competition; bristling with excitement and sensation; home to ambition and the celebration of sweet success; and the place where the community suffered from, and lived through, calamity and cataclysm. In this sense, the local canvas of ancient Greece was as rich and diverse as the human experience itself.

Place-Identity and Boundedness in a Connected World

It has often been remarked that the world of ancient Greece was shaped by fragmentation. Josiah Ober speaks of an "ecology of city-states" (2015, 21), implying that Classical Greece comprised countless poleis that were both united under a shared culture and segregated at the same time, similar to one another, yet different. Multiple circles of identity tied the city to the local, regional, and universal Panhellenic horizon. The pervasive study of these identities in literary traditions and material evidence is at the heart of our discipline. As the conversation continues, we are repeatedly reminded of the methodological challenges and conceptual caveats that permeate the debate. Modifiers of identity—for instance, ethnic identity, cultural identity, gender identity, or micro-identity—have been found as a convenient way out of the dilemma, but here too, scholarship warns us that these branches cannot easily be separated from one another. Where modified strands of identity appear, the isolation is heuristic rather than real, formulated in response to practical needs in the organization of scholarship. What figures as a modified register of identity in research, in real life was, and always is, inextricably intertwined with other circles of identity.[2]

The rise of place as a conceptual paradigm in the human and social sciences, while remarkable in itself, has resuscitated yet another identity in scholarship. In the words of Peregrine Horden and Nicholas Purcell, there is a staggering new interest in the study of places with a "distinctive identity derived from the set of available opportunities and the particular interplay of human responses to them" (2000, 80). Spurred by extensive and exciting conversations about the social constructions of space, the study of definite place has been brought to the scholarly agenda with full force. The trend is further supported by the creative application of Global Positioning Systems (GPS) in the human sciences to collect, sort, and visualize spatial data, which empowers research on the question of how location determines a community's place in the world. With the arrival of a wealth of new conceptual and technological advances, inquiries into place and identity have gained an all-new momentum both in and across a variety of disciplines, including history and historical geography, sociology, anthropology, and the neurosciences. Along the way, the notion of an identity of place has joined the canon of modified identities.

The study of place-based identity targets the linkage between people and the world around them—for instance, how people develop attitudes about urban designs, landscapes, environments, and ecosystems. The resulting spatial psychologies all feed off of place in one way or another. Place provides the real or imagined frame of reference for the identity that is associated with it: for politicized forms of identity, such a local point of reference appears quintessential (Ulf 2009, 224). Unlike a local identity, commonly understood as a sentiment of belonging to a locally confined group of people, the identity of place is energized by place itself. It is filled with meaning that relates to and derives from locality. This is also why identities of place and their expression in custom and culture have the capacity to cut across groups that are otherwise often segregated or marginalized. The identity of place blurs social divisions and hierarchies, although it obviously doesn't discard them altogether. Shaping images—real and of the mind—of local distinctiveness, the identity of place reverberates across different segments of society. Beyond the group(s) within, it also informs the way in which people from outside (travelers, visitors) experience a particular place. Couched in a discrete locality, it inspires a local discourse environment (below) that is discernable from other such environments.[3]

The interplay between place and identity is both obvious and complicated. In the study of ancient Greece, the alliance is undercut by the dynamics of two powerful movements. The first is the issue of displacement. It is easy to see how the enforced displacement of individuals, groups of people, or entire societies disrupts sentiments of belonging to and association with place. For the world of Classical Greece, it has been argued that migration, displacement, and mass relocation, voluntary or enforced, were not only central to the survival and viability of Hellenic culture but key to its success. Exile and diaspora were prominent features in Greek society—so prominent that they qualify as landmarks in the formulation of a Greek migrant identity (another modified identity).[4] All the while, it is worth recalling that the majority of all Greek city-states, though they experienced the anguish of war, natural catastrophe, or violent civil strife and the displacement that came with these horrors, were settlements with a remarkable continuity in place, many of them throughout Graeco-Roman antiquity.

For the age of the so-called Great Colonization, from the eighth century BCE to the end of the sixth, several cities exported sizeable proportions of their inhabitants overseas. It is debatable just how sizeable the number of emigrants was. The *Stanford Polis Project* has calculated that only 8 percent of all known poleis (eighty-one in total) embraced the role of a mother-city—that is, they sent out colonies or piggybacked onto another city's colonizing activities. Ancient Greece has been labeled a wandering culture, but throughout the long duration of their history, many cities had only limited or no bonds with diaspora populations on the remote shores of the Mediterranean or the Black Sea from previous acts of displacement.[5]

The second jeopardy relates to the first, yet it weighs more heavily. It is the notion of connectedness in general, which significantly complicates the twin concept of place and identity. It has become a truism to note that everything is connected to everything else (see "Linked," Albert-László Barabási's popular study on the science of networks [2002]). Networks adhere, argues Barabási, to relatively simple laws and structures; in fact, this simplicity explains why they are so pervasive. As the network expands horizontally, it doesn't just imprint upon its local nodes (societies, economies, groups of friends, etc.), it alters the morphology of their being. Among the most eminent consequences of this is the transformation of the time and space continuum into which local nodes are typically nested. Time is felt differently, simply because of the high volume and speed of communication. Place, too, forfeits its physicality. For network participants, location, distance, and physical boundaries no longer play a critical role in many relationships, as these are overcome by new modes of communication and a sense of proximity, for good or for ill.

Social media users will immediately attest to the force at stake, as will those of us upon whom the social media communications of others (e.g., tweets) are forced via more traditional news channels. Network societies, in the description of Manuel Castells, adhere to a grammar of loosely structured, horizontal connections that marginalize more conventional categories such as "top and bottom" or "center and periphery." In a network society, the new benchmark is one of belonging to the network as such. Effectively, the development of a connected mindset is not only determined by a new degree of linkages and information flow, but by the tacit consent of participants to adhere to the recalibration of time and space as dictated by the network.[6]

Such a formative quality of the network is certainly also true for its most extensive manifestation, that is, in the global context. Approaches to the history of premodern societies through the lens of global network science have become immensely influential. In the study of the ancient (Greek) Mediterranean, the notion of globalization has become a salient paradigm.[7] Recent research has demonstrated how, from the Archaic period, shifting horizons of engagement created a new kind of Hellenic convergence in the Mediterranean basin. In this approach, the Mediterranean figures both as an analytic unit of and backdrop for the investigation, which has given rise to the label Mediterraneanization—an awkward term, to be sure, but the emphasis on process rather than timeless Mediterraneanism is important. Mediterraneanization thinks through the obvious: that is, that locally encoded, bounded cultures are never pristine but are energized by connections near and far. Material evidence casts a spotlight on those connections and their resonance in everyday practices: for instance, in securing raw materials, developing crafts, trading objects, and the conspicuous consumption of imported goods. Drawing on advanced readings of materiality and its entanglement with human practice as it transpires from cultural theory, Mediterraneanization studies shed new light on how people in Graeco-Roman antiquity experienced the world and how this experience was shaped by networking activities across the sea.[8]

Local boundedness was an important part of the mix. Indeed, Mediterraneanization suggests that the interrelations between bounded cultures were so deeply entangled that this altered the conventional binary of local and global. Each end of the binary infiltrated the other; both were intertwined, and the relation was exposed to accelerated adaptation and change over time. This is how, and why, the word *glocal* has entered the debate, which has become so prominent in recent humanities and social sciences research. According to the conventional cycle of cross-fertilization between the local and the global, globalization triggers an increasing sense of disconnection from the local, or delocalization. This fuels a new need of locality; beyond its casual meaning of having a location, the term denotes the long-standing patterns that emerge from the association with the local, including all expressions of local culture, knowledge production, and communal conviction, each one in relation to the local horizon that inspires it. In its most immediate variant, this need of locality inspires the sentiment of localism: that is, a mindset that prioritizes the sum of these local expressions and experiences over alternative sources of meaning from outside the community. Localism, in turn, challenges the basic tenets of globalization. *Glocal* indicates that the rotations in this cycle happen all at once, signaling a hybridization of the ways in which existing sociocultural practices are recombined with new forms and in new practices.[9]

In a study that is nothing short of ingenious, Irad Malkin has made these tenets fruitful for the scholarly exploration of ancient Greece. His recent book on connectivity in the Greek Mediterranean (2011) examines the multiple networks of colonization, commerce, and religion that allowed Hellenes near and far to interact with increasing frequency. This "small Greek world," Malkin argues, witnessed a persistent increase in its connectedness. The necessary prerequisites in infrastructure and technology behind this are easy to pin down: improved navigation at sea and developing road networks on land; increasing volume of trade in response to the rising demands of urban societies; advanced security of travel, and so forth. Yet Malkin's analysis extends beyond such material improvements. Drawing on network theories that are inspired by social media communication on the internet, he explains how networks constitute a particular type of social morphology. We just noted how networks are prone to trigger a shift in the mindsets of those who engage in them, and how they undermine the juxtaposition of near and far. In the concrete terms of ancient Greece, and according to Malkin: despite the vast distances between them, the Greeks of the Mediterranean basin occupied a world that was both large and small at the same time. The paradox is resolved with reference to the omnipresence of tightly meshed networks that provided the infrastructure and interface of interaction. In this "Hellenic Wide Web," the boundedness of place was subject to high-powered connectedness that added its own taste to prevailing identities of place.

Hybridization does not nullify the inherent quality of the local—on the contrary. Arjun Appadurai has suggested that networking and globalization processes be viewed not as heavy-handed developments that force themselves onto defenseless, passive local worlds. Instead, he charts globalization as a "localizing process," one that happens also "from below" rather than being top-down only. This view fully appreciates the role of the local as a feeder of universal networking processes. Appadurai's model warns us not to subscribe to connected master narratives that discount complex combinations of local diversity, difference, and distinction. A similar warning was issued by Tamar Hodos, who advocates for the deconstruction of global generalizations that occlude the "multicoded nature of cultural materials and beliefs."[10]

It is intriguing to see how this aspect of globalization, its reliance on bounded place and local culture, takes stock, implicitly, of Fernand Braudel's *longue durée* of social, economic, and cultural developments. In his masterful examination of Mediterranean microhistories, small areas of land and their parochial communities, Braudel detected a striking resilience of local thought and action. This long duration of history in the microrealms of the Mediterranean was out of sync, Braudel argued, with the great waves of *histoire événementielle*, the history of events and people who were tied together in the unified space of the Mediterranean. Each of these histories followed a different pace and trajectory. Appadurai's "globalization from below" adjusts this view, evoking a quintessentially post-Braudelian picture: the bounded, geographically determined microregions of the Mediterranean appear as powerful engines in an equally powerful process of network exchange. Rather than a mere vignette of a *longue durée*, Appadurai's local is not out of sync with the global but equally dynamic, fast-changing, and multicoded.[11]

The galvanizing amount of scholarship on networks, connectivity, and exchanges in and across the ancient Mediterranean has altered the landscape in classical studies. While the strengths of the approach are evident, few have commented on the limitations of the network paradigm to capture the vertical depths of the lived experience—in power relations, social configurations, cultural expressions, and so forth—that was so characteristic of the Greek city. We will return to this aspect further below. As the Mediterranean convergence took shape, radiating fascination and buzzing with opportunity, the vast number of people continued to live in bounded environments that were formative to their everyday social, economic, and mental positioning. In their world, the identity-forming force of place was omnipresent. We will get a better sense of this when we explore how place was fused with local custom and culture.

(Local) Custom Is King

In Greek literature the local figures as a sphere where cultural distinction meets with definite place. The two are interlocked, each drawing inspiration from the other. Pindar declared in a renowned passage that "custom is the king of all" (frag. 169a Race). The Greek word for "custom" here, *nomos*, also means "usage" and "law." There is a lively debate about what precisely Pindar meant by *nomos*. From Herodotus, who also cites Pindar's lines in 3.38.4, it is clear that the notion of habitual practice, and in this sense custom, was among the most common understandings of Pindar's verses.[12] Reference to the governing force of custom shows an alert sense of diversity. It implies a multicoded nature of materials and beliefs, the type of fragmentation we encountered above and that is so critical for our assessment of Greek culture. Communal practices might be carried out in one way or another, implies Pindar, whereby the judgment of proper conduct, its accordance with custom, largely depends on preconceptions that are entrenched in society. Similar to what Michel Foucault labeled a regime of truth, Pindar's rule of custom emanates from a wide range of communal convictions that allow societies to steer through the vagaries of their everyday existence. The verdict that something is "done in this way or that" or "not done at all" is informed by self-referential loops of social practice rather than careful deliberation, loops that adhere to implicit codes and collective symbols; to patterns of meaning and repertoires of reasoning; and to a particular type of knowledge that is in itself "nomological," imparting all interpersonal communication in society with the guiding force of *nomos*. We note that the validity of taken-for-granted routines and their translation into regimes of custom, appropriateness, and truth are subject to boundaries. They are confined by society. In each society reigns a different regime of custom or truth.[13]

We do not know the point of reference of the "custom is king" fragment—that is, whose custom? In Herodotus, the discussion is couched in the comparison of Indian and Greek customs, with Persia in-between. From Xenophon's writings, we learn that the force of *nomos* not only played out in different civilizations. In the everyday lives of the Greeks, the most common arena for the rule of custom to commence was that of the small city-state. Citing the Pythia as his authority (a universal authority!), Xenophon states that "to follow the custom (*nomos*) of the polis" is the sure compass to navigate through the shoals of appropriateness. Local custom, he asserts, is "the right way" (*Mem.* 1.3.1). Despite all Hellenic communality and cultural coherence, each city-state fostered its own regime of truth. It is difficult, if not impossible, to determine the proportions of universal coherence and local idiosyncrasy; presumably this, too, varied from city to city. Be that as it may, in the lived experience of the polis, local custom was king.[14]

The fusion with place provided further charge. Greek literature of all ages was fascinated with the physical entrenchment of *nomos*. Ever since Homer's poetry, we detect an almost voyeuristic interest in discrete place and local practice—and the translation of both into social order. For instance, the Phaiakians enjoyed "unfailing abundance" (*Od.* 7.99) derived from their fertile fields as much as from good governance. The Lotus-eaters were consumers of intoxicating flowers from a "rich land" (*Od.* 23.311) that sent them to peaceful apathy. The infamous Cyclops, insolent and lawless dwellers in hollow caves on mountains, lacked every societal advancement whatsoever (*Od.* bk. 9). Arguably, these examples are drawn from remote fantasy corners of the Mediterranean world. Yet the same curiosity in place shines through in the portrayal of local distinction in Greece itself. Countless examples in the Homeric epic identify cities with topographical markers that evoke images of a real environment (steep, grassy, stony, etc.). Identification of sites through human practice expands on the idea: while some cities were "famed for walls," "well-built," "rich in flocks," others were renowned for "warriors well-skilled in fight" or "of horses best by far."[15]

In each of these examples, local distinction was highlighted through the amalgamation of human practice with place. By the fifth century BCE, it had become a common exercise to list local labels in the form of literary chains that were as elegant as they appeared erudite. It is again Pindar who attests to the idea in an exemplary manner. From the Taygetos, he reminds his audience, comes "the Lakonian dog, the smartest creature for chasing down prey; goats from Skyros are best for milking; arms from Argos; the chariot from Thebes; from Sicily of the splendid fruit seek a sophistically manufactured mule car." The comic poet Antiphanes (fourth century BCE) enumerated "from Elis the cook, from Argos the cauldron, from Phlious wine, from Corinth bedspreads, fish from Sikyon, flute girls from Aigion, . . . perfumes from Athens, eel from Boiotia." Visual representations lent vividness to the voice. In Eupolis's *Cities* (performed around 420 BCE), the allied cities of Athens were brought onto the stage as chorus, each one displaying its local characteristics.[16] Enumerations such as these were subject to context and convenience. Also, the issue of positionality weighs heavily on how we read each stated example; we shall return to this below, when the discussion of local idiosyncrasy will be led in a more detailed manner (chapter 3). The mindset is, however, revealing, as it pays attention and gives voice to the diversification of cultural expertise in ancient Greece.

Much later, by the second century CE, Ptolemy of Alexandria proposed an all-new literary genre to capture this diversity. Ptolemy's topic was world cartography (*geōgraphia*), a subject that saw the world as a single, continuous entity. To highlight this universal trait of *geōgraphia*, he contrasted it with what he called *chōrographia*, that is, the study of definite place (here labeled *chōra*, "country"; see below). In Ptolemy's words, chorography "sets out the individual localities, each one independently and by itself, registering everything practically to the least thing therein, for example harbours, towns, districts, branches of principal rivers, and so on" (*Geog.* 1.1). Chorography was characterized by small-scale, often minute perspectivation, a compartmentalized endeavor. But as Ptolemy continues, he asserts that different economies of scale between geography (big picture) and chorography (small picture) did not translate into corresponding economies of meaning (lots of meaning vs. little meaning). For the geography of place "deals above all with the qualities . . . of the things it sets down" (1.1); hence its quest both for plurality and peculiarity. Chorography thus traced the outlines of a particular entity, one where the quantifications of scalar geography were outweighed by the embodied experience.[17]

Ptolemy's *Geography* reminds us that the epichoric world of the city not only spoke to physical realities, but carried its own weight as a discursive quantity. This notion, too, stretches back to the beginnings of Greek literature. The Homeric tradition might have satisfied all sorts of fascinations across the sea, yet not everyone shared in this allure. Among the most outspoken writers to praise the small world in which they lived were Hesiod of Askra and Theognis of Megara. Indeed, it is captivating to see how the dichotomous opposition of global (Homer) and local (Hesiod) is foundational to Greek tradition. In antiquity, this was articulated by means of an imagined poetical contest in which both singers were judged according to the value their poetry had for the polis. We note in passing that Homer, the most eminent voice of distant worlds, was defeated by Hesiod, notorious for his local attitude. In the contest between glamorous globalization and parochial polis, the latter won first prize.[18]

Like Hesiod, Theognis had traveled quite a bit (just how far is debated), and, like Hesiod, he declared his hometown the ultimate place where he would pursue his goals in life. As we shall see, this appreciation of place was neither necessarily topical nor was it driven by sentiments of nostalgia, let alone the desire for deceleration. What appeared as a local backwater to others was a source of meaning to Hesiod and Theognis, a realm where human ambition was given place. In the later sixth century BCE, Phokylides of Miletus praised the "small polis on a rock" as a spring of social meaning, because it provided its inhabitants with purpose and mindfulness, even if they lived in a difficult location ("on a rock": chapter 2).

The idea of a small place as stage of meaningful communal interaction is also prominent in Greek political thought. Archytas (c. 428 BCE), acclaimed polymath from Taras, was said to have established the theoretical foundations of studies of place and its ontological quality, although we know only a little about his teachings.[19] One generation later, the field was in any case altered by Aristotle. According to Aristotle, one of the main characteristics of a polis was that its people lived in a common locality (a *koinōnia tou topou*), where they shared laws, engaged in economic activities, and had sex (*Pol.* 1280b). In Aristotle's view, communal action was at the heart of the polis; hence the emphasis on various types of human agency (politics, economy, religion, lovemaking, etc.). Yet, in order to play out in a purposeful manner and, effectively, allow various groups of people to form a community, their agency required a definite place. Again, in Aristotle's words, the condition of the good polis did not commence unless its participating members "inhabit one and the same place" (*topos*: 1280b37). He also offers an example: if Megara and Corinth, situated on either side of the isthmus, had a contiguous city wall, joint laws, and other regulations to govern their affairs collectively, they still wouldn't be a city-state, because this dual city lacked a prime quality of the polis—its inhabitants did not live in the same spot.[20]

Curiously enough, Corinth did actually embark on a dual city project for a few years in the early fourth century BCE, not with Megara but with its southern neighbor and longtime rival, Argos.[21] If, according to Aristotle, the integration of two cities did not result in a new polis, because its inhabitants did not live in a common locality, then a further issue arises: the question about the size and shape of local place. The answer requires a full-fledged attempt to conceptualize the local in ancient Greece. Before we turn to this, however, our findings so far merit the discussion of a first, exemplary image of an identity of place.

Local Approximations: Valley, Vine, and Views of Centrality

We have now established how the nexus of place and culture was a commonplace in Greek renderings of the world. As much as the omnipresence of networks might have fostered a connected mindset, this ethos is only understood when complemented with the prevailing sentiment of place. In Xenophon's *Hellenika*, we find an exemplary case of how such a sentiment translated into the lived experience of the community. Our example comes from Xenophon's discussion of Phlious, a city-state in the northeastern quadrant of the Peloponnese. Situated two kilometers north of the modern town of Nemea, ancient Phlious was a microcosm of its own. The settlement occupied a low ridge on one side of a valley that is ringed by high mountains. Two extensive archaeological and geoarchaeological survey projects have brought to light the complex relation between human agency and the natural environment in the Phlious basin.[22] The Asopos River winds through the plain to Sikyon about 20 km north on the Corinthian Gulf. The alluvial soils of the Phliasia, in conjunction with the prevailing microclimate, provided ideal conditions for the cultivation of wines and grains. The former was a celebrated brand label already by the fourth century BCE. Today, the plain is almost entirely used as vine-growing region of the famous Nemean wines, including its famed Agiorgitiko grape, a much-appreciated commodity on markets around the world.[23]

According to the estimations of the Copenhagen Polis Centre, the combined territory of city and hinterland, *astu* and *chōra*, was about 135 km^2, which made Phlious a mid-size town. Xenophon (*Hell.* 5.3.16) states that the city had five thousand adult male citizens (≈ twenty thousand inhabitants?), a number that seems exaggerated both in relation to the polis territory and to what is known otherwise about the size of Phliasian military contingents. But even when we prefer a lower figure, it is clear that Classical Phlious was among the most populous settlements in the Peloponnese.[24]

Geopolitically, the Phliasia was not located on a major travel artery, yet it was only a short distance away from the main highway into the Peloponnese, the road from Corinth to Argos through the Nemea Valley five kilometers to the east. Near the crossroads of the movements of armies, goods, and ideas, the Phliasians occupied a special place. Xenophon relates how the land—that is, the narrow topography of acropolis, urban center, countryside, and border forts in the hills—provided the backdrop for a special kind of local attitude. The inhabitants of this polis, he found, embodied a degree of loyalty and stout endurance (*karteria*: *Hell.* 7.2.17), even under the grimmest of circumstances, that made them exemplary among the Hellenes. In support of this verdict, Xenophon adduces a plethora of military encounters in the Phliasia (7.2.2–23). Each of those incidents documented how the Phliasians held on to their place: they fended off invaders, often through tactical operations in the urban terrain itself; they secured supply lines along itineraries that were known to the locals only; and they struggled, and succeeded, with the task of repatriating exiled citizens and restoring their previous rights and ownership of landed property in the *chōra*.

FIGURE 1.1. View across the plain of Phlious, from the agora to the west. In the background, the Phliasia is bordered by the Arkadian mountains. © 2018 Hans Beck.

Xenophon's narrative is evidently exaggerated and charged with moral undertones. At some point in the 380s BCE, due to Agesilaos's intervention, the government of Phlious changed to an oligarchy. Praise for the loyalty of the new citizen body to Sparta and to Agesilaos in particular, Xenophon's longtime friend and admired hero, appeared a natural thing. If Phlious's loyalty, as Xenophon suggests, extended to the years after the Battle of Leuktra, despite enormous pressures from outside, such praise was even more deserved. Note, however, how Xenophon's treatment of the city also shows sympathy to the previous democratic regime, which displayed similar characteristics (*Hell.* 5.3.10–17). It is therefore too simple to dismiss Xenophon's assessment on the grounds of personal bias.[25]

Beyond the challenges from critical analysis of the literary account, the quest for local distinctiveness is complicated by universal paradigms as we encounter them in the Phliasia. For instance, the city's locality, on a slanted hill that descends toward a fertile plain with rich water supplies (fig. 1.1), was something that Phlious shared with countless other city-states; the settlement pattern was so common that it found its way into Aristotle's discussion of the ideal location of a state.[26] The same goes for the agricultural produce in the *chōra* (olives, wines, and grains), which represents the food groups of the so-called Mediterranean triad; although, as we shall see, it is debatable how compelling this modern concept is in relation to the evidence from antiquity (see chapter 3).

With these caveats in mind, there were formidable local distinctions. The climate in the microregion of the Phliasia (altitude 270–80 m) is noticeably different from that in the upland plain of Arkadian Stymphalos (altitude 642 m) in the west and the Sikyonia to the north, with its marked maritime conditions. Differences in temperature and barometric pressure cause significant local winds in the neighboring territories, particularly in the fall, whereas the Phliasia is pleasantly protected. Sandwiched between the Argolid and Arkadia, with its typical inland weather conditions, Phlious marks an intermediary spot between maritime and continental climate zones. The relative secludedness of the valley has attracted sedimentological and microclimatological studies that inform predications about local vegetation patterns as early as the Pleistocene.[27]

Relations with their neighbors informed the way the Phliasians viewed the world. Most of the surrounding cities were, arguably, more potent than Phlious itself: Sikyon, Corinth, Argos, and Mantineia all fall within the radius of 45 km or less—that is, less than a day's journey on horseback. In politics, local conversations were thus tacitly shaped by a hardwired reality: as inhabitants of an independent city-state, the Phliasians couldn't ignore the fact that they were exposed to the vagaries of power politics in the Peloponnese and beyond. Much of Phlious's localism was relational, formulated and sharpened in juxtaposition to the political and economic success of others. If we follow Xenophon, the Phliasians responded to this with a sense of steadfastness. In the attempt to stand their ground, the locals, in all likelihood, drew inspiration from the land as such. Xenophon portrays both the city and its hinterland as battlegrounds, with enemies mounting walls on ladders; defenders showering them with arrows; skirmishes over supplies in the countryside, and so on. Yet the land was more than a battlefield. Beyond violent eruptions such as the ones described by Xenophon, the Phliasia provided a rich source of meaning to its inhabitants.[28]

When Pausanias visited the city in the second century CE, he found it flourishing (2.13.3–8). At least a dozen religious and profane sites were well maintained. Among these, he saw a grove of cypress trees and a sanctuary on the acropolis, both of which were "of ancient times" (3). There was also a bronze statue of Artemis, which appeared old (5). In the marketplace, Pausanias saw a bronze goat mostly covered with gold; the votive offering was made to protect the most precious Phliasian commodity, the vine, which at the time of the rising constellation of the Goat was threatened by overnight frost. In close vicinity to the goat stood the tomb of the celebrated tragedian Aristinas, son of another famous playwright, Pratinas (6). Both were native sons of Phlious. They had competed in tragic competitions in Athens and elsewhere in the first half of the fifth century BCE. Their works were among the most eminent pieces of the local cultural legacy; we can easily imagine how they were put on stage in the nearby theater that Pausanias also saw (5). In conjunction with a sacred stone or building structure that the locals referred to as "navel" (*omphalos*: 7), Pausanias learned from his informants that the people of Phlious viewed their valley as the center of the Peloponnese; hence the idea of the *omphalos*. According to another tradition, the city prided itself on a visit by Herakles, who had passed through, the locals explained, on his return to Greece from Libya. Memories of the visit were kept alive by a shrine with an ensemble of stone sculptures that recollected a legendary banquet scene showing Herakles and his Phliasian hosts (8).

Pausanias's description, along with Xenophon's stories from the battlefield, have triggered a fair number of attempts to identify the scattered archaeological remains in the plain, albeit with limited success. The likely identification of the site of Keleai (Paus. 2.14.1), an extra-urban sanctuary where mystery rites in honor of Demeter were performed and that might have been connected to the city by a paved road, is a notable exception.[29] The methodological challenges at this intersection of archaeology and literary analysis are obvious. More often than not, the age of monuments and landmarks described by the second-century CE traveler is difficult to ascertain. Take the case of the partly gilded goat in the agora, dedicated to protect vine stocks against frost damage. Praise for Phliasian wine in the Classical period (above) suggests that its cultivation was more than just an agricultural activity; long before Pausanias's days, it was a matter of local distinction and pride. Climatic conditions in the plain will have changed little over time, so the threat of frost damage was presumably perpetual. In light of such jeopardy, aversion rituals must have appeared an apt strategy of communal self-immunization against potential losses of the grape harvest. While the general constellation is clear, it is unclear when the Phliasians dedicated the bronze goat in the agora.

With the challenge of time comes that of changes in meaning. When Pausanias heard legendary tales from his informants, both the narrative and the meaning of those traditions varied immensely over time, from their inception and early dissemination to his own days. At least in the cases where Pausanias speaks of "ancient" stories and practices or buildings of old, it is commonly assumed that they relate to traditions from the Archaic or Classical periods, the grandeur of Greece, which Pausanias had found so captivating. But often we can't go further than that in our attempt to pinpoint time.[30]

Traditions about the *omphalos*—also encountered by Pausanias—almost certainly sprouted in the fifth century BCE. From the 430s BCE and through the fourth century, a series of silver coins from Phlious bear a wheel with four pellets, one in each corner of an incuse square on the reverse (fig. 1.2). Their weight follows the Aiginetan standard, which indicates easy exchanges with emissions from the economically powerful mints in Sikyon and Argos nearby

FIGURE 1.2. Drachm (left) and hemidrachm (right) from Phlious (420 BCE). The zodiacal wheel is identified by four pellets in an incuse square. A unique feature on Greek coins, the four pellets appear on local emissions until the seizure of Phliasian coinage after 322 BCE. Courtesy of the American Numismatic Society, 1968.57.48 and 1964.59.9; cf. also *BCD* 41 and 43; Head 1911, 409.

that used the same standard. In conjunction with the oxen on the front, the series might reference agricultural productivity. On some emissions, the depiction is both more schematic and abstract, which indicates that there is more at play here than farming. Scholars have suggested that the circle and pellets might be understood as the zodiacal wheel; pellets in particular were a common reference to the stars. Also, in some emissions, the iconography of the wheel amalgamates with the letter Φ, for Phlious, which further propels the propagated relation between city and zodiac. If this interpretation is correct, we find here the symbolic representation of the four geographic directions coalescing in Phlious. Although the coins do not display the *omphalos* itself, they play on the idea of centrality. The longevity of the series, which runs unchanged for the longest time in the Classical period, further supports the interpretation that the visual language of the coins gave voice to a prevalent way in which the people of Phlious saw themselves.[31]

The great Pausanias commentator James G. Frazer has declared long ago that it is "of course absurd" (1898, 3:81) to think that Phlious was at the center of the Peloponnese. But the quest for geographical exactitude misses the point. What is more intriguing is the mindset behind the claim. Recent research on the spatial dimension in the narrative of Herakles's visit to Phlious reveals how the story was situated at the crossroads of several far-flung, mythical genealogies. As such, Herakles's stay in Phlious was part of "a radiating web of associations" that fostered a sense of connectivity. At the same time, the story was localized in place and validated by a landmark in the local topography, the shrine of Herakles, which tied those associations together. We should not be mistaken to read this part of the tradition, its localization in the microcosm of the valley, as a local ingredient in the legendary fabric of Herakles and his Cycle of Labors, a genuinely local contribution.[32]

If this is the case, it doesn't take much to see how the local tradition of Herakles corresponded with the story of the *omphalos* and the idea that the

Peloponnese gravitated around Phlious. Similar to the role of a relay station, which the Phliasians assigned to themselves in the Myth of Herakles, the *omphalos* tradition articulated an imagined centrality, a world view that put the city at the center stage of affairs, in the Peloponnese and beyond. In an astronomical sense, it meant that the zodiacal wheel was centered on Phlious. Such an interpretation of the alignments, in turn, must have found resonance in the local calendar and festival cycle, as corresponding examples from Argos, Delos, Sardis, and, of course, Delphi attest. Already, Jane Harrison has pointed out that reverence of the *omphalos* usually was associated with the worship of Gaia, Mother Earth; hence, the alignment of the stars was mirrored in another semantic layer of boundedness in place. Moreover, representing the cosmos with Phlious as the imagined central point on map, this idea also replicated and corresponded with the everyday experience of the Phliasians and the location of their city in the valley around them. Readings of the alignments and of local place complemented one another. The navel tradition thus captured a sociocentric mindset in its pristine form, an assessment that not only prioritized the local community, but was geared toward and validated by the community and its settlement location. To the Phliasians, this was at the heart and soul of how they saw their place in the world.[33]

Survey archaeology adds to the picture. In their examination of the site, the Nemea Valley Archaeological Project (see Wright et al. 1990) investigated how the Phliasia related to the overall regional scope of the project. Literary evidence contributes little to the understanding of the nature and frequency of the relations between the Nemea and Phlious valleys. Poor access routes across Mt. Trikaranon, from Phlious to Kleonai, posed a significant challenge. The distribution of numismatic evidence, however slim, suggests that there was a lively exchange between the inhabitants of both sides of the mountain. Curiously enough, this contact did not fuel Phliasian interests in the Nemean Games; Phliasian coins are mostly absent from the hoard finds in the Sanctuary of Zeus at Nemea. In other words, and as one would expect, there was some exchange between Phlious and its neighbors in the next valley; yet the network of grand-scale Hellenic exchange, as documented by the Nemean Games, seems to have bypassed the city. The *Nemea Valley Archaeological Project* has conjectured that the Phliasians might have preferred to stay away from political and economic competitions over the Nemea Valley, which was often in the hands of powers located at a significant distance.[34]

These observations remind us that the traceability of networks does not imply that every city felt automatically inspired to engage in the corresponding networking activities, or engage in them with the same intensity. In an opening note in Plato's *Phaedo* (57a–b), Echekrates of Phlious states that "nowadays none of the Phliasians go to Athens at all, and no stranger (*xenos*) has come from there for a long time"; effectively, Echekrates desires to learn about the details of Socrates's trial, which gets Phaedo going. The statement is a literary convenience, although it is clear that the trope would have fallen flat if Phlious and Athens had maintained vibrant, everyday exchanges with one another.[35]

We now have a better sense of how the local horizon mattered to the people of Phlious, how place provided the underpinnings of communal agency. Much of the city and *chōra* looks generic, but upon closer examination, we notice how the Phliasia provided the scenery for a distinct discourse environment. As so often, the local discourse is mute in our sources; we are well advised to take Xenophon's comments on a discursive culture of stout endurance with a grain of salt. In this sense, our quest for the local resembles that for dark matter: its traces can be observed only through resonance in other visible manifestations that provided a frame of reference. Beyond manifestations in politics, local sentiments also found their expression in a local Phliasian script, and in material culture, ceramics, mints, and more.[36] At the most foundational level, these manifestations were fueled by a definite place, the meaning the Phliasians assigned to it, and the orientation they received from it in return. It is difficult to assert exactly how the identity of place played out, but we sense that it wielded tremendous impact over the people of the Asopos Valley.

Beyond Pottery and Politics: The Deep Frame of the Local

The oscillating nature of Greek culture, between universal and idiosyncratic expressions, has always put the local horizon on the agenda of scholarship. There surely has been, and continues to be, immense interest in the local imprint on politics and culture. The latter is most prominently associated with, and traceable in, countless local pottery styles, with all conceptual caveats in establishing and defining the rubric of local ceramics. Precisely how those styles emerged in relation to regional styles is a matter of significant debate; this nexus, too, between local and universal and multiple layers of hybridity in-between is a key topic in classical archaeology. Incidentally, it is useful to remember that the vast amount of pottery (90 percent and up) from virtually any find spot in Aegean Greece is what is conventionally called local ware, although the interest this local ware receives in scholarship is disproportional to its availability. The field is dominated by studies in posh import ware: much fewer in number, yet artistically more refined, more precious and polished, such imports speak to questions of far-flung connectivity and exchange. They are also of a higher display value in museums and exhibitions around the world.

In politics, the study of local administration and governance has been the lifeblood of approaches to ancient Greece at all times, beginning in antiquity with the famous collection of 158 constitutions of Greek city-states compiled by Aristotle and his school. The polis, with its strong notion of autonomy and freedom, advocated for by an exclusive body of citizens and expressed in robust city ethnics (Hansen and Nielsen 2004, 55–69), was itself the most visible and most vocal expression of political diversity. Greek poleis might have looked alike, but despite all universal protocols and governing principles, the conduct of politics followed idiosyncrasies that were thoroughly local. In the arena of law-giving, it has been argued that the general features of Greek law were not only outbalanced but actually surpassed by substantive diversity and specificity. In their discussion of the unity of Greek law, the leading experts in the field see the organization of justice as the constituent core of the legal "system" of ancient Greece, although the pitfalls of the universal paradigm are obvious. In the legal sphere of the polis, arrangements were often quirky and the degree of local idiosyncrasy bewildering.[37]

Between pottery and politics, there is a wide expanse of local manifestations that have all been given careful consideration in scholarship. In some cases, this has led to the establishment of entire branches of research: for instance, the study of local scripts and dialects, epigraphic habits, rituals and festivals, calendars, coinage, and more. While these expressive dimensions of the local are relatively well understood, its inherent repertoire of values, meanings, and creative forces is as yet unexplored. Beyond the traditional view that sees local as an attribute, one which we encounter in so many matter-of-fact manifestations, there is a vast array of implicit strategies that were reflective of and, in turn, inspired by the local world. Local, in this sense, is not only a signifier of content and cultural practice, but a foundational quantity. As we shall see momentarily, the quest for this deep frame of the local and the normativity it lends to human agency is not entirely new. Indeed, significant scholarly advances have been made in disciplines and fields that are largely segregated and often compartmentalized. An integrated approach toward a comprehensive sociology of the local has yet to come.[38]

It is worthwhile to survey some of the broad trends in the human sciences that inform the exploration of the local in ancient Greece. The research behind each of these is of enormous magnitude; hence, we cannot offer more here than a series of (very succinct) outlines. Four areas stand out: (1) advances in the conceptualization of space and place, effected by what has been greeted as yet another scholarly turn, the "spatial turn"; (2) research on neighborhoods and their role in the process of local stratification; (3) the decoding of cognitive and sensory perception patterns of the local, a swiftly expanding field also in the neurosciences; and (4) the study of local knowledge cultures.

Localized Interaction and the Spatial Turn

The sheer frequency of scholarly turns in recent decades is somewhat ironic—among others, the spatial, the performative, the memorial, and the network turns, or the subsuming of all of these under the all-inclusive culturalist turn. But there is more to this than scholars boasting about ever-new epistemological quantum leaps. As Karl-J. Hölkeskamp (2015) has observed, the quality of each turn in the human sciences lies in the more modest advances from shifting accentuations, thematic extensions, and theoretically and methodologically refined approximations. While none of these advances constitute ground-shaking discoveries as such, their interplay does. The much-cited thick description of human agency and culture, often subject to the mechanics of cross-reference, circumscription, and repetition, not only inspires such interplay but actually necessitates it. At the intersection of multiple turns grows the progress in the decoding of their common denominator: that is, "the cultural conditioning of the human existence and the reality-shaping force of . . . social practice."[39]

It has been observed that cultural conditions and social practices require place, an environment where human agency melts into the realness of society. In our discussion of identities of place, we noted in passing how place energizes the present debate. We're beginning to see how and why the cultural turn cannot go without place. As remarked by Michael Werner and Bénédicte Zimmermann in their conception of entangled history, or "histoire croisée," the cultural turn emphasizes "the specificity—indeed, the irreducible nature—of the local." In turn, such emphasis contributes to "refining our understanding of the differentiated functioning of societies and cultures" (2006, 30). In other words, localized interaction requires the study of the local itself. There is nothing petty to this approach. The local is formative, comprehensive, and all-embracing.

We are well advised to recall that the entire array of interpersonal interactions in place has come under the scrutiny of scholarship. The city itself, its urban layout, design, and ethics, has attracted tidal waves of assessments and theories that are variously informed by data across time and space. Among the latest branches of urban theory is the rethinking of local/global configurations within the city, brought about by the extensive reach of mercantile capitalism. The corresponding transformation of urban environments has been labeled a "reglobalization" (Short 2006, 61), indicating that the local development (e.g., land prices, visual culture) causes a back-ripple that steers global trajectories. Reglobalization alters the way in which the city is experienced. In its most recent variant, marked by the arrival of virtual infrastructures and the hybridity they superimpose upon the realness of place, the notions of delocalization and disconnection from place describe the transformation of the urban experience; the catchphrase of the "global village" beautifully (and deceptively) idyllicizes this transformation. It is impossible to foresee the outcome, yet at this point it has become utterly clear that Richard Sennett's axiomatic formula of "flesh and stone" (1996)—the intricate and also innate unity of the urban designs and bodily conceptions, and the sway that each exerts over the other—is deeply wavering in our world today.

Here, too, in the modern city of cosmopolitanism and hybridity, the local is not marginalized, let alone superfluous. As the economic exploits of faceless corporations transform the urban environment, we detect another, more benign dimension of the global village: that is, that local circumstances are often assessed and indeed shaped by global discourses of a more humane quality than sheer profit-making: for instance, local conversations about environmental issues, social justice, and equity, or political leadership ("frontline democracy"). Throughout these examples, the local horizon of the globalized city is a place where vastly disparate realms, discourses, and identities merge into one.

Within the city, the premodern city in particular, real place has been identified as a force majeure in societal (inter)action, including media communication, the exercise of elite rule, and the conduct of religious and civic rituals. It has become commonplace not only to see the various ambiences of urban space (e.g., sacred and profane, urban and sub- or extra-urban, public or private spaces) as stages for the performance of social practice, but also to explore their innate capacity to govern the conduct of affairs. Procession rites—intracity processions and those of a more peripheral or liminal nature—are an obvious example of the complex dialogue between human agency and its embeddedness in an environment that is in itself charged with multiple modes of meaning: for example, sacred spots, monuments, demarcated realms, and places of memory. Often those modes are in complex conversation with each other, a process that has been aptly called intersignification, which highlights the connection in the visual language and meaning among physical objects. The corresponding fabric of shared traditions and memories, their monumentalization in place, assigns a distinct quality to place. We will return to the inherent distinction between place and space below and, indeed, throughout this book. Urban environments are subject to ongoing development and change (of function, design, meaning, etc.), and with change come cultural reappropriations and redefinitions, each one in a vexed conversation with long-lasting notions, sentiments, and trajectories of place.[40]

Between Local and Domestic: The Neighborhood as an Intermediary Scale

The neighborhood provides a special frame of reference for localized interaction. All settlements, low-density urbanism as much as more massed urban layouts, share the existence of neighborhoods in one way or another, for purposes of administration, social hierarchy, life quality, and so forth. Commonly understood as residential zones that have considerable face-to-face interaction and distinctive physical and/or social characteristics, neighborhoods have received tremendous attention in recent years, in the human sciences in general as well as in the study of the ancient Mediterranean world. The reason for this comes from a smorgasbord of burning topics that we noted in the previous section, including issues of health, sustainability, social justice, and economic development, the latter also in conjunction with the desire to endorse, or creatively rebrand, existing local identities of place. Resolutions to any of these issues depend on their realization in functional localities that are categorically different and that each foster the process of local stratification and diversification: zones of production and trade, districts, public places. Among this kaleidoscope of sublocal localities, the neighborhood reserves a special place simply because of the sheer volume of interactions that occur in it and the time that is spent there, as well as the subtle continuity that both provide to the human existence.

The questions of how to identify neighborhoods in the premodern city and to recreate corresponding neighborhood experiences from the diverse bodies of archaeological, textual, documentary, and geospatial evidence are notoriously difficult to answer. As Michael Smith, a pioneer in the exploration of neighborhoods in premodern Mesoamerica, and Juliana Novic have pointed out (Smith and Novic 2012), the urban and social clustering in neighborhoods is itself subject to, and reflective of, diverse settlement types. A universal feature shared by cities and towns around the world, the neighborhood is a gateway to the understanding of entire settlement cultures.

The study of neighborhoods in ancient Greece is situated between these poles of universalism and cultural specificity. It is difficult to overestimate the role and function of the neighborhood in the convoluted processes that scholars subsume under the label of the rise of the polis—that is, the emergence of a "new concept of living in Archaic Greece" (Lang 2007) that was driven by the gradual division of the settlement into distinct, functionally segregated spaces.[41] Sublocal units, such as *phylai, obai, kōmai, dēmoi*, and the like, were organizational landmarks in the increasing complexity of the Greek city. There is an endless debate about the nature of those units, whether they were kin-based or the result of more convoluted socio-spatial dynamics (or both). Although not neighborhoods in the genuine sense, it is worthwhile to remember that, for as much as we can tell, sublocal units such as *phylai* were not disconnected from place either. Some of those units (e.g., the Megarian *kōmai* or Corinthian *merē*) were crafted in response to the physical environment of the city and its surrounding territories. In cases of a pronounced person-based nature, for instance, in *koinanes* and *hetairiai*, individual affiliations with the group usually depended on quotas of landed property and/or agricultural produce, which further rooted them in the land. Effectively, *koinanes* or *dēmoi* also had the capacity to shape a neighborhood experience, beyond their assigned functions in the administration of the citizen body. It is easy to see how, and why, in some of the earliest pieces of Greek legislation, the organization of residential zones was governed by the polis through, for example, property regulations and resolutions of boundary conflicts, inheritance laws, or regulations for new arrivals in the city. Governance of the sublocal locality, no matter how defined, was part and parcel of Greek legal and political culture.[42]

We note, not without regret, that our understanding of sublocal space receives only limited input from material evidence. Neighborhoods are difficult to identify and analyze from archaeological data. Outside of Athens and its demes, which have been studied with so much insight and zeal by Hans Lohmann, the most promising case studies include the excavations in Olynthos in Northern Greece and Halieis in the Argolid, located in a place of supreme strategic importance at the mouth of the Argolic Gulf (Ps.-Skylax 50.2). Each city had a clearly defined life, with no layers of habitation in the post-Classical period that complicate the analysis. They are generally considered paradigmatic for the understanding of urban settlement patterns in the fifth and fourth centuries BCE. In one section of Halieis's lower town, in a more extensive excavation area, archaeologists have unearthed the remains of three housing blocks, two streets, and one major through road. The homes in this neighborhood all share certain features: for instance, the layout arranged around an open courtyard from which various rooms opened. The room types in each *oikos* include not only the so-called men's quarter (*andron*), kitchen, and bathroom, but also oil press rooms, workshops, and other rooms of economic activity. Judging from the archaeological data, the term *residential zone*, in a rigid sense, therefore appears as a misnomer to describe the neighborhood experience. In Halieis and elsewhere in ancient Greece, the urban layout was not only subject to the diversification of functional localities, but to the mixing and blending of functions within each of these localities. This mixing also happened in the neighborhood.[43]

Greek literature complements our picture. The topic is prominent in Hesiod's poetry. Multiple references to neighbors (*geitones*, sing. *geitōn*) make it clear how vital, and at times, precarious neighborhood relations were in the early Greek city. We ought to add that it is not entirely clear if the term *geitōn*, the root of which surely had something to do with land (*gē*), was used for the holder of the bordering property or, more likely, larger sections of the town.[44] "If any mischief happens on your estate (†*enkōmion*)," Hesiod states in *Works and Days*, "the neighbors (*geitones*) come straightforward [*scil.*, to aid you]"[45] (344–45). A bad neighbor, on the other hand, is "a great plague; but a good one is a great blessing" (346). The praise was neither topical nor misty-eyed. In light of volatile farming conditions and the vagaries of agricultural activity, healthy neighborhood relations were closely tied in with not only the success of individual farms but the well-being of the community as a whole. The concept of mutual support between *geitones*, helping each other out in reciprocal relations that were "oiled by lending and borrowing" (Osborne 1987, 94), was considered critical to the flourishing of all. It is not surprising, given the immediacy of social relations in the neighborhood, that many rituals pertaining to the strategy of overcoming communal crises were relegated to, or located in, the context of the sublocal realm (see chapter 4). Between *oikos* and polis, the neighborhood was charged with its own social meaning.

Home: Embodiment and Cognition

That the local triggers a distinct embodied experience is an axiomatic idea. We have already noted in passing that place stimulates a sense of attachment. Odysseus's longing for home, a state of mind that causes him, among other reactions, to weep, is in many ways the foundational story of *nostos* in Western literature, of homecoming to a place that is experienced in a particular way. Home and its relation to place is a multidimensional concept in a multidisciplinary and diverse field of studies. The recurring ideas and associations were surveyed in a critical literature review by Shelley Mallett (2004), who reminds us of the complicated interplay of place, feeling, practice, and/or an active state of being that permeates the experience of home. We will disentangle the complicated helix of physiological, psychological, and emotional strands of this archaeology of home in chapters 2 and 3. At this point, it is important to note that the experience of place, beyond the stimuli it receives from culture, is governed by intrinsic processes in the human body itself. The medical corpus commonly associated with the name of the Greek physician Hippocrates conjectured that sentiments like Odysseus's longing for home, his homesickness, were sparked by a physiological condition: wistful anxiety, the Hippocratic writer found, stimulates the excessive production of black bile in the blood, which causes pain among those who suffer from it.[46]

In the seventeenth century, Swiss medical scholar Johannes Hofer opened an all-new chapter when he described homesickness as a psychopathological disorder. Studying the anxiety of Swiss mercenaries who had fought away from home, Hofer argued that their homesickness and subsequent mental disarray were actually withdrawal symptoms, caused by the removal from a soundscape: the sound of cow bells, to be precise, which Swiss soldiers were accustomed to hearing in their daily lives and which marked the core of their experience of home. "Swiss Disease" was emblematic of what Hofer labeled *nostalgia*, a neologism combining *nostos* with the Greek word for "pain" (*algos*). Hofer's notion of nostalgia fostered the idea that the experience of place was not merely subject to physiological processes but was a complex psychosomatic condition.[47]

In the 1990s, scholars began to apply more analytical approximations and to rescue the sense of place from idyllic images and ideas. Much of this has happened in lively, cross-disciplinary studies that were essential parts of the scholarly turns described above. In this line of investigation, research on the "senses of place" (Feld and Basso 1996) resonated in ethnographic evocations and theories of local dwelling, a culture-driven approach that explores how people encounter places, how they experience, embody, and perceive them, and invest them with meaning. Our interest, at this moment, rests less with culture than with advances that concern cognition patterns in the human body. It is intriguing to see how recent discoveries in the neurosciences complement the theoretical framework of the human sciences. In collaborative research that won them, among other distinctions, the 2014 Nobel Prize in Physiology or Medicine, Edvard Moser, May-Britt Moser, and John O'Keefe revolutionized the understanding of spatial cognition processes in the mammal brain. Cognitive neuroscience has demonstrated how place cognition is subject to the firing of so-called grid or place cells in the hippocampus, the brain area where memory and navigation are located. Moser, Moser, and O'Keefe discovered that grid cells in the hippocampus interact extensively with the neighboring entorhinal cortex. It was there, in the entorhinal cortex, that the researchers were able to see a pattern in the firing of place cells as test animals moved through place. The traces of the pattern resemble a near-perfect geometric form (a hexagonal lattice), which suggests an innate navigation matrix. Greeted by the Nobel Committee as the discovery of "an 'inner GPS' in the brain that makes it possible to orient ourselves in space," the work of the research team is a landmark step in the decoding of spatial awareness. Beyond the medical implications, especially in the field of Alzheimer research, the discovery of the brain GPS promises new insight in the cognition of local environments and the interaction between the neural code of place-experience and extrinsic stimuli. At this fruitful juncture of the neurosciences and the humanities, the local has become a sphere of intense fusion of neural codes and culture.[48]

Local Knowledge

Commonly understood as the knowledge developed and accumulated over time by a local community, local knowledge is a rich repository of embodied and collective ways of knowing. We detect the same dichotomy here that we encountered earlier: local knowledge is typically painted as static, fixed, often backward, and parochial. Compared to the progressive designs of connected, cosmopolitan, and global knowledge systems, local knowledge is belittled as irrelevant to larger concerns. At best, it is seen as traditional and folkloristic. While preserving traditions that are of voyeuristic curiosity to the outsider, the quality of local knowledge is seen in its capacity to store memories that bear little relevance in a world of fast-paced change. We presume local knowledge is limited by location and confined in meaning.

Anthropologist and pioneer in the field Clifford Geertz (1983/2000) has long argued for a profound re-conceptualization. Local knowledge, he demonstrates, is not merely the knowledge *of* and *in* place, but a craft that is driven by place itself. The distinction is important. The former, the accumulation of knowledge about place, immediately highlights the strategic value of a knowledge system that allows communities to connect to place and to maximize, for instance, the economic, ecological, or militaristic benefits of this connection. But the force of local knowledge doesn't end there. The contextual dimension, the boundedness of knowledge in place, also marks the beginning of an exciting transformation, one in which local knowledge is turned into a high-powered cultural currency. General claims about the validity of knowledge systems and the hierarchy among them, according to Geertz, are not only not helpful, they obfuscate the true quality of local knowledge: its specificity, predictability, self-evidence, and reliability. In the lived experience of society, abstract ways of knowing are not inevitably of a higher order than contextual knowledge. Indeed, the identification of these domains, their ascribed contents, and implicit order, as Ngũgĩ wa Thiong'o (2012, 27–43)

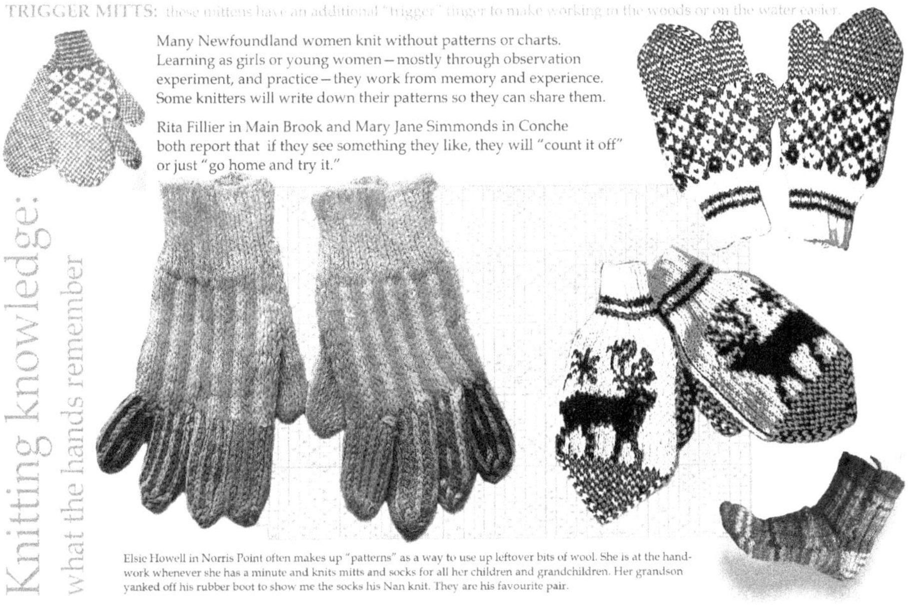

FIGURE 1.3. "Knitting Knowledge: What the Hands Remember." Folio originally published in *Towards an Encyclopedia of Local Knowledge: Excerpts from Chapters I and II*, © 2017 by Pam Hall. Reproduced with permission of Breakwater Books and ISER Books.

teaches us, is in itself not universal but part and parcel of a cultural separation of different ways and genres of knowing. In the arena of social meaning, the assemblage of local knowledge easily challenges the authority of abstract and remote knowledge repositories.

Pam Hall, in a combined art-and-research project entitled *The Encyclopedia of Local Knowledge* has recently charted the vectors of local knowing in communities in Newfoundland, Canada (figs. 1.3 and 1.4). Drawing on hundreds of local informants who, much like Pausanias's *epichōrioi*, unravel the intricate and locally enshrined ways of knowing for her—for instance, the meaning of place names, artisanal practices, or food idiosyncrasies that are inspired by distinctive climatic conditions—Hall traces the constitution of local knowledge repositories and their role in society. Not only do the general traits of knowing-your-place become visible; the situatedness and context of the knowledge practices she describes shape precisely the predictability and specificity we just noted. Moreover, she finds that locally encoded knowledge is never static or fixed but in deep conversation with other systems of knowing (global, scientific): knowledge of seasonal local pathways and waterways complements GPS navigations; handmade boots from harp seal go with GORE-TEX outerwear; the preparation of protein-rich foodstuffs and corresponding preservation practices are in a dietary dialogue with import goods; and so on.[49]

SALT, DRY, BOTTLE, CAN: On Preserving More than Protein

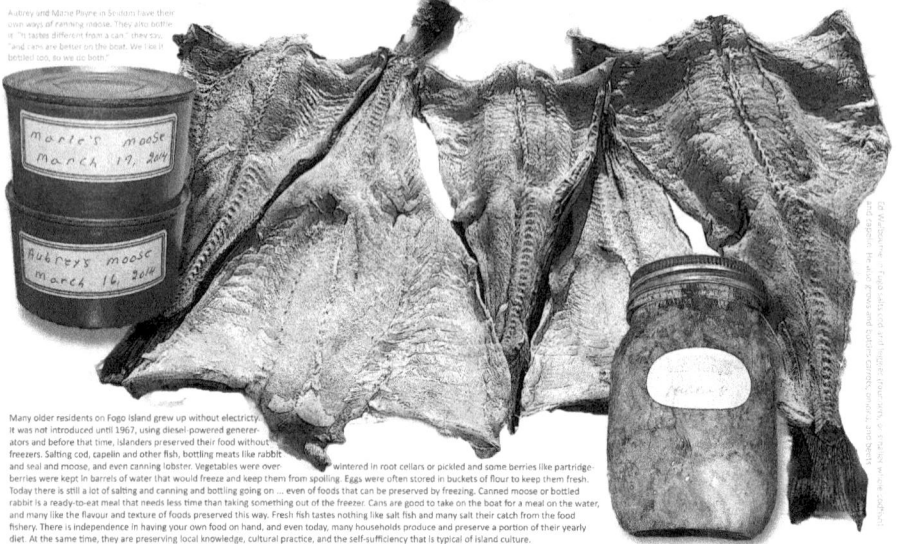

FIGURE 1.4. "Salt, Dry, Bottle, Can: On Preserving More than Protein." Folio originally published in *Towards an Encyclopedia of Local Knowledge: Excerpts from Chapters I and II*, © 2017 by Pam Hall. Reproduced with permission of Breakwater Books and ISER Books.

As we have seen, the innate quality of local knowledge as an aggregation of cultural shifts, full of nuance, heterogeneity, and ambivalence, makes the local way of knowing or doing something a reliable exercise. It also renders purpose. In its most outspoken form, this quality of local knowledge creates an entire branch of meaning, something that art historian Pamela Smith (2004) has labeled an "artisanal epistemology." As local craftspeople seek to develop designs and enhance skills, their action is, at varying stages of awareness, reflective of place. Rather than following rule-bound schemes, they resort to local practices to navigate errors and improvise spontaneous solutions. At times, this amalgamation of skill, materiality, and local practice translates into full-fledged expressions of an identity of place. The distinguishable shape of trigger mitts from St. John's, Newfoundland, that make working in the woods or on the water easier is as much a testimony to this as the design of Räuchermännchen from the Erzgebirge, used to burn cone incense. Both have generated entire industries of production and trade that have long surpassed the local context. Their commercial success, however, is grounded in and supported by the deep frame of a local knowledge culture.

Our sketch arrives at a conclusion that is almost diametrically opposed to the common perceptions of local knowledge noted at the beginning. Local knowledge motivates us to look beyond global forms of knowing and question the self-evident authority that the universal paradigm claims for itself. Knowledge *of* and *in* place not only makes larger visions possible; it is a quintessential condition for those visions to play out in a real-life knowledge environment.

Conceptualizing the Local in Classical Greece

At the beginning of Plato's *Republic* (327a), Socrates sets the scene by saying that on the previous day he had trekked down to the Piraeus to attend a festival held in honor of Bendis, Thracian goddess of the hunt. The cult was new in Athens, and Socrates was curious about the spectacle. He was pleased with the procession of the Thracians, which was particularly captivating, but that of the locals (*hoi epichōrioi*) he also found delightful.

While Bendis and the introduction of her cult into Athens have received due attention in scholarship, our interest in the passage naturally gravitates to the *epichōrioi*. The most common English translation is "locals." Likewise, "natives" is used sometimes, although its colonial baggage weighs heavily. The adjective *epichōrios* is referenced in *LSJ* as "in" or "of the land." When applied to people and animals—and gods, as we shall see in chapter 4—*hoi epichōrioi* are beings of the country (in Attic also *houpichōrioi*: Soph. *Oid.* 1046). Material goods and attitudes can be "of the country" or "in use in it," similar to the less frequent *topikos* (local, of place). There is a curious spatial semantics at play, inspired by the wide gulf of meaning of *chōrion* (place, spot, district) and of *chōra*, "hinterland." In French, *les gens du pays* or *les gens du coin* resonate a similar meaning, as does the German word *Einheimische*, which also adds a flavor of home. Plato's *epichōrioi* are juxtaposed with the Thracians, people from away. Note how the opposition is not framed in terms of citizens (*politai*) vis-à-vis noncitizens. High-powered claims about law and politics are not at stake here. Rather, the contrast is casual, avoiding questions of status and entitlement. "Our folks here," Plato implies, "did a good job of cultural appropriation. Not as good as the Thracians themselves, but nice." The Thracians resided in Athens; hence, they shared the same *chōrion* as the Athenians, but, more generally speaking, they adhered to a cultural regime that was not typical of the Athenian way of life.[50]

The semantics of place are interrelated with cultural conduct. Rather than a mere geographical concept, the local is deeply interwoven with social and cultural currents. The subtle meaning of *chōrion* might have evoked a rural background and, implicitly so, a degree of deprecation; we noted earlier that such a meaning, too, falls within the possible semantic horizon of *locals* in English and *les habitants* in French. In their conversations about culture regimes elsewhere, the Athenians notoriously looked down upon the localness of others, equated here with ruralness or backwaterness. But this is not at all what Plato has in mind here. When Socrates speaks of *epichōrioi*, he evokes a particular point of view, a degree of knowledgeability. The perspective is not dissimilar to that of *astoi* (sing. *astos*), "residents" or "townsmen," and, in this sense, insiders who are knowledgeable about local ways, although it is debated just how much *astoi* were to be equated with *politai*, "citizens." Beyond the complicated issue of legal entitlement, the semantics of place resonate very differently in all three terms. While the word *politēs*, by the Classical period, had "eschewed all connotation of territoriality" (Cohen 2000, 53), *astos* signals complicity: from the pre-Classical record on, *astos* carried the meaning of the local insider who is physically present and hence in the know about the city.[51] *Epichōrios* shares some of the same semantic field, but, through explicit reference to *chōrion*, the notion of land reverberates stronger. Much like Pausanias's local informants, who guide the global traveler through the intricacies of countless local knowledge cultures, Plato's *epichōrioi* are experts in cultural traditions that relate to place. They are active agents of an identity of place. Arguably, the eagerness to engage in cultural appropriation processes was itself a vibrant facet of an Athenian identity of place, built into the DNA of the city, but this is not the point here.[52] When locals stage a foreign parade, they transcend the boundaries of tradition, knowledge, and self-reference. Vice versa, when foreigners hold a parade in Athens, the stage might be local, but the ceremony is not. Bendis was the domain of the Thracians, who had their own ways, their own culture regime. They resided in Athens, and, most likely, they, too, were susceptive to the prevailing identity of place. But to label them locals would have been a stretch.

The spatial connotation of *epichōrios* merits further discussion. Can we be more precise about the geography of the local in the Classical Greek variant? And how can local, in turn, advance our reading of Greek culture and society? First, we would need to establish local place as such. In doing so, it is important to recall that the local plays out in two arenas of spatial semantics: the physical and the imagined realm. As a physical space, the local is the manageable, accessible realm through which individuals navigate in their everyday lives. Such an embodied experience implies multiple groups of human agents. It expresses itself in a kaleidoscope of functional localities in which group relations are realized—for instance, neighborhoods (above) and places of artisanal or agricultural productivity; hence, the distinction between the urban center and the countryside. Religious and profane places, again associated with demarcated locations in the polis territory, were also subject to divergent strategies of communal maintenance.

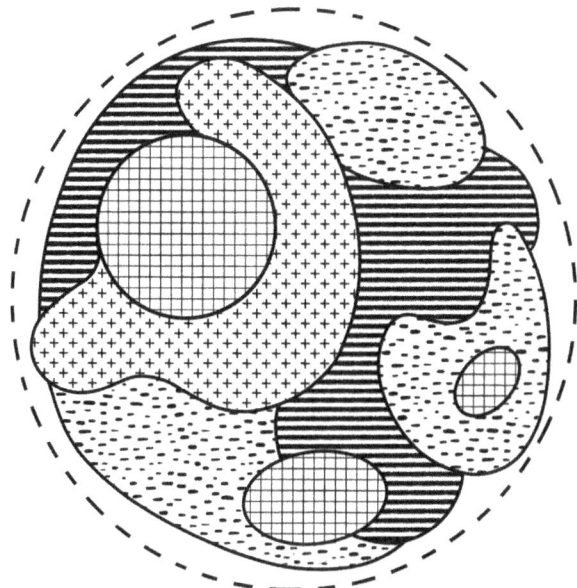

FIGURE 1.5. Outline of local accumulation, real and imagined. The physical local comprises irregularity, diversity, and convolution, as indicated by coded areas. The dashed circle depicts the imagined local as a unifying force.

Survey archaeology has disclosed a tremendous florescence of activity in the countryside of many city-states in the Classical period. The distribution of sites (farmsteads, hamlets, shelters) is indicative of a strategy to take advantage of divergent conditions in the *chōra*, for instance, in soils, wind, sunlight, the occurrence of quarries and mining opportunities, and so forth.[53] Moreover, archaeologists detected a diverse mixing and blending between and within functional localities, which reinforces the picture we encountered earlier in the examination of residential zones (fig. 1.5). Rather than assuming neat segregation—for instance, between living quarters and production spaces, or between city and hinterland—we are advised to view the local world of the polis as a tapestry of localities that were both malleable and permeable, stitched together into a convoluted "space syntax" (Bill Hillier). The local realm of the farmer in the countryside was not the same as that of the barber and perfumer in the agora, nor of the *kapeleion*-keepers who sold wine to the residents of their neighborhood. What united these sublocal localities was that they were all parts of the same imagined lifeworld.

How large is the radius of local engagement? The answer to this question depends both on cultural assumptions and circumstances of mobility.

Effectively, scholarly attempts to scale the local horizon differ widely, depending on the area, time, and culture under investigation, or all three. Our own experience today betrays how deceptive the local can be. For instance, in the so-called locavore movement, spawned as a result of issues of food sustainability and eco-consciousness, participants typically restrict themselves to the consumption of food that is grown within a radius of one hundred miles, or 160 km, a number that is neat and arbitrary at the same time.[54]

The Classical Greek city had its own scales. With the great majority of inhabitants being peasant farmers—Hans-J. Gehrke (1986, 18) has suggested a number as high as 80%—the local radius was subject to the daily commute of farmers to their fields in the countryside, usually a short ride or walk from their homes in the city. John Bintliff has calculated a distance of not more than five or six kilometers, or less than a two-hour walk. If farmers lived in villages or hamlets, they would find the distance between their homes and the marketplace in the city equally manageable. The question is of course complicated by huge discrepancies in the natural environment. Mobility schemes are distorted by differences between travel on flat land, step climbs, or the crossing of rivers and runlets. Recent GPS research on the countrysides of Hermione and Methana in the southern Argolid has gauged the temporal and physical realities in both cities. The emerging picture of least-cost paths and path distances suggests that, while daily commutes of up to three hours (one-way) were generally possible, the highest density by far of farmsteads in the *chōra* fell within a ninety-minute radius, or about 5 kilometers.[55]

The Bintliff diameter translates into a *chōra* size of about 80–110 km², to which we would add the area of the city itself: depending on the urban environment, another 5–20 km². The resulting grand total has been found typical for many city-states. In its inventory of 1,035 poleis, the Copenhagen Polis Centre (CPC) collected, among other things, all information relating to the size of city-state territories. The resulting scheme, the CPC urges us, should be read in the context of significant variation between different regions of Aegean Greece. Many regions of the Greek world show pronounced landscape profiles and distinct settlement patterns; also, often enough, settlement sizes fluctuated over the time period covered by the CPC. But the trend is revealing: while some 60 percent of all attested cases had a territory size of 50–100 km², the next category (up to 200 km²) comprised only another 20 percent. Only 10 percent had a middling territory of more than 200 km², with a very few statistical outliers over 1,000 km². On the other end of the spectrum, only about 10 percent had a territory of less than 50 km².[56]

What we learn from these numbers is that the landscape of the average city-state was experienceable. In other words, the knowledge of people about their local area was acquirable through firsthand encounters with place, and it was communicated directly and between individuals who were, in principle, equally familiar with and knowledgeable about the quotidian horizon. This triangle of place, knowledgeability, and communication marks not only a landmark trait of the local, but also a decisive distinction between local and nonlocal realms. Greek cities maintained vibrant networks of interaction with each other in the regional sphere. Indeed, as we will see shortly, no matter how far-reaching occasional connections might have been, the highest volume of linkages with others happened precisely there, within the regional horizon. In the regional sphere, human agency was subject to subsidiary modes of communication. Longer distances precluded daily interaction; hence the organization of exchanges via scheduled peer polity-meetings—for instance, periodical market days, joint parades and athletic contests, the celebration of festivals, or the conduct of politics—all of which were typically carried out under the umbrella of a *koinon* or amphiktyony, or both. In the lived experience of the local and the regional, we note that Greek city-states resorted to categorically different strategies: one strategy was governed by directness, autoreferentiality, and complicity; the other by intermediary contact and periodic exchange.[57]

At this point our definition of local segues into the second arena of spatial semantics, which is more demanding than the measuring of distances: the local's inherent quality as a metaphorical or imagined place. This quality extends the local experience to an imaginary circle of individuals and, eventually, an imagined community (Benedict Anderson 1983/2016). It has long been argued that the metaphorical manifestation of space is in dialogue with the physical world but also separate from it. As we have seen, physical space segregates, in that it shapes multiple localities that exist in proximity to and within each other: we noted the existence of multiple functional localities in one and the same local realm. Social space, on the other hand, in the words of Henri Lefebvre, suggests "actual and potential assembly at a single point, or around that point. It implies, there, the possibility of accumulation" (1974/1991, 101).

The possibility of accumulation is highly contextual. First, it is informed by real-life constellations—for instance, infrastructure and technology. The natural environment, too, galvanizes the idea of accumulation, in that it provides a canvas for the projection of social space (e.g., a valley, plateau, island, etc.). This does not imply that the environment—its topography and geography—wields a deterministic force over society. If anything, the causal relation went in the opposite direction. As David Harvey (1979/2006, 275; cf. Crumley, Lennartsson, and Westin 2017) has demonstrated, the social quality of space is not determined by geography but is defined through human practice: that is, through an ongoing, complex, and often nonlinear negotiation in the course of which space is made subject to, and appropriated by, the governing ideas of society. Identities of place, no matter how deep the conversation with place, are always the result of the human imagination.

In Greece, the imagination of accumulation was fueled further by its embedding in a peculiar lifeworld, one where the epichoric purview was both the stage for conversations about togetherness and an authoritative source of reference. In the definition of Edmund Husserl, the lifeworld is a realm that is driven by self-evident validity from intersubjective experience rather than abstract or universal propositions (e.g., from science). Regardless of its shape and size, the foremost horizon of the Greek lifeworld was the polis; we have already seen how the city-state was the base-unit of local regimes of truth. In the lifeworld of the city, public conversations—in politics, culture, and so on—combined many of the traits that we have discussed earlier, but they were also amendable to a condition that we only encounter now in our discussion of the imaginary local: that is, to the strong fusion of lifeworld and locality, forged by a constellation that is best characterized as a local discourse environment.

In the open-air culture of the Greek city, public discourses were, in principle, visible and audible to all. The general openness of communications in—for instance, the theater, street, agora, or in spaces that were reserved for the conduct of religion and politics—facilitated lively and often heated conversations. With no clear-cut opposition between public, political, and profane communications, public conversations were always of a variegated nature; hence, the quest for one single discourse and one coherent public opinion misses the point. The local discourse environment of the polis was thus shaped by a polyphony of voices and a plurality of realms where conversations between shifting groups of speakers and audiences took place. Despite complex and nuanced differentiations within, the unifying element of the discourse was that voice and place were bracketed by the horizon of directness; the local delineated a communicative boundary.

At the same time, the conversation was energized by and received critical input from the local. Through this amalgamation with the local, the discourse environment provided public deliberations with a robust frame of reference. Conversations *in* the polis were often identical with conversations *about* the polis; as we shall see in chapter 5, the intricate role of citizens who were the makers, adjudicators, and keepers of history created a rather peculiar circle of self-reinforcement. This is again not to suggest that there was ever only one theme up for debate, let alone one public opinion. Rather, whatever conversation there was drew on long-term sentiments, conditions, and beliefs as they prevailed in place: for instance, images of primordial descent and ownership of the land, the social reality of economic practice, cultural distinction, communal expertise, the legacy of ancestral calamity, and so forth. These sentiments predetermined the course of the conversation. And, as the debate unfolded, they rendered validity to communal assessments. This quality made the local discourse environment similar to an echo chamber: energizing the imagination of local collectivity, uniqueness, and distinction, it endorsed local readings of the world writ-large. In turn, this amplified ideas of uniqueness.

Our inquiry into the fusion of lifeworld and locality reveals a lively dynamic of mutual cross-fertilization: drawing on the idea of potential accumulation in the local world of the polis, this imagination was expressed in and made possible by a discourse environment that suggested precisely this, the assemblage of all in one place. This metaphor of local implied more than a firm footing from which to struggle forward. In the rapidly changing world of Classical Greece, it made the imagined local an anchor that stabilized quotidian interpersonal relations; a resource that powered communal strategies of distinction and competition; and a venue where the past intersected in a meaningful way with the present, binding everyone together by the familiarity with their local world.

The inherent quality of *epichōrios* derived from the double meaning of local: its territorial and metaphorical traits. As an ontological concept, the Greek local mingled physical and imagined realms, married relational and contextual categories, and manifested an integrated discourse world in which the local was both the platform for the expression of social meaning and a source of reference. In light of a pluriverse of city-states, we should expect a rich combination of these traits, with varying weights and proportions. In Phlious, for instance, we came across what might be called an ideal-type convergence of physical and imagined local place: as we have seen, the territory size was average; imaginations of the local, stereotypical. The union of Corinth and Argos, alluded to by Aristotle (above), incorporated an extensive territory, one that exceeded the horizon of quotidian experienceability. The land will have made it difficult to speak of the union as local, but what disqualified the double-state of Corinth and Argos most definitely was the complete lack of an imagined quality of local; the two cities each had their own epichoric imaginaries. Athens, on the other hand, had an even larger territory (c. 2,500 km^2), much too large and too profoundly heterogeneous to qualify as local in any grounded sense. Indeed, the demes throughout Attica each constituted their own local worlds, almost in beautiful compliance with the Bintliff diameter, both manageable and calculable in terms of risk and opportunity.[58] And yet Plato's Athenians could be easily called *epichōrioi*, because they were so successful in crafting an imagined community that propelled the idea of accumulation, from Eleutherai to Rhamnous and from the Piraeus to Sounion (see also chapter 2). We sense that the Greek local was a fluid, permeable concept in itself. What united the many shapes of *epichōrios* was a spatial ontology that related its inhabitants to the domain of their local horizon—real, imagined, or both.[59]

We now have established the spatial dimension of local place. Its cultural dimension is another question; we turn to this question throughout the subsequent chapters when we delve into assorted local arenas. Some further conceptual deliberations are necessary. They are pertinent to the exploration of the local and the gravity it wields over the lived experience in a connected world.

As we have seen, network approaches provide us with a compelling picture of ubiquitous connectivity within Aegean Greece and across the Mediterranean. The investigation typically gravitates toward the horizontal spread of exchanges: how far the network extends, who participates in it, and so on. We noted earlier that questions such as these have generated a good deal of genuine excitement about the discovery of (inter)cultural dialogues, traceable, for instance, in the development of hybrid material styles, the advancement and spread of expert knowledge, and the more mundane experience of people whose quotidian horizon was reflective of a world full of connections near and far.

This said, it is notoriously difficult to gauge the depth and meaning of network structures. One of the prevailing, although mostly implicit tenets, is to jump from frequency and extent to scales of meaning: the wider the network and the more connections, the more meaningful. For instance, in discussions of the Hellenic convergence in the Mediterranean, the so-called *theōria* has received much attention. *Theōroi* were envoys sent by a city or sanctuary to announce a particular festival held in their place of origin. Depending on the significance of the games, the catchment area and related travel of *theōroi* differed in the distances that were covered. Wherever the *theōroi* roamed, they were received by *theōrodokoi*, their local counterpart, as it were, who offered them hospitality. Both *theōroi* and *theōrodokoi* are amply attested to. In some cases, as in epigraphic dossiers from Epidauros, Delphi, Argos, Athens, and Hermione, the surviving lists of festival embassies reveal elaborate theoric travel itineraries. The inscriptions have been studied in great detail; they play a landmark role in conversations about the connected Greek Mediterranean.[60] As official documents, issued by the polis, published in the public sphere for everyone to see, and inspiring viewers to project their own mental map of distant horizons, the lists have been taken as crown witnesses of a Greek network mentality. Indeed, it has been posited that the "sum of all *theoriai* may be perceived as a 'hypernetwork' that connected the entire Greek world."[61]

In a similar vein, approaches to the institution of guest-friendship (*proxenia*), a busy field of research in classical studies at all times, have been fully brought under the spell of the network turn. Evidence for the *proxenia* is both broad and large. The epigraphic material comes from all corners of the Mediterranean and all periods, with a body of surviving inscriptions ranging in the ten thousands. This, in turn, has inspired audacious predications about the governing views behind the institution. The most in-depth study of the material to date, conveniently supplemented by the interactive database *Proxeny Networks in the Ancient World*, posits that "[i]ndividual poleis viewed their proxenoi en masse as geographically distributed networks. This wider perspective is crucial . . . as a context for interpreting individual grants."[62] In other words, the critical determinant in the award of proxeny honors to individuals elsewhere was the institution's capacity to enhance the city's networking capacities.

We engage in this discussion in more detail in chapter 5, when some of the epigraphic material is put to the test. For now, it suffices to observe that it is not entirely clear how occasional ties with others via guest-friends and *theōroi* were indicators of a deeply entrenched, connected mindset. The conjecture is neither inevitable nor self-evident. Graphic representations of a city's networking activities (including proxenic ties) tend to chart horizontal linkages across any given region, often conflating multiple layers of time as well as vastly heterogeneous connecting counterdots (cities, courts, individual benefactors, etc.). The resulting image is highly suggestive; it implies coverage. From the viewpoint of the Archaic and Classical Greek city, however, its linkages were most likely not seen as measures contributing to a systematic indexing-exercise. For the polis, its links radiated outward from the core of the community. Whatever territorial coverage existed was subject to the idea of centrality. Connections differed in weight and depth, and were subject to a spatial hierarchy. As we move ahead with our exploration of the local horizon, the graph in figure 1.6 serves as a template of how the polis viewed its multiple linkages and connections with others.

Measures and weights are adapted from the calculation of territory sizes carried out by the Copenhagen Polis Centre, with calibrations to four *chōra* sizes from 50 to 200 km². As we have seen above, about 80 percent of all Archaic and Classical Greek city-states fall into this range. For the lowest and highest 10 percent of territory sizes (i.e., less than 50 km² and significantly more than 200 km²), the outline would look different. For one, the few poleis

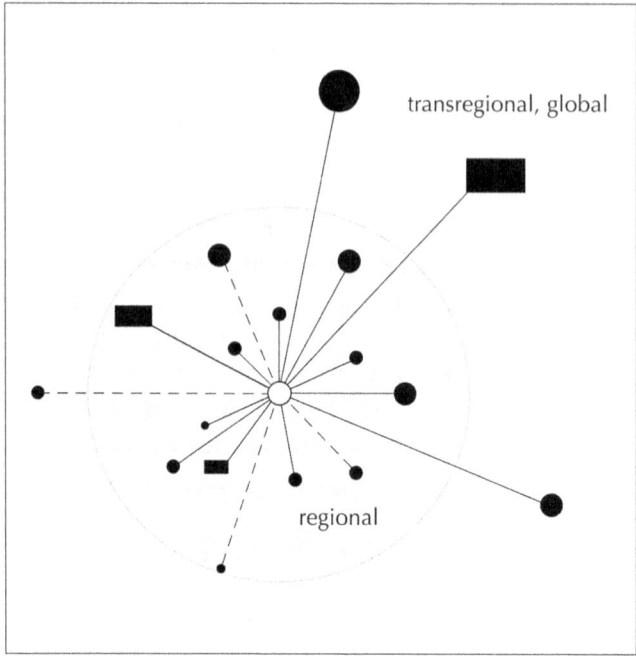

FIGURE 1.6. Connectivity compass, tracing linkages radiating out from the local into translocal realms. Reference to actual coordinates of longitude and latitude is not intended. Rectangles symbolize bodies and institutions (amphiktyonies, federal organizations, military alliances), with different weights and catchment areas. Dots represent other cities, according to a four-weight scale, adapted from the CPC: poleis with territories ≤ 50 km^2; 50–100 km^2; 100–200 km^2; ≥ 200 km^2. Dotted lines indicate weak, ephemeral links; continuous lines, more stable ties.

with very extensive *chōrai* and a "fame factor" at the highest end of the spectrum (Sparta, Athens, Syracuse) would have had a significantly higher connectivity rate, in the regional context and beyond. Vice versa, the smallest city-states, for instance some of the Phokian or Arkadian communities, had a lower connectivity score.[63]

The graphic of figure 1.6 builds on the relational aspect of three spheres of interaction: local, regional, and universal or global. In the regional realm, it also represents the idea that exchanges were subject to real distances: connections with neighboring cities were, by default, more frequent than with more remote poleis (e.g., on the fringes of the region). In this sense, regional connectivity was dictated by geographical scales of near and far, by natural barriers, travel routes, and so forth. In the transregional/global sphere, scales are compressed. This is deliberate. Military alliances led by Athens and Sparta, the two most obvious candidates for a large rectangle, might have been based at a distance of two or four days travel from the local, across rugged terrain or the sea, or both. But those differences didn't alter the picture. From the perspective of the local, they were all far away, which meant they required modes of communication that were more intermediary than in the regional realm. In the same way, if the local maintained proxenic ties overseas, differences in real distance did not inevitably translate into different perceptions of the linkage as such. The main idea was that the distance was far, somewhere on the edge of the horizon.

The prevalence of regional connectivity becomes more pronounced when we consider the implications of central place theory. It was again John Bintliff (2002) who observed that the distribution of Classical poleis was catered toward the provision of economic services and relay stations, which, in turn, allowed for maximum capitalization of agricultural resources. On average, Bintliff calculated that the marketplaces of cities and towns in central and southern Greece were separated by about fifteen kilometers. This observation endorses the suggested typical size of combined urban and *chōra* territories. It also implies that the majority of exchanges was girded by the regional sphere. Religious and/or political organizations naturally intensified exchanges within the *ethnos*. Across the boundaries drawn by the politics of regional identity, archaeologists have traced a lively entanglement in microregions united by distinct natural features and favorable lines of translocal communication—for instance, in the Kephissos Valley from Phokis into Boiotia, in the human geographic triangle of Eretria, Tanagra, and Oropos, the Western Argolid, or around the Isthmus of Corinth. Extensive research in each of these microregions, among others, has brought to light busy and buzzing exchanges; their radius rarely extends more than 20–30 km. It is curious to note, although we will discuss the details only later (chapter 5), that the overall majority of grants of *proxenia* also falls within the scales of the regional *ethnos* and/or geographic microregion.[64]

One final comment on demography. Josiah Ober reminds us (2015, 84–89) that, while the vast majority of city-states fall into the 50–200 km^2 range of territory sizes, demography offers a different picture. He estimates that 80 percent of all people in Classical Greece lived in poleis with a territory size of more than 200 km^2, with a disproportionate concentration in the two megacities, Athens and Syracuse.[65] In other words, four-fifths of the people inhabited 10 percent of all cities and hence lived under the conditions of a higher connectivity rate than our compass suggests. Vice versa, the model of polis connectivity suggested here applies to only 20 percent of the entire population.

The point is well taken. In what Ian Morris (1998, 13–36) has characterized as the central Greek area, we encounter a particularly crowded world of city-states, including many around the 200 km^2 mark. Circumstances there, in

Central Greece, the Peloponnese, and the Cycladic and Ionian islands, were less imbalanced than elsewhere in the Greek Mediterranean. The principle of multiplied local spaces in a dense natural environment, each one with its own gravitational pull, proved to be particularly potent in the central area. If, as we argue throughout this book, the everyday experience was shaped by the epichoric horizon, then the principle of multiple, small-scale, and compartmentalized worlds of local meaning constituted a force in its own right. Regardless of its population size, the local (any local, really) had the capacity to generate meaning, which makes the interplay with universal manifestations of Greek culture all the more exciting.

Roadmap through This Book

If, as I believe, the prioritization of the local is a typical societal response to the challenge of expanding worlds, then localism is a transhistorical theme, hidden in the past and present in societies around the globe. Its encoding, intensity, and form are, however, deeply entangled with culture. Notions of, for instance, resistance to global trends or the rise of hybridity from local/global cross-fertilization, in arenas as divergent as materiality, lifestyle, or religion, might appear as self-evident dispositions, but their practice is in fact not obvious at all. As a fruitful concept in the study of history, inquiries into localism and the local require context. Indeed, one of the main weaknesses of the network turn is that it takes the inherent value of the network for granted, regardless of the cultural entrenchment of linkages, nodes, and clusters.

Scholars have brought to light in recent years a wealth of approaches to globalism and globalization in the Hellenistic world. Among the main findings of this type of research is that, from the Age of Alexander, sentiments of "belonging and isolation" (Ager and Faber 2013) became increasingly intertwined with a growing sense of cosmopolitanism: the delicate balance between local and global was tipped by a new quality of the global. This new quality, it has been argued, also triggered an identity crisis at the local level. In a world that had grown substantially larger, the expansion of previous worldviews required a profound adjustment of meaning and orientation.

The earliest traces of this need for readjustment are usually associated with Diogenes the Cynic's coining of the term *kosmopolitēs* around the mid-fourth century BCE. It has been rightly observed that Diogenes's point, rather than heralding the arrival of a full-fledged concept of a "citizen of the world," was mostly a "dramatic, parrhesiastic act of self-identification" (Chin 2016, 134). As a diagnosis of a societal state of being, the verdict of identity crisis was in any case not confined to Diogenes's days. I would argue that this type of challenge has been a common trait of Greek culture of all times, from the so-called Age of Colonization through the Classical period, and beyond. With it, attitudes and dispositions of the local were always probed, challenged, and, effectively, renegotiated. The ways in which the realignment played out were neither set nor stable, but malleable over time. In other words, while place remained principally the same, inspiring long-standing patterns of meaning, this long duration of the local was exposed to shifting parameters. Our test case from earlier in this chapter, the local sphere of Phlious of the fourth century BCE was different in many ways from that of the fifth century, as was the world around it.

Classical Greece, under scrutiny here, offers an intriguing example for the study of localism. Its basic ecology—united under a high-value currency of culture but politically fragmented into countless small places and a narrow, varied environment—provides both an exemplary configuration and a wealth of data through which the prioritization of the local becomes visible. In turn, and partly as a consequence of this ecology, Greek localism was destined to evolve along a dynamic trajectory, powered by the energy of vivid interaction and competition. This charge is felt even more when we turn to core Greece. For the most part, this book roams through the narrow terrain of the central area: the corridor stretching from Phokis and Boiotia across the Isthmus of Corinth and into the northeastern Peloponnese. Only occasionally do we leave a 100 km radius around the Isthmus of Corinth, although occasional jaunts into places further away, on Sicily and in Ionia, are inevitable. On the whole, however, the conversation takes place in a genuinely small Greek world.

The body of evidence for this type of endeavor is fragmented and rich at the same time. Fragmented, because our sources hardly ever allow us to unravel the local discourse of any one place in a stringent and coherent manner. Traces of the ontological quality of the local appear as spotlights in our sources rather than as continuing stories, and they pop up in poleis hither and yon, often unpredictable, sometimes random. It is tempting to point to the obvious, that the writing of ancient history is hardly ever a consistent enterprise to begin with; we never meet the expectations of what is believed to the be "the full picture," if such a thing exists. From a more constructive point of view, I feel that the fragmented nature of the evidence itself lends a structuring force to this study, not only in that it imparts countless local aperçus, but that it inspires a nonlinear narrative that traces the path to local distinctiveness.

This does not, however, dispose of the more basic challenge of how the topic is approached. Once we move beyond the spotlight of the moment, often captured in narratives of conflict and war, our sources are extremely rich, both in terms of quantity and quality. The human encounter with the local is engrained in categorically different types of evidence—literary and nonliterary, material and immaterial, anthropological and environmental. Add to these the more indirect manifestation of local, nuanced, subtle, and oblique: we have already noted how the quest for this type of evidence resembles the tracing of dark matter through which a pronounced local signature becomes visible. The obvious implication of all this is that the quest for the local draws on diverse research strategies to collect, process, and contextualize data. In this sense, the study of ancient Greek localism is located at the very crossroads in the present day where the conceptual language and grammar of many disciplines in the human sciences have come under reconsideration. In our discipline, the new benchmark is the creative integration also of fields, applications, and toolkits beyond those traditionally associated with the study of the ancient world.

Our journey to the local lifeworld of Classical Greece begins with the notion of attachment to the land: we explore how the rise of the Greek city was complemented by the appropriation of place, definite as well as metaphorical, fusing the meaning of the present day with high-powered images of the past (chapter 2). Subsequently, we immerse ourselves in the local as a cultural currency. The human sense of place is driven by sensory recognition and interpretative choices; no matter how deep the neurological encoding, the regime of the senses is always subject to the reins of culture. We trace both in our discussion of communal excitement—from the sensation of local taste and food traditions to pride in local skill sets and to the excitement of athletic spectacles and public performances. In the world of Classical Greece, the excitement of place was magnified by the fact that the land was inhabited by humans and supra-human beings alike. Indeed, the grounding of Greek religion in place marks one of the landmark principles in the repertoire of locally enshrined values and meanings. We turn to this in chapter 4. The final section examines the intricate question of how the conduct of politics was governed by ideas of the local (chapter 5). In particular, we explore how polis societies were susceptible to and geared toward a genuinely local reading of the world. In the arena of history and politics, too, the local was in persistent conversation with the wide horizon of Greek affairs. As we shall see, such exposure to the demands of a connected, fast-paced world did little to undermine the local's ability to provide purpose and offer orientation.

2

Attachment to the Land

> "A small and orderly polis on a rock is better than foolish Nineveh."
> PHOKYLIDES, frag. 4 Gentili/Prato

In the sixth century BCE, Phokylides of Miletus left no doubt about his affection for the small Greek city. His praise of local ambience echoed the voices of Hesiod and Theognis, who had declared their respective hometowns the ultimate place where they would pursue their goals in life, for good or for ill. The trope of a parochial lifestyle is notoriously prominent throughout *Works and Days*. Travel to Chalkis, across the straits that separated Euboia from Boiotia, was the maximum Hesiod was willing to consider (*W&D*, 651–67). Likewise, Theognis had journeyed "to Sicily, the vine-rich plains of Euboia and to Sparta, splendid city of the reed-nourishing Eurotas," but nothing else was dearer to him than his *patria*, his homeland (783–88). Journeys to faraway lands held no appeal to Hesiod and Theognis. They weren't their thing.[1]

Phokylides, too, appears to have been immune to the glamour of the world far and wide. The appraisal went beyond personal choice. His statement is usually understood as an early reference to the normative force of the city-state as a political aggregation, with a growing sense of self-governance or, avant la lettre, *autonomia*. Note how Phokylides's polis was "orderly" (*kata kosmon*) and in this sense "orderable." Organization *kata kosmon* corresponded with, and was in turn made possible by, another quality of the polis: namely, that it was "small" (*smikros*)—both virtues played out in the manageable world of the local horizon first and foremost. Phokylides's city was built on a steep hilltop, "on a rock." This might signal that it had good natural defenses. The image is one that occurs frequently in the *Iliad*, where Greek cities are described as steep or scanty (Kalydon: 2.640; 14.118). But there is more at work than defense strategies. The impression is that the inhabitants of these cities in rough terrain cultivated a particular sense of place. They occupied a spot that was neither rich nor necessarily pleasant, if this is the right way to put it. Often the most basic resources were hard to secure. Several cities in Phokis had no immediate water source available. Their inhabitants regularly trekked to the next spring or creek to obtain drinking water. The natural environment put limitations on the potential to grow. Yet the cities were well-thought-out by their people, who maintained and cherished them, evidently because the place meant something to them.[2]

As this chapter explains, the place of the polis inspired a series of links—relational, contextual, and spatial—between the community and its land. Each one of these links was filled with and gave rise to narratives of attachment. In chapter 1, we asserted that this normative quality of place is the main predicate of locality. Consequently, as we explore the various narratives of attachment to the land, the foremost concern is with how they were charged with a special social meaning. From the outset, it is intriguing to see how Nineveh, today's Mosul in Iraq, the most captivating metropolis of the Assyrian empire, lacked such charge, at least according to Phokylides. It is portrayed as "foolish" or, literally, "meaningless" (*aphrainousēs*). In this sense, Nineveh's fame as a grand capital was outweighed—or outdone—by the orderly yet sometimes charmless Greek city. In the contest between imperial megacity and parochial polis, the latter scored higher. In the following sections, we explore how Phokylides, and the inhabitants of Greek city-states in general, might have arrived at such a conclusion: how, in the aftermath of the Bronze Age, the association with the land originated from the nuclear world of small, disconnected communities; how it translated in the Archaic period into stories of intricate relations with the land; and how the resulting sentiments shaped a territorial mentality that lent local weight and meaning to the Greek city.

Grains, Orchards, and No Shellfish

The origins of an unyielding attachment to the land lay in the early days of Greek history. When the Mycenaean palaces fell, this triggered a ripple of disconnect among the settlements that survived the downfall. With the crash of the palaces came the collapse of the transregional networks of Aegean exchange. Regardless of whether we perceive the network ties between the Bronze Age palaces as strong or weak links, as one- or multidirectional, as decentralized or hierarchical, or as a combination of these that played out differently between different networking agents, once the central nodes of the web had faded, the network as such disappeared. Whatever the inhabitants of the palaces had enjoyed by means of their transregional connectivity had slipped from the hands of those who lived among the ruins. This was also true for the small towns in the countryside to which the palace had served as a relay station, thereby connecting them to the orbit of the Aegean world. In the rural areas of the palatial domains, the demise of the center left hamlets and villages to fend for themselves. Their ties with the palace prior to the downfall have recently been profoundly reconsidered. As a result, the understanding of the redistributive nature of this relation has gained new depth. But again, no matter how the interaction between the palace and its satellites in the countryside had actually played out, after about 1200 BCE the link was broken.[3]

The site of Nichoria in the southwestern Peloponnese captures this schism. Nichoria was most likely a sizable town with 600–800 inhabitants whose settlement enjoyed some wealth. Indeed, it has been conjectured that, in the expanding Pylian kingdom, Nichoria rose to become a flourishing regional center. Most likely, it was the place attested as *ti-mi-to-a-ke-e*, wielding administrative control over the area across the Likodimo ridge, known as the Further Province. Frequent references in the Linear B tablets to the head official, the *qa-si-re-u*, as well as to numerous local landholders (the notorious *te-re-ta*) suggest that the town took the lead role in this corner of Pylos's domain. All the while, the local *qa-si-re-u* and his followers seem to have operated under less restrictive conditions than, for instance, the local dependencies of Mycenae in the plain of Argos.[4]

Following the old orthodoxy of a complete wipeout, the excavators of Nichoria had initially thought the settlement was deserted after the fall of Pylos, but subsequent readings of dispersed sherd finds in the layers after 1200 suggest otherwise. Unlike the palace at Pylos, which was no longer occupied, the settlement at Nichoria continued, albeit on a reduced scale.[5] Analysis of animal bones from the ridge suggests that, from the eleventh century, the inhabitants sustained themselves through pasturing of domesticated animals on the hilltop and in the plains below—mostly cattle, but also smaller numbers of sheep, goats, and pigs. Deer bones betray hunts in the surrounding woodlands. At the same time, the archaeological record speaks to planting, harvesting, and storing activities that responded to the natural cycle of the year. In the lowlands, where there was no shortage of water, grains (wheat and probably barley), grapes, olives, and vegetables were grown with increasing intensity. These finds indicate that the Nichorians were farmers, herdsmen, and hunters alike.[6] It is striking to see that these activities were carried out in a discrete environment. Although the sea was only two kilometers away, the almost complete absence of shellfish from the records implies that the inhabitants did not venture far from their hilltop, and certainly not toward, or across, the sea.

After about 950, a few shared motifs between pottery from Nichoria and Sparta signal early interaction with Lakonia, albeit on a limited scale. We should be cautious not to overstate these scant finds. Confined to its flat-topped ridge, Nichoria was a parochial hideout, which allowed its settlers to organize their food supplies and carry out their fundamental household crafts in the immediate vicinity of their village.[7] Naturally, such a lifestyle instilled a growing sense of attachment to the place itself—the ridge as the shelter of their habitation, the fertile bottomlands as a rich source of agro-pastoral foodstuffs, the nearby woods as hunting grounds. In this environment, the Nichorians had everything they needed to survive. Besides, their isolation in one remote spot of the Peloponnese left them without many choices. For much of the Iron Age, Nichoria's trajectory was bound to the local horizon.

North of Pylos, along the western shores of the Peloponnese and into the Ionian Sea, circumstances on Ithaca blend into this picture. Yet the lens through which conditions there become visible is also different. Odysseus's famous habitat has not yet been found, although the palatial building complex near Aghios Athanasios, in the northwestern corner of the island, is now treated as a hot candidate by Greek archaeologists; however, due to a lack of public funds, excavations there were suspended in 2009. Be that as it may, it is amply clear that no single palace existed on Ithaca that matched Pylos in grandeur. Local protogeometric pottery developed from Submycenaean styles, which suggests a continuity of some habitations across the divide of 1200.[8] Unlike those at Nichoria, the finds from a sanctuary on the isthmus of Mt. Aetos point to a measurable degree of transregional exchange from the ninth century, if not earlier. Excavations brought to light not only imported ceramics but also bronze, ivory, and amber, among other precious foreign items. These finds should not be understood as signs of the longevity of Bronze Age networks of trade and exchange. Rather, they resonate with what Irad Malkin has labeled a regional clustering: given the island's strategic location in the Ionian Sea, which put it on the map for anyone who traveled across the adjacent Aegean and Adriatic regions, it is easy to see how Ithaca rose as a localized node in transregional routes of communication.[9] A similar development is attested for Perachora and its Sanctuary of Hera on the westernmost tip of the Geraneia promontory, which occupied a vital traffic node in navigations across the Corinthian Gulf from the tenth and ninth centuries BCE.[10] Amid this emergence of new seafaring routes, the scattered settlements in the area of Vathy and ancient Alalkomenai lived from small-scale farming. Their agricultural regime was shaped by the climatic conditions typical to the islands of the Ionian Sea. In the valleys and narrow plains, olives were harvested, along with grapes from sloping vineyards, and grains.

More precious were the crops from pear, apple, and fig orchards, high in fiber and essential minerals. Fig trees in particular were characteristic of rocky Ithaca, due to their ability to survive in arid edges of the cultivated land. In the mountains, a variety of wild herbs (e.g., sage, thyme) added to the local flavor of foodstuffs.[11]

This is the backdrop to Odysseus's story. The *Odyssey*'s theme is one of an archetypical homecoming, *nostos*, with the protagonist desperately "longing to return to his home and his wife" (*Od.* 1.13). This striving for family and home—as much a state of being as a physical place, the *oikos* from which he was "longing to see the smoke curling up" (1.58-59)—is amplified by the way it is couched in the depiction of Ithaca. Much like our mercenaries who suffered from Swiss Disease (chapter 1), Odysseus's mental state is wholly subject to the desire to return to his native land, his *gaia* (1.21). It is among the poem's great dramaturgical moments that, when he finally completes his journey after countless adventures afar, Odysseus is so battered that he does not recognize Ithaca. Highlighting his state of disarray and the sense of estrangement it fosters, the singer states that Odysseus, upon his return to Ithaca, "didn't recognize just where he was. He'd been away so long. . . . all things seemed strange to [him], the long paths, the harbor with safe anchorage, the sheer cliffs, and the luxuriant trees. So he jumped up and looked upon his native land, and then he groaned and struck his thighs with the flat of his hands. Mournfully he said: 'Where am I now? Whose country have I come to this time?'" (13.187-89, 194-200). Pallas Athena fills him in:

> "Stranger, you're a fool, or else you've come from somewhere far away, if truly you ask about this land. Its name is not unknown—not at all—many men have heard of it, all those who live toward the dawn and rising sun, as well as all who dwell towards the gloomy darkness in the west. It is a rugged place, not fit for driving horses, yet not too poor, although not very wide. There are countless crops and wine-bearing grapes. There's no lack of rain or heavy dew, a fine land for raising goats and cattle. There are all sorts of trees and watering holes that last throughout the year. And so, stranger, the name of Ithaca is even known in Troy, which, they say, is far from this land of Achaia." (13.237-49)

Up to this point in the epic, references to Ithaca are mostly generic, with little attention to detail. Athena's attention to the features of the land announces that the narrative segues from adventures abroad to the world of Odysseus's home. Note how herding is captured: the land is not fit for horse breeding, but good for goats and cattle. Farming conditions are portrayed somewhat broadly, but there is reference to some characteristics—the island was notorious for its vineyards and abundant orchards. In sum, it is a rugged place, not too poor but not too rich either, yet certainly fine enough to sustain a good life. Listening to Athena's words, it doesn't take Odysseus long to grasp that he has arrived in his homeland, even though he is cunning enough to keep up his cover and withhold expressions of joy for the time being. The concluding act of his *nostos* thus begins in book 13 with Odysseus reconnecting with his *gaia* and everything it meant to the hero. Its vegetation, harbors, farmlands, herding grounds: these images of the land assure Odysseus that his *nostimon imar* (1.168), the day of his sweet return, has finally come. The word *nostimos* signals genuine sensual excitement: a culinary word in the modern Greek language today that means a pleasing taste because it triggers sentiments of home, Odysseus' *nostimon imar* speaks to the full breadth of the sensory phalanx. It signifies a deep emotional reunion with everything he had longed for, for so long.[12]

In book 24, toward the very end of the poem, this importance of the land in the process of homecoming resurfaces. When the *nostos* is complete, after the suitors have been killed and Odysseus has reclaimed his *oikos*, he reaches out to his father, Laertes, who lives on a removed farmstead. Odysseus catches him, significantly enough, shoveling a plant (24.226–27). Laertes doubts Odysseus's story, but his doubts are cast aside with the following:

> "Come, I will also point out to you the trees which you once gave me in our well-ordered garden, and I, who was only a boy, followed you around the garden and asked you about this and that. It was through these very trees that we passed, and you told me their names and what they all were. You gave me thirteen pear trees, ten apple trees, and forty fig trees. And rows of wine too you said you would give, fifty of them. There was corn planted between each row, and they yield fruits of every kind whenever the seasons of Zeus weighed them down." (24.336–44; see also 244–48)

To verify his identity, Odysseus references the family estate, the agricultural land and its crops, and everything he had learned as a young man about farming and plant growing from his father. The land is a force that unites generations in their efforts to cultivate it; it equates to home as such. The conversation about orchards and grains thus puts an empathic closure to the *nostos*, indicating that Odysseus is reunited with his land. Only now has the hero arrived home in the fullest sense of the word.[13]

While the archaeological record tells a developing story, Homer's poetry looks at the Mycenaean world from the rearview mirror of later centuries. At the intersection of both perspectives, Homeric attitudes toward the land overlap with our findings in Nichoria. As we have seen earlier, after the downfall of c. 1200, settlements across Aegean Greece were left to fend for themselves.

Without the administrative finesse and technical know-how of the palaces, they strove to sustain themselves through hunting, farming, and herding, all of which were carried out in a small-scale environment. The high number of local pottery styles in the postpalatial period impressively highlights this confinement. For the first two centuries or so after the collapse, most of the small subsistence economies had little contact with the outer world. Some regions were of course hit harder than others. In Messenia, Achaia, and Boiotia, for instance, the degree of desertion and, effectively, local isolation was higher than it was on Euboia or in the Argolid (the geometric pottery of Argos, we ought to add, has been found to be clearly local in its styles). All the while, this disconnect should not be misinterpreted as a condition that inevitably put settlements on the road to failure. Archaeological finds from Phokis, Opuntian Lokris, northern Thessaly, and eastern Attica near Perati suggest that many of these local settlements fared relatively well. Some were even of formidable size, with necropoleis of two hundred tombs and more. Analysis of skeletal minerals points toward predominantly terrestrial animal protein in the diet, similar to the pattern we encountered in Nichoria.[14]

Along the Kephissos corridor in Phokis, diverse evidence hints at a combined agro-pastoral regime that persisted for much of the Iron Age. In the case of Elateia, supplies seem to have been sufficient enough to take in populations from nearby sites, adding to the city's role as a local center. At Kalapodi, bronze finds from the Geometric period betray a lively activity, although the evidence speaks mostly to a limited horizon: the main traffic routes of offerings point toward the upper Kephissos valley, Malis, and Southern Thessaly (Pherai).[15] Finally, the afterlife of the late Bronze Age tholos tomb of Kazarma near Arkadiko suggests that the surrounding village fared fairly well among the Mycenaean ruins. In the post-Mycenaean period, the tomb apparently became the focus of an ancestor cult, as illustrated by the ritual sacrifice of animal bones and drinking vessels there. It is unclear how much the small settlement owed to its strategic location at the highest point on the Mycenaean traffic corridor through the Argolid. The Iron Age occupants of Kazarma in all likelihood led a mostly secluded life.[16]

From about 1000 to the time of Homer, the local settlements of Greece witnessed a steady increase in exchange that outbalanced their state of isolation. We noted above how in Nichoria around 950 the first Lakonian sherds appear among the archaeological stratum referred to as Dark Age 2. Increasingly regionalized pottery styles, fibulae, pins, and luxury items such as the ones we encountered in the sanctuary on the isthmus of Mt. Aetos on Ithaca further enrich the picture of reemerging exchanges. The question of how these contacts should be understood is a difficult one, and there is a general danger in jumping too quickly from contact to connectivity. For instance, some of the attested objects might have arrived at their final destination through intermediaries, such as shepherds or fishermen who acted as go-betweens among different settlements. In that case, the contact was mostly perfunctory. In other instances, and upon closer examination, attested traces of exchange might not speak to long-distance connectivity at all.[17] The available evidence does not automatically suggest that these villages immersed themselves in a transregional network society. Unlike in the Bronze Age, there was no stable exchange that allowed them to, for instance, adjust everyday practices such as the organization of food supplies to the possibilities provided by a connected world, or to reconfigure those practices in light of a new networking mentality.

On the contrary. All regional differences set aside, what the Dark Age settlements of Greece had in common was that they developed a sense of attachment to their land and its surroundings, simply because it was the one vital resource that guaranteed their survival. As we noted earlier, pastoralism and seasonal occupation of hamlets were typical practices that, at times, complemented the subsistence strategies of many settlements. But the developing picture of habitation patterns puts a significant challenge before the so-called pastoralist hypothesis, which posits seasonal roaming as the predominant form of subsistence. It seems clear that the idea of a transient lifestyle, as a widespread phenomenon, carries only so far.[18] In sedentary agrarian communities, on the other hand, attachment to place is a common feature. As we will see shortly, in the Greek world this gave rise to a particular body of stories and traditions that placed the interplay between land and people at the heart of communal self-beliefs.

Meanwhile, not every community succeeded in the struggle for survival. Some were abandoned, such as Nichoria in the mid-eighth century; it is futile to conjecture how, and why, their settlements came to an end. Lefkandi, an Iron Age powerhouse and notorious for what was at the time the largest monumental building in mainland Greece (shortly after 1000 BCE), went through revolving cycles of ups and downs. A vibrant relay station in regional exchanges and trade contacts as far as the Eastern Mediterranean, Lefkandi was a sizeable settlement, although there is some debate over the extent and nature of the community. Toward the end of the eighth century, the settlement collapsed and was abandoned.[19] Others, such as Askra or Panopeus, lingered on, but they never really evolved into vibrant towns. Yet others thrived. For the more successful towns, the relation to place became stronger in subsequent periods, amplifying over time. The sites of these future city-states evolved into local points of reference: soon enough, place not only provided the canvas for the projection of communal values, but it became a compass of orientation. This twofold quality of place made the early polis meaningful to its inhabitants. How much might be a matter of debate, but apparently more meaningful than "foolish Nineveh."

Born of the Earth, or from Dragon Teeth

Colonial ventures through the Iron Age Mediterranean broadened the horizon of many early city-states. The foundation of settlements far afield extended the sheer radius of action, as did the participation in the trade of goods between the mainland and the distant shores of Sicily, Southern Italy, and the Black Sea region. With this came an all-new degree of connectivity, although, as we have seen in chapter 1, the nature of the emerging networks and their ability to trigger a shift in the mindsets of those who engaged in them is open to scrutiny. The motivations and reasons behind what was traditionally labeled the Great Colonization have in any case been thoroughly revised in recent research, as postcolonial theory has become the benchmark for how we converse about the nature of Greek settlements overseas. In fact, the term *colonization* had already fallen out of fashion before the arrival of the postcolonial paradigm because it implied a coherent movement and a uniform trend that triggered it, neither of which were the case. True, the conventional renderings have the narratives of Herodotus and Thucydides in their favor. But there is also a sense of healthy skepticism about the cut-and-dried organization of colonial enterprises, as is implied by both authors.

Take the issue of agrarian crisis, which, following Herodotus, has usually been regarded as one of the prime movers. Against this view, archaeologists have questioned the basic belief that the demand of rising populations, coupled with their concentration in new urban centers, put city-states before an omnipresent challenge. In Corinth, for instance, the growing urban population had access to an extensive hinterland of up to 900 km². By means of comparison, the territory of most poleis did not exceed much over 100 km². What is more, the Corinthian hinterland does not betray any traces of overpopulation, nor is the quality of the soil poor for agricultural exploitation; quite the contrary holds true. It appears that the Corinthians had everything they needed to feed a growing population. And yet Corinth was one of the main colonizing powers of the day.[20]

In a similar vein, while the demography of Chalkis, Eretria, and Megara, all major colonizing agents, indicates a formidable increase in population from the eighth century BCE, this rise appears to have been less dramatic than is sometimes assumed. Few scholars today subscribe to the belief that

Chalkis and Eretria came to blows over the agricultural produce in the plain between them, the so-called Lelantine Plain, because of swiftly rising population figures and the hunger this generated. The agricultural capacity of each was healthy enough to keep supplies in sync with the growing number of people. There was no agrarian crisis that triggered waves of emigration, let alone an event as fantastic as the Lelantine War.[21] Similar to Megara and Euboia, the town of Askra, although significantly smaller, experienced no shortage of land either. Askra was not a prosperous place but nonetheless successful enough to take in new citizens from elsewhere. Hesiod's *Works and Days* portrays an agricultural ambience of grain crops and grapes, draft animals, and livestock (goats and sheep) that were at the heart of self-sufficient farming activities. On the whole, this should summon the scene.[22]

These observations are exciting because they challenge the widespread assumption of crisis and collapse in the agrarian sector during the early Archaic period. In fact, they turn the old orthodoxy on its head. For if the rising city-states of the mainland had enough farmland and herding grounds available to sustain their populations, and they fully exploited these opportunities to build their communities, then the agricultural background of early poleis must have been in itself more developed, and impactful, than often assumed. By extension, this verdict also applies to cities that are typically associated with extensive mercantile activities and long-distance trade.

With the agrarian lifestyle playing such a prominent role, it comes as no surprise that the spatial awareness of separate realms of the city and its countryside, the *chōra*, became a key factor in the emergence of the polis. In a study that appears as ingenious as it is controversial, François de Polignac uncovered the way in which the agricultural exploitation of the land in the late ninth and eighth centuries resonated in new cult practices that revolved around the fertility of the soil. His model has come under attack within a decade of its publication, because it associates sanctuaries in the countryside with corresponding urban centers at an early time when their relation was still fragile, open to negotiation. The territorial character of the festivals discussed by de Polignac seems, however, too obvious to be dismissed. Venerating the rural deities that nurtured the community, those ceremonies were usually performed in peri- or extra-urban sanctuaries that were located on the fringes of communal land—or, more precisely, of what would become communal fringes along the way. The ritual, segmented with processions through the countryside, mediated the relation between the people and the deities that guaranteed the well-being of their settlement. There is ample evidence. In Selinus on Sicily, the sanctuary of Demeter Malaphoros, "the Fruit-Bearer," embodied this triangular notion of territorial demarcation, spatial differentiation between city and hinterland, and reconciliation with a goddess of fertility. The *temenos* of Apollo Hyakinthios, located a few kilometers southwest of Sparta and associated with the great hero of vegetation, acquired a similar role in Spartan society. In Argos, the interdependence between the city and countryside was forcefully articulated through the integration of the sanctuary of Hera, which lay in the periphery of the polis, about 9 km from the urban center.[23]

We elaborate on this more fully below when turning to the issue of religion and the countryside (chapter 4). For now, the idea of spatial differentiation sets the scene for another important expression of the sense of place: that is, as settlement patterns and spatial concepts of the polis evolved from the eighth century, so too did legendary traditions that proclaimed an innate bond between the people and the land.

In their conversations about communal origins and primordial descent, many city-states acknowledged that they originated from wandering heroes who had arrived in Greece to take the land from earlier peoples there. The elusive Pelasgians were usually referred to as indigenous inhabitants of "Greece before Greece"—that is, before the advent of Hellenic culture. According to Herodotus, Hellas itself was called Pelasgia in the distant past (2.56.1).[24] Hence, the broad stream of legendary tales of descent depicted the Greeks as migrants who, under the leadership of illustrious culture heroes, had come to Hellas from abroad. In a key passage, Herodotus surveys the populations of the Peloponnese (which itself bore the name of a wandering cultural hero, Pelops from Phrygia). According to his account, most of its inhabitants had arrived in their present lands from elsewhere: Aitolians, Dryopians, Lemnians, Dorians from outside the Peloponnese; Achaians after wanderings within. And then there were the Arkadians and Kynourians, who were "autochthonous and remain settled in the same places that they had inhabited in the past" (8.73.2). Unlike the immigrant peoples of the Peloponnese, the latter two had always been there; they had possessed their land since time immemorial.[25] In a similar vein, the Athenians claimed autochthonous status for themselves through Erichthonios, the legendary king of Athens, who was said to have been *gēgenēs*, "born of the soil."[26]

The claim of autochthony heralds a forceful link between people and the land. The notion appears as a universal paradigm that can be traced in various civilizations and across different periods of time. But as a particular variant of the broader concept of indigeneity, autochthony is also specific to the culture that nourishes it. In Canada, for instance, several indigenous peoples pursue the idea that they originated from the earth. Inuit myths of descent relate that all humans were made from *niaqutait*, hummocks of earth. At the dawn of time, the land (*nuna*) governed reproductive and alimentary cycles—the earth was the beginning and the end of all life—until humans gradually acquired certain skills that enabled them to become agents of their own, next to earth, sky, and animals. Fostering the idea that they were initially born of the earth, the close association between the Inuit and the land translates into a series of mutual obligations that condition the well-being of all agents. If, on the other hand, people violate the equilibrium, the perpetrators will suffer the inevitable retaliation from those who have been harmed (earth, sky, animals). Such retaliation is extremely dangerous, as it will most likely interfere with the already marginal existence of the Inuit. The indigenous connection with the earth therefore creates a mutual bond between people and land. Yet, although the people are born of the land and have lived on it since the beginning of time, they do not actually own the land. Inuit consider themselves *nunaatigiit*, "those who share the land," which articulates the belief that the land cannot be owned; it is common to all. Despite claiming a strong and existential relation with the land, these traditions do not instill the Inuit with the sense that they are the rightful owners of the land. In Western Canada, the Nisga'a Nation, which resides in a relatively small territory, shares a similar set of self-beliefs. Like the Inuit, the Nisga'a are sometimes described as hunter-gatherers, which seems to set them on a different footing than sedentary societies. But such a dichotomy is easily overstated, as the degree of movement varies over time, and hunter-gatherer subsistence clearly doesn't preclude the idea of attachment to territory. On the contrary, despite the Nisga'a Nation's movements, attachment to the Nass Valley is a prevalent notion. Due to the cultivating acts of a trickster there, the valley epitomizes a storied landscape that gives shape to what makes the Nisga'a who they are.[27]

Greek autochthony shared some of these traits, but it was also different with regard to others. The word that is used by Herodotus to describe the indigenous trait of the Arkadians is *autochthōn*, which captures the idea of occupation of the land since earliest time; in this sense, it resembles the English word *indigeneity*. More specifically, the term implies that *autochthones*, in the plural, were "born from the land itself."[28] Herodotus's Arkadians were autochthonous through their foundation hero Arkas, who was regarded as bringer of Arkadian customs and culture. But note that Arkas himself, unlike the Athenian Erichthonios, was not earthborn; he was the son of Zeus and a local nymph named Kallisto. The quality of Arkas as an autochthonous hero was that he was the first to establish a link between the Arkadians and the land. This extended, through filiation, to all of his descendants.[29] What made the Arkadians autochthonous then was, in Herodotus's words, that they "remain settled in the same places that they had inhabited in the past." There is a vital temporal link here between the present day and the past that is grounded in place. Indeed, Herodotus goes on to explain that the notion of perseverance in an autochthonous lifestyle is just as strong a criterion of autochthony as the bond with the land as such, for the Kynourians, Herodotus continues, "had become thoroughly Dorian . . . with the passage of time" (8.73.3). This does not void their autochthony, but it does jeopardize the ties between the present day and the time of origin of their group. The variations of different conditions of autochthony and their ranked hierarchy is clear: the Athenians were descendants of an earthborn king, and they had treasured their autochthonous legacy ever since. The Arkadians originated not from the earth but from a culture hero, and they maintained the spatial ties and cultural ways over time. By contrast, the Kynourians qualified as autochthonous because they stuck around, disregarding the link that united them with the soil.

At Thebes, these various shades of autochthony coalesced. Established by a foreign culture hero, Kadmos of Phoinikia, the *ktisis* of Thebes comprised a somewhat bizarre sequence of events. Kadmos was led to the site of future Thebes at the behest of the Oracle at Delphi, which had instructed him to follow a cow until she lies down exhausted, and then found a city there. Once they reached the designated site, some 110 kilometers away, Kadmos eagerly got to work but was attacked by a dragon while collecting water from a nearby well. The monster is taken down with the help of Athena, who advises Kadmos to sow the dragon's teeth, which in turn give rise to a band of fully armed warriors, the so-called Spartoi, "the Sown Men." However, the Spartoi begin killing each other on the spot. Only a handful of them survive the slaughter to become the ancestral forefathers of the Thebans. The account thus reconciles the idea of autochthony, in the sense of earthbornness, with the idea of a culture hero from abroad, whose action (notably the slaying of the monster) renders the land inhabitable. The Thebans never abandoned this place, maintaining the local tie to their origins over time. Their claims for indigeneity were thus based on the triad of autochthonous descent plus cultural and spatial continuity.[30]

There are several interpretative challenges. As always with Greek foundation myths, there was no single, authoritative version; rather, there were countless divergent local traditions, which, taken individually, were never static or stable over time. Consequently, much of Kadmos's story and the sowing of the Spartoi had become already a matter of dispute among ancient writers who attempted to rationalize the narrative. For instance, in an account from the fourth century BCE, the Spartoi were understood as a warrior band that was assembled by Kadmos from all over the earth; hence their perceived earthboundness. In a different reading, from the same time, Androtion conjectured that the Thebans must have been so alarmed by the military prowess of Kadmos's band that they appeared to them as natural warriors—and so emerged the idea of their birth in full armor.[31] In modern scholarship, the convoluted nature of the legend has sometimes led to the dissociation of the narrative strands of Kadmos and the Spartoi, which might not have amalgamated before the later sixth century. Such a late combination of both tales is not impossible; indeed, the boastful claim for autochthony might have been inspired by similar narratives, as they were prominent across the border in Athens. But in order to make for a meaningful blend, both strands must have been significantly older. It is best to assume, then, that Kadmos's story mirrors a narrative piecemeal of the early Archaic period.

In her examination of Theban and Boiotian foundation myths, Angela Kühr disclosed how the key themes of Kadmos's *ktisis* developed over time and in space, and how this related to the process of ethnogenesis in Boiotia. Kühr casts light on the idea of earthboundness as it shines through at various moments in the story. Before Kadmos is attacked by the dragon, he is about to offer a sacrifice to Ge (Mother Earth), signaling reconciliation with the divine. The sacrifice is meant to establish harmony between the settlement and the land on which it will be built. As we have seen, the slaying of the monster was not only a civilizing and cultural achievement, but it also unlocked the resources of the land (fig. 2.1). As the dragon occupies a critical spot—the well of Ares on the nearby Hill of Ismenios—it is only with its removal that the water source becomes accessible, allowing the settlers to make use of it in their efforts to cultivate the soil. There is a sense of fertilization of the land traceable here that can be detected in other variants of the legend too. In Euripides's *Phoinikian Women*, the chorus points to this thought by praising the agricultural prosperity effected by Kadmos: his *ktisis* made Thebes "in the plains rich with wheat, and where the lovely waters of Dirke pour over the land, the green and deep-seeded fields" (644–46).[32] Finally, the dragon itself is a chthonic creature that establishes a bond with the land. He is labeled as *gēgenēs* ("earthborn"), and his teeth are sown back into the earth, from where the Spartoi rise. The story of death and rebirth translates the idea of autochthony from a wild, uncivilized world into a new order, where earthbornness endures in Kadmos's city. When Kadmos, in the next episode of the saga, marries Harmonia, in the same spot where the *ktisis* was performed and in the presence of all gods, the legend concludes by presenting the foundation of Thebes in precisely this light of a new cosmogony. As is highlighted in Kühr's analysis, one of the main traits of the legend is thus the rise of a new civil order that embraces old and new.[33]

FIGURE 2.1. Black-figure kylix from c. 550 BCE (Rider Painter). The iconography captures the moment when Kadmos takes possession of the land. Fighting the dragon who occupies the well, represented here by a typical fountain house, Kadmos defeats the forces of wilderness and unlocks the natural resources necessary for his city-foundation to thrive. The cup is of Lakonian provenance, the scene is therefore sometimes identified as Apollo slaying Python. Both themes appear prominently in the works of the Rider Painter and on other pieces of Lakonian pottery at the time. The Spartan clan of the Aigeidai traced their heroic pedigree to Kadmos, who was venerated in a hero shrine in Sparta. Beyond the Theban reading of the story, the tradition was entangled with Lakonian interpretations of how the encounter on the Ismenian Hill mattered to Spartan society; see Nafissi 1991, 365–69; Malkin 1994, 100–102; Lupi 2018. Image Rights: Collection Campana 1861, E669. © bpk / Musée du Louvre, Paris. Printed with permission.

It is commonplace to interpret the claim for autochthony as a powerful strategy of city-states, in the Classical period and beyond, in their competition for recognition and renown. Most evidently, such interpretations are inspired by Athenian boasts of the city's autochthonous nature. On the road to Salamis, when Gelon of Syracuse demanded to lead the maritime forces of the Hellenic League against Persia, his proposition was brushed aside by the Athenians on the grounds that "we can demonstrate that we have the longest lineage of all, and [we] alone among the Greeks have never changed our place of habitation" (Hdt. 7.161.3). In the debate over military leadership, the claim for autochthony was employed as a gesture that speaks to an innate quality of the Athenians, allowing them to substantiate their demands vis-à-vis those of others. In the genre of funeral orations, the argument occurs as a rhetorical device that reminds citizens that they lived in a community of fate, with one common ancestry.[34] Following this avenue of interpretation, Nicole Loraux has taught us that the notion of autochthony also created a mental interface between citizens and the democratic polis. Fostering the idea that all Athenians were ultimately—and equally—born of Mother Earth, such kinship strengthened the communal ties among the Athenians, male and female citizens alike. The sentiment of collective earthbornness thus fueled the idea of equality among the citizen body and filled the mental space of democracy with life.[35]

Readings of autochthony such as those of Loraux consign the topic to the realm of "big politics," to democracy and warfare. Just as, in the Athenian discourse, autochthony was superior to migration (we will turn to this momentarily), so was democracy to oligarchy. As we have seen earlier, the Thebans might have tapped into the contest too by brewing their own story of combined wandering and earthbornness. There is, however, another trait to the topic, one that is more subtle and mundane. Claims to autochthony were not staked by superpowers such as Athens and Sparta alone. As we have seen above, the Kynourians, of whom little is known otherwise, proclaimed a similar status for themselves; their call for autochthony gained them some notoriety in Herodotus. To the north of Kynouria, less than fifty kilometers away, the people of Phlious voiced similar claims. Their settlement was initially called Arentinos or Arantia and traced itself back to the earthborn hero Aras. When Pausanias visited the village, ideas of Aras's earthbornness still reverberated; his story was entrenched in, and in turn reinforced by, the natural environment and a vibrant cultural topography.[36] The foundation myths of Argos, halfway between Kynouria and Phlious, reported that Argos, too, was established by a hero who himself had sprung from earth—at least, this is what the Argive historian Akousilaos said.[37]

What follows from these instances is that many city-states garnered the idea of earthbornness, either through land genealogies that aligned the community to a common ancestor who was born of the soil, or through a culture hero who laid the foundation of its sociopolitical and economic existence in a spot that was never since abandoned; or both. The associated stories not only wove a strong mental tie between the people and the land; they rooted the inhabitants *in* it. The land, the *chōra* in particular, was the place that provided the people with more or less rich resources. At the same time, it was a commodity of immaterial value. Its topography was charged with traditions of indigeneity and narratives of descent, and in a great many cases the soil was itself the ultimate source of a common ancestry. In a swiftly changing world around them, with ever new forms of contact and exchange, legends of earthbornness invited an inward-looking perspective. They were the anchor that grounded the city in place.

It would seem that legends of wandering and migration precipitated a somewhat looser association with the land. At least this is what Athenian ideology implied. In a very prominent spot in his history, in the early sections of book 1, Thucydides expresses his belief that prosperity and cultural advancement were long-term consequences of sedentariness. Tied to a soil that was not exceedingly fertile, he argues, the Athenians did better than others because they occupied their land without interruption. Continuous habitation allowed for ongoing improvement in agricultural techniques, while the relative poverty of the soil skirted the jealousy of outsiders. Other areas of Greece, Thucydides continues, such as Thessaly, Boiotia, and most of the Peloponnese, were blessed with more fruitful lands. Yet their richness invited factionalism and attracted invaders, so that in turn they suffered from multiple waves of migration. These ruptures were precisely the cause that stilted economic growth. By means of comparison, Athens was the better, more stable, and more sustainable society (1.2.4–6).[38]

The connection between sedentariness and a prosperous way of life is already prevalent in Herodotus, who juxtaposes the autochthonous Athenians with the "much-wandering" (1.56; cf. 7.161) forefathers of the Dorians. The binary feeds off the Dorian foundation saga as preserved in the tradition of the Return of the Heraklids, among the most prominent myths of migration. In a version that was nourished at Sparta, the legend represented Spartan rule over Lakonia and beyond as the result of the recovery of Herakles's inheritance. Once the Heraklids had returned to the Peloponnese from their exile in "windy Erineus" (Tyrtaios, frag. 2 Gerber), after multiple moments of success, setback, and suspense, they distributed the land among themselves by lot. Lakonia fell to the twin brothers Eurysthenes and Prokles, great-great-great-grandsons of Herakles. With Sparta counting among the legacies initially bestowed upon Herakles by Zeus, the return of his offspring completed their quest for rightful restoration of the divine order.[39] Yet the twin brothers weren't considered *archēgetai* of Sparta, or founding magistrates. The actual *ktisis* occurred only under their son (Agis) and grandson (Eurypon). Yet Eurysthenes and Prokles weren't the first settlers in the Eurotas valley either. According to heroic genealogies as they took shape in the Archaic period, the first mythical king in Sparta was Lelex, son of Poseidon or Helios. According to another tradition, he was earthborn. Among his offspring were a daughter Lakonia and a son Eurotas, who were considered the eponymous heroes of the land before the *ktisis* was initiated by Agis and Eurypon.[40] Across the Aegean, the eponymous founder of the Ionian city of Miletus was a hero of the same name. But the city had a pre-life, as it were. In the earlier time, a certain Anax was either referenced as a giant or was the first king of the city, who was considered to have been born from the earth. The later Milesians intermingled with his descendants.[41]

The observation of protracted beginnings bears some relevance. As we have seen, Herodotus posits a binary of autochthony and wandering. Yet he also offers a more nuanced appraisal. True, the Spartans/Dorians were wanderers. But at the same time, although a migrating tribe, they were considered by Herodotus (1.56) as genuine Greeks from the dawn of time. Once they had arrived in the Eurotas valley, their pedigree amalgamated with that of another foundation figure, that of Lelex, an autochthonous hero. Through Lelex, the tradition of wandering Dorians was partially and creatively enriched with the motive of autochthony. The Ionians, on the other hand, were the archetypical descendants of the earth. But Herodotus states in the same passage that they were not of Hellenic but of Pelasgian origin, which put a dent in their pristineness. In other words, there was a moment of recalibration that blurred Athenian claims for earthborn descent.

Between the origins of time and the cultural act of *ktisis* were multiple moments of intermingling and blending that allowed for a narrative reconciliation between earthbornness and wandering. The standard binary of autochthony and migration should thus not be overstated. In some sense, the orthodox view of opposition is counterintuitive to the fabric of Greek foundation myths. As these stories covered a remote past, they were just as convoluted, volatile, and widely adaptable as the vagaries that came with the long duration of time. Wandering and earthbornness pointed to registers of origins that were categorically different. Yet with each one going through many phases of narrative blending, it is doubtful whether autochthony evoked stronger and more resourceful ties to the land than the legacy of migration. In the mental map of most poleis, both registers can be detected. They almost appear as the base pair of a helix. The main difference was the scale with which each one was represented. In Athens, autochthony was the more dominant base; in Sparta, the notion of wandering. Between these binary ends, we find many nuances.

By now it should be obvious that the relation to the land was expressed in various ways: tales of earthbornness, of wandering peoples and heroes, of sedentariness, either since the dawn of time or from the *ktisis* of the city. All of these inspired a unique sense of place. In their stories of belonging, city-states not only revered the land for its capacity to feed them, but they also nourished the belief that the land told them who they were and where they came from. It is difficult to determine when these stories surfaced; their very nature makes the call for any one moment of origin a fruitless exercise. In some cases, especially with regard to Ionian and Dorian legendary tales, scholars have argued that the extreme charges of each legend as propelled by their major protagonists, Athens and Sparta, were the products of only a relatively late period, somewhere in the sixth century BCE.[42] On the whole, it is most likely not wrong to see the roots of these stories somewhere in the early decades of the Archaic period. As such, they coincided with the first waves of transregional connectivity and exchange as brought about by the earliest colonial enterprises. The idea of autochthony then marked a notable counterpoint to expanding worldviews. As aristocratic adventurers, entrepreneurs, and colonists traveled farther, their communities at home fostered high-powered stories of association with place. It might not come as a surprise that, as time went on, the poleis of the Classical period developed their very own local responses to the changing circumstances in the world writ large.

Emerging Mentalities of Territory

By the later fourth or early third century BCE, the Boiotian cities of Koroneia and Lebadeia were implicated in a dispute over their borderlands. As both were members of the federal league of Boiotia, the case was brought before the *koinon* for arbitration. The subsequent judgment was chiseled in a round limestone column that demarcated the boundary in what the text calls "the [Troph]onian (?) land." The *koinon* decreed that the border should henceforth run "along from the source where the water flows from the ridge to the Altar of Zeus."[43] What triggered the dispute is unknown. Since the contested area of Mt. Laphystion is treacherous terrain, it is unlikely that agricultural issues or the cultivation of (sacred) land fueled the conflict. Some scholars have pointed to quarrels over grazing grounds, while others entertained the idea of tangles over access rights along the southwestern shores of Lake Kopais, including the lucrative business of cutting reeds and harvesting eel (chapter 3). From the reference to the Altar of Zeus, yet others have inferred that the bone of contention lay in access to the shrine and its administration. It may well be that any one of these reasons was at the heart of the dispute, or a combination of them. But, as we will see in this section, it is also conceivable that none of the suggested causes had anything to do with it at all.[44] Instead, the dispute might have been fueled by a complex negotiation of spatial attitudes within and between both cities. In the course of this, an alert sense of territoriality emerged that, almost inevitably, required each polis to formulate its claims over the treacherous strip of land.

We already noted in passing how, in the course of the Archaic period, the nucleation of settlements occurred in tandem with various processes of spatial differentiation: between center and periphery, city and *chōra*, and places of the living and the dead. The growing awareness of communal space that was in itself inherently diverse was further inspired by the arrival of written law and its prominent occupation with property issues. Recent explorations of the interrelationship between land laws and institutional power in the early polis demonstrate how communal views of the territory were shaped also by the ongoing protection of the property of individuals. Elaborate laws of ownership added both to the rise of a "territorial jurisdiction," a geographically demarcated space in which those laws were binding, and to the "metajurisdictional authority" of the polis: that is, its capacity to wield power over the land of the city.[45]

Territorial organization of the polis as a whole, through the creation of subunits of the land, for instance demes, *merē*, *phylai*, and so on, complemented the picture. The best example of such an organization of the polis land that was both sophisticated and highly artificial is of course the case of Athens and Attica in the later sixth century BCE. Kleisthenes's famous reform of the Athenian territory into *phylai* and *trittyes*, amply evidenced in the literary and epigraphic tradition and traceable also in scattered material remains of deme-structures across Attica, provides the most telling attestation of the corresponding territorial mindset. In the words of Greg Anderson (2003), the reform amounted to nothing less than the creation of an imagined political community: as the spatial awareness of a shared territory met with the creative force of politics, this enabled the Athenians to push the mental boundaries of their city-state beyond the realm of daily interactions. The true success of the arrangement was that it allowed the people of Athens to experience their city as one imagined local community, despite the large territory. The reforms bridged the gap between physical and imagined manifestations of the Athenian city-state.[46]

In other cities, the pervasion of the hinterland by means of an elaborate territorial organization played out with similar sophistication. A recent systematic study of Greek *phylai* has brought to light how corresponding measures in Sikyon and Argos, although targeting a smaller territory, articulated a spatial mentality that inspired both cities to organize their lands in a tight, seamless fashion.[47] For neighboring Corinth, the corner marks of a developing territorial mindset have been uncovered in an exemplary manner. Situated in a spot that connected the city to all major traffic routes on land and sea in Central Greece, the urban center of Corinth itself was located in a congenial place. From the lower end of the northern slope of Akrocorinth toward the area of the emerging agora, the settlement stretched out across a series of limestone terraces that allowed easy access to veins of water underneath. The site was not only rich in agricultural resources from the surrounding lands, but had ample supplies of water and building materials. Under the rule of aristocratic clans, the notorious Bakchiads and then the Kypselids, the settlement development was driven by the typical triangle of urban nucleation, spatial pervasion of the *chōra*, and politicization of power structures. From the early Archaic period, we can trace the emergence of connecting axes between several concentrations of houses and tombs in the hinterland that both eased and intensified the exchange. These routes and first roads speak to a settlement growth not only through the extension of the urban core but through an ongoing incorporation of clusters of houses that evolved along those streets. Similar to procession roads through the countryside (above), those traffic roads expressed and inspired a robust sense of territoriality among daily travelers.

It is unknown when this sense translated into a new, comprehensive organization of the Corinthian polis land. By the Classical period, the territory was divided into eight districts (*merē*) that correlated with eight *phylai* of citizens; the latter were subdivided in two *hemiogda* each ("half-eights"), which, in turn, comprised an unknown number of *triakades*. It would be misleading to search for exact parallels with Athenian *trittyes* and *phylai*, but the Corinthian model obviously betrays a similar interplay between politics and the pervasion of space. Much as in Attica, and presumably somewhat earlier, the land and people of the entire Corinthia were integrated into a coherent, territorialized city-state. The spatial integration not only enforced territorial attitudes within, but signaled claims over the land vis-à-vis the neighboring cities.[48]

We shouldn't be puzzled to observe, then, that disputes such as the one between Koroneia and Lebadeia were commonplace in the Classical period. If we follow the sources, more often than not they evolved seamlessly from grievance to allegation and aggression, with little time for nonviolent conflict resolution. Once the first acts of violence were committed, they generated more grievance, followed by more hostility. To be sure, there is a solid body of attested cases of interstate arbitration, and the available evidence is probably only the tip of the iceberg. If this is correct, then the number of border conflicts, violent and nonviolent, will have been higher than the sources imply. Grievances were fueled by many reasons. With limited farmland available and indistinct borders in a muddled terrain, feuds over agricultural and pastoral lands were a quotidian occurrence. The quarrels over the plains around Amphissa were the most famous, or infamous, example. Comprising some of the most fertile soils in Central Greece, yet surrounded by the rugged natural environment of Mt. Parnassos and its foothills, the plains were a hot spot for disputes. The issue was further complicated by the fact that the *hiera chōra*, the sacred lands of Delphi, were by and large indistinct from the Amphissan territory. Disputes that arose from farming or herding were thus easily fused with charges of sacrilege and religious crimes. In the course of time, some petty border disputes that had originated from local grievances there quickly evolved into full-blown warfare on a regional or a Panhellenic scale.[49]

The case of Amphissa also demonstrates how agricultural feuds were intertwined with conflicts that arose over the attempt to shape spheres of interests and exercise power beyond the local arena. John Ma has emphasized that the capacity for war and interstate violence in disputes with neighboring communities were vital features of the Greek city-state and its self-understanding as both an autarkic and autonomous body. The point of Ma's assessment is that this tendency toward micro-imperialist action did not come to an end with the arrival of a new macrostructure of power politics in the Hellenistic period. Rather, it developed into a forceful, if not destructive, dynamic that responded to the realities of the Hellenistic world. Indeed, warfare can be shown "to have been structurally as important for the local communities as for the great empires" (2000, 357). What matters here is not so much the persistence of the pattern in the Hellenistic period under the new circumstances of the day, but the more general tendency of polis communities to compete for translocal influence, establish domains of microregional leadership or hegemony, reach out for exploitation of their neighbors, and, if at all possible, extend their territories. There might be a tendency to overstate the ubiquity of war in ancient Greece, but the verdict of a volatile state of neighborhood affairs by and large holds true.[50]

The military means and mechanics have been studied by many. Field archaeology has brought to light the full array of armament measures with which city-states organized their surrounding countryside. The most notorious example is again Athens. The systematic review of archaeological remains, in conjunction with literary and epigraphic sources, has allowed scholars to reconstruct the way in which the Athenians cast a network of defenses over Attica. Combining frontier towers and walls, military highways, and signal stands, the Athenians established a robust lineup of fortifications. Inland, between the city and its frontiers, the *chōra* was permeated by a corresponding network of roads, communication lines, and strategically located assembly points. Organized, preclusive defenses existed from the early Classical period. In the fourth century BCE several demes also received defense walls, while the countryside was further shielded with rubble camps. Remains of the fortifications in the northwestern quadrant of the Athenian *chōra*, in the borderlands with Boiotia, document the point. Landscape archaeology in the Mazi and Skourta plains, near Oinoe, Eleutherai, and Panakton, underscores the way in which the neighboring parties clung to their part of the territory. Although the frontier zone often took the shape of an intermediary space, characterized by a state of in-betweenness, both Athenians and Boiotians staked their claims through monumental structures and physical markers of presence. From the Athenian point of view, these measures suggested that the polis territory had morphed into what has been called, although somewhat ambiguously so, "Fortress Attica."[51]

Military facilities provided the infrastructure for guard and patrol policies. With citizen-soldiers levied mostly for combat and campaigns, the greater part of manning border stations and surveillance of the countryside went to the body of ephebes, or young citizens. In the aftermath of the Peloponnesian War, all operations in the countryside were put under the command of the *stratēgos* of the *chōra*, whose sole resort was the defense of Attica.[52] Thucydides, in a much-cited passage, reports that the "newest" men (*neotatoi*: 1.105.4; cf. 2.13.7) were enlisted to assume paramilitary duties in the country. They were either identical to, or operated in conjunction with, patrol units that are referred to in the sources as *peripoloi*, "those who are going the rounds," under the command of their *peripolarchos*. From Aristotle's description of the Athenian ephebic program, which is supplemented by hundreds of so-called ephebic inscriptions, we learn that the cadets were stationed in guard-posts from where they patrolled the borders and the *chōra*. This service also aimed at helping the ephebes to familiarize themselves with the major roads, paths, and lines of long-distance communication that structured the polis territory.[53] One of the largest border forts was in Eleusis in the northwestern corner of Attica, which was also a prominent station for ephebic contingents. Fortress Attica ended here.[54]

To the west, across the foot of the Kerata range, the neighboring city of Megara had established a similar system of beacons, defenses, watchtowers, and communication hubs with which the Megarians attempted to fend off potential situations in their borderlands. Their fortified polis land, Fortress Megara, as it were, extended as far as Aigosthena on the Corinthian Gulf, which made the Megarid a strategically aligned countryside and allowed its inhabitants to coordinate the movement of troops from several outposts and in different sectors (fig. 2.2.).[55] To the north, in Boiotia, the federal *koinon* maintained a network of signal towers and beacons, fortified outposts, and supply nodes that transformed the region into a fortress of its own. Evidence from inscriptions indicates that the local communities of Boiotia supplemented

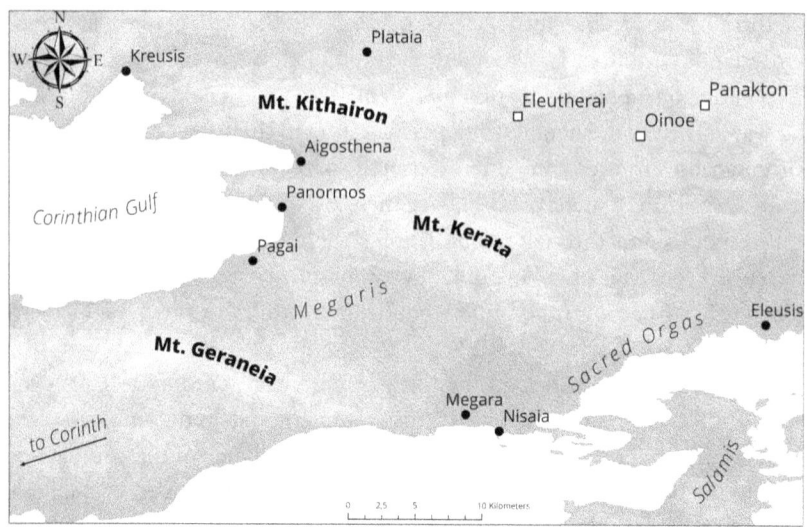

FIGURE 2.2. The entangled borderlands of the Megarid, Attica, and Southern Boiotia.

the league's policy and employed their troops to safeguard their territories. To this end, several Boiotian cities had their countryside patrolled by platoons of ephebes who, much like their Athenian counterparts, dealt with brigandage and small raiding parties, and also watched for enemy encroachment. In Thespiai, these units were assisted by so-called "chief dog handlers" who patrolled the *chōra* to enhance its security. Although the evidence for dog guards and escorting ephebes comes from a slightly later period, it is very likely that these measures were in place by the fourth century BCE. What's more, this appears to have been the case for other ephebic programs in the region also, in Megara and in Eretria on Euboia.[56]

By the later Classical period, then, the entire microregion between southern Boiotia, the Megarid, and northwestern Attica was covered with surveillance and communication networks with which poleis screened their borders. Moreover, as Megara, Athens, and Thespiai surveyed their respective frontiers, the demarcation of polis territories instilled them with the sense that their respective *chōra* was an integral part of the city. Connected to the urban center by lines of transportation and communication, fortified with military structures, and patrolled by units that were mounted by the polis, the citizen body endorsed the attachment to its territory. Its integrity and inviolability were forceful markers that steered local self-beliefs of the polis and its exchange with others. We encounter here an intriguing trait of the microregion that complements its previous characterization as a space shaped by unifying natural features (chapter 1). For instance, for the microregion along the shores of the Euboian Gulf, survey archaeology has brought to light a growing economic and cultural entanglement of the cities of Eretria, Oropos, and Tanagra. In the lived experience of their inhabitants, formal and informal interactions across the Straits of Euboia forged a network of short-distance exchanges. At the same time, intercommunal competition, fueled also by membership in different federal states and long-standing military alliances, invited a rigid approach to territory issues. In Eretria, the rural countryside of which has been most extensively researched, Sylvain Fachard was able to unearth the traces of a systematic fortification of the *chōra* and its settlements—through walls, watchtowers, forts, and rubble enceintes. The militaristic measures were complemented by a thorough, in-depth political organization of the Eretriad in districts and demes that covered the entire polis territory. Demarcating and securing borders in liminal lands were thus indispensable practices to support the claim of full authority over the *chōra*. With them, the notion of polis borders itself became part and parcel of a territorial attitude.[57]

It is worthwhile to explore this further. In what might be called a commonplace of the Greek mindset, the realm beyond the polis and its surrounding *chōra* was usually imagined as a place of wilderness. This juxtaposition of civilized and wild terrain was so prominent that it expressed itself in a variety of legal, religious, and cultural institutions that were designed to overcome the anomaly—and anxiety—associated with marginal lands.[58] Since the ordered world of the polis was a fragile achievement, its liminal zones were in particular need of what Arjun Appadurai has labeled a "special ritual maintenance" (1996, 179). The most obvious way to safeguard the fringes of the polis land was to put them under the authority of the gods and their border sanctuaries, which also enhanced the ties between the periphery and the rest of the polis land. Such a desire to seek divine sanction in the process of boundary drawing resonates in the publication of boundary inscriptions in frontier shrines, a practice that placed the agreement under the authority of the gods. The inscribed stele recording the federal arbitration in the dispute between Koroneia and Lebadeia (above) might well have been erected in the sacred precinct of Zeus that is referred to in the text; the Altar of Zeus would thus have sanctioned the federal decree, turning the border between both contestants into a sacred line.

In the border region between Megara and Athens, along the Sacred Tract (*hiera orgas*), a stretch of unbounded land, the Athenians set up a border stone in the mid-fourth century BCE, explaining that the Oracle of Apollo at Delphi had commanded people to leave the land untilled.[59] The language from other border inscriptions provides ample evidence for similar involvement of the divine. In a related vein, it is interesting to note that the idea of sacred borders was so deeply rooted in Greek thought that the term *sacred line, grammē hiera*, was also applied to the boundary between the opposing sides of a checkerboard.[60] Publishing the mutual borders in a sanctuary and placing them in a religious context implied, on the whole, that the polis had received "the imprimatur of the gods" (McInerney 2006, 47). In turn, the practice instilled communities with the sense that their territory, from center to periphery and back, comprised one integral body of land.

No matter how integrated the territory of the polis, and no matter how tight the actual defenses along the borders, the truth is, of course, that the frontiers between Greek city-states were never sealed or rendered impermeable. Indeed, much of the actual defensive infrastructure and the corresponding military strategies were conceived of to fight enemies once they had already entered the polis territory.[61] But this does not dismiss the general notion of a territorial or defensive mentality, as Josh Ober (1985) has posited with regard to military designs. As we have seen above, the ephebes played an eminent role in the formation of such a mindset. Their duties in the countryside were first and foremost of a military nature; border patrols, safeguarding grazing grounds and farmland, and protection from raiding parties were admittedly small-scale operations, but they were nonetheless of great importance to the settlers in the *chōra*. Yet the experience of cadet school went further. It has become fashionable to view the ephebeia as an institution that administered a rite of passage. On the brink of manhood, young adolescents were introduced to cooperative forms and patterns of behavior, as they were considered formative by the polis. With this came the powerful experience of temporal marginalization from society and the civilized realm of the polis. We revisit this theme below when the discussion turns to the topic of local worldviews; we explore how the polis synced the attitudes of adolescent youths with those of the citizen body as a whole (chapter 4). What is striking at this point is that, while the ephebes were charged with the protection of the countryside, this task was much more than a military assignment. It fostered a strong link with the location of the polis and its land as such.

Beyond its intrinsic value as an agricultural point of supply and backbone to military prowess, the *chōra* was a source of social meaning. For instance, in the stories of autochthony and primordial descent that we encountered earlier, the land served both as a backdrop and as an actual stage of foundational acts that were considered formative to the community. More than simply reminding citizens of the stories that were associated with specific locations and features in the country, the environment vouched for the validity of those legends and their communal importance. This quality of the territory was expressed also in the traditions surrounding sacred groves, rivers, and divine springs, "sites of exceptional purity" (Bonnechere 2007, 27) whose worship was rooted in belief and ritual.

There was a specific local trait of supernatural beings, as they were inseparably tied to and identified with concrete places in the *chōra*. Nymphs were inseparable from the landscape. They were associated with topographical features of the land, including springs, mountains, trees, and caves (fig. 2.3). In a similar vein, river gods commonly correlated with the polis territory. In Akarnania, worship of the Acheloos river was expressed in the mythical traditions of several cities. The Alpheios in the western Peloponnese was venerated in Pisatis and Triphylia, along with its many tributary rivers, which were equally personified; Alpheios's legendary tradition was closely intertwined with that of a nymph, Arethusa. In Boiotia, the legendary fabric of the Asopos was interwoven with the foundation myths of a whole bunch of cities along its shores.[62]

There was a deep epichoric tenor to those traditions. At Thespiai, which, according to Pausanias, was named after Thespia, one of the daughters of Asopos, the countryside was home to Herakles's hunt of a local monster. The hunt was also the occasion when Herakles had sex with the fifty daughters of Thespios—either with all of them in one night or with one at a time in fifty subsequent nights—a story that was valued by the sanctuary of Herakles at Thespiai. While the precise location of the sanctuary is unknown, there is good evidence for several shrines and altars of Herakles in the immediate vicinity, which suggests that Herakles's heroic story was inscribed in various places in the city and countryside.[63] In the same style, the famous Fountain House of Theagenes at Megara was said to be supplied with waters sacred to the Sithnidian nymphs that are described as local, *epichōrios*. One of these had sex with Zeus, and the resulting child, Megaros, escaped Deukalion's flood in his youth by taking refuge in Mt. Geraneia to the west of the Megaris. The name of the mountain range was connected with Megaros's temporary flight, and up until Pausanias's day, there was a liminal sanctuary nearby that was most often connected with this story.[64]

Legendary tales of Herakles and Thespios's daughters no doubt inspired ephebes and citizen soldiers alike in more ways than one. Megaros's tradition of heroic parentage, exile, and return obviously also resembled the most emblematic ephebic saga—that is, the tale of Theseus and his coming of age, with all of its impact on Athenian society.[65] What combines these with other traditions is that they were inscribed in the topography of the land. Patrolling the *chōra* and defending it against invasions and encroachments was more than a (para-)military exercise, and the protection of landbound resources was not confined to agricultural commodities alone. As guards of the territory, the

FIGURE 2.3. Terra-cotta calyx-krater, believed to be of Athenian origins (Metropolitan Museum of Art, 52.11.18; Beazley archive number 14714. © bpk / The Metropolitan Museum of Art. Printed with permission). On this krater from the fourth century BCE, the intimate relation between people, place, and local meaning is articulated in a compelling visual language. The side depicted here shows the apotheosis of Herakles, who can be seen at the top of the vase riding in a four-horsed chariot. At the bottom, there is a funerary pyre. Athena is shown running near, gesturing toward a group of nymphs who are holding water jugs, just about to be thrown onto the pyre to put out the flames. On the other side, Amymone defends herself against a gang of satyrs. Saved from their attacks by Poseidon, she had sex with him and bore Nauplios (Hes. frags. 157 and 234 Most). The daughter of Danaos and Europa, Amymone was a quasi-nymph: the spring and river Lerna across the bay from Nauplion (Argolid) were assigned to her. In Euripides (*Phoin.* 187–88), Poseidon struck the spring with his trident, which is why it emerged from three fissures. Connected by the power of water, both sides of the krater play on the intimate relation of (demi)gods and (water) nymphs; their foundational union is evidenced by real place. Moreover, through the permanent presence of the water, this union becomes both tangible and meaningful, amplifying the sentiment of attachment to the land.

ephebes, among others, shielded realms that infused the world of the polis with local meaning. In turn, we see that the territorial mentality, as expressed in warfare, and the more general attitude toward the land as military, agricultural, and sanctioned space were interrelated. As the city-states engaged in ever-increasing translocal exchanges, assertions of their land at home and their attachment to it extended in depth and scope. More than ever before, the land of the polis was a meaningful place.

Poleis without Territory: An Afterthought on the Land

In a study from 1939, Austrian scholar Franz Hampl explored the political and judicial manifestations that governed the notion of polis territory in the Classical period. Noting that the predicates of statehood in Greece drew on the base category of people rather than territory, Hampl argued that if the polis was dissociated from its territory, this did not necessarily undermine its quality as a city-state. In the cases under scrutiny, which were mostly drawn from the Athenian empire and its dealing with allies in revolt, the citizens of defeated cities were allowed to maintain their settlement but lost ownership over their polis and private lands. Hence, Hampl concluded, they became "*Poleis ohne Territorium*"—that is, poleis without territory.[66]

This view has been challenged by many, and there is no need to recall the scholarly debate in detail here. Following Thucydides's famous remark that "the polis is its men" (7.77.7), who seems to have referenced Alkaios (frag. 426 Campbell), it is a truism to assert that in their conceptual approach to the polis the Greeks highlighted the importance of people and governance. All the while, the land was an important, integral component of the city-state from its earliest formation in the Archaic period. The scholars of the Copenhagen Polis Centre (1993–2005) have done a magisterial job in disentangling all conceivable strands of what a polis was. Their work leaves no doubt that it comprised both a community of citizens and a settlement in a given place or locale—despite the fact that this place might at times have been occupied by someone else.[67] The conventional English translation of polis, "city-state," captures this complementary meaning of people and land; the trend toward "citizen-state" is merely one of prioritization, emphasizing a shift from the urban and territorial connotation of polis toward the status group of citizens, rather than dismissing the idea of territory as such.[68]

The verdict of "poleis without territory" reminds us, however, that the relation to the land and the contextual ties that emerged from this need for locality were always fragile, vulnerable to the dynamics of—sometimes violent—change. As the vagaries of warfare inevitably shaped different degrees of dependency, many cities suffered territorial losses of different scales. For instance, the occupation of another city's territory during campaigns, raids in the *chōra*, or acts of annexation, often followed by forced dislocations, posed an obvious threat to the link with the land. Such acts of war jeopardized the city's territorial integrity, and they also left their mark on how subsequent conversations about the land were led and mental maps of the territory were drawn. Among the most extreme outcomes of war, if the population was not killed altogether, was the disconnect of the survivors from their native land, much along Hampl's line of inquiry. But even in this case, the tides of war usually turned at some point: Athens, according to Themistokles, was still a polis despite the temporary loss of its territory to Persia in 480 BCE (Hdt. 8.61.2); it regained control over the city and countryside within a few days after the Persian defeat. In the quarrels of the Corinthian War, the polis of Corinth effectively split into two states, one supported by Sparta, the other in political union with Argos (chapter 1). For some time, both these Corinths occupied separate strips of territories in the city, the acropolis, the countryside, and the harbor at Lechaion. In 373 BCE, the Thespians lost ownership of their polis to the Thebans but were able to recuperate from this blow within a few years. The Thebans themselves lost their city in 335. They established it only some twenty years later, albeit on a much-reduced scale.[69] In each of these cases of dispossession and recovery, the changing fortunes of war triggered highly charged narratives of attachment to the soil. Yet, needless to say, the ties between the citizens and their land were never cut during periods of dispossession. The land mattered, even if it was temporarily lost. And if the loss was permanent, we would imagine that the grudges were as well.[70]

We can only conjecture how deep the attachment went, but the general point is clear. The sentiment in any case wasn't confined to the major stakeholders in Greek power politics. Nothing documents the force of long-standing attachment more than the challenges faced by the city of Megalopolis in the aftermath of the Battle of Mantineia (362 BCE). When the fighting parties were ordered back to their homes, many soldiers of the contingent from Megalopolis did not return there. Instead, Diodorus (15.19.1-3) informs us, they went to their *patrides*, their original home communities. Megalopolis was established in the decade before the battle, when several Arkadian towns, up to twenty or maybe more, were told by decree of the federal league to relocate a substantial portion of their citizenry to the newly established city. In the general confusion after the Battle of Mantineia, many of these new citizens of Megalopolis took the opportunity to turn their backs on the federal project. It is unclear whether the villages that had initially participated in the synoikism were abandoned altogether or, more likely, remained intact, albeit with a reduced number of inhabitants. The number of recalcitrants was in any case substantial. It was high enough for the remaining Megalopolitans to plead to Thebes for help to prevent further exodus from the city. The rebels, for their part, sought the support of Mantineia and other Arkadian cities. The conflict was solved when a Theban dispatch unit arrived that raided some rebel settlements while threatening others. Through force, the Thebans compelled the recalcitrant faction to change their home back to Megalopolis. Outgunned, so to speak, by the Theban army, they were left with no other choice than to comply.[71]

The quarrel over Megalopolis's population was, at least in part, fueled by the same factional strife in Arkadia that had led to the Battle of Mantineia in the first place. At the same time, the contrast between the new megacity and the villages that were synoikisized in the course of its foundation couldn't have been bigger. Many of the dislocated people came from towns in the Mainalia, northeast of Megalopolis, and the Parrhasia range, running north to south from Mt. Lykaion to Lykosoura at an altitude level of about 250 m above the plain. Both were fairly impenetrable mountainous regions. The air is considerably lighter to breathe up there, especially in the hot summer months, when the plain of Megalopolis is hit by dry heat waves. The terrain itself invites small-scale herding and seasonal movement of livestock rather than large-scale farming. Effectively, many of the settlements in the region did not exceed the size of hamlets and farmsteads, with the exception of a few fortified locations. As we note in chapter 4, the habitation pattern in the Parrhasia provided the backdrop to a curious military engagement of the youths in ritual and sacrifice there.

Megalopolis, on the other hand, was designed as a monumental urban project, with an impressive political and religious infrastructure. Beyond its doorstep, it absorbed the administration of the cult center of Zeus Lykaios in Parrhasia. The city itself had robust defenses and was envisioned to develop into a vibrant commercial center. It is uncertain how much of this building program was realized already in the first years after the foundation, but the trajectory was unmistaken. Also, Megalopolis's location in the western Arkadian basin, where the Alpheios, Helission, and other rivers flow together, allowed its inhabitants to establish an agricultural regime on a grand scale. With the foundation, an all-new thrust toward the rearing of horses arose in the region. The main challenge was that there was too much water at times, but once the problem of seasonal flooding was resolved, the city had access to ample food supplies from its surrounding *chōra*.[72]

The Megalopolis project bore the signature of the major federal cities Mantineia, Tegea, and Kleitor in northern Arkadia, with the settlements from Mainalia and Parrhasia tagging along. According to Pausanias (8.27.2–6), each of these parties dispatched two *oikistai*, or city-founders, whose work received support also from other Arkadian federalists. Pausanias declares that there was significant enthusiasm about the city foundation, which promised to provide the league with a sizable new center.[73] Megalopolis served as a military and commercial bulwark there against Sparta, which clearly added to its attraction. Yet when it came to the abandonment of homes and the relocation of people, the tasks were not shared equally. Pausanias's list of those who were ordered to move speaks mostly of Mainalians and Parrhasians, along with some smaller communities. The federal project appeared attractive, but to those who were asked to abandon their homes and bring the city to life, this task bore little, if any promise. Some Parrhasians, most eminently the Lykosourans, changed their minds at the last minute and withdrew from the project. Others were made to comply and leave their homes by force (Paus. 8.27.5). Despite its grandeur, the new city held no charm for them. Clearly, the idea of a "great city" did not align well with the lifestyle of mountain folks. We are reminded of Phokylides's opposition between large Nineveh and the small polis. The people from Mainalia and Parrhasia might not necessarily have thought of Megalopolis as a place that was *aphrainousēs*, "foolish." But they weren't drawn to it either. It seems they preferred their villages over the new foundation, despite the complete absence of worldliness and their poor location. Actually, they might have preferred their homes precisely because of this lack of pulsating, big-city life.[74]

3
Senses and Sensation

> "They used to go to the agora wearing robes all of purple,
> not less than a thousand in all,
> boastful and exulting in the splendor of their hair,
> drenched with the scent of artfully fashioned perfumes."
> XENOPHANES, frag. 3 Gerber

According to Xenophanes of Kolophon, his fellow citizens enjoyed a lavish lifestyle. Picture the scene. When the Thousand, the ruling elites of the city, gathered in the marketplace—the term *agora* used here is most likely a synonym for "assembly"—they wore their finest couture: they were dressed in exquisite robes, their hair elegantly styled and bedecked with ornaments, bathed in extravagant scents. Add to this attire, presumably, corresponding footwear and jewelry, and the public appearance of the Kolophontian citizen is complete. On another occasion (frag. 2 Gerber) Xenophanes declares that all Hellenes—including his compatriots, we would think—were fanatics when it came to sports. The Olympic Games in particular attracted so much attention that the polis showered its victorious athletes in prize money and distinctions even more than usual. Under such circumstances, it should come as no surprise that the Kolophontians weren't cheap, nor modest, when it came to partying and drinking; on the contrary. Following Athenaios, the referencing source of Xenophanes's fragment, we learn that some Kolophontians were so enfeebled by constant drunkenness "that they never saw the sun rise or set" (*Deipn.* 12.526a). The local world of Kolophon resembled the luxury-fevered city in Plato's *Republic*. Control over the extensive plains along the Halis and Astes rivers equipped the people with prosperity and wealth. The wealthy actually seem to have outnumbered the poor. In the display of their wealth, they fueled the public image of a decadent polis addicted to every pleasure. To borrow James Davidson's (1997) famous book title, by the first half of the 6th century BCE, Kolophon appeared to be a city of "consuming passions."[1]

In Xenophanes's writings, the discussion of local habits in Kolophon is intertwined with an unambiguous invective. To the social critic, the city's devotion to luxury and glamour was not only an aesthetic problem but also indicative of harmful priorities. Things went wrong when the Kolophontians followed the ways of the neighboring Lydians, Xenophanes asserts, whose political demise, despite their riches, made them all-time champions of "unprofitable luxuries" (frag. 3). Although the Lydians could have served as fair warning, Kolophon was intransigent. When Xenophanes was a young man in his mid-twenties, around 546 BCE, the city fell to the Persians, who established a "hateful tyranny" (frag. 3). Many Ionian cities were known for their love of luxury, and Kolophon wasn't the only Greek city in the region to fall under Persian rule, after all. Yet, while others flourished under foreign domination, Kolophon did not. Its prosperity dwindled. Soon enough it was eclipsed by its rising neighbor, Ephesos.[2]

Xenophanes's voice reflects several conceptual issues that inform the investigation in the present chapter. The first is the interplay of cultural communality and local idiosyncrasy. In their conduct of the social practices, the Kolophontians were like many other Greeks: for instance, fascination with athletic competition and a vibrant symposiastic culture that included, if need be, heavy drinking were cultural commonplaces. In Sybaris, on the other side of the Greek Mediterranean, the citizens were equally notorious for the lavish dress and glamorous ornaments they wore to political gatherings. Perfumes, too, were amply used by prosperous men and women. The production of fragrances made from a mixture of vegetable oil and scent-bearing plants was widespread, and a large selection was available, from local products to expensive scents from reputed perfumeries elsewhere. Judging from the sheer volume of exported *aryballoi*, Corinthian iris perfume was most likely among the top labels, as was a brand called Megalleion produced in Ephesos. These practices, among others, were cultural commonplaces rather than local particularities.[3]

Why was Kolophontian lavishness then so objectionable to Xenophanes? He speaks of *askētoi chrimata*, "artfully crafted unguents," a description that has no inherent pejorative meaning. By contrast, in the acclaimed symposium poem, Xenophanes praises the "fragrant ointment" (frag. 1) in use at convivial celebrations. Scholars have noted the opposition between both verdicts—one praising the application of perfumes, the other critiquing it.[4] What sets the two passages apart is a more fundamental opposition between moderation and extravagance. The symposium poem celebrates a banquet brimming with good but plain food and drink: wine, cold water, "sweet and pure; golden loaves lie near at hand, and the noble table is loaded down with cheese and rich honey" (frag. 1, lines 8–10). The scene is dominated by frugal foodstuffs. By extension, pristineness also applied to the ointment that was passed around to symposiasts to avoid drunkenness. Indeed, Xenophanes advises his audience to drink with moderation, so to avoid moments of disgrace on the way home. His admonition is in line with late-Archaic poetic traditions, where polis and symposium where inextricably related themes. In Solon's poems and in the *Theognidea*, the aristocratic banquet was a microcosm and a model of the community as a whole and, thus, an indicator of the city's well-being overall. Hence, proper conduct and the avoidance of excess were quintessential. The contrast between the moderation of Xenophanes's symposiasts and the exalted allures of the Thousand couldn't have been greater. While the symposium poem propels the idea of moderate consumption and an ethically grounded expression of status, the Thousand at Kolophon are critiqued for undue excess in both. In other words, Xenophanes's quarrel was not so much with perfumes, or any other goods that were associated with a distinguished lifestyle for that matter, but with fancy and exuberance, and how they were showcased in public.[5]

Clearly enough, the Kolophontians shared in the broad canon of Hellenic traditions. Universal Hellenic customs guided everyday life. However, those customs became locally encoded when translated into quotidian experience. Subject to regional dynamics and local circumstances, the expression of shared customs often took the particular, if not peculiar, twist toward idiosyncrasy. At Kolophon, this meant that the display of conspicuous wealth and adoption of strategies of social distinction evolved into normative allure. Maybe such exaggeration was fueled by a dynamic of increase and rivalry with Kolophon's Ionian neighbors, such as nearby Ephesos first and foremost, whose citizens were not known for a frugal lifestyle either. The appropriation of universal practices by individual city-states was thus energized not only by the macrocosm of cultural exchange but also by the local context. As we will see in the sections below, place fostered the formation of local idiosyncrasy, filling cultural practices with local meaning that was recognizable—both to the locals and to outsiders—as a notable departure from the universal template.

The second conceptual premise follows from this: the issue of positionality. Xenophanes's poetry did not serve as a mouthpiece for Kolophon. He didn't talk on behalf of his fellow citizens; rather, he talked about them. In the Olympia elegy (frag. 2), such a constellation of "them" and "me" arose through harsh opposition between what many Hellenes prioritized in life and what Xenophanes believed was best. Feeling his advice was unappreciated by his fellow citizens, he left his hometown at the age of twenty-five (if we can trust his record), wandering about for sixty-seven years, "bearing myself from city to city" (frag. 45; see also frag. 8). His critical attitude toward his countrymen and their resistance to his teachings thus led Xenophanes to turn his back on the place. His position, effectively, changed from that of a critical observer within to that of an expat. Whatever we learn from him about his hometown comes through the voice of someone who was an insider and an outsider to the local world of Kolophon at the same time.[6]

This has important implications for the way we read our sources. Simon Goldhill (2010) recently pointed out that the language of cultural mapping has its own grammar. In particular, there is a marked difference between assessments such as "this is how they do things there" and "this is how we do things here." Both expressions draw on distinct strategies of complicity and inclusion. The former, "this is how they do things there" resembles the mechanics of cultural stereotyping. Much like the etic eye, it looks at others from the outside, assigning to them various qualities that appear curious enough to be targeted. It is easy to see how this technique transitions to the critiquing or mocking of local idiosyncrasies elsewhere. In its most flagrant form, it segues into strategies that assert identity through alterity or othering, joining coarse expressions of ethnic discrimination and disparagement.[7]

By contrast, "this is how we do things here" is fueled by a different positionality; it hails from another source of knowledge. This is the emic perspective, that of the insider, who is not only knowledgeable about local practices but in complicity with the group that subscribes to them. As this chapter shows, the epichoric self-awareness of polis communities extended to a wide spectrum of local practices. Regardless of how these were branded (or mocked) by others, they mattered to the locals. Filled with purpose and meaning, they constituted what we specified earlier as a local regime of truth. As part of everyday experience, this regime was based on preconceptions that determined how a communal practice was performed; hence, it signaled that the conduct was correct and proper, performed in accordance with the local way. We encounter here the same social and cultural quality of the local that we detected in chapter 1: while overlapping with spatial approximations, it is also and in principle separate from geography. Other Hellenes might have thought what they wanted about the look of the Kolophontian assembly-goers, but to the Thousand, it was the appropriate way to attend their gatherings. And, presumably, it was the only way. Shabby attire and bad smells were unwanted in the agora at Kolophon.

Reference to sight and smell hints at the third conceptual premise that derives from Xenophanes. The phalanx of human senses has recently entered the world of historical scholarship, generating new interest in the cultural dimension of sensory perception. Far from being a straightforward issue, the notion of sensation—that is, the awareness of stimuli through senses and the subsequent cascade of excitement it triggers across the nervous system—has come under close scrutiny. Smell, for instance, as pointed out by Neville Morley, always works through "a combination of the physiological and the psychological or cultural" (2015, 113). On the one hand, the physical presence of certain scents triggers the experience of smell. On the other hand, the recognition of scents depends largely on interpretative choices that steer people toward a particular reading of olfaction. Some scents trigger universally negative responses because of the potential threat, or disease, associated with them. Beyond these, the sensory interpretation of smell results from cultural conventions and traditions. In this vein of inquiry, scent has not only an aesthetic dimension; it also allows people to situate themselves in, and connect to, the world around them.[8]

Maurice Bowra once famously remarked that the Greek light is a unique sensory experience. Its strength and sharpness impose a secret discipline on the eye, shaping the edges of the terrain both against the colors of the sky and in contrast to the soil. Such clarity in sight, Bowra argued, had "a powerful influence on the Greek vision of the world" (1957, 11). The same can be said about the air and the scents it carries. In chapter 1 we saw how Mediterranean vegetation patterns are subject to the necessity of perennial plants to adapt to the seasonal distribution of rainfall and, for the most part, the absence of frost. The characteristic flora is therefore basically similar throughout Aegean Greece; olive trees, cypresses, and pines are found in many places (yet all three prefer different soils). This commonality does not rule out significant variations in regional climates.[9] With swiftly changing altitude levels over short distances, these variations translated into microclimates: pockets of land in which the temperature, humidity, and precipitation differed significantly from other contained climate zones nearby; for example, Herakleides Kritikos remarked how the two flanks of Mt. Pelion in Southern Thessaly constituted vastly diverse ecosystems (*BNJ* 369A F 2.9). Microclimates such as these not only gave rise to distinct vegetation patterns, they also provided aromatic stimuli affecting how the environment was experienced—stimuli of pristineness, or, in Bowra's sense, a clarity that sometimes has a euphoric sensation to it, as many travelers today will testify. It should come as no surprise that the Greeks thought of the places that encapsulated this experience—for instance, groves and meadows—as spirited realms that were of key importance to the exercise of local religion (see chapter 4).

In the Greek mindset, cities were associated with epithets that signaled their distinctiveness: "seven-gated Thebes" is a catchy example. In Homer's *Catalogue of Ships*, many epithets are drawn from topographical features and characteristics of place. There is a long controversy among scholars over whether those epithets are, like many more in the *Iliad*, generic and conventional or more specific. Many factors relate to this question, including issues of syntax and meter, but none effectively discount the point that whoever provided the basic materials for the *Catalogue*, "obviously knew the Greece of his day quite well."[10] Kalydon, as we have seen earlier, is "steep" (2.640); Aulis "stony" (496); Hermione, with its enclosed natural harbor, embraces "a deep gulf" (560); Lilaia lies by "the springs of noble Kephissos" (522). Other references to place resonate more strongly with the senses. Thisbe was notoriously "dove-haunted" (502)—we almost hear the doves fluttering around the pigeon loft. Isthmia and Epidauros were "rich in grapes" (537, 561), while Pyrasos in Thessaly was "flowery" (695). Haliartos was "grassy" (503), while Pteleos's meadows were "deep in grass" (697); deep grass is a common vegetation pattern of the elm tree (*ptelea*, in Greek). As we have seen in the previous chapter, Odysseus's estate on Ithaca was rich in orchards. Ithaca itself has no epithet in the *Catalogue*, but Aigilips, one line earlier and a place in the domain of the island, was "rough" (633). The air on Ithaca and Neriton, both "covered with waving forests" (632), was filled with the scent of fruit-trees and spices that grew so prominently on the island, mixed with a breeze of salt from the sea. All of these were innately familiar to Odysseus, and they triggered in him the feeling of attachment to place.[11]

The same is true for other sensory environments. We don't need to travel as far as Kyrene to experience a distinct smellscape: the intense smell of silphion, a plant that was used both for seasoning and medicinal purposes. According to Theophrastus (*Hist. pl.* 3.6.1; 6.3.1; see also Antiphanes, frag. 216 *PCG*), the resinous milky juice obtained from the stem served as a panacea; it had a rich, voluminous smell. Although notorious, silphion wasn't the only plant to render a place unique. The name Marathon most likely derived from the fact that the bay in Northern Attica was "covered with fennel," its tall flowered stocks dotting the landscape. Consumed on its own or used as a food condiment, fennel is known for its sweet, anise-like, aromatic fragrance that fills the air. Its full-bodied scent also makes it a common base ingredient for herbaceous perfumes and scented oils. Near the precinct of Aphrodite in Sikyon grew a hawthorn that, according to Pausanias, was found nowhere else on earth. Its use in sacrifice shrouded the ritual with a distinct smell (2.10.5-6). The roots of arum at Mt. Pelion, already spotlighted for its diverse microclimates, diffused a rich, if not intoxicating scent: its smell seemed to be pernicious to snakes, yet to humans it was sweet, "like the bouquet of thyme in bloom" (Herakleides *BNJ* 369A F 2). In the villages of the Parrhasia range and in southern Arkadia, where the air is lighter than elsewhere in the Peloponnese, the winds whirl through the crowns of deciduous trees, including many walnut trees, with their characteristic sprawling branches and thick tops. Near modern Analipsi, in the small village of Karyai (literally "Walnut Trees"), this scenery was the backdrop to a commemorative festival that was rich in epichoric song and dance. To the people of Orchomenos and Chaironeia, the smell of seasonal wild flowers—white lilies, roses, narcissi, and irises that sprouted in their *chōra* and were used in the local perfume industries— announced the familiarity of home. On Kos, known for its cypress trees and their evocative, soothing scent, the cult of Apollo Kyparissios was associated with a corresponding grove in the precinct of the Asklepieion; the durable, scented wood was placed under the authority of the god. In Epidauros, the scent of pine was ubiquitous. The cones and nuts of cultivated pines played an important role in healing and ritual in the sanctuary of Asklepios.[12]

These examples are drawn from different contexts. They are united, however, by the fusion of physical and cultural encodings of sensory perception as we described it earlier. In each case, the experience was at once determined by the presence of certain scents and the interpretative choices that followed. The connection between place and air was so prominent that it had already inspired scientific approaches in antiquity. To the author of the Hippocratic treatise *Airs, Waters, Places* (fourth century BCE), knowledge of air, wind, and the impact they wielded over people's health was of critical importance. He therefore advised his medical students that whenever they came to a city they ought to assess the winds, in general terms and in relation to how they were "locally distinct (*epichōrios*) in every place (*chōra*)."[13] As we have seen earlier, the same author took a medical approach toward homesickness (chapter 1), which complements the notion here. In their connection to the land, the Greeks drew on distinct smellscapes that added nuance and depth to the sense of belonging (fig. 3.1). More often than not, the sensation was subtle, yet it was precisely this implicitness that made the "smell of home" such a powerful experience.

In the present chapter, we explore how cities sparkled with local sensation. We will examine three major themes. Each one merits a book-length discussion in its own right; much of the following is therefore programmatic in character. In each theme, we see that the land was the real or imagined backdrop to an excitement that was quintessentially local. The first section deals with the issue of taste and how the everyday uses of food and drink informed locally encoded cuisines. The second section extends this approach to local skill sets and expertise in material culture as sources of local distinction. In the third, we examine athletics and communal celebrations in song and dance, presumably the most gripping arena of local distinction. To be sure, some of these sensations drew on and were, in turn, fueled by performances

FIGURE 3.1. Didrachm from Selinus, late sixth century BCE. The city was known for its wild celery (*selinon*), which is shown on the obverse. The plants, with their wedge-shaped leaves and arcuated stalks, have a coarse taste and distinctive smell, filling the air with aromatic flavor. Image credit: Courtesy of the American Numismatic Society (1989.93.1). See also Marconi 2006, 75; Cutroni Tusa 2010.

before audiences beyond the polis. As we will see along the way, however, accentuating tastes, cultural capacity, and athletic success invited the city also to cultivate strong ties to the local.

Local Idiosyncrasy and Stereotyping: The Excitement of Taste

Take the boat from a port in Central Greece and head north. After a few days you will reach the Hellespont. At the narrowest point of the straits, in a commanding strategic spot on the Asiatic shore, lies the pulsating city of Abydos, rich in precious minerals and fish. Many visitors, however, did not come for the fish. By the later fifth century BCE, Abydos was famous for its loose women. The Athenian orator Antiphon implied that young men from all over Greece journeyed to the city to take advantage of the promiscuous attitudes of the women there. Male fantasies were fueled further by the prominence of Aphrodite Pornē in the exercise of local cults, although the temple of Aphrodite "the Prostitute" might have come into existence only later, toward the end of the fourth century. Feeding off the mindset of sexual exaltation, the one local food delicacy Archestratos (frag. 7 Olson and Sens) associated with the city in his *Life of Pleasure* were oysters, meaty and full in flavor. Abydos's image was that of a cultural stronghold on the Outer Rim. Its location on the fringes of Hellenicity made its inhabitants susceptible to bodily pleasures of all sorts, including seafood and sex, and the pleasure-enhancing relation between the two recognized by many experts.[14]

We have already noted the mechanics of positionality at work here. What the Hellenes—men in particular—imagined Abydos to be like was one thing; the local conversation was another. More likely than not, the Abydonians would not have thought of their women simply as fair game for travelers. The cult of Aphrodite Pornē was in any case charged with local meaning. According to Neanthes from nearby Kyzikos, it was inaugurated to commemorate the heroic deeds of a prostitute who had helped to set the city free after a period of foreign occupation. Just as our reading of Aphrodite Pornē requires a more nuanced interpretation, so too does the notion of exquisite oysters. Like the consumption of lobster, a bottom feeder, oysters are generally considered less of a culinary extravagance in communities that have the ability to harvest them than in those that don't. In Greek antiquity, oysters were not necessarily considered a gourmet treat that is best enjoyed raw; they were also used as an ingredient in broths and other ordinary cooked meals. To the Abydonians, their meaty oysters might have been more mundane than Archestratos implied.[15]

It is nevertheless intriguing to explore the local culinary traditions of Abydos further, or those of any other city-state, as much as this is possible. To begin with, Peter Garnsey has reminded us (1999, 13) that, while the food consumption in Aegean Greece generally follows the taxonomy of the so-called Mediterranean diet and its triad of cereals, olives, and the vine, it is easy to overstate the uniform character of this diet. There was immense local variation across the Greek world. Once again, it emanated from differences in the natural environment and the divergent vegetation patterns between plains, mountain sites, coastal regions, and deep forest surroundings. But local variation did not result from nature alone. It was also the outcome of the creative way in which the culture of food was built around local conditions. Claude Lévi-Strauss (1964/1969) observed long ago that food gives us access to the human mind, as people make deliberate choices about what they eat and how they prepare their meals. Similar to our assessment of scent earlier in this chapter, choices in taste (and distaste) are of an interpretative nature, mirroring the attitudes and convictions of those who savor them and of the community to which they belong. Resulting dietary regimes and their translation into cuisines—often with minute guidelines for the selection, preparation, cooking technique, and consumption—are not only indicative of cultural conventions, but are themselves a forceful expression of them. Typically, the guidelines are passed on from one generation to the next, which grants an ancestral authority to them, further enhancing their ability to bring people together. Eating is thus not just a biological necessity and a signifier of culture, but also a process charged with memory and meaning. Regardless of whether or not that meaning is embedded in a plain meal whipped up from humble ingredients, in rich recipes with tantalizing tapestries of spices and seasonings, or in the intense experience of cooking an animal whole in a pit in the ground, each of the corresponding flavors allows people, individuals and collectives alike, to orient themselves in time and place.[16]

This is the juncture where food studies enter the terrain of 'food and identity.' The topic has become immensely fashionable, in scholarship and in popular academia, as it allows audiences to draw connections between multiple micro-/ego-histories as well as their own lived food experience.[17] In corresponding inquiries, local perspectivations are not only omnipresent, but actually inevitable. Local cuisines are typically viewed in juxtaposition to waves of transregional economic exchange and cultural transfer in larger formations—for instance, in the Roman or the British Empire. In such a constellation, the local is a culinary cosmos where foreign eating habits coalesce with cuisines that are already in place. The process is one of ongoing adaptation and change, at both ends. While foreign food practices are not introduced without adjustment to local conventions, these local conventions themselves leave their imprint on the universal paradigm. Along the way, the two amalgamate. For example, it was demonstrated how the multilayered relations between local and imperial elites in Roman Gaul were also negotiated, and effectively mediated, through evolving patterns of food consumption that were reflective of the cultural traditions of the respective stakeholders. Food not only has the capacity to articulate identity in oppositional terms, but it can help to reframe identities according to cultural currents.[18]

Such a mediating quality of local cuisine, as a facilitator of cultural reciprocity, has much in its favor. With this in mind, the local trait of food regimes in Classical Greece requires further conceptualization. The thrust toward self-subsistence prioritized, as such, the consumption of foodstuffs that were available locally. Aristotle (*Pol.* 1252b 27–53) famously declared autarky both the ultimate goal (*telos*) of the Greek city and its best state of being. The idea clearly didn't obviate interest in trade relations. But the strong link between autarky and genuinely political goals, autonomy, and the absence of dependence upon any foreign power put the notion of self-subsistence at the heart of the city's public conversations.[19] Practical issues added to the picture. The components of the Mediterranean triad are generally suited for export, including long-distance transportation across the sea. But the risks were considerable, as were the costs. Consequently, cities usually resorted to imported supplies only if they were forced to do so: for instance, because of a shortage of local supplies. Another reason for imports was that food items from elsewhere were of a higher quality than the local produce, or weren't locally produced at all. In landlocked Tegea, a fishmonger from Argos regularly sold his catch from the Argive Bay. Allegedly, the man carried his goods with a yoke around his shoulders to Arkadia, quite a feat over thirty-five kilometers of rugged terrain. The fish must have been priced accordingly. Dry-salted sea bream from Cadiz, available from a delicatessen dealer in the agora of Corinth, show that fish lovers there cast their nets even wider.[20]

Imported goods thus rose to the status of desired commodities that spoke to the economic power and taste of their consumers. As such, they signaled an elevated lifestyle—another example of oppositional group-identity formation through food.[21] The ostentatious consumption of imported wines, always identified by place, for instance from Mende, Chios, or Peparethos, is an obvious example; in the case of Maroneia, the place-brand promised rich, flowery scents of nectar. Eel from Lake Kopais in Boiotia is another example. The only other notable source of exquisite eel was Sikyon, known for its marine, scaleless conger eel. But the Boiotian catch, although regrettably expensive, was championed by most consumers. The distinction went both ways. While in high demand in fish markets throughout Central Greece and praised by gourmands with the necessary purchasing power, eel from Lake Kopais was a product of distinction and local pride among the fishing communities around the lake. The Hellenistic historian Agatharchidas reports that the people of the region, "after putting wreathes and throwing barley corns on them like sacrificial animals, while praying to the gods sacrifice the largest of the eels from Lake Kopais." The cheerful custom is explained as ancestral. Presumably it extended back quite some time.[22]

If imports compensated for a shortage in local supplies, such a shortfall was particularly pressing if it occurred with the third component of the triad, that of cereals, because of their primary role in the everyday diet. At the most basic level, meals consisted of *sitos*, a baked cereal such as bread or barley cake. On exceptional occasions, the *sitos* was paired with the more pleasurable *opson* ("relish" or "made dish"), referring to meat or fish. Given the exquisiteness of the latter, the word was sometimes used as a synonym for seafood, but it really applied to any prepared complement to the staple.[23] In lack of an *opson*, the most common side-dishes (*paropsides*) to go with the *sitos* were vegetables and pulses—dried peas, beans, lentils, or chickpeas—which were appreciated for their high levels of protein and fiber, and also for their availability all year long; they ripen several times. Grains and other vegetables (onions, celery, beets) were suitable for long-distance shipment, yet only with substantial transportation costs and risks, while other legumes were less suited to a journey: for instance, cabbage and turnips. Even over shorter distances between neighboring communities, transportation was complicated by the fact that animals needed resting places and ample amounts of fodder (oxen, in particular), which again drove up the price.[24]

All this is not to suggest a return to primitivist views of the ancient Greek economy so famously propagated by Moses Finley (1973). It is a matter of debate just how far and frequently goods and individuals traveled. According to Finley, markets were shallow, and transaction costs high—that is, expenditures of resources, time, and effort to acquire information to organize transportation and reduce risks. Both posed a high threshold to profitable trade, which is why many, Finley argued, avoided market transactions altogether. Many scholars have objected to this, pointing to how the primitivist data eschewed both archaeological data and the quantification of evidence. New Institutional Economics alerts us that the issue is further complicated by social and cultural practices that contribute to and widen the canon of activities more commonly associated with economic conduct. Be that as it may, the practical constraints to trade and market exchange were real. They remind us that, wherever material evidence hints at long-distance exchanges and embryonic integrated economies, such entanglement did not automatically topple the local food repertoire. In the lived, quotidian experience, practical concerns brought produce from self-subsistent agrarian activities to the table first and foremost.

Thucydides claimed in a well-known passage of the *Funeral Oration* that the Athenians had of course long surpassed all inhibitions: "Produce of the whole earth flows upon us, and we are fortunate enough to enjoy goods from abroad as if they were our own as much as the products from home" (2.38.2). Although evidently a hyperbole, the image was not entirely wrong in the sense that Athens, by the fifth century BCE, had become the largest import economy of Aegean Greece. But the point here is also that Athens's trade volume and the lifestyle it facilitated were indeed exceptional. The entire argument in Perikles's speech rests on the assumption that the Athenian achievement was not representative of circumstances elsewhere. It is intriguing to contrast Thucydides's statement with a fragment from his contemporary fellow Athenian Poliochos (frag. 2 *PCG*), who has one of his protagonists describe his everyday diet: "A small barley-cake kneaded full of bran was what each of us had twice a day, and some figs. Sometimes we braised a mushroom. And if there was a bit of rain, we caught a snail. And there were local vegetables and a bruised olive, and some wine of dubious quality to drink."

It is impossible to pin down the context or even who the speaker was (an Athenian, someone from elsewhere, an Athenian elsewhere?); many questions remain open. It is dazzling to see, however, that the word for "local" vegetables used here is *autochthonos*, "born of the land." Poliochos might have played a joke, as vegetables are always grown of the land, yet it is also possible that *autochthonos* was used in the sense of the more common term for "local," *epichorios*, and that this was what Poliochos had in mind, setting up a contrast between local food and more refined imported goods.[25] Poliochos's picture was most likely not overtly skewed. For many Greeks, this was a dietary reality; note how the three food groups of the triad are present. For sure, the cities of Aegean Greece engaged in all sorts of trade and exchange networks that allowed for transactions of material goods, but this does not refute the more general point that in their daily food consumption the majority of Greeks relied on supplies that came from the surrounding countryside, from where they were brought into the city. Survey archaeologists have suggested that the least accumulative cost-distance marker ran in the range of a 2.5–5 km radius from the urban center (see chapter 1). The availability of local foodstuffs from within that radius, its agricultural produce and what might be collected from wild-growing plants, determined the basic diet of many communities.[26]

The foodstuffs listed above grew in many places of Aegean Greece, with varying degrees of abundance and quality. For instance, while cabbage grew throughout, the climate conditions in the Megarid were almost ideal for its cultivation. In neighboring Attica, with its slightly lower levels of annual rainfall, the climate seems to have been less suited for cabbage. In cross-border exchanges, cabbage was not only an agrarian commodity but also the inspiration behind all sorts of stereotyping. We will return to this shortly.[27] Multiple occurrences of the same crops did not imply, however, that they played the same role in each local cuisine. The incorporation of locally available food into everyday diets is not an automatic process, as Igor de Garine (1979) has observed. When nature intersects with nutrition, local cuisines feel the impact of cultural awareness. We have already noted how food consumption is an important medium of self and social projection, as it allows people to articulate and reassert patterns of belonging. The precondition is that a group has agreed upon common practices of preparation and consumption—that is, that both the diet and its associated tastes are considered to be socially acceptable. Public feasts in the polis, Pauline Schmitt-Pantel's imaginative *la cité au banquet* (1992), where everyone received a share in the sacrificial food and, at least in theory, all ate together, highlighted this need for social acceptance. They also reinforced the idea that choices of taste reinforced the solidarity of the group.[28]

What was tasty in one polis was not necessarily so in another. In the early 3rd century BCE, Lynkeus of Samos, brother of the historian Duris, made fun of Athenian meals. In his play *The Centaur*, the main character, a man from

Perinthos, found Athenian foods "nothing at all to satisfy the belly." Along with his companion, a man from Rhodes ("neither of us enjoys Athenian dinner!"), he took offence at the dining habit of serving different food items on many small plates; all he wanted was one large plate with one food item (frag. 1, from Athenaios 4.131f–132a). Writing roughly one generation before Lynkeus, Diphilos of Sinope, a contemporary of Menander, joked about idiosyncrasies in taste as they prevailed in different cities, and how he found some of them bizarre. One of the main characters in his *The Woman Who Left Her Husband* is a chef who inquires into the local background of the guests who are expected at a wedding party. The head of the event is puzzled by this question, but the cook rebuts: "This is a chief part of my art, master, to know beforehand what mouths are going to eat. Suppose you have invited Rhodians: no sooner have they entered, you must give them the largest catfish or *lebias* to enjoy, served piping hot. . . . Or suppose they are Byzantians, soak all you serve to them in bitters, with quantities of salt and garlic. For they have so many fish in their part of the world that they are all clammy and full of phlegm" (Athenaios 4.132d–e).

Menander, in his *Trophonios*, similarly highlights the importance of local taste. Once again, where his guests came from makes a difference to the chef: "These little island foreigners, for example, are brought up on all kinds of fish just out of the water, and so they are not attracted to preserved fish. If they eat it at all, they do so without spices, and welcome more gladly forcemeats and highly seasoned dishes. Your average Arkadian, on the other hand, living far from the sea, is caught by oyster-bait, while the Ionian, bloated with wealth, makes his chief dish of *kandaulos*, and foods that provoke desire" (from Athenaios, 4.132e–f; see also 517a). The *Trophonios* would be an interesting play to have, since its main hero's claim to fame came from his ability to eat infinite amounts. Maybe he also indulged in high quantities of *kandaulos*, a meal that, according to Hegesippos of Taras (fourth century BCE), was made of boiled meat, bread crumbs, cheese, anise, and fatty broth. Initially of Lydian origin, *kandaulos* became a high-end delicacy in many Ionian cities, yet not without local variation. There were at least three versions of the dish ranging from sweet to savory, says Athenaios, to whom this variety was indicative of Ionian indulgence in all kinds of luxuries (516d). It would be interesting to know which kind of *kandaulos* was favored by the Kolophontians, of whom we have heard so much at the beginning of this chapter.[29]

Curiosity spurs us to dwell on the topic of local food distinction for a short while. The island of Thasos was renowned for its wine. Its full body, refined with pleasant notes of apple, made it a much desired good throughout Aegean Greece in the fifth century BCE. The most frequent iconography of Thasian coins—depictions of the wine god Dionysos or of an ithyphallic satyr and a nymph—show us that the people of Thasos took pride in their local wine, partly because of the sexual disinhibition it bestowed upon its consumers.[30] In Tanagra, its reputed wine—according to Herakleides Kritikos (1.8), it "held the first place in Boiotia"—played an equally important role in epichoric traditions. In later periods, a local guild of vinedressers oversaw its cultivation. Chefs or sacrificial butchers were also numerous enough in town to be united in another association, that of *mageiroi*.[31] The Megarians preferred the more frugal goods that determined local dietary distinctions. According to Apollodoros of Karystos (third century BCE, from Athenaios, *Deipn.* 7.281a), they savored rolls of cabbage, sometimes stuffed with pork. We have already noted how cabbage grew prolifically in the Megarid. Apollodoros speaks of "cabbage-vending Megarians," who are content to boil their vegetables. If we follow Athenian writers from the Classical period, the Megarian menu was determined by what was considered to be poor man's foods throughout. Other than cabbage, turnips, onions, and flat-cakes, the Megarian palette was marked by a pronounced love for garlic and strong salt from the saltpans on the coast facing Salamis. In Aristophanes's *Acharnians* (526), Megarians are depicted as "garlic-stung." Kallias, poet of the Old Comedy, added "Megarian sphinxes" (frag. 23 *PCG*), most likely a slang word for "prostitutes," to the mix of mediocre local produce.

From Megara across the Isthmus, the inhabitants of several Achaian cities treasured more hearty meals. According to Aristophanes of Byzantium (third century BCE) they indulged in a dish called *kreokakkabos*—chunks of chopped meat, blood, and fat cooked in a sweetened broth. The Thessalians had their own version of this dish called *mattye*, made from wild game birds that were hung unplucked to retain their blood, and cooked whole in a fatty soup. Subsequently, the bird was served smothered with stewed vegetables. In Sparta, notorious for its culinary regime and opaque dining practices, the local variant of this dish went by the name *epaikleia*. The broth that was used was the famous, or infamous, Spartan black broth (*melas zōmos*), and the meat came mostly from partridge and goose. Some of the most delicious geese were, however, not found in Sparta, but in Orchomenos and other Boiotian cities. As we have seen, the main delicacy there was, however, the giant eels the inhabitants harvested in Lake Kopais. The *sitos* that went with the eel in Boiotia was called *kollix*, although we do not know how *kollix* differed from other bread types. The local variety of breads and cakes was in any case extensive. In Eretria, ninety kilometers to the east of Orchomenos, the local bakers baked breads that were so distinct that they forged the local epithet of the city: "white barley-meal Eretria."[32]

The data assembled in these paragraphs derives from a diverse body of sources, each one with its own context and agenda. This makes it difficult, if not impossible, to approach the material from a coherent perspective. The interpretative challenges are real. For instance, the topical image of the swaggering cook, so prominent in Athenian comedy, makes us wonder just how Menander's comments were inspired by popular theatrical themes and narrative purposes. The dislike of Athenian dinners displayed by the man from Perinthos in *The Centaur* is easily understood as a caricature of a simpleton who lacked the sophistication needed to enjoy an exquisite meal. Also, the dynamics of positionality are omnipresent. For Megara, for example, it was demonstrated how frequent mockery in Athenian comedy was designed to portray its inhabitants in a condescending manner. The result was an "antithetical relationship" (Florence 2003, 51), one where Megarians served as a negative counterpoint to Athenian civic values and cultural advancement. "Men of Megara, why don't you go to hell!" shouts Hermes in Aristophanes's *Peace* (500), which captured the prevailing sentiment. The same can be said of the Arkadians, drooling over oysters in Menander, because of their remoteness from the sea—and from everything else, we might add. Labeled by their fellow Hellenes as notorious "acorn-eaters" (Hdt. 1.66.2), the Arkadians in all likelihood didn't really eat acorns (most sorts are too high in bitter tannins to be enjoyed by humans; see Mason 1995). As was pointed out by Jim Roy (2011), the image of uncivilized foodstuffs was inspired by the perceived cultural backwardness of the region. The Arkadians had their own ideas about what a typical meal (*deipnon*) should include. When Hekataios visited the region, they told him that they enjoyed barley cakes and pieces of barbecued pork. The local historian Harmodios (chapter 5) explained how this diet translated into festival banquets in the Arkadian town of Phigaleia.[33] The difference between emic and etic perspectives reminds us of the dynamic force of cultural stereotyping. While food consumption in Arkadia was believed to be indicative of the wild, uncultivated character of men and country, the refined tastes of Ionia spoke to the decadence and licentiousness of the people there. Reference to Arkadian, Ionian, or Achaian eating traditions also recalls the conceptual challenge of dissecting the local sphere of food regimes and separating them from those prevailing in realms that were of a deliberately translocal nature (chapter 1).

Despite these interpretative difficulties, the examples discussed here nonetheless cast some light on the exciting process of shaping local food regimes. They indicate that local foodstuffs, their preparation and presentation, were reoccurring themes in the communication between Greeks. Local distinction not only allowed communities to position and brand-label themselves, as it were (Thasos is an excellent example), but also provided a drawing board on which to map cultural variation. The conversation about local food habits—by statements of the obvious, mockeries, or insults—was led before the wider horizon of what Hellenic culture was (and, presumably, what it wasn't). All the while, this type of cultural communication reasserted and endorsed the idea of the fragmentation of Hellenic custom into countless cities, each one contributing its own currency to the web of culture.

As the conversation gained both in breadth and depth over time, it fostered the rise of a new narrative genre, one that was dedicated to the connoisseurship of food, drink, and the infinite variety of local recipes that guided both. By the late fifth century BCE, Philoxenos of Kythera published a first cookbook entitled *Deipnon*, which was referenced by the comic poet Plato (frag. 189 *PCG*). Among the followers of Socrates was a man from Megara named Terpsion—a speaking name, "Mr. Pleasure"—who authored a brevier in which he taught his readers what foods to avoid.[34] But the real breakthrough came with Archestratos of Gela, allegedly a student of Terpsion's. In the 340s BCE, he put together what would become the first comprehensive narrative account of the cuisines of Aegean Greece. Written in dactylic hexameter, his *Hedupatheia*, or *Life of Pleasure*, (sometimes it was cited as *Gastrologia*) was a huge success. The fragments of the poem survive through Athenaios, 62 of them in total, or approximately 330 verses, that have been calculated to amount to about one-third of the overall text. The fragments attest to an extensive geographical range of local cuisines, from Archestratos's native Magna Graecia to Asia Minor. Once again, we sense how the conversation about food was intertwined with the dialogue about Hellenicity, cultural dynamics within, and demarcations vis-à-vis the non-Greek world.[35]

The poem was a commanding literary construct, one in which countless local cuisines and dining practices merged into a sizzling survey of food and drink, and the pleasures they provided. Beyond the literary edifice, Archestratos offered a colorful kaleidoscope of cultural assumptions and culinary values that were reflective of his times. The most recent editors of the text, Douglas Olsen and Alexander Sens (2000), have restored the internal structure. The opening sections were concerned with cereal products, the *sitos*, followed by a discussion of side dishes: vegetables, pulses, and the like. The greatest part by far of the *Hedupatheia* was, however, dedicated to the *opson*. It is easy to see how fish and seafood outstripped the excitement of beetroots, and more so because of the ambiguous place of fish in Greek food culture. Its source of special sensory pleasure made it the ideal target of all sorts of moralistic discourses. Archestratos left no doubt as to where he stood in such deliberations. A bon vivant through and through, he had traveled far and wide to collect information on "where each food [and drink] was best" (frag. 3). Along the journey, it is striking to see how his findings were fused by various local knowledge cultures; we have already encountered such a formative force of local knowledge in chapter 1.

In Erythrai, as the fisherman would have assured Archestratos, mullet fish was only great if caught near the shore (frag. 42). Cow-tongue fish was enjoyable in Chalkis on Euboia only in the summertime (frag. 33). Fat gilthead from Ephesos was not to be missed; its local name was "little Ionian" (frag. 13). Parrotfish from Kalchedon were agreeable, but the ones from across the straits, from Byzantion, were "nice and big, with a body as large as a circular shield" and hence preferable, provided they were prepared in a sophisticated fashion established by the Byzantians; among other preparations, this involved a coating of cheese and olive oil (frag. 14). The purchase of grey mullet from Aigina indicated connoisseurship for sure (frag. 43), while sharks and rays from Miletus were by far the most delightful (frag. 47). Nothing beat eel from Lake Kopais—although the catch from the Strymon river came close—for they were "both long and of amazing girt" (frag. 10). Parion had superb bear-crabs; Ainos on the coast of Thrace, large mussels; and Abydos, its meaty oysters, as we learned at the very beginning of this section (frag. 7).

Dining among Carnivores

In fragment 5, Archestratos advises that from among "the gifts of fair-haired Demeter," some of the finest barley comes from "seven-gated Thebes." As with the examples listed above, the reference doesn't imply that the Thebans necessarily built a food culture around barley. From what we have seen in the previous discussion, there was a positional asymmetry between the perception of local food habits by outsiders and how locals themselves saw their culinary world. More often than not, we find it difficult to see through the lens of the latter. The basic grammar of local food regimes should be clear by now, but the details of how they played out in individual city-states remain painfully obscure.

Thebes offers one of the rare exceptions. The city had access to large quantities of arable land, comprising two *chōrai* rather than one. To the west, the Teneric Plain extended about ten kilometers up to the hills of Onchestos near Lake Kopais, while the wide, treeless Aonian Plain to the north covered a territory of 70–80 km^2. Both expanses were very fertile in antiquity, with some sections experiencing too much water in winter, and thus tending to become marshy. Unlike in neigboring Attica, where the soils are patchier, with a mixture of rendsina and red soils, the land in the Theban *chōra* is rich, light loam

FIGURE 3.2. Theban stater from the early fourth century BCE. Obverse, Boiotian shield; reverse, volute crater with a rosette above, emblematic of the rich flora in the Theban countryside. The series of this period generally reference Heraklean and Dionysiac attributes, often in combination with symbols of rich agricultural produce, including grapes and barley. Image credit: Courtesy of the American Numismatic Society (1944.100.20096).

that easily retains moisture, allowing the cultivation of crops during periods of drought. The location of Thebes therefore offered a combination of fertile land, natural communication lines, and the presence of rich water springs, including the one on the Kadmeia that we encountered earlier. It was there that Kadmos slaughtered the dragon (chapter 2). The springs of Dirke, Melia, and Oedipus, each one the locus of fateful legendary traditions, were also in the immediate vicinity of the city. In sum, Thebes comprised a highly nucleated urban environment and a rich hinterland, indeed, "more green pastures than any other city in Greece" (Herakleides BNJ 369A F 1.13), with plenty of vine, olives, and crops, all easily accessible within the critical cost-distance marker of a few kilometers. The settlement structure in the countryside indicates that the Thebans had established an agricultural regime that allowed them to maximize the revenues from as far as the edges of their *chōrai*, with little if any losses from the challenge of longer distances from the city.[36]

Riches in water and fertile soils favored the cultivation of grains and, effectively, large quantities of fodder crops. In turn, fodder supplies were key for raising livestock. Whereas the hilly edges of the hinterland provided an ideal grazing environment for sheep and goats, the grassy plains of Thebes were suited for herding cattle in abundance. Cattle were notoriously expensive to raise and used for labor, serving as beasts of burden and transport animals. In most cities, cattle were consumed only when slaughtered for major sacrifices. The Thebans, on the other hand, seem to have had so many of them that they could afford to include beef in their regular diet. Kleitarchos related in the first book of his *History of Alexander* "that the Thebans were mean-spirited and stingy when it came to food, preparing meals of ground meat in leaves and boiled vegetables, anchovies and other small fish, sausages, beef-ribs and pease-porridge" (*BNJ* 137 F 1). The moral charge of the passage is unmistakable. Couched in the narrative of Alexander's destruction of the city in 335 BCE, Kleitarchos's description of the diet of the Thebans was indicative of their corrupt character; the intellectual conjecture being, as so often in ancient literature, that culinary habits had moral consequences. Athenaios, who is the referencing source (148d–f), goes on to joke that the Persians, when served such foods by their medizing hosts in the Persian Wars, were destined to lose the Battle of Plataia even before the first shot was fired (see also chapter 5).

There is another way to read Kleitarchos's Theban food regime. First, the mix of different types of meat betrays a craving for animal-based foodstuffs. Aristophanes, in *Acharnians* 876–80, foreshadowed Kleitarchos's observation by introducing an unnamed Boiotian character who brings to Athens all sorts of wild game, "geese, hares, foxes, moles, hedgehogs, cats, lyres, martins, and otters." Most likely, the point was a parody of the local penchant for meat. The appetite for low-quality meats nicely overlaps with Kleitarchos, who speaks of ground meats and sausages. These were usually considered a poor man's dish because they were made from the throwaway parts of the butchered animal that could easily be blended with less desirable meats: dog, fox, otter, or any other animal in Aristophanes's list. Beef ribs (*schelides*, in Greek), on the other hand, did not count among those meats. Pherekrates, a slightly older contemporary of Aristophanes, speaks of "mouth-melting *schelides*," along with "boiled pig's trotters with the most heavenly smell" and "delicious pork ribs browned and resting" as most sizzling meat dishes (frag. 108.13 *PCG*). In *The Knights* (362), Aristophanes himself describes beef ribs as power food, instilling men with physical strength. Although beef was generally too costly to be consumed on a regular basis, for most of the Classical period, the Thebans were economically positioned to make beef part of their quotidian diet.[37]

Recent research in the field of osteoarchaeology confirms that meat consumption at Thebes was high by all accounts. Exploring the dietary profile of the inhabitants of Classical Thebes, Efrossini Vika, Vassilis Aravantinos, and Mike Richards (2009) performed a $\delta 13C$ and $\delta 15N$ isotope analysis of the bones of thirty humans from a fifth-century burial site. The results show a formidable rise in nitrogen values, usually associated with dietary increases of protein. In their explanation of this unexpected and unparalleled increase,

Vika and her collaborators entertain the idea that the Thebans might have consumed more freshwater fish from Lake Kopais than usually thought. Also, as a result of more intensified agricultural practices, the Thebans appear to have fertilized their fields with manure. Effectively, the consumption of cereals grown on manured soils would have triggered the elevation of protein values. The third possibility, which should be considered alongside the others, was "a more systematic exploitation of animal sources [that] led to increased consumption of either meat or milk and milk products" (2009, 1078).[38]

The Theban habit of consuming large amounts of meat continued throughout antiquity. Among their fellow Hellenes, this inspired the image of dedicated carnivores and other slanderous designations that came to be considered stereotypical of the Theban character. Pindar appears as the earliest witness of the famous saying of "Boiotian swine" (*Ol.* 6.89–90). In all likelihood, this was also inspired by dietary traditions. Herakleides Kritikos declared that the speech of Theban men was "unpleasant and wearisome" (*BNJ* 369A F 1.20) and that they were known for their violent character (F 1.14–16). Moreover, Herakleides's characterization of Thebans as dumb, simple-minded people merges into a cascade of other negative character traits, Theban and Boiotian alike. His assessment culminates in the minute enumeration of Boiotian cities, each one with its own local defects (insolence at Thebes, arrogance at Anthedon, officiousness at Koroneia, pretentiousness at Plataia, stupor at Haliartos, and so on: F 1.25). Polybios found the Boiotians gluttonous. The Thebans in particular devoted themselves, he claimed, to eating and drinking; some Boiotians had "more banquets in a month than there were days in the calendar" (20.4–5). Three centuries later, Plutarch stated that the Athenians "say that we Boiotians are dull, senseless, and stupid, mostly because of our gluttony. They were also the ones who called us swine" (*Mor.* 995e). The note derives from the *Treatise on Vegetarianism*, where Plutarch elaborates that eating meat "is not only physically against nature, but it also makes us spiritually coarse and crude" (we have already encountered the conjecture between diet and morality in Kleitarchos). So there is an extrinsic theme here that plays out in Plutarch's text. Also, the voice of prejudice is unmistakable, and the dynamics of positionality obvious: outsiders, the Athenians, said that their neighbors were gluttonous meat-lovers; consequently, they were dull, senseless, stupid. As we have seen, this stereotyping had a long history in antiquity. But no matter how others judged them and their eating habits, the Thebans treasured their own food choices, and they actually built a local cuisine around them. The love of all kinds of meats was part and parcel of this.[39]

The Sensation of Skill: Material Culture and Local Brand-Labeling

As we have seen in the previous section, food and drink allowed the city to establish powerful links to place. The selection, preparation, and consumption of foodstuffs were deeply grounded in, and reflective of, the local horizon. However, food was only one among other expressions of an identity of place. The daily usage of casual items, such as ceramics, might be an unremarkable practice as such, yet it imprints a particular type of meaning upon society. As scholarship in the field teaches us, there is a wide gulf between the utility and meaning of material objects. In the words of Michael Dietler (2010, 59), "objects materialize cultural order." Archaeologists have turned to a context-based approach that focuses on the interplay between producer and consumer, which further helps to unlock the cultural meaning of objects and the visual sensation (décor, design, etc.) emanating from them. Much like food regimes, ceramics can be read as an embodiment and expression of strategies of local distinctiveness—for example, through the application of creative designs or manufacturing qualities, or both. Since artisanal and artistic expressions are themselves representative of communal values, norms, and habits, they also impart a sense of belonging. This sense is again magnified through repetition over time. Material culture is thus not only a prism through which we see the daily life of past societies but, more importantly, it is a mirror of society itself, one that "encompasses the social production and reproduction of meaning."[40] Our subsequent discussion of manufacturing traditions in four cities along the Central Greek corridor, all from within a limited geographical radius, illustrates the case. Each data set involves rather different elements and craft skills.

Given that a high proportion of their land was used for pasturage, the Megarians were notorious for raising sheep and producing wool. According to Aristotle (*Pol.* 1305a25–26), in their violent competition for influence in the polis in the later seventh century BCE, some aristocratic leaders made it their strategy to slaughter the grazing flocks of their opponents, underscoring the value of sheep wool. Soon enough, local spinners developed their own clothing style, the so-called *chlanis*, a durable, short woolen tunic. Later sources credit a certain Nikias of Megara with the invention of a particular fulling process that was applied (Plin., *Nat.* 7.57). Unsurprisingly, the dress became the object of ridicule in Athenian comedy and was subjected to various condescending comments (Aristophanes, *Acharnians* 519; *Peace* 1003). All the while, Megarian *chlaniskia* were a desired export product. Known for the fine quality of their wool, they were appreciated both as ready-to-wear clothes and as good winter dress. According to Xenophon (*Mem.* 2.7.6), some

Megarians made considerable profit from their production and trade, in the Saronic Gulf and beyond.

About the same time as Xenophon, Diogenes of Sinope mocked the Megarians for their ignorance and vulgarity. With Diogenes, who "would rather be a ram belonging to a Megarian than his son" (Ail. *Var.* 12.56), we see the pendulum of positionality in full swing. Whatever the implication of the mockery—animals will not have mattered more than sons—it is easy to imagine that Megarian sheep breeders were invested in their stock rams, which were so critical for successful flock management. Just as outsiders associated the wool *chlanis* with Megara and manufacturing skills there, the Megarians took pride in its production. As we have noted earlier, Pamela Smith (2004) has labeled such communal expertise an artisanal epistemology (chapter 1). In the Megarian case, corresponding expert ways of knowing and handling embraced all steps of the production chain: from the more generic animal husbandry and sheering to the specific skills of dying, spinning, and weaving that were applied to make the *chlanis* distinct. It is notoriously difficult to assert just how exactly these practices translated into social meaning, but this difficulty does not render void the general observation that the garb was both an expression and reassurance of a Megarian identity of place.[41]

On the other end of the Saronic Gulf, the people of Hermione were known for a different craftsmanship. In the words of the great German scholar of historical topography, Alfred Philippson, Hermione "on land could be reached only via treacherous paths through rugged mountains" (1892, 49). Some sixty kilometers away from Argos, the city was in a peculiar position. Scholars identified a rift in the sacred geography of the Argolid. While the central plain appears to have been Hera's domain, with a high frequency of corresponding cult sites there, in the region around Hermione worship of Demeter was particularly prominent. In the city and its *chōra*, there were at least five sanctuaries associated with her cult: Demeter Chthonia; Demeter on the Pron; Demeter Thermasia, itself a branch of the liminal Demeter in the borderlands toward Troizen; and Demeter and Kore near Bouporthmos. The cultic idiosyncrasy speaks to the secludedness of the southern Argolid. Leadership of Argos was undeniable, but as a port town on the edge of the Saronic Gulf, Hermione and its main traffic routes were oriented toward Aigina, Megara, and Athens. We note that the fastest connection to Argos itself was by boat.[42]

In Aischylos's *Agamemnon* (959–64), Klytemnestra implies that the palace in Argos had large resources of purple dye (*porphyra*) at its disposal that were gained from local sea snail farming. Supplies were used for dyeing robes and all kinds of decorative tapestries. But the production was complex. It involved the baiting of sea snails, the extraction of the glands, and the subsequent transformation of the secretion from the glands into dye, a multistep process that made purple garments notoriously labor-intensive and costly. Effectively, they were objects of great luxury and distinction. Agamemnon tragically warns that their lavish display in his home might attract "the gods' jealous eye" (948).

Hermione, renowned for the wealth of its fisheries and seashells, was most likely the place of origin of Argive supplies of purple dyes. Seizing the Persian imperial treasury in Susa, Alexander, according to Plutarch, acquired exuberant riches, including large quantities of purple dye from Hermione (*Alex.* 36; cf. Arr., *An.* 3.16.7; Strabo 8.6.12). The stated figure of five thousand talents in weight raises suspicion, but other aspects of Plutarch's account, such as the method of long-term preservation of dyes, have been confirmed independently by archaeological work on purple-dyeing sites elsewhere. If the reference on Hermionian dyes in Susa is found trustworthy—and there is nothing to suggest that it isn't—then the Hermionians must have perfected the art of purple snail fishing. On the pointed promontory of the city, archaeologists discovered rich deposits of snail shells that were used in the construction and repair of fortifications. Others suggested that seashell farming also resonated in local cult practices at the temple of Aphrodite Pontia and Limenia (Paus. 2.34.9–11). Without a doubt, the dying industry produced vast quantities of shells over time, which were ideal for secondary usage in other economic activities as well. Note that in the fourth century BCE Hermione did not have much more than four thousand inhabitants, which suggests that many of them were involved in the production of purple in one way or the other. The organization of labor might have inspired connected production processes across the Argolid. Excavations in Argos have brought to light a high volume of crushed murex shells in a well that was attached to what archaeologists believe was a dye-house. Most likely, the animals were brought to Argos for processing, rather than farmed in Argos itself. Hermione is then the most obvious candidate for providing supplies. Its inhabitants not only mastered the creation of purple dyes by means of a multilayered production process, but, in light of tremendous harvesting capacities, they also provided supplies to other dye-stations elsewhere.[43]

Returning to the Megarid via land, two-thirds along the way, the road bypassed the territory of Sikyon. The Archaic and Classical city lay in the coastal plain near the Corinthian Gulf where today's Kiato is, before it was moved to the plateau further inland, where archaeologists have excavated the remains of the Hellenistic and Roman settlement. The plain's fertility was proverbial. Alluvial deposits from the weathering of the neighboring rocks that were washed into the plain by rivers and torrents created ideal conditions for olives and grapes. Geologically, the territory of Sikyon consists of a series of step-like sedimentary terraces that descend from Mt. Kyllini toward the Gulf. As a result of formation processes relating to these terraces, the land of Sikyon has significant amounts of pale, limestone-rich marl clay and occasional pockets of iron-rich terra rossa. The clays were found to have an ideal plasticity; they are particularly suitable for forming and firing pottery.[44]

It has long been conjectured that the excellent clay quality supported Sikyon's pioneering role in the production of ceramics and the visual arts. Boutades of Sikyon (late seventh century BCE) was believed in antiquity to have been the first clay modeler. Around the same time, Myron, a leading member of the local Orthagorides family, offered what Pausanias (6.19.1–2) called two bronze *thalamoi* to the Sanctuary of Olympia after his victory in the horse race there (canonically 648 BCE). Presumably these *thalamoi* were objects of superior architectural design, although their nature is not entirely clear. Made of bronze, they speak to what would soon become the famous Sikyonian "school" in toreutics, or the art of bronze sculpturing. Judging from references to bronze workers and bridle-makers "from Aigialai" in Linear B texts from Pylos and Thebes—according to Pausanias (2.5.6), Aigialeia was Sikyon's earlier name—the recognition of metallurgical skill sets seems to have extended far back. In the fourth century BCE, the renown of this "school" reached its all-time high with Lysippos of Sikyon, who was traditionally regarded to be among the most distinguished bronze sculptors of the day. Among Lysippos's mentors figured Eupompos of Sikyon, who was the founding father of yet another local "school"—that of painting. Eupompos's fame was later eclipsed by Apelles, a native of Kos and master painter of ancient Greece, who had studied for some time in Sikyon with Eupompos's successor, a certain Pamphilos.[45]

The final and most tangible data set comes from Tanagra in Boiotia, about a day's walk from Megara, our first example in this section. Removed four kilometers southeast from the modern town and nestled in a landscape that today is dominated by the Schimatari Airbase, ancient Tanagra was situated where Mt. Kerykeion descends toward the Asopos river. The site can be accessed via a dirt road that forks from the main drive to Agios Thomas.[46] In the early 1870s, local farmers discovered a large Classical and Hellenistic necropolis at Kokali, in very close vicinity to the ancient city. The tombs yielded a high volume of terracotta figurines that were sculptured from casts. Surfacing at a peak time of historical Classicism, the elegant and artistically designed statuettes quickly caught the attention of European art markets. During the "Exposition universelle de 1878" in Paris their popularity fueled

FIGURE 3.3. Tanagra figures: three females draped in himation, with typical accessories (330–280 BCE). © bpk / Musée du Louvre, Paris. Inv. MNB 559, 452, 494 (left to right) = *Tanagra. Mythe et archéologie* # 118, 120, 119. Printed with permission.

a sheer Tanagra-mania. Soon enough, it also instigated the production of a considerable number of forgeries, but that is another story. Typically 20–30 cm high, the figurines represent mostly young women and, in a few cases, youthful males (fig. 3.3). The female sculptures are usually dressed in sumptuous clothing, sport sophisticated hair styles, and present striking poses; they are further accentuated with fancy accessories, such as sunhats (the characteristic *tholia*), earrings, fans, or floral wreaths. Dresses are tightly wrapped around the body, with fabrics and folds depicted billowing in motion. With the earliest examples dating from the second half of the fourth century BCE, the drapery foreshadows the arrival of Hellenistic art and its fascination with movement. Before firing, the figurines were coated with a liquid white slip that enhanced the effects of subsequent coloring with watercolors, further highlighting their appearance. The Tanagra figurines certainly captured the attention of the ancient observer as much as they inspire anyone today with an interest in the artful representation of "female elegance, beauty, and charm."[47]

The purpose of the figurines is a matter of significant debate. In light of an overwhelming variety of postures, gestures, and details it might be best to account for multiple contexts in which they were used, from grave goods to talismanic objects to portraits of "ideal" femininity, either in a ritualized or a more casual, everyday setting. The number of surviving pieces is revealing. Ranging in the thousands, their production must have shaped a formidable industry at Tanagra, including the supplies of workable clays and colors, coroplastering (the fabrication of the models that were used for the molds), and the artistic finish of each figure. The manufacturing process underlines the idea of mass production. Like the Chinese Terracotta Army, albeit as miniature pieces, the heads were produced separately, presumably to resemble the looks of their owners (in the Chinese case, this is much contested), and then attached to the prefabricated body. Based on the analysis of color pigments, scholars were able to identify a significant range of workshops in Tanagra, operating on different scales. Their output can be traced through many find spots in the Mediterranean world. In the course of the Hellenistic period, the Tanagra figurines appear to have reached the status of a global commodity that was associated with Hellenic culture, in mainland Greece as much as on the fringes of the Greek world.[48]

Each of the examples introduced above is indicative of a delicate balance between the local and the wider world in which it was nested. To be recognizable as the creative cultural output of a specific place, textiles and other material goods had to be made available through economically and culturally interconnected trade routes; hence, association with the local required interconnectivity with others. The local, in other words, was in persistent conversation with other locals. Network studies inspire us to think big about those conversations, across geographical barriers and to the remote corners of the Greek world. Upon closer examination, however, it is not altogether clear what was actually communicated. For instance, the evidence from Tanagra and its wide circulation in the Mediterranean world suggests an impressive degree of connectivity. Corresponding charts of dispersal and distant find spots support this picture. Yet at the same time, they conflate a variety of information that is best kept apart. For one, the timeline during which the figurines were produced and traded (if indeed they were traded) spans approximately four centuries, from the later fourth century BCE to the early Imperial period; Mediterranean connectivity evidently experienced profound changes during that time. Second, the circumstances under which the Tanagran ladies arrived in their later archaeological find spots, in Tanais, Babylon, or Etruria, are obscure. By the later third century BCE, the high demand for figurines led to their production in other places, including Tarentum and Alexandria. With the establishment of secondary workshops of production that satisfied the demands of local markets, the *chaîne opératoire* from Tanagra to, say, Persia, was neither linear nor unbroken. In such a scenario, the artistic biography of the figurines attests to changing preferences in cultural consumption in the Hellenistic world in general; hence, their status as global commodities was the result of a complex mediation between local patterns in cultural consumption and tectonic shifts of global exchange. There might have been a back ripple to Tanagra, but the city's main contribution was that it energized these processes, providing local supplies—real and/or through the inspiration of a new style—to markets near and far. From the fifth century, various workshops made terracotta figurines, in Boiotia and adjacent territories, but the evolving brand-label from Tanagra became the bellwether of all.

We sense how entanglement in the web of Hellenic exchanges triggered a pronounced identity of place. Take the case of Sikyon and Corinth, only some twenty kilometers apart. Unsurprisingly, the soils in the Corinthia are similar to those in the Sikyonia, especially in the lowland coastal strip along the Gulf. Clay work and ceramics production had an equally influential tradition in Corinth. Indeed, according to later sources, Boutades, pioneer in clay modeling and inventor of terracotta antefixes (decorative masks that were attached to gutter tiles on roofs), was said to be from Corinth rather than Sikyon. Scholars have concluded that the former, Corinth, was the more likely candidate for propelling the new roofing style of decorative terracotta. Be that as it may, the rival traditions cast a spotlight on the competing claims of both cities over their respective cultural creativity. In Corinth, in the so-called Potter's Quarter, archaeologists have discovered a high volume of maiden figurines with what today are typically labeled "Sikyonian" folds in their skirts. The conclusion is that those pieces were manufactured by Sikyonian craftsmen in Corinth or, more likely, by local potters who imitated the Sikyonian style. As was pointed out by Angela Ziskowski, the Sikyonian-style *korai* thus offer an exciting example of the Corinthians integrating a foreign "stylistic practice into [their] own repertoire of production."[49] We may safely assume that the same was true for Sikyonian styles in clay modeling, toreutics, and certainly painting, with so many artists traveling there to work with the renowned experts of the local school.

Dynamic cultural exchange has long been identified as the main engine of artistic advancement in Aegean Greece. It is a truism to note that in light of omnipresent entanglement, the artistic and artisanal skills of individual cities were always reflective of multiple styles and trends; there was no pristine local style. At the same time, much of the creative potential that we detect resulted from local competition—that is, the desire on the part of individual communities to improve existing styles through the adaption, alteration, and application of a local trait. This is precisely what happened in the case of the Tanagran ladies. Scholars have puzzled over how a parochial place such as Tanagra could have emerged as a hot spot for artistic production. In their desire to solve the riddle (a self-inflicted one, to be sure), some have turned to Athens to identify a viable point of origin. Today, it is widely held that the stylistic design was also inspired by Athenian ateliers that manufactured statuettes of stock figures from Menander's *New Comedy*. In what is the most consequential formulation of this view, the association of the figurines with the city of Tanagra is geographic alone, a pure happenstance. In this reading, their manufacturing technique, iconography, and style attest to Athenian cultural hegemony, with next to no regard for Tanagra itself.[50]

The hypothesis of "Athenian Tanagras" is not only problematic in terms of art history: arguments from coroplasty and stylistic comparison fail to deliver a conclusive picture. More fundamentally, it starts from a wrong assumption, a misappreciation of Tanagra as a local world in its own right. This is not to deny that there was a rich cultural intersection that cut across the border lands between Tanagra and Attica—how could this have been otherwise? Much as in the case of Sikyon and Corinth, there was a lively cross-fertilization of Attic and Boiotian/Tanagran ceramic styles which, in all likelihood, would have influenced the design of the ladies in one way or another. Other cities in Boiotia, too, had a rich tradition in the production of miniature terracotta statues. Yet none of this reduced Tanagra to the role of a passive recipient of cultural innovation from elsewhere. By the second half of the fourth century BCE, the local world of Tanagra was driven by a cultural development of its own, reaching back some two hundred and fifty years in time. As indicated by Albert Schachter, by the early sixth century BCE the city displayed "a fairly high level prosperity" (2003, 102) and a good deal of accumulated wealth. Despite changing fortunes in the Classical period, Tanagra controlled a sizeable hinterland. Its territory was in any case larger than that of Sikyon, an acclaimed pioneer in arts and design. Hailing from Tanagra (rather than Thebes), Korinna's lyric poetry pays rich homage to the local horizon of her hometown and the ontology of its place: its topography, local traditions, and language. At the behest of the muses, she also addressed the "white-robed women of Tanagra" (frag. 655 Campbell), evoking a distinguished culture of female appearance. Korinna's lifetime is notoriously difficult to ascertain. Even if we acknowledge a later date—that is, the early Hellenistic period (Berman 2010), it is clear that the passage gains significance through reference to something that was time-honored, something typical of Tanagra because it was deeply entrenched in its local culture. In other words, elegance in the public appearance of women was emphasized, and this reverence went back quite some time. Artistic representations of this elegance drew almost naturally on cultural input from elsewhere. But when this input hit the local scene, it gave rise to an all-new artistic creation.[51] In such a rendering of Classical Greek culture, there is no need for unidirectional infusion from Athens. The parochial horizon of Tanagra—and that of Sikyon, Hermione, or Megara, for that matter—was not a hindrance to cultural productivity; rather, it was a powerful engine that drove the desire of those communities to brand-label themselves before the eyes of their fellow Hellenes.

Indeed, redefining the state of the art of something was a key strategy for fostering a recognizable identity of place. It is telling to see how this strategy might have traversed into concrete policy. We note that the aforementioned Pamphilos, who had attracted Apelles to Sikyon, also initiated a law that made the education of the city's youths in the art of painting obligatory, presumably at public expense. According to Pliny (*Nat.* 35.36) this amounted to nothing less than the birth of the liberal arts. More important for our discussion here, Pamphilos's education measure betrays that, in the attempt to foster Sikyon's recognition as a cultural hub, the Sikyonians also competed for the best visiting artists to come and add to their fame. Moreover, the goal to enhance the profile of Sikyon as center of the arts inspired the people to implement a concrete measure, one that extended the local brand-labeling to a training program for the youths of the polis. The example offers a rare glimpse of how various "schools," in Sikyon and elsewhere, added to the local discourse environment. As knowledge centers with a recognized expertise in a given field—in medicine and healing, the arts, or philosophy—the corresponding schools were both indicative and the result of a lively connectivity across the Aegean. At the same time, the hub of learning was rooted in place, not only through its widespread association with a particular city, but within the community itself, where it contributed to a particular identity of place.[52]

Again, the Sikyonian example does not imply that we should assume a seamless translation of skill into social meaning. Our attempt to grasp the process through the output of the arts and material culture is further complicated by the fact that local economies were never monolithic; as we have seen, the art of painting was only one of several in Sikyon. And Megarian tunics were but one trade item in Megara. Nor should we tacitly assume that the production process was handled by citizens alone and, hence, that it generated communal meaning in a straightforward manner. For Athens, it has been demonstrated that the perfume industry was largely in the hands of metics. It was even posited that the market was dominated by certain metic "dynasties of perfumers."[53] Although somewhat hyperbolic, the verdict hints at the interpretative challenges that follow for our reading here. Hermione was too small to leave the purple dye production to the citizens alone, although there is no way to be sure about this; as we have seen, the dying industry might have utilized work forces in Argos also. Similar labor practices were most likely adopted in the manufacturing tunics at Megara. In the communal domain, artisanal epistemologies were complicated by social hierarchy and diversification.

The emerging caveats are not insurmountable. For instance, in a recent study that revisits the topic of dress and identity in ancient Greece, garments, accessories, and hairstyles are understood as embodied social practices and as sensory experiences that are multiply charged with meaning. Highlighting the profound way dress impacts the construction of ethnic, class, and gender identities in ancient Greece, the author disentangles the contextual meaning of dress at all critical junctures in the span of a life, from the cradle to the grave (Lee 2015). In light of polyvalent identities, we might assign another interpretative layer to dress: that is, its capacity to embody, and express, a distinct identity of place. Spartan women wore a notoriously short dress with slit skirts, their "thighs showing bare through the revealing garment" (Eur. *Andr.* 598). No matter how men fantasized about this, the outfit was associated with Sparta as such. *Chitōnes* from Amorgos were renowned for being see-through, because they were made from a type of wild silk that was not from the island but traded through it (Aristophanes, *Lys.* 150–151; Lee 2016, 91). Male minds will have found this inspiring, but more important here is the point that the Amorgonian *chitōn* was an identifiable commodity that came from a particular place. The women of Megara wore a local garment called *aphabrōma*, a dress that was associated with the epichoric tradition of the wife of one of the city's founding figures, a certain Habrote. The Megarian women didn't like their *aphabrōmai* and attempted to break the dress code on various occasions; each time, "the god prevented them by an oracle" to do so (Plut., *Mor.* 295 a–b). Theban women wore their hair bound up in a crown on their head, which "the locals" (*enchōrioi*), according to Herakleides, called a *lampadion*, or "little torch" (*BNJ* 369A F. 1.19). These and similar examples testify to the embodiment of local tastes and traditions.

Each of these features required a particular kind of local knowledge of weaving, tailoring, or braiding. Following Pam Hall's work on local knowledge cultures in Newfoundland (chapter 1), it is captivating to observe how locally bound styles and the knowledge that is applied in their production process shape the self-perception of communities. Woolen trigger mitts from St. John's are charged with a commensurable identity of place. In the same vein, wool sweaters from the Shetlands that are knitted from yarns of numerous color shades in a local technique, the famous Fair Isle style, have become an emblematic cultural and economic commodity of the Shetlands. In neither case, Newfoundland or the Shetlands, is the production process today necessarily handled by locals. What is local are the knitting techniques, design templates, and at times also the raw material—in this case wool—which make the final product a recognizable commodity.

Similarly, the best *auloi* of Classical Greece, the celebrated single- or double-fluted wind instrument, came from the western and southern shores of Lake Kopais in Boiotia. Theophrastus notes that the thick reeds in that corner of the lakeshore were of a particularly high quality: the flora there benefitted from the way in which marshland and lake were diked to form separate wetland resources. The region was known in antiquity for its advanced water management (Horden and Purcell 2000, 245–246). Thick tufts of reed are a prominent feature in the landscape around Orchomenos until the present day. By the 5th century BCE, the local species was the primary source throughout the Greek world that was used in the production of mouthpieces with ample vibration, the key determinant of a great sound. From his epichoric informants Theophratus learned how the local *aulos* industry, built around the reeds, had its own cultural history: it had its own technical jargon for raw materials, adhered to a unique production cycle throughout the year, and responded to the developments of sounds, styles, and musical tastes overall. To the people of Orchomenos, *aulos*-making was more than an economic activity. It was a source of local pride and global renown.[54]

In each of these cases, its cultural creativity enabled the city to claim a particular artisanal epistemology and, effectively, declare distinctiveness in a world that was much larger. Such orientation through brand-labeling emanated from within. Megarian *chlaniskia*, Theban torches, Tanagran sunhats, and Sikyonian folds—among an infinite number of similar expressions of local culture—speak vividly to the gravitational pull that drew polis inhabitants to their local world: their boundedness in the land, the respective skills they developed in correlation with place, and the success the combination of both bestowed upon the community.

Pride and Praise: The Local World of Sports

The town of Phigaleia in southwestern Arkadia had little to pride itself on. Located on a rocky promontory above the Neda River, it was curbed by steep ravines on two sides and a semicircle of mountains on the other two, with no room to grow. Of all cities in Arkadia, Phigaleia presumably possessed the most extreme mountain location. The site beautifully captures Phokylides's "small polis on a rock" (chapter 2). In its mountainous *chōra* were a few satellite villages, often not more than some scattered hamlets. One of these clustered around the Sanctuary of Apollo Epikourios at Bassai, six kilometers as the crow flies to the northeast. The construction of the first monumental temple there in the decades on either side of 600 BCE was the one thing that put Phigaleia on the map. The other was the city's native son Arrachion, three-time champion at the Olympic Games and among the most renowned pankratiasts ("all-fighters") in Greek antiquity. Arrachion, so the tradition went, was strangled to death in the finals of 564 BCE but on his last breath broke his opponent's toe, thus forcing him to release his lethal scissor hold. In honor of such bravery, the referees proclaimed Arrachion victor and crowned his corpse. His hometown remembered him for centuries. On his visit to Phigaleia, Pausanias saw Arrachion's statue in the agora, which he considered to be of old age. Signs of decay were omnipresent, yet Arrachion stood tall. His fame was a source of pride. In all likelihood, although this is not attested in our sources, he was the recipient of a hero cult, which would have provided a ritual context for the commemoration. Through Arrachion, the people of an otherwise relatively unremarkable city were able to connect to time and place, and orient themselves in the vagaries of life.[55]

Victory in athletic competitions spurred some of the most boastful expressions of local pride. As we saw at the beginning of this chapter, the Kolophontians were eager followers of the Grand Four at Olympia, Delphi, Isthmia, and Nemea. According to Xenophanes, if their athletes were victorious in any of these, they showered them with money and honors.[56] But the relation between athlete and polis was not governed by economic transactions alone. Take the case of Ageus from Argos, winner in the long race, or *dolichos*, in 328 BCE at Olympia. As soon as he had crossed the finish line, Ageus wanted to announce his victory to his hometown; allegedly, he managed to deliver the message there on the very day of his triumph (Eus., *Ol.* 113). According to Google Maps, the walking distance between Olympia and Argos amounts to 152 kilometers, which casts doubt on the historicity of the passage. Yet the implicit desire to break the news at home as swiftly as humanly possible speaks volumes to the taxonomy of relevance. Beyond the moment of triumph in the stadium, the truest impact of victory showed itself when the news hit the hometown. It was there that sensational narratives unfolded, where victory shaped what Leslie Kurke (1991) has called a multi-layered "economy of *kudos*," or economy of praise.

Athletes participated in the games on their own account: that is, as individuals rather than representatives of their city. Yet the cities' ties to the contest were strong. A two-way exchange of festival delegations, so-called *theōroi*, constituted a formal link between polis and games. *Theōroi* traveled from the sanctuary to the cities, proclaiming a festival truce and issuing invitations to participate. From the end of the fifth century BCE, their local hosts, the *theōrodokoi*, are known from many inscriptions, which also allows us to trace the itinerary of such sacred deputies throughout the Greek world (see chapter 1). In the reverse direction, cities sent their own *theōroi* who, more like state-pilgrims, observed the games and represented their communities among the festival crowd. When the herald announced the names of the victorious athletes before the assembled audience in the crowning ceremony, this included mention of the athletes' hometowns; by implication, the announcement always honored the *theōroi* present. The native city was also mentioned in all official records, such as victory lists and other transcripts. In short, we see an intriguing interplay between city and sanctuary, one that was facilitated and shaped by the athlete and his agonistic performance. This intermediary role made athletes identification figures par excellence.[57]

Many cities threw lavish parties upon their return. When Exainetos of Akragas, second-time winner in the stadium race at Olympia in 412 BCE, came home, he was said to have entered the city in a parade of three hundred chariots that were led by the champion himself, mounted on a quadriga. This, or rather the morning after, was also the occasion when the symbolic value of crowns of laurel, olive, celery, or elderberry was topped with other distinctions—honorary membership in the city council, seats of honors, or tax exemptions—and also with "real" capital. In some cases, cities went out of their way to pay their victors exuberant cash funds.[58]

The economy of *kudos* was thus not subject to one-time transactions. Rather, it had its own time line. Arrachion's example illustrates that the dedication of victory statues—at home in the agora, in the sanctuary where the victory was won, or in both locations—was among the foremost strategies to facilitate long-term conversations. A great many examples of statues and honorary documents survive in the archaeological and literary record that inscribed victory into the urban environment of the community—so many that the issue hardly requires further elaboration here.[59] Once again we detect an alignment between the economy of praise and the expenses involved. When Tellon from Oresthasion in Mainalia in southern Arkadia won the competition in boy's boxing in 472 BCE, his hometown dedicated a statue to Olympia in recognition of its native son. An assembly place of the Peloponnesian League, Oresthasion was otherwise unremarkable—so unremarkable that its local elites maintained burial shrines in Phigaleia. When they commissioned the statue, the citizens probably had to scrape their money together to pay for the project. Tellon's victory was a moment of pride that was worth the effort.[60]

Putting the athlete in the middle of the community (literally so: most commonly in the agora), victory statues had a tremendous communicative capacity to encapsulate communal self-esteem and inspire future traditions. In a more general sense, narratives of athletic vigor aligned with other combat traditions: for instance, those of heroic warriors or hunters (Fontenrose 1968). What made those traditions so compelling was that the champions—in battle or in sports—were members of the polis community—that is, inhabitants could say that "he was one of us." Moreover, as the defining traits of belonging to the community were clustered around the role model citizen ("he had fought staunchly in battle"), champions in war and at the games appeared as icons of a combative ethos, one that, if fulfilled, guaranteed the well-being of the community. It is not surprising, therefore, that several Olympic victors received heroic honors in their hometown. Examples include, among others, Polydamas of Skotussa (pankratiast in Olympia, 408), Theagenes of Thasos (boxing champion, 480), and Euthykles of Lokroi Epizephyrioi (pentathletic champion in 488 BCE; see chapter 5). Each of their associated hero cults has been studied in great detail, with scholars having identified a fine line between heroic veneration of the individual and the statue as a "magical double" (Kurke 1991, 150). For example, the statues of Polydamas and Theagenes—not the athletes themselves—were believed to have healing powers. In both instances, the respective hero cults were construed around the monument rather than the person. All the while, the secondary veneration of the athletes' genius highlighted the community's desire to reconnect with the past, charge it with meaning in the present day, and perpetuate it into the future. Under such circumstances, the economy of *kudos* appeared as a lasting obligation, drawing on the statue and its genius as communal resources from within—in a metaphorical sense, from within the citizen body, as much so as, literally, from within the town.[61]

Athletic victory at the Grand Games of Olympia, Delphi, Nemea, and Isthmia inspired economies of praise that fed off universal interaction and its reception at the local level. The economy of *kudos* was subject to local dynamics, energized by parochial narratives, and tied to place. But it also drew on the prestige that came from afar, the honor and distinction of victory in a competition that was carried out before the wider audience of the Hellenes. Some sanctuaries had a wider catchment area than others (fig. 3.4). For Nemea, for instance, it was demonstrated that while the games there attracted a similar pool of athletes as the competitions in Olympia, the crowd of spectators was less far-reaching (Nielsen 2018a, 169–229). This does not,

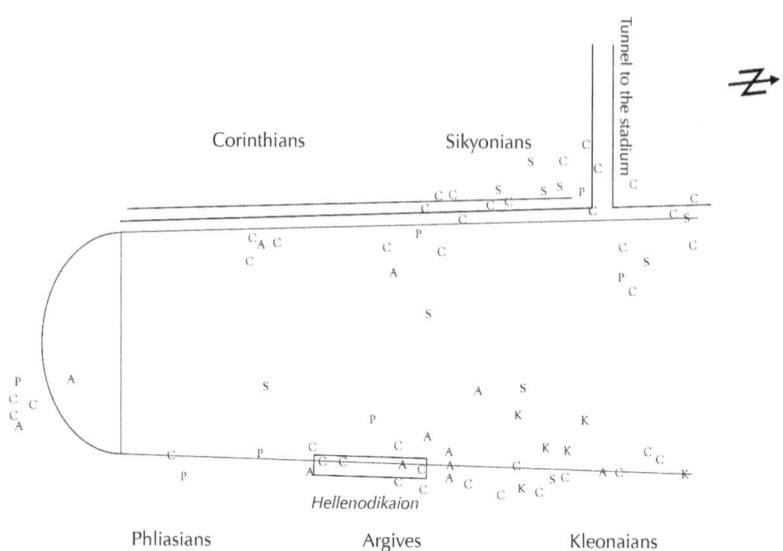

FIGURE 3.4. Distribution of coins in the stands of the stadium at Nemea from the Classical and early Hellenistic period (sample size: 153 pieces). The distribution has been found to provide additional insight into the use of the facility. With the majority from mints in Argos, Kleonai, Corinth, Phlious, and Sikyon, the coins indicate that the audience came mostly from neighboring cities, within a day's walk. Although coins were discovered scattered about the stadium, several local clusters have been identified, which are interpreted by the excavators as "cheering sections" or fan blocks. If this is correct, the coins bear witness to groups of spectators who rallied together in support of their local athletes. See Knapp and MacIsaac 2005, 27–30 (fig. is based on their plan).

however, undermine the general interplay between local and universal systems of meaning, each one energizing the other.

Nothing illustrates this better than the case of Euthymos of Lokroi Epizephyrioi, a boxer who was victorious at Olympia in 484, 476, and 472. His native town commissioned honorary statues for him at home and in Olympia (see *IvO* 144). Both dedications gave rise to various heroic traditions. According to Pausanias (6.6.4–11), when the statues were struck by lightning on the same day, the rattled Lokrians received an oracle from Delphi urging them to venerate Euthymos as a hero while alive and as a god after his death. Presumably, then, Euthymos's veneration as a hero began during his lifetime, and new layers were added to his legend over time. For while Euthymos was born the son of a certain Astykles, the locals (*epichōrioi*: 6.6.4) claimed— much in line with Delphi's advice for divine honors—that he was the son of the river god Kaikines. The river bed of the Kaikines was the political border between Lokroi and its belligerent neighbor, Rhegion. It also demarcated the Lokrian cosmos as such, with all its idiosyncrasies. On the one side of the river, observed Pausanias, the cicadas, insects with a very peculiar stance in Greek mythology and attributes of the Muses, chirped as usual; whereas on the Rhegian side of the river they were quiet. Euthymos's association with the Kaikines put the hero in place in more ways than one. All the while, tales about his return from Olympia were interwoven with Odysseus's visit to the region during his *nostos*. In particular, Euthymos was said to have driven out an evil spirit from the city of Temesa, situated on the opposite side of the Italian toe from Lokris, who had resided in Temesa ever since Odysseus had landed there. We note that Lokroi Epizephyrioi, a relatively young colony, was founded only around 600 BCE. And yet Euthymos, the boxer hero, allowed the Lokrians to assert a claim to antiquity, link themselves to the epic tradition, and write themselves into its narrative arch. We will return to this interplay between the epic tradition and local narratives shortly.[62]

Communal identification with the victorious athlete is usually viewed in conjunction with the rise and early development of statehood in Greece. As the expression of an aristocratic ideal and lifestyle for most of the Archaic period, athletic distinction was initially prone to fuel forces that were counterintuitive to the integration of the community and the institutionalization of politics. This centrifugal nature of athleticism only gradually gave way to a more integral picture, one in which the polis, rather than an aristocratic clan or faction, capitalized on the distinction of its champions. The tacit assumption behind this integration, or absorption, of achievement into the collective of the city is that the victory was won in competitions of the Grand Four. In their role as facilitators of peer polity interaction and transregional exchange, the games of Olympia and Delphi appear as landmark events, with pivotal importance for the rise of the Greek state.

What about local games? In addition to the four Crown Games, we find a rich variety of *agōnes* that were held locally and regionally. Local games were part and parcel of Greek athletic culture. Not surprisingly, some of them were staged in emulation of the Grand Four. Following the same logic of distinction through competition, they attest to a vibrant exchange of shared social values, and they document how those values translated into the local horizon. Local games, too, left their mark on the development of the culture of athletic competition, permeating the same ideas as the Grand Four did. Louis Robert has famously remarked that there had been an "explosion agonistique" in the Hellenistic and early Imperial periods, indicating that there was a quantitative jump in local games in Greece from the third century BCE. By implication, the number and role of local *agōnes* in the pre-Hellenistic period are typically considered low. Preoccupation with Olympia and Delphi as beacons of cultural advancement relegates local games to the realm of pettiness. It is difficult to avoid condescending conclusions about games held in the shadow of the Grand Four. From some of the most eminent scholars in the field, we hear the verdict that local games "may not have had more than a local or regional appeal." They are generally introduced as "less important contests" than the prestigious Crown Games.[63] This begs an important question: less important to whom?

Upon closer examination, the diverse body of evidence betrays a frequency of local games in the fifth and fourth centuries that posits them as a force with which to be reckoned. Scattered examples are found throughout the Greek world, from the Chersonese in the northern Aegean to Kroton in southern Italy to Megara and the Arkadian heartland in the Peloponnese, where local games are attested to for both Tegea and Mainalos, home of the famous boy-boxer Tellon. In Euripides's *Alkestis*, when Herakles returns Alkestis to her husband after freeing her from the clutches of Thanatos (Death), he declares that he had found "some people (*tines*) holding a public contest, an occasion worthy of an athletes' toil. . . . Those victorious in the light events won horses as a prize, while those in the heavier events, boxing and wrestling, won cattle, with a woman in addition. Since I happened to be there, it seemed a shame to let slip this chance for profit combined with glory" (1025–31). The casual character in which this is told suggests that Euripides references common practice: local games can be held anywhere, on a multitude of occasions. All the while, the imaginative scene is captivating, full of excitement. There is nothing petty about the fight. It was in a heavy contest with Thanatos himself, a gripping battle between two supreme champions, that Alkestis was rescued and brought back to life.

As the most emblematic athlete of all, Herakles's prowess was venerated in many local sports contests. A fifth-century prize vessel from Thespiai is inscribed to honor victory at the "Herakleia at Thespiai" (*SEG* 37.387), evidencing a contest there. In nearby Thebes, the people had their own *gymnikos agōn* in honor of Herakles, which was held in conjunction with the city's annual festival of the same name.[64] The example of the Herakleia at Thebes is revealing because it is indicative of a trait of local games that is often underappreciated. Much as with the Grand Four, where the athletic events were couched in a religious context, many polis festivals had an agonistic component. Indeed, the *gymnikos agōn* was a prominent part of the overall celebrations. The experience was magnified when held in conjunction with a polis festival, at the juncture of communal conduct of religion and ritual.[65] Thomas Heine Nielsen has collected evidence for 155 local *agōnes* of the Archaic and Classical periods across Aegean Greece (this does not include the gymnasium games that were held in every city), and in an attempt to provide a "guesstimate" beyond the attested cases, he posits that the number most likely "ran into several hundreds" (2016, 39). The vast majority has slipped out of our record and may remain elusive forever, but this does not weaken the general observation that local athletic games were both a frequent feature and a source of excitement in the life of polis societies.[66]

Naturally, local games did not produce world-renowned champions in the way Olympia did, but they did allow their audiences to enjoy the spectacle of athletic competition. Every polis held *agōnes* in the gymnasium, competitions of the citizen youths who underwent athletic and military training (see also chapter 4). While these gymnasium games were confined to participants from the polis, the local games discussed here were open to athletes from elsewhere. Just how far their catchment area went beyond the polis is difficult to assert. In general terms, the mobility of the majority of athletes was more limited in pre-Hellenistic times. The Amphiaraia at Oropos, for which we can trace the itinerary of some of their victors, suggest that in the fourth century BCE champions there were only modestly mobile.[67] Audiences certainly traveled even less. They came from a regional radius: the maximum distance many spectators were able to manage was one or two travel days; as we have seen earlier, this is also confirmed by the predominant composition of the crowds at Nemea. So there is no reason to suggest that local events, by and large, attracted many spectators from afar. The audiences of local games may or may not have found the local contest as captivating as that at Olympia. But to most of them, this would have been a hypothetical comparison. The spatial dynamics of Panhellenism (Michael Scott) put Olympia on the mental map, but actual travel to the sanctuary was never a real option for many. Games that were held in the polis or in a nearby sanctuary, on the other hand, provided a realistic opportunity for them to experience the excitement of athletic competition. It allowed locals to get a glance at some of the iconic athletes of the day. In turn, it made them feel that their city was worthwhile for those athletes to visit and to appear in their games.

There are examples of traveling super athletes. Diagoras of Rhodes, for instance, was a *periodonike* who had championed in boxing competitions at each of the Grand Four, winning a total of nine crown victories. The man was a living legend; later traditions would likely have made him even greater. His performances were spectacular, sometimes bone-chilling. On one occasion, he was said to have killed an opponent in a fight at Delphi. Yet Diagoras didn't restrict himself to appearances at the Grand Four. According to Pindar (*Ol.* 7), he fought and prevailed at local games on Rhodes, in Athens, Argos, Arkadia, Thebes, and other Boiotian cities; Pellene, Aigina, and Megara, much to the delight of the audiences in those places. Theaios of Argos, wrestling champion at Nemea around 463 BCE, at Delphi, and at Isthmia, was also a two-time winner of the local Heraia in Argos. This was the occasion when most of his fellow citizens saw him perform (Pind., *Nem*. 10). Aristagoras of Tenedos, on the other hand, had collected a fine slate of victories in local pankration and wrestling competitions as a young man. A potential Olympian champion, he actually never performed there because his parents wouldn't let him (Pind., *Nem*. 11). Finally, there was the sensation of hippic contests. By the later sixth century BCE, the sanctuary of Athena Itonia near Koroneia hosted a chariot race, although it is difficult to discern some of the most basic features of the event. The contest was the prime opportunity for the people along the southern shores of Lake Kopais to attend a hippic *agōn* and enjoy the bristling excitement—riders, horses, technical equipment, roaring crowds—because of the sanctuary's convenient location less than a day's walk from many Boiotian cities.[68]

The sensation of the moment was one thing; its translation into the storied world of the city, another. Generally speaking, the world of sports invited communities to distinguish themselves through competitions that were either unique or followed a unique script, or both. For instance, the aforementioned Amphiaraia included a contest among sophists that was apparently only held there (later fourth century BCE). Twenty-five kilometers west, in Tanagra, audiences were drawn to a rather different contest: the violent spectacle of rooster fights—something of an acquired taste that was considered a local specialty in Tanagra. Other cities distinguished themselves through a lively culture of rhapsodic competitions, a form of contest that had its roots in the Archaic period and that was particularly prominent in Boiotia, while several Thessalian poleis held hippic *agōnes* that were carried out under the specific rules of the Thessalian triad. At the local level, the canon of disciplines and statutes at the Grand Four was thus counterbalanced by a broad agonistic diversity.[69]

Such diversity added to local preferences for certain competitions; indeed, some cities specialized in, and developed a taste for, specific disciplines. Take the case of Onomastos of Smyrna, who was the first victor in boxing at the twenty-third Olympiad in 688 BCE. According to the sources, he was responsible for writing the rules of boxing competitions in general. From what we have established earlier, his hometown surely would have granted him all sorts of awards and honors. Moreover, it is not unlikely that Onomastos's fame triggered a boxing boom in Smyrna, with young men emulating their champion, although, admittedly, this is pure conjecture.[70]

Other examples of local specialization make such a conjecture not unlikely. Racing teams from Elis highlighted the fact that their victories were won with horses from their city. By doing so, they hyperlinked their success in sports with another local tradition, that of Eleian horse breeding. According to later traditions, the Eleians called their agora a hippodrome because they trained the horses there. The local practice put the animals both metaphorically and factually in the heart of the community. Kroton, across the Ionian Sea, produced a striking number of Olympic champions in two disciplines: wrestling and the stadium run. Starting in 588, the Krotonians gained twenty Olympic victories over the course of one hundred years. This exceptional record has been explained in terms of Kroton's outstanding role as medical center. In the sixth century BCE, the city was renowned for its advanced knowledge in medical and therapeutic sciences. Presumably, the Krotonians used this expertise not only for healing purposes, but also to maximize the training of their athletes through appropriate diets, an elaborate fitness program, and exercises that increased physiological strength and the locomotive system. If this is correct, we detect here a curious amalgamation of two local discourses, in medicine and athletics, each one informing the other.[71]

Maybe this was also the case in Thebes. Since the later fourth century, the statistics of Theban champions at the Grand Four indicate a significant increase in successful pankratiasts, especially in the competitions among boys and youths. Sebastian Scharff (2016c), who has compiled the evidence, argues that the trend was anything but coincidental. In light of the city's recent plight, in 335 BCE, the Theban community attempted to project the image of a vital, youthful place. The best way to do this was to promote the training of combat sports, especially the pankration (or *pammachos*, as it is labeled in victory epigrams), which soon became a local specialty. The Thebans—qua Thebans—couldn't have made a better choice. It is anecdotal to note that, according to Athenaios, athletes in combat sports were known for their high meat intake; superstar boxer Theagenes from Thasos, whom we encountered earlier, was reported to have eaten an entire bull (10.412d–413f). We are tempted to recall the famous, or infamous, Theban dietary habit of wanton meat consumption (above). It is possible to see a link here, and if so, we might get a hunch about how various things came together in Thebes—dietary traditions, lifestyles, sports, power politics—to craft a unique local environment.

Local Tunes

The praise of athletic achievement in song was one of the most exciting expressions in the conversation about sports. Epinikian song, with its thick script of enthralling sound, powerful stanzas, anthemic lyrics, and coordinated choral dance deeply moved the audience. We note in passing that songs were regularly performed on occasions that abounded with other types of sensory excitement, including the one that comes with the consumption of large amounts of alcohol. The Greek conception of wine as a symbolic incarnation of the divine on earth will have added its own twist of exaltation. Pindar, in any case, said that his songs put people in a state of jollity described as *euphrosyna* (*Nem.* 4.1), a condition that caught "life at its song-filled best" (Burnett 2005, 239). And song was a forceful marker of an identity of place. Claude Calame (1977), among the most eminent authorities in the field, has long remarked that this quality of choral lyric poetry, its local boundedness, was one of the defining spheres of Greek chorality. Polybios, in a widely known passage, commented that instruction in local song and dance was among the prime aspects of youth education. Speaking of Arkadia, he declares that, "trained to sing in measure the hymns and paeans in which by traditional usage they celebrated the local (*epichōrioi*) heroes and gods" (4.20.8), the people there treasured a song culture that was deliberately local, allowing them to connect to place and orient themselves in the world.

It's a commonplace to note that athletes and their families usually hired poets from afar to sing the praise of victory. Hence, the task of composing songs was outsourced to foreigners. The works of the great choral poets of Archaic and Classical Greece are thus typically seen as representative of Panhellenic song. The term is a misnomer; we discuss this in more detail below when we return to the issue of song and prayer in ritual (chapter 4). Strictly speaking, there was no such thing as a Panhellenic song, neither in the genre of victory odes nor in ritual. This is not to deny that the surviving corpus of *epinikia* is indicative of how local communities engaged in conversations with others and how these conversations defined some of the basic traits of Hellenicity through common themes and forms, and a joint performative culture in which both where rooted.[72]

We ought to bear in mind that poets were hired to compose songs for specific events. The poet's challenge was to capture the concreteness of the moment—a specific constellation of people, place, cause, and event—and craft a coherent whole through music. In turn, poets received very locale-oriented gifts and benefits, such as lifelong privileged seating at festivals (*proedria*) or proxeny honors, which again highlights the local context. Barbara Kowalzig (2007, 68) has posited that, at its baseline, panegyric poetry reflects the interests of the local community that commissioned it.

The local backdrop to epinikian song requires full appreciation. Musical performance was a privileged medium to underscore and celebrate prevailing discourses, distinctions, and, in this sense, identities. More often than not, *epinikia* were recited in effective first-person voice that allowed every member of the group to recognize themselves in the performance. The stanzas of choral song followed each other in unbroken sequence, and the complex repetitions of rhythm and melody, although unidentifiable to us today, reinforced the song in ways that were compelling to the ancient audience, allowing them to share in an "experience of victory extended and made imperishable."[73] Since the poet typically was an outsider and hence an extra authoritative voice, this lent even more weight to the music. Finally, the practice of circulating songs after their performance invited the articulation of local distinctiveness and its advertisement to others. In panegyric poetry, local achievement and idiosyncrasy merged into a "supra-local background" where they were appreciated by audiences in the polis.[74]

The local itself was an anchor point of praise. Bakchylides calls on "the local born Muse (*Mous'authigenēs*) [who] summons the sweet din of pipes, honoring with victory songs the dear son of Pantheidas" (2.11–14). In the same vein, Pindar, in an ode for Psaumis of Kamarina, victor in the mule-car race at Olympia (*Ol.* 5, from 448 BCE?), addresses the local nymph of the city, the daughter of Oceanos. The song then continues to celebrate the topography of Kamarina through which Psaumis traveled on his return from the Peloponnese: "the sacred grove, Pallas protector of the city, and the river Oanis, and the local lake (*enchōrion limnan*), and the sacred canals with which Hipparis waters its people, and swiftly builds a tall-standing grove of steadfast dwellings, bringing this host of citizens out of helplessness into the light" (5.9–14). In *Nemean* 7, Pindar references the urban topography of Aigina, praising the pentathletic champion Sogenes for living in a house that has a temple of Herakles on either side. These examples bear ample testimony to the prominence of local place in song. They reveal an encoding of victory songs that was rich in meaning, an extra-textual web of allusions to place, people, and traditions that stood at the heart of the local community.

The most effective strategy for articulating local distinction was, however, alignment with divine genealogies and the heroic tradition. At first glance, such tapping into the epic cycle speaks to the universal dimension of epinikian poetry, rather than the local horizon. We have already seen how Lokroi Epizephyrioi, for example, linked up with the epic tradition through its superstar boxer, Euthymos, and how this was done in an attempt to increase the city's local profile. The eleven odes for young athletic champions from Aigina by Pindar illustrate this strategy of enhancing local visibility through universal narrative. The Aiginetan songs adhere to a coherent frame. Ample in scale, well textured, and composed around a central mythical theme, Pindar's songs fully met the taste of his audience: a rich local aristocracy that prided itself on social values that it saw epitomized in its young athletes. This is, in any case, the impression we get, considering that the commissioning families engaged Pindar over and over again, from the 490s BCE to the 440s. All of the Aiginetan songs were *epinikia* composed for performance in Aigina itself, situating the music firmly in the local context.[75]

The heroic pedigree of the Aiginetan elites clustered around the myth of Aiakos, first legendary king of Aigina and son of Zeus and a local nymph (Hom., *Il.* 21.189; Hes., *Catalogue of Women* 145.1 Most). Aiakos was said to have had three sons, Phokos, born by the sea nymph Psamathe, and Telamon and Peleus, from a union with a dryad named Endais. Her name was a speaking name, from Engaios, "In the Earth," which is why scholars extrapolated a double sense of belonging from the family tree. As descendants of the seabound nymph Psamathe and the earthbound Endais, the tale allowed the Aiginetans to see themselves as "masters of the sea but fully human and belonging to the soil of their land."[76] We have already encountered the corresponding paradigm of attachment to the land through earthbornness in chapter 2. But the myth didn't end there. After conspiring to murder their brother Phokos during a contest, Telamon and Peleus fled from their homeland. Peleus went to Thessaly, where he had sex with Thetis to father Achilles, while Telamon would become the father of Ajax the Great. Through the Aiakid family legend, then, the local aristocracy of Aigina maintained prime relations to gods and heroes alike, with a pedigree that was far-reaching and utterly local at the same time.

The earliest ode that survives for an Aiginetan champion is *Nemean* 5 for the boy pankratiast Pytheas, son of Lampon (c. 483 BCE). It begins with reference to the sculptures of the new Temple of Aphaia that was put up in the 490s on the site where the previous temple had burnt down about a decade earlier. The new pediments were boastful exclamations of the Aiakid myth, with Telamon playing the central role in the eastern pediment and Ajax, his son, dominating the scene on the western pediment. Pindar's poem claims to bring movement to sculptures that are otherwise bound to stand idle in place (lines 1–2), animating them through the power of choral song. The claim is as metaphorical as it is real, for the ode swiftly merges into a full-blown narration of the Aiakid heroic genealogy, artfully construed around Peleus's wedding (lines 7–39). Only in line 40 do we arrive at Pytheas's family, when Pindar references his maternal uncle, a certain Euthymenes who had excelled in games at Nemea, Megara, and also at home.[77] The next stanza, in the firstperson, jumps from individual achievement to communal emulation, emphatically declaring "I rejoice that all of the city strives for noble rewards" (lines 46–47). After praise for Pytheas's trainer (an unusual acknowledgment in itself, but this is not the point here), the ode returns to a monument set in stone, the heroic altar-tomb of Aiakos, where the chorus deposits crowns of veneration (lines 53–54). The song-animated journey through the Aiginetan legendary cycle thus concludes by means of a ring composition, from one physical place to another, the Temple of Aphaia to the Altar of Aiakos.[78]

Throughout the ode, the boy champion Pytheas remains silent, almost invisible. And yet he is key to it all. Embodying the virtues not only of his family but of the entire community, and inspiring, together with his uncle, his fellow citizens to strive for "noble rewards," the athlete is iconic of a local heroic tradition, an intermediary who allows the community to connect with its past. Those past ties situate the Aiginetans in the broad stream of Panhellenic legends, but, more importantly, they add depth to the local horizon. The referenced monuments were real anchors in the urban environment of the city, fostering the veneration of and reconciliation with the divine, and the religious practices that related to these monuments turned the mythical past *of* place to a lived past *in* place. As victorious athlete, Pytheas was an intermediary between heroes and men. His song wasn't simply an articulation of local pride. It was a source of orientation in its own right.

In *Nemean 6*, which honors not just one champion but five generations of Bassids who had collected a total of twenty-five victories at the Grand Games, such an intermediary function is made even more explicit. Men and gods share the same mother, Gaia (Earth), forming a strong bond of kinship, despite being kept apart by distinct powers (lines 1–4). The most recent champion in the long line of Bassid champions, a boy-wrestler named Alkimidas,

> now makes this kinship obvious to all,
> that the valor is like crop-bearing fields,
> which in changing seasons give rich nurture to man from the plains,
> and then rests to regain its strength. (lines 8–11)

The boy adds to the fame of his family, as have others in the past; indeed, the line stretches back to their ancestor Praxidamas, who was the first Aiginetan champion at Olympia (lines 16–18, in 544 BCE). Two other champions, Kallias and Kreontidas, distillations of Bassid excellence who are shrouded in an almost mythical aura (lines 34–45), were associated with Praxidamas. From these, the ode segues into lands as remote as Ethiopia and to legends as compelling, as it were, as that of Achilles. Time discriminates the past from the present, but in the Bassid display of strength the audience is invited to detect a more permanent trajectory, one in which linearity gives way to cyclicality. As time marches forward, hero-like qualities of the family surface in every generation, a condition that is compared with the seasonal flourishing of "crop-bearing fields" which give "rich nurture to man." Athletic stardom thus overcomes the perishability of the moment. It reminds the audience of their sacred relation to Gaia, and this reminder is evoked in the most emblematic image of the local: the image of rich fields that are a source of life to the polis.

We have seen in this section how the world of sports threw polis communities into a state of excitement. Athletic competition at the Crown Games (Olympia, Delphi, Nemea, and Isthmia) is generally viewed as the pivotal event of sports entertainment, but our examination has brought to light a lively interplay between transregional athletic contests on the one hand (the label is itself problematic for Nemea and Isthmia, judging from their limited catchment areas) and those on the local level on the other. Success at Olympia instilled athletes and their hometowns with effusive pride, but, statistically speaking, with participants from hundreds of poleis, a limited number of disciplines, and an interval period of four years, the hope of many city-states for victory never materialized. The local world of agonistic competition, by contrast, was in reach, tangible. Athletic stardom is a common feature in other premodern cultures and societies, but the heightened significance of the competition as such—the sincerity with which it was carried out, its general open-endedness, and the renown that was drawn from it—added a unique texture to the agonistic culture of ancient Greece.[79] In the Hellenic variant, and due to the particular role of athletes in it, stardom in sports fed into a broad array of cultural conversations. Athletic games were not only *agōnes* between athletes but between competing local communities that tried to excel in the display of cultural capacity in order to gain the prestige it lent to its proprietors. In this rivalry for recognition, the athlete was an epitome of the local, an icon of values and self-beliefs, a critical link that tied the polis to its heroic roots in time and place. Long after the dust of the competition had settled and the athletes were gone, songs of praise continued to sound through the streets of the city. The circumstances in the world writ-large changed quickly, but the songs remained the same, inspiring future generations and instilling in them local pride, self-esteem, and orientation.

4

The Gods in Place

> "Dearest of men, please let us do no further harm. What we have is enough to have reaped a terrible harvest. There is sufficient grief already: let us not get blood on our hands. Go now, honorable elders, to your homes [yielding to fate] before you suffer. These things must [be accepted] as we have done them. If, I tell you, a cure for these troubles were to appear, we would accept it, after having been so wretchedly struck by the heavy talon of the evil spirit. Such are the words of a woman, if anyone sees fit to learn from them."
> AISCHYLOS, *Agamemnon* 1654–61 (trans. Sommerstein)

Toward the end of the *Agamemnon*, Klytemnestra's desperation pushes her to do something that is nothing short of daunting. For the longest time in the play, she had presented the murder of Agamemnon as an act of salvation. By killing her husband, she had argued, she averted an evil spirit, or *daimōn*, that had resided in Atreus's house ever since the crime of Thyestes's feast. Yet now, suddenly, she changes her tune and portrays herself as a victim, as part of a community much larger than that of her house that has been hurt by the same *daimōn*. More suffering will come to all Argives if the grievances between them cannot be resolved. Highlighting the need for healing, Klytemnestra proposes a three-pronged argument. First, she amplifies the threat of the imminent situation; if not contained, its outcome will be more detrimental than the terrible harvest it has already provoked. In light of such jeopardy she stresses, second, that the elders, and with them everyone in Argos, will be harmed. Third, she takes this negative implication of community—a community in suffering—turns it around, and charges it with the positive prospect of healing, if the Argives only stand together. Klytemnestra endorses this thought of unity and belonging by underscoring her integral role as a woman among the community of Argives. So, what had once begun as a sacrilegious crime in the house of Atreus grew into a family disaster, a burden borne from an ancestral fault. Toward the end of the *Agamemnon*, this fault is again magnified, reminding the Argives that they shared the same fate, not in a doctrinal statement, but as a point of contention between the lead actors and the way they might overcome the crisis before them.[1]

Contention and dissent, with their ability to spark stasis, or civil war, were threats to polis communities at all times. Civil strife put the entire city at risk. In its most extreme case, it led to the exile, enslavement, or slaying of substantial parts of the population. Competition in frontline politics thus always had the capacity to throw the community into disarray; at times it threatened its very foundations. Divided or not, the decisions of the citizen body always produced an immediate impact on the polis. In politics, with its uninhibited capacity to steer affairs, the Greek city was the epitome of a self-governing— and self-responsible—community. This type of self-responsibility energizes the ideology behind what scholars have labeled a community of shared fate. The term has become a commonplace in globalization research, despite the thorny legacy it has carried over time.[2] It posits that the trajectory of communities is not determined by cultural, religious, or political bonds alone. Rather, a community of shared fate implies that the constituent group faces exposure to forces emanating from both conscious choice and the unintended consequences of choosing—for instance, climate change or epidemic threats. Social scientists have observed that fate communities are typically evoked under extreme duress. Triggered by a situation of urgency or disaster, the pronouncement of suffering surfaces as a reminder of what is at stake if danger strikes: famine, warfare, pestilence, or, in Klytemnestra's case, the talon of an evil spirit.[3]

The Argive example reverberates with some of these traits, such as an extrinsic threat, a pressing urgency, and the prospect of healing. At the same time, it signals that the idea of communal fate was rooted deeper in Greek thought than the necessity to face the situational challenge suggests. Greek polis communities viewed themselves as groups that shared a common descent, with a joint pedigree and with blood ties through which the citizens could trace their heritage back to legendary heroes and founding fathers. The *patris*, the literal fatherland, suggested self-containment and self-support, cohesion and continuity over time. It helped to forge strong bonds of obligation from one generation to the next. The ancestral fault thematized in the *Agamemnon* illustrates this, for better or for worse. Atreus's crime against his brother Thyestes had occurred in the generation before Agamemnon and Klytmnestra; although committed in the past, it continued to contaminate both Atreus's house and his *patris*. The *miasma*, the pollution of an uncleansed crime, lingered on to haunt the Argives, with one atrocity leading to another. As long as the initial crime was not purged, the community as a whole was infected by catastrophe.[4]

At Thebes, Oedipus's tragic deeds had an equally detrimental effect on the city. Many years after his marriage to his mother, Iokaste, Thebes was struck by a plague of infertility, which affected its crops, livestock, and all people. When Oedipus sets out to unravel the roots of the crisis, tragedy takes its course, irreversible, with terror and might.[5] Atreus's legend and the Theban Cycle are uncompromising examples of crime. The slaying of one's father and subsequent marriage to one's mother, the feasting on one's own children, and so on: the accumulation of anger, anguish, and atrocity is so extreme that the horror leaves us breathless. Throughout these incidents, the notion of *patris* aggravates the repercussions of a shared-fate community: if evil strikes in such a scenario, there is no escaping for anyone.

Hesiod is less bone-chilling. In *Works and Days* he alerts the audience to what is at stake for their community. Commenting on the need for righteousness, Hesiod projects the image of a parochial environment, a small town in which no crime goes unnoticed by the gods, let alone unpunished. When Justice (*Dikē*) is expelled from the polis, by crooked decisions or wrongdoing, she will return to the people and their accustomed places (*ēthea*), clad in darkness, bringing harm to the men who drove her out (*W&D* 217–24). Hesiod dwells on this thought, headlining the interplay between the evil deeds of a few and the fate of all:

> As for those who give straight judgements to foreigners and to their own people alike and do not deviate from what is just, their polis flourishes, and the citizens bloom. Peace is about the land, fostering the young, and wide-seeing Zeus never marks out grievous war as their portion. Neither does Famine attend straight-judging men, nor Blight, and they feast on the crops they tend. For them, Earth (*Gaia*) bears plentiful food, and on the mountains the oak carries acorns at its surface and bees at its centre. The fleecy sheep are laden down with wool; the women bear children that resemble their parents, . . . the grain-giving plough land bears them fruit. But for those who occupy themselves with violence and wickedness and brutal deeds, Kronos' son, wide-seeing Zeus, marks out retribution. Often a whole community (*xympasa polis*) together suffers in consequence of a bad man who does wrong and contrives evil. From heaven Kronos' son brings disaster upon them, famine and with it plague, and the people waste away. (*W&D*, 225–43. Trans. West, modified)

The moralizing tone is unmistakable, as is Hesiod's disgust at the town leaders and their crooked judgments; elsewhere they are branded as swallowers of bribes (264) who occupy themselves with depravity. Moreover, Hesiod enhances the authority of the passage by weighing in with his expertise as a farmer. This suggests the integrity of a man who works the fields with his own hands and who is an obvious authority on crops and agricultural produce—someone who knows what the absence of supplies does to the town. All the while, there is a deep conviction at play here that energizes Hesiod's "gospel of work and justice" (Strauss Clay 2009, 71). It is the belief that social conditions are poised precariously between prosperity and sundry disasters, the one close to the others, with only a thin line separating them. While justice leads to prosperity, the well-being of man, his *oikos*, and of the entire community, injuries to justice are detrimental to all.

Jean-Pierre Vernant (1974; 1979) has identified the institutions that balance the human existence in light of such volatile pursuits of fate. In Vernant's ingenious reading of *Works and Days*, the road to redress was marked by the ethics of sacrifice, agriculture, and family, with the demands of each surfacing and playing out in all facets of quotidian life. Note how these institutions were entrenched in local configurations: the household, the town and its neighborhoods, as well as the surrounding fields. The message is clear. Vernant's balancing institutions are grounded in daily interactions, while the human condition itself is tied to place. Shaping its own future and fortunes in the confines of a local environment, the small town was at the heart and soul of the shared-fate community. If everyone adhered to the demands of life in an righteous, ethical manner, the city prospered from one generation to the next. If the community deviated from the path of righteousness, it attracted divine intervention, with disastrous consequences for all. At least this is how Hesiod had it.[6]

We learned in the previous chapter how the local sets off cascades of epichoric excitement. Inspired by the uniqueness of the land and contributing to a particular identity of place, the local swathed the communal experience of the city. We explore this quality of the local further in the present chapter, albeit in a more existential sense. There is a profound and indeed exciting shift in scholarly conversations about Greek religion taking place today, especially with regard to the neat (sometimes too neat) separation between universal or Panhellenic dimensions on the one hand and local configurations on the other. We turn to this general theme first, to get a better sense of where communal strategies of coping with crisis were located, and how this localization of religious practices mattered. We then proceed to the study of festival calendars and epichoric cults. The polytheistic nature of Greek religion invited variation in ritual and sacrifice. In so doing, it diversified religious practices in prayer, song, dance, offerings, processions, and so forth. It is staggering to see how these practices were intrinsically tied to the local, that is, how they were informed by locality and, in turn, how they infused the local with meaning. The ephebes played a critical role in this process. As young men and future citizens, they were instrumental in the preservation of religious meaning. We explore this capacity of ephebes as agents of locality in the final section of the chapter.

Beyond the Binary: Mapping Local Religion

Greek religion is usually understood as a fabric woven from different threads. Emanating from the great transregional sanctuaries of Olympia and Delphi, the Panhellenic thread provided the Greeks with a universal belief system—a common pantheon, joint mythical traditions and rituals—and its grounded expression in *ta hiera*—that is, in sacrifice and cult. According to Herodotus (8.144.2), those shared sacrifices were among the defining traits of Hellenicity. The second thread introduced contrast and diversity. It is associated with the polis as a place of religious conduct. In their communication with the divine, citizens turned to a broad array of religious practices that were anchored in and sanctioned by the polis. For instance, the cults and sacrifices of the polis were administered by city officials, carried out before the assembled crowd of citizens, and governed by prescriptions of the community. Greek religion was thus what Robert Parker has labeled an "embedded religion" (1986, 265; cf. Eidinow 2015). Its conduct followed a local dynamic: it was tied to the cults and deities of the polis, to the sacred covenant the citizens had established with the divine, and to the good fortunes this covenant was believed to bestow on the people. This preeminence of the polis in religious affairs has sparked the idea that Greek religion was quintessentially a polis religion, implying that the polis mediated the entire slate of relations between the citizens and the gods. We cannot ignore the eminent role of the local in the conduct of Greek religion. At the same time, and despite all local encoding, there was a strong thrust toward universal paradigms.

In accordance with the orthodox picture, and reinforcing the binary between universal and local, we find that the common interpretation subscribes to an implicit taxonomy of relevance. Delphi and Olympia are often seen as the epitome of Greek cult practice, marking the central nodes in a Panhellenic web of worship. In the absence of key organizing principles and a single source of authority such as a holy text, they also wielded the greatest religious impact. This interpretation is inspired by the celebrity factor of Delphi and Olympia, whose renown in the ancient world is beyond question. Also, it feeds off of a perceived dichotomy between universal and local spheres of Greek religion, each one wielding its own weight. The universal flaunts connectedness: in it, cities from distant shores link back to the Greek mainland through grants and dedications, *theōroi* travel far and wide, joint ritual practices homogenize the Greeks in the conduct of their *hiera* across the Mediterranean and beyond. The local sphere is inhibited by its confinement to place and its limitation to a low number of participants. Local religion has therefore been circumscribed as subject to a small horizon and, according to the traditional view, deemed to be of low significance.[7]

The oppositional localization of Hellenic religion has recently been called into question. Examining the antipodes of the Greek religious experience, Julia Kindt has argued that the binary of local and universal builds on a series of dubious premises; indeed, she posits that the duality is "a false dichotomy" (2012, 130–31). The point of Kindt's departure is marked by the quest for local infiltrations at Olympia. Conflict and competition were of course two of the key principles that steered the performance of cities in Olympia and Delphi. The religious and cultural conformism was always balanced by the competitive behavior of polities who—despite their cultural cohesion—did not shy away from challenging each other. At times, they boasted about their capacity to jeopardize another polis' existence. This competitive edge has led some to question the usefulness of the term Panhellenism altogether, although such a move seems to downplay the politics of belonging at work in both sanctuaries.[8]

What is more important here is that the expression of a competitive ethos, for instance by means of dedications, donations, or displays, adhered to a peculiar grammar. Dedications at Olympia were addressed to a universal audience, implying that they needed to be understood by all. At the same time, they were subject to local reasoning that added its own spin to the universal. For instance, the vast majority of war dedications were of a local nature. They attested to grievances at the local level by referencing rivalries between neighboring communities and grievances that arose from a local history of violence, one in which many claimed victory, yet few ever emerged as permanent winners. In a series of bronze inscriptions from the late sixth century BCE from Olympia, Orchomenos celebrates victory over Koroneia, Thebes over Hyettos, and Tanagra over another community whose name is lost.[9] This same spirit of troubled neighborhood interaction inspired the deposit of treaties and alliances that were placed under the surveillance of the god. The earliest examples from Olympia include a binding agreement between the Sybarites and the neighboring Serdaioi in southern Italy from c. 550 BCE and a similar treaty between Anaitoi and Metapioi, in which the participants declare that there shall be friendship for fifty years. On the Peloponnese, around the same time (between 550 and 500), the copy of an agreement between Elis and Heraia was deposited in the sanctuary.[10] These examples attest to the growing authority of Olympia in a swiftly expanding Hellenic world; the importance of the sanctuary as a showcase of Hellenicity is beyond question. All the while, it is noteworthy to recall that each of the underlying acts of violence was local through and through. Although the dedications were made on a remote Panhellenic stage, the radius of daily interactions was confined to exchanges with neighboring cities and the regional horizon.[11]

In addition to context and cause, the local permeated the display of cultural traditions. At Olympia, the Eleians had a great deal of sway over who was entitled to make dedications and where they were put. It seems that cities could not request a specific place for their offerings but were at the mercy of the Eleians. Things were different with the dedication itself. City-states were generally free to determine its shape and style, and they hired a craftsman or a team of craftsmen to carry out the work according to availability and budget. Effectively, dedications reflected the tastes and traditions of the commissioning communities. In other words, the poleis established what they wanted to say and how they said it.[12]

With messages ordained by different bodies of citizens, the meaning of dedications might not always have been as clear as one would expect. Indeed, the Altis in Olympia was a tapestry of local variation. For instance, the intricate details of the Boiotian victory dedications that we encountered above may very well have escaped many visitors: when were those battles fought, over what grievances? In a similar vein, when Pausanias marveled at a statue of a certain Theognetos of Aigina, winner in the boys wrestling competition, he was puzzled to observe that Theognetos held "the fruit of the cultivated pine and a pomegranate" (6.9.1). Pausanias muses over the meaning, conjecturing that they must have gone back to a "local tradition" (*epichōrios logos*). Similar articulations of the local were detected by Pausanias in the peculiarities of onomastics, which sometimes adhered to a local tradition (*epichōrion*: 5.21.12), and in certain expressions that were used by locals only (*epichōrioi*: 5.21.2). In all these instances, the local inflections required explanation. As so often during his travels, Pausanias had to rely on his expounders of local matters. This was also the case at Olympia, the one place that was iconic of Greek culture like no other. In light of omnipresent local diversity, even an eminent expert like Pausanias encountered the limitations of his cultural literacy in Olympia.[13]

The people of Sikyon chose another expression of their localism in the sanctuary. Their treasury was built from calcareous sandstone, a type of stone that was not used in other buildings in the sanctuary. It was suggested by Wilhelm Dörpfeld that the stones were originally quarried in the Sikyonia where this type of sandstone is commonly found. Likewise, the first Sikyonian treasury at Delphi, a rectangular colonnade, was built from stones of Sikyonian provenance. The decision to quarry local stone and export it to Delphi and Olympia might have been motivated by practical considerations, as neither sanctuary was close to marble sources, and the stone around Olympia was of no great quality. The Sikyonians solved this problem by bringing in their own building material. But this might also have had a deeper meaning. Scholars have long argued that the local use of stone from the *chōra* in monumental building projects in the urban center of the polis generally tightened the bonds between city and country; the corresponding buildings symbolized the profound connection between them. If this is the case, then there was more to the Sikyonian decision than practicality. Drawing on natural resources from home, the Sikyonians relocated their countryside, in part, to each precinct, placing it under the authority of the gods. Effectively, this anchored the city in both sanctuaries: literally, metaphorically, and symbolically. And this, in turn, also reconnected the treasuries with their home. The move was a bold one, documenting self-sufficiency and strength. It articulated the indissoluble bond between the people of Sikyon and their land.[14]

These observations illustrate how religious conduct in Olympia was subject to the desire to articulate a marked local agency. Dedications followed a Panhellenic script, while at the same time they impersonated the local world of the city that had taken the initiative. In such a scenario, the strands of religion weaved together local and universal paradigms. Both spheres were entangled, implicit one in the other.

It is curious to see how on the other end of the orthodox binary, that of the city-state, the polis forfeits some of its gravity in scholarship on Greek religion. In light of exciting new discoveries from the exploration of sub- and translocal arenas of religious conduct, the concept of polis religion is faltering. Polis religion, in the much-cited words of Christiane Sourvinou-Inwood, builds on the idea that each city "was a religious system which formed part of the more complex world-of-the-polis system. . . . [D]irect and full participation in religion was reserved for citizens, that is, those who made up the community which articulated the religion" (1990, 295). Sourvinou-Inwood extended this claim by stating that beyond their polis, Hellenes were reduced to the status of *xenoi*, guests or strangers, if participating in the *hiera* of Greeks elsewhere, including the sanctuary at Olympia. Again, in the words of Sourvinou-Inwood, "The polis had ultimate authority in, and control of, all cults, and polis religion encompassed all religious discourse within it" (307).

We have already noted some of the basic points in support of this view, including the overlap of religious personnel and public office holders in the city, and the citizens' capacity to stipulate laws and religious prescriptions that were binding on all. Yet the idea of polis religion also raises doubts. First, the margins of religious activity were much messier than the cut-and-dried concept of polis religion suggests. The case of the so-called Marathonian Tetrapolis in Northeastern Attica, for example, a cult organization that is well attested to in epigraphical sources from the fourth century BCE, demonstrates how its links with the religious administration of the polis were but one scale of ritual and cult performance in the lives of those who participated in it. Manifesting itself in a series of local sanctuaries and shrines, all within a day's walk from each other, the religious activities of the association cut across four Athenian demes in the region. What united them was their coordinated response to the physical environment. Rather than adhering to administrative borders, the sanctuaries were stitched into the plain of Marathon and its adjacent mountain ranges, following the natural lines of communication and exchange. While some of the Tetrapolis's religious infrastructure overlapped with that of the polis, in other ways it was completely separate from it.[15]

Jan Bremmer, originator of the phrase "messy margins of polis religion" (2010), has identified a wide range of religious practices on the fringes of the city, which further undermine the idea of polis religion. The strands of magic and mystery cults, for instance, are commonly associated not with the polis but the *oikos*, which is why the corresponding practices are tagged as expressions of domestic, private, or personal religion, implying that they were not mediated by the polis. The term *popular religion*, with its high currency in religious studies, is also used at times to lump individual expressions of religiosity into a single category, one that was not mitigated by the city-state. It is certainly right to assert that expressions of personal religion lacked the coordination and dogma to monopolize the establishment of religious meaning. But this did not, of course, make them less influential, or less important, to those who subscribed to them. Within the city and on its fringes, we encounter a plethora of religious expressions that had nothing to do with the organization of the polis.[16]

Bremmer's messy margins extend also to the regional realm. The vast amount of research on Greek *ethnos* and federal states in recent decades, including its focus on the processes of ethnic identity-formation and togetherness, has brought to light the pivotal role of sanctuary sites beyond the polis. Their dualistic nature as "platform[s] for the expression of tribal cohesion and . . . as centers of political interaction" (Beck and Funke 2015a, 24), made federal sanctuaries a lively feature in the conduct of politics and religion. Kalapodi in Phokis, the Sanctuary of Zeus Homarios in Achaia, and the cult site at Messon on Lesbos bear witness to such conduct in an intermediary space, variously labeled as federal, regional, or translocal. In some of the earliest regional amphiktyonies, we detect a similar dynamic. For instance, in Onchestos in Boiotia and in Kalaureia on Poros, we see how cult centers that were initially local in nature gradually extended their radius of recognition into the micro-region around them. The Archaic history of Onchestos, a forerunner to the great regional sanctuary of the Classical and Hellenistic periods, teaches us how local cult places might emerge to become central nodes in a web of regional clusters. On the level of sheer practicality, their earliest monumental building programs were made possible only by means of the joint efforts of the communities who settled around them—hence, the literal meaning of *amphiktyones*, "around dwellers." The rise of a new sense of religious regionalism was accompanied by economic entanglement and political cooperation.[17]

An altogether different way of looking at Greek religion comes with the lens of place. Polis religion makes a tacit equation between the city-state and its local environment, which demarcates the sphere of religious conduct. Sourvinou-Inwood was, of course, well aware that the conduct of polis religion played out in different constellations of locality. For instance, while some sacrifices were subsumed under the rubric of central polis cults, others were relegated to subdivisions of the polis territory or of the citizen body: demes, phratries, and so on.[18] To reconcile such sub-polis activity with polis religion, Sourvinou-Inwood argued that the latter were merely compartmentalized branches of a greater entity; effectively, they supplemented the grand architecture of polis religion. The overall equation of polis religion with the local horizon remains intact.[19]

Such a rendering leaves us with an additive approach toward local religion: polis by polis, cult by cult, neighborhood by neighborhood, each one subscribing to an underlying unity of belief, yet maintaining its own ritual grammar of ceremonial prescriptions, prayers, dress codes, and so on for priests, priestesses, and participants alike. For instance, many cities celebrated the Thesmophoria, but not everywhere at the same time of year; only in Eretria were the sacrificial meats grilled in the sun rather than on the fire. The festival of Agrionia was celebrated differently at Orchomenos in Boiotia than it was at Chaironeia, less than ten kilometers away. In Boiotia alone, a total of nineteen different cult variants of festivals in honor of Apollo have been identified, with an even higher number of local epithets, each one identifying the character traits exhibited by the god in a particular place.[20]

Hellenic religion was, however, not merely a summation of diversity. The conceptual value of place isn't simply restored by means of a jigsaw that brings together countless pieces of local distinctiveness. The pieces themselves merit further examination. It is fascinating to see how the local wielded normative force over Greek beliefs. In the polytheistic world of ancient Greece, the polis was a home to gods, heroes, nymphs, and also demons. As we have seen earlier in this chapter, the Argives were under the spell of a divine spirit that resided with them, for good or for ill. In the *Suppliants*, Aischylos speaks of "the gods who possess the land" (704–5) and of *enchōrioi daimones* (482), "the spirits in the land," who exercise authority over the citizens. The meaning of *enchōrios* resembles that of its cognate *epichōrios* in that both relate to the native land of the polis, its *chōra*. But the prefixes also attest to a semantic difference. Whereas *epichōrios* designates something as "of the land," with a formidable breadth of meaning, ranging from cultural expressions to agrarian produce and mythical traditions, all at the local level, the usage of *enchōrios* appears more restrictive. The literal translation of "in the *chōra*" or "in the land" may or may not invoke overtones of indigeneity, but on the whole it is fair to assert that *enchōrios* is used mostly with reference to the inhabitants. Unlike the attributive meaning of "of the land" (*epichōrios*), *enchōrios* relates to the ontology of place. In Aischylos's script, the *enchōrioi theoi* are part of this ontology.

In our examination of tales of earthbornness, we have already noted how the inhabitants of Greek cities were tied to the land through primordial descent from gods, heroes, and nymphs, whose presence was detected in specific topographical features of the *chōra* (rivers, groves, caves: see chapter 2). On a prominent occasion in Thucydides's *History*, this cohabitation of people and the divine is further explicated. The scene is set in the countryside of Plataia in 430/29 BCE, where the Spartan army under king Archidamos had pitched its camp to launch an assault. The Plataians, in distress, sent envoys who reminded the Spartans of a previous exchange of oaths whereby the Plataians were protected. These oaths were witnessed "by our gods in the land" (*theous hēmeterous enchōrious*) as well as "the gods of your [i.e., the Spartans'] fathers" (*theous humeterous patrōous*: 2.71.4). The plea, it is well known, falls flat, and the Spartans attack, but before the first blow is delivered, the gods are invoked again. This time, the Spartan king is the speaker, who calls "the gods and heroes in the country" (*kai tōn theōn kai hērōōn enchōriōn*: 2.74.2) to witness, as they hold the land (*gē*) of Plataia.[21]

Irene Polinskaya (2013) observed that the distinction made here between the gods in the land and the gods of the fathers is made carefully. It acknowledges both the place that is addressed and the perspective of the speaker. When the Plataian envoys speak of their own land and the divine spirits that reside in it, they emphasize their ties through reference to the *enchōrioi theoi*. The Spartans no doubt had their own gods in the land, but that is not at stake here, nor is the conflict about their land. Hence, they are referred to as *patrōoi theoi*. Archidamos subscribes to this view by evoking the Plataian gods and heroes as *enchōrioi theoi* also. In more general terms, they would have been addressed as the traditional gods of the Plataians. Yet as the incident relates to the land the war parties are in, and since the quarrel related to that land, this immediacy is expressed in the words of *enchōrioi theoi*. As the debate unfolds, the city and countryside of Plataia are conceived of as a shared landscape, occupied by humans and the divine alike. The main quality of the local cosmos is that it provides the backdrop for the existential relation between human and divine inhabitants.[22]

The local horizon here is not reduced to a canvas for segregation and idiosyncrasy. Rather, it is indicative of a religious system of its own. In our attempt to map such a system and measure its meaning, we detect three genuinely local traits: First, the ties between the human and the divine played out in the concrete, manageable environment. Most corresponding practices in ritual and sacrifice, while inspired by universal paradigms, occurred in the local community: we established, however, that the notion of polis religion is too rigid to capture the essence of this local encoding. Despite the apparent similarity of the terms, polis religion and local religion signify different things. Unlike polis religion, local religion indicates that the religious system is subject to place rather than to political manifestation. The difference becomes also visible when we recall the ontological quality of the local. Delphi and Olympia wove local religion into a wider web of meaning, but they were removed, through sheer physical distance, from the lifeworld of the polis, which made their role also hazier. The local conduct of religion, on the other hand, was immediate, filled with self-evident practice and meaning.

This leads us to the second trait of local religion. As key expressions in the relation with the gods, cult and sacrifice were performed in the same place where those ties commenced. There are countless examples that speak to the spatial fabric of Hellenic religion (see also below): rites of procession through the countryside that paid homage to each minute topographical feature of the *chōra* and its divine spirits; the veneration of places of memory that encapsulated the origins of the community; or the hymnic evocation of prayer and song that was not only performed in relation to place, but actually localized the god or goddess: the act brought the divine to life in place. Indeed, the choral performance of song and dance, so ubiquitous a form of religious worship, facilitated a unique fusion of people and place. In the words of Leslie Kurke, Greek chorality was "a machine for the production of pure presence, conjuring the gods and merging chorus members and audience alike with the divine for the space of the performance" (2012, 218). When Apollo was evoked in prayer, the time-space continuum shrank—it melted into the local horizon. The very nature of Greek religion magnified the sense of attachment to place, a sense that was foundational to the way in which local communities saw themselves.[23]

Third, such localization was inspired by, and in turn geared toward, the cultic topography of the city—its landmark features, including rivers, hills, caves, groves, and so forth—that was part and parcel of the religious communication. The divine wasn't simply there; its presence called for particular forms of veneration. Vice versa, such veneration fostered the ties to the local horizon.[24] From Hyettos in northern Boiotia comes a curious example that offers us a unique glimpse into the deep connection between place and religion. Rich in deposits of magnetic iron ore, the land around the city was used in Classical antiquity for various mining activities. The exploitation of magnetite is traceable also in the local ceramic production, which underscores its importance in multiple branches of the local mixed economy. Pliny (*Nat.* 36.128), following a source from the late fourth century BCE, identified distinct features of magnetic ores from Hyettos to which he also assigned certain healing capacities. The people of Hyettos picked up on this. In a local sanctuary that was also visited for healing purposes, Pausanias saw an old cult image that he describes as a shapeless, unpolished stone (*lithos*, 9.24.3). This somewhat crude appearance should not be mistaken for negligence or carelessness—on the contrary. To the people of Hyettos, the *lithos*, most likely a chunk of iron ore, was the embodiment of divine presence in their land, an epichoric manifestation of the god. Presumably, the lump was not as inspirational as a pleasant spring or a shadowy grove. Yet no matter how awkward its appearance, to the people of Hyettos it was a witness to the sacred covenant with the gods in their land.[25]

In the Shadow of Olympia

Xenophon captures for us a local religious ambience par excellence. When settling near Skillous in the Peloponnese, in the 380s and 370s BCE, he purchased a land lot from funds he had once deposited in the temple of Artemis in Ephesos and that had now been returned to him.[26] Unlike the modern village further to the east, ancient Skillous was located outside today's Makrisia, stretching from the Profitis Elias to the north, where archaeologists have found abundant evidence for a sizeable Classical settlement. Xenophon's plot was somewhere in the vicinity.[27] On his land he built a shrine and small temple, just as he had pledged during the campaign in Asia Minor. In the *Anabasis* (5.3.7–8, 11–13) he declares that the site of the new *temenos* for Artemis resembled that of its paragon in Ephesos. Both were adjacent to rivers named Selinus, and both are described by Xenophon as rich in fish and mussels. Moreover, the lot in the Peloponnese was ideal for hunting deer, fox, marten, and the like. The precinct was of significant extent; it included a meadowland and tree-covered hills, suited for the rearing of swine, goats, cattle, and horses. The immediate surroundings included a grove of cultivated trees, which produced all sorts of dessert fruits. No wonder that Xenophon's initiative soon became a formidable success. In fact, the cult flourished so much so that he took

> the tithe of the products of the land every year in their season and offered sacrifice to the goddess, all the citizens (*politai*) and the men and women of the neighbourhood (*hoi proschōroi andres kai gynaikes*) taking part in the festival. And the goddess would provide for the banqueters barley meal and loaves of bread, wine and sweetmeats, and a portion of the sacrificial victims from the sacred herd as well as of the victims taken in the chase. For Xenophon's sons and the sons of the other citizens used to have a hunting expedition at the time of the festival, and any grown men who so wished would join them; and they captured their game partly from the sacred precinct itself and partly from Mt. Pholoë, boars and gazelles and stags. (*Anab.* 5.3.9–10)

We hear the entrepreneur talking in these lines, the man who makes things happen. If Xenophon set his mind on a precinct in honor of Artemis, he did it right. All the while, the initiative illustrates how the conduct of *ta hiera*, while adhering to a universal pantheon, was firmly rooted in place. It was subject to the environment of Skillous, its physical features, its flora and fauna, and these in turn infused the enterprise with meaning. Xenophon was eager to highlight the similarities between his Artemis cult and its more famous counterpart in Ephesos. Skillous is presented as a miniature model of Ephesos, evidently to boost, and to boast about, its importance. Ten kilometers to the southeast, on a hilltop on Mt. Lapithos, another Artemis sanctuary was located, that of Artemis Limnatis.[28] Xenophon's foundation was not necessarily in open competition with the older Artemis cult there. Yet the new foundation certainly strove for recognition. Note how the precinct at Skillous gains authority because its territory was located near the river Selinus. Just like its counterpart in Asia Minor, the Selinus in the Peloponnese was rich in seafood: fish and freshwater bivalves.[29] The name Selinus was not uncommon for creeks and runnels in the Hellenic Mediterranean because of the wild celery (*selinon*) that grows spontaneously along river beds (chapter 3). Presumably this was the case also for the banks of both Selinus rivers in question, in Asia Minor and the Peloponnese.

The Selinus provided further room for religious meaning. On their hunting trip, the party parkoured through the precinct and the nearby hills of Mt. Pholoë to the northeast of Olympia. The chase traversed through a sizeable territory. Its most liminal point was about twenty kilometers away, a distance that could be covered in a day, including the return trip, before sunset, if need be. Xenophon suggests that the area was rich in all sorts of game. Its wildlife

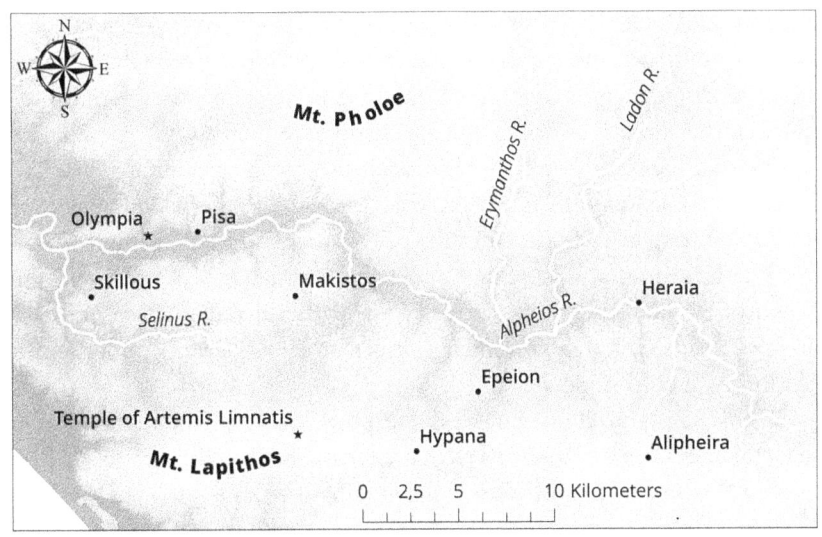

FIGURE 4.1. The storied world of Skillous and surroundings.

was widely recognized in Pausanias's times (5.6.5). Mt. Pholoë itself lay across the Alpheios, a stream that carried rich mythical traditions about the river god of the same name. One of these traditions recorded how Alpheios was driven by an excessive desire for a local nymph, Arethusa. Fleeing from his advances, Arethusa leapt into the sea and surfaced again in Sicily, bursting from the ground in the form of a freshwater spring.[30] In the shadow of Mt. Pholoë, home of the Peloponnesian centaurs, the hunters entered another realm that was as rich in wild boar as it was in mythical traditions. The most famous of these clustered around the centaur Pholos who had entertained Herakles on his hunt for the Erymanthian boar. It doesn't take much imagination to see the hunting party follow the trails of this mythical chase, fathers and their sons, inspired by Herakles's exemplary prowess. At times the hunting party might have made it as far east as to the Erymanthos river, a storied shire. In the woodlands, they were reminded that the centaur Pholos, Herakles's host there, was the love child of Melia, a local tree nymph, and a rustic *daimōn* named Selinus. Thus closed the circle of tales that radiated from Xenophon's *temenos* by the riverbed of the Selinus into the microregion of the Alpheios Valley (fig. 4.1).[31]

The hunting trip from Xenophon's shrine across the Alpheios covered a landscape full of mythical traditions. The stories plugged into universal traditions, however malleable. At the same time, they were locally embedded, energized by place. To be sure, the gravitational pull of Olympia must have been felt everywhere; indeed, Xenophon's initiative to establish a *temenos* for

Artemis was made possible only because of the transregional fame of Olympia.[32] At the same time, the epichoric festival carefully eluded Olympia and its lands. Avoidance of Olympia might have been due to the desire to respect Eleian interests in the region. As many have pointed out, Xenophon's situation on the south banks of the Alpheios was somewhat precarious. The Spartans had settled him there, yet Spartan claims to the region as part of their genuine sphere of interest in the Peloponnese were met with objection by Elis. The last thing Xenophon wanted in this situation was to provoke the people of Elis and, effectively, see his cult jeopardized and estate confiscated, or worse. Indeed, Xenophon managed to maintain peaceful relations with Elis throughout his time in Skillous.[33]

Be this as it may, Xenophon's cult worked without Olympia. As we have seen, the annual celebrations were characterized by the ethics of reconciliation. In this sense, the festival was inspired by the same stabilizing institutions that we encountered earlier: sacrifice, agriculture, and marriage. The latter—marriage and the *oikos*—played a critical role, one that was visibly placed above the polis community and its political and/or religious organization. Xenophon refers to his sons as participants in the chase, as well as to the sons of other citizens. Yet the festival was not confined to Skillous and its *politai*, for Xenophon goes on to speak of those living nearby as participants in the sacrifice—men, women, and children alike. The impression we get is that the circle of celebrants was determined by proximity, not political status. Whoever lived in the vicinity was invited to attend, the citizens from Skillous as much as the free inhabitants from nearby farms, hamlets, and smaller settlements south of the Alpheios river.[34]

The cult of Artemis at Skillous is sometimes seen as a private rite and an example of personal religion; effectively, this calls into question what the case teaches us about Greek religion overall. Indeed, Xenophon's religiosity led him to inaugurate the cult on his own initiative, and the administration appears to have been in the hands of his *oikos*. We already noted above how such a localization of religious conduct on the margins of the polis does not inevitably point to low relevance. The festival was not an expression of sanctioned polis religion, but this did not diminish or marginalize its meaning. The key to Xenophon's festival was its double entrenchment in place and in what Kostas Vlassopoulos has labeled a "composite polity" (2007, 151): a community of people whose daily interactions were not only governed by the high-powered ideas of political belonging but by fluid constellations at the local level.

It is obvious at this point that the exercise of local cult practices cannot be easily pigeonholed. Ties to the polis and to universal practices are undeniable, but beyond these poles, the local horizon added its own colors to the religious fabric. In the ongoing struggle to seek reconciliation with the divine, the small world of everyday existence was an eminent source of religious orientation and meaning.

Local Time

Now that we have established how the local imprints on religion and ritual, it is time to move to some of the concrete manifestations. To begin with, it is worth recalling that few aspects of polis life were so openly subject to local dynamics as the organization of time. The Greek city-states of the late Archaic and Classical periods adhered to a luni-solar calendar. The immediate challenge was to sync the cycle of moon-based months with sun-based seasonal activities, farming and agriculture in particular. There was no consentient solution. Every polis handled the issue differently. To fill the gap between the lunar and the solar year, the twelve lunar months were usually appended with intercalary periods of varying lengths. But since the practice of adding these intercalary periods differed from polis to polis, this meant that the calendars of neighboring cities were often out of sync at a very basic level.[35]

There were no universal datelines or annual landmarks, such as a common New Year's Day, either. In other words, there was no customary Panhellenic calendar at play. The Persian Wars would have been the most obvious candidate to inspire a common political commemoration across mainland Greece, but when such a celebration was inaugurated, it was done only several generations after the event, and it didn't come without friction. In the meantime, the members of the former Hellenic Alliance all commemorated "their" Persian Wars at a different time in the year and employed different commemorative strategies (chapter 5). The closest the Greeks came to a shared calendar was the festival cycle of the Panhellenic Games, the Olympian calendar in particular, with its four-year period. Yet Olympia's calendar was not made to suit all, nor was it created with this goal in mind in the first place. The Olympian cycle allowed conversations about the duration of time. This quality of reckoning in Olympiads was of particular value in the evolving genre of historiography, when the narration of affairs between multiple city-states required a common chronological frame of reference.[36]

Other contexts bear witness to the communicative quality of the Olympic dateline. One of the earliest references to Olympiads outside the sanctuary, a sacred law from Selinus from the later sixth or early fifth century BCE, stipulates that a certain sacrifice must be performed before "the truce, in the fifth year, before the Olympiad occurs" (*SEG* 43.630; 45.1413: column A, lines 7–8).

Although this reference is sometimes understood as a chronological reference, the law itself was most likely not dated after Olympiads but according to the calendar at Selinus. Rather than adhering to a Panhellenic calendar, the surviving text decrees that a certain ritual needs to be concluded before the *ekecheiria* period: that is, the sacred truce guaranteeing safe passage to and from Olympia. The *lex sacra* from Selinus attests to an awareness of the Olympic cycle and truce, and it bespeaks the recognition that both enjoyed among the western Greeks. As an annual time-keeping practice, however, the Olympic cycle was not in use in Selinus.[37]

When communities counted time, they turned to annual lists in which the years were identified by civic magistrates. In many cities, the year was named after the so-called *archōn eponymos*, an official who gave his name to the year in which he held his term. In light of such reliance on local year-counts, the Olympian calendar was useful when conversations about time went across borders; ancient attempts to synchronize local dating practices in various cities indicate that it was notoriously difficult to reconcile eponymic calendars of different provenance.[38] It is intriguing to note that the Olympian calendar, which is used on many stelai in the sanctuary itself, was actually not Olympian but predicated upon another local calendar, that of Elis, according to which the Olympic Games were held alternately after intervals of forty-nine or fifty months—depending on where the Eleian calendar was with its local intercalation.

Time-keeping was a local affair, inspired by prevailing idiosyncrasies. The New Year started at different times in different places. Scholars have identified certain preferences among cities to enter the New Year at the solstices in June and December or the equinoxes in March and September, but the variety of annual beginnings exceeded the choices provided by these solar events. In Thebes, the New Year started in the month of Boukatios (December); in Megara, in Petageitnios (November); in Miletus, in Taureion (April). In Athens, the best attested case, the first month of the year was Hekatombaion (July).[39] These differences were further complicated by variations of when individual months started, due to observational discrepancies. Furthermore, the names of the months themselves differed significantly, even between cities that are often considered connected by bonds of ancestry, migration, or political cooperation. The so-called Ionian calendar, the most notorious example of an ethnically connected calendar, reveals commonalities as much as it speaks to local variations among those who used it.[40] The Dorian calendar (if not a mirage altogether) is now better understood through CT scanning of the Antikythera device. The machine records local calendar idiosyncrasies as they prevailed in Corinth, which is commonly considered part of the

Dorian family of calendars. By means of comparison, of the six months that are explicitly attested for the calendar in Sparta, three do not appear among the complete list of the Corinthian calendar from the Antikythera mechanism.[41] It is noteworthy that the device contains two dials that measure the Olympiad cycle and the so-called Kallipic cycle (seventy-six years), which speak to its broader purpose to measure universal astrological constellations. As we have seen, the city-states had no means to provide such a universal time-reckoning.[42]

Add to this variety the opaque calendars observed by religious associations and other subdivisions of the polis to organize their activities: the aforementioned Marathonian Tetrapolis maintained, of course, its own sacrificial calendar that was separate from that of the largest deme of the association, Marathon (Lambert 2000). The bewilderment is complete. Referencing Plutarch's sighs over so much local time-keeping (*Arist.* 19.7), Robert Hannah has concluded it is easy to be "utterly confused" (2013, 355) over the organization of time in the Classical Greek world.

Local Worship and Worshipping the Local

The festival calendar governed the cycle of religious events that revolved around the community's well-being. It ordered the sequence of celebrations that were held to honor the sacred covenant between the community and the gods.[43] Much of this was geared toward the celebration of chthonic cults. As Renate Schlesier (1991–1992) reminded us, chthonic gods and goddesses were not found to live on Mt. Olympos or in the sky but in the land itself. Their earthboundness invited a particular type of worship; in turn, this type of veneration was articulated in a distinctive ritual grammar, including fertility rituals, harvest feasts, and procession rites through the countryside that honored the gods of the land. We have already heard that the *chōra* was a spirited place, rich in signatures of divine powers, heroes, and nymphs. The chthonic gods were of utmost importance among these, since they underscored the sacred relation with the land. Three stood out: Dionysos, god of fertility and vine; Artemis, goddess of the fields; and Demeter, deity of the earth and of agriculture, who was intimately associated with the seasons and the harvest. Veneration of these chthonic gods was a recurring theme in the annual festival calendar.[44]

Sanctuaries of Demeter, as is well known, were usually situated in the countryside. In Corinth, the temple precinct was located on the way from the city to the plain (Paus. 2.11.2). To the north of Corinth, in the Megarid, the sanctuary of Demeter Malophoros was located in the harbor town Nisaia, approximately 2.5 kilometers away from the urban center of Megara. The situation there resembled that in Selinus on Sicily, where the sanctuary of Demeter Malaphoros was placed on the western fringes of the *chōra*, where the plain merged into a line of hills running north to south, providing the countryside of Selinus with a marked natural boarder. Some twenty-five kilometers west of Corinth, in Sikyon, a holy grove called Pyraia was home to the sanctuary of Demeter Prostasia and Kore. In its grove, there was also a temple called Nymphon (Paus. 2.11.3; Plin., *Nat.* 35.151–52).[45]

Further to the west, archaeologists made the sensational find of unique examples of Archaic Greek paintings on wood. The pieces were found in 1934 in a cave on Mt. Helidorea near the village of Ano Pitsa, in the municipality of Xylokastro. Located twenty kilometers from Sikyon, the cave was actually closer to Pellene. The rugged terrain in the area would have made it difficult for either city to wield permanent claims over the site. Ongoing quarrels between Sikyon and Pellene, in the course of which the settlement of Pellene was moved at least once, further complicated the issue of boundary drawing. Ano Pitsa was on the radar of both cities.[46] The panels date from the second half of the sixth century BCE; they are the earliest of their kind. Of the four polychrome boards, the best-preserved depicts a group of females who approach an altar to the right. On the left, behind the women, a bearded male is visible. Their party is accompanied by two musicians and a small figure, leading the sacrificial victim, a lamb. The scene has been variously interpreted as a family sacrifice or as a ritual of a female cult. The surviving parts of the inscription name two women dedicators, Euthydika and Eucholis, whose sacrifice is "dedicated to the nymphs." One of them carries a tray with two conical *lekythoi* and a decorated *pyxis*, a box that held a sacrificial cake or incense for the offering.[47]

The lineup suggests a procession of the group to the cave in the *chōra*, although the diminishing scale of the adult figures and the perspective of depth it creates might indicate that they are already assembled around the altar. Either way, the board depicts a chthonic ritual in honor of the epichoric nymphs there. The sacred grove with its Demeter temple and Nymphon in the territory of Sikyon, along with the holy cave of Pitsa in the nearby border lands give us a superb impression of how the countryside was a place bristling with the presence of gods, nymphs, and divine spirits. Much like the ritual space of the Marathonian Tetrapolis and Xenophon's Artemis precinct, the spirited lands between Sikyon and Pellene suggest that the exercise of religious practice was not always and clearly not inevitably integrated into the high-powered organization of the polis. The approach to local cult practice

FIGURE 4.2. Sacrifice to the nymphs from the cave at Pitsa. Credits: NAM A 16464, National Archaeological Museum, Athens. Photographer: Giannis Patrikianos. © Hellenic Ministry of Culture and Sports/ Archaeological Receipts Fund (Law 3028/2002). Printed with permission.

merits revision in this sense, too. It requires us to think outside the dichotomy of city versus *chōra*, and beyond the charged ideas associated with communal fringes. Only when we delve into the rural realm, beyond major cities and settlements, will we be able to grasp one of the landmark principles of Greek religion: its deep association with and its anchoring to the land.

In chapter 2 we have noted, more generally, that this chthonic trait was also articulated in processions from the city to the extra-urban sanctuary, so-called centrifugal processions, that encapsulated a complex agenda of territorial demarcation, spatial differentiation between city and hinterland, and reconciliation with the gods. We turn now to three examples that provide us with a better sense of how procession rituals were carried out and how the role of the land played out in practice.

The first example is also one of the earliest pieces of evidence that survive to illustrate the ritual grammar of a procession through the countryside. It derives from an inscription that records the march of a Milesian cult-ordinance along the Sacred Way from Miletus to Didyma. The sanctuary of Apollo at Didyma was widely connected beyond the local horizon. Its network of relations enhanced its prestige in the Greek world.[48] At the same time, the inscription makes it obvious that the sanctuary was a local force of its own. The cult law describes how the so-called Molpoi, addressed as "crown-bearers" (*stephanephoroi*), traverse the distance between the city and Didyma. The relevant passage pays close attention to the topographical features along the way, and how each of these inspires acts of reverence on behalf of the Molpoi. As they depart from the city,

[t]wo sacred stones [*gylloi*] with garlands are carried, one is placed beside the image of Hekate before the gates [of Miletus] and a libation of undiluted wine is poured; the other is put beside the doors in Didyma. After this they walk along the plateau until the road hits the hills, from there up into the woods. And they sing paians first at the image of Hekate before the gates, before Dynamis [between the city and the summit], then to the nymphs in the meadow on the hilltop, then at the altar of Hermes Kelados, then to Phylios near Keraiites, then before the statues of Chares. And near Keraiites they offer a skinned [sheep] in the all-sacrifice year, and to Phylios they offer incense [or a sacrificial cake] every year. (*Milet* 1.3.133 = *LSCG* 50, lines 25–31)

The cult law of the Molpoi has naturally attracted much scholarly attention. The inscription is dated according to a formula that we encountered earlier in this chapter: an eponymous magistrate is listed in the opening section (line 1), an *aisymnētēs* named Philtes, son of Dionysios, whose term in office is otherwise attested for the year 450/449 BCE. The surviving stele is a copy from the second century BCE of the initial law that was put up in the Delphinion in Miletus, the cult seat of the Molpoi. In its original form, the inscription presents an immensely rich document of singular importance not only for the study of Milesian history in the fifth century BCE, but of Greek sacred laws overall.[49] What matters for our purposes here is the alignment of the procession of the Molpoi with the local topography. Archaeologists were able to trace most of the Sacred Way, disclosing its longest stretches between the city and the sanctuary. The road was about 16.5 km long and 4–7 m wide. Apparently, it was paved over the entire distance. The hilltop mentioned in the text has been identified with the summit of the Stephania Ridge. The halt for praising the nymphs on the hilltop has also been discovered. In a meadow that is situated just before the highest elevation along, the remains of a sanctuary and a spring were found, together with a votive sculpture, a seated figure inscribed to the nymphs. Toward the end of the journey, along the final stretch of the road, the remains of the statues of Chares have been found; they are on display in the British Museum today.[50]

The combination of evidence from epigraphical and archaeological discoveries helps us to understand how the ritual was governed by place. Note how the religious narrative was inspired by the physicality of the *chōra*. The individual sections of the journey were all associated with epichoric deities and local heroes respectively: the first stretch with Dynamis, presumably the personification of magisterial "Power" at Miletus. The ridge and hilltop were home to local nymphs. Descending from the Stephania hill, the following leg was hemmed with altars of Hermes, with the local epithet Kelados, and Phylios, presumably a local hero. In the final section, the Chares group, while initially set up in honor of a local ruler from the sixth century, obtained the status of heroic worship over time. With this, the ensemble was charged with local meaning.[51]

The procession paid homage to each site with prayers, songs, and sacrifice: to Hekate, goddess of crossroads and entrance-ways, when their journey began traversing the space outside the urban centre; throughout the countryside, with reverence to several local heroes and nymphs; and at the final destination of their trip, when the second holy stone was placed beside the doors in Didyma. Reverence for heroes and spirits in prayer and song not only reinforced the local cult, it also magnified the religious experience. From what we have learned in the previous chapter about the nature of song, the processional songs performed by the Molpoi were in all likelihood *epichoriōs*, both their lyrics and tunes. The same goes for the offerings to Phylios. Depending on whether this was an incense sacrifice or the offering of a flat cake—scholars are divided here—the preparation would have followed a local recipe.[52] It has been pointed out that the consumption of wine along the route is not attested to in the document, and it is conceivable that no alcohol was consumed throughout. But at least the pouring of libations at the beginning and end of the journey entailed the use of wine in the ritual. It is reasonable to assert that this, too, came from local produce.[53] Finally, the Molpoi would have worn special clothing on their journey—headgears, robes, shoes—that highlighted their status and religious authority. It has been argued, rightly so, that among the main functions of the procession was the desire to connect the outlying sanctuary of Didyma with the center of the polis at Miletus. The ritual was thus in line with a developing sense of territoriality among the Milesians, as we have noted it earlier. At the same time, it speaks to the relation between the local and the exercise of religious practice. The procession of the Molpoi adhered to a local dynamic: its religious props were locally encoded, and their application subject to a regime of local *nomima*. Moreover, the local wielded impact over the ritual. In the religious system at Miletus, the cult activity of the Molpoi was governed by the topography of the land, which provided the ceremony with a stage for the exercise of religiosity and filled it with a particular local meaning.

The ordinance of the Molpoi was intertwined with the organization of the polis, but we ought to add swiftly that they were not identical with it. Their procession was not inclusive in the sense that it did not assemble the citizen body of Miletus. As cult ordinance, the Molpoi traversed on behalf of their community; they were not a community in motion. We thus encounter another variant of a local religious group configuration here. The lines between such groups and the polis community were blurred. But this did not make the procession a less forceful expression of an epichoric cult.[54]

The second example derives from Thebes. The festival of the Daphnephoria was among the most splendid polis celebrations there. Held in the month of Alalkomenios (May), in an eight-year cycle, the festival girded the arrival of Apollo's laurel and its cathartic powers against *miasma*, or spiritual pollution. Reconciling communal relations with the gods, the Daphnephoria played a critical role in securing the city's well-being. Upon reception of the laurel, the branch was carried through the town and the surrounding *chōra*. In its most basic form, the *pompē* followed the same ritual dynamic of staking territorial claims through the veneration of epichoric deities that we have encountered before.

The details are known from the Imperial or Late Antique author Proklos, whose work survives in Photios's *Bibliothēkē* (tenth century CE). Commenting on different genres of song—iambic poetry, hymns, dithyrambs, and paians— and their local development, Proklos also discusses the chapter of *partheniai*, so-called Maiden Songs. His description of the *daphnephoria*, which belong to this group, is couched in the wider discussion of song and its role in ritual. It is worthwhile to paraphrase the entire section. Proklos (*Chrestomathia* 25, from Photios's *Library* 321a–322a) says that

> an olive branch is decorated with laurel and other flowers. A bronze globe is attached to the top, from which other smaller balls are suspended. Another ball is placed in the middle of the olive branch, smaller in size than the one at the top, with hanging strips of purple bands. The base of the branch is adorned with a saffron-coloured cloth. For the Boiotians, Proklos asserts, the bronze globe at the top was representative of the sun and Apollo, while the globe in the middle represents the moon, and the smaller suspended balls are the planets and stars. The purple bands symbolize the days of the year, as they number 365. At the head of the festival party, a young boy marches with his father and mother. His closest relative holds the olive branch. The *daphnephoros* then follows, holding the laurel in his hand. He has flowing hair and wears a golden crown. Also, he is clothed in a gleaming dress that falls to his feet, and he is wearing special sandals of an Iphikratic style. The leading group of the procession is accompanied by a choir of girls, holding branches of supplication and singing hymns.

It is difficult to disentangle the various layers of time that intermingle in the account. For instance, Iphikratic foot gear, boots introduced by the famous Athenian general that were light and easy to tie, sets the mid-fourth century as a *terminus post quem* for this detail; just how much after is unknown. The idea of a year's length of 365 days was not commonly accepted much before Caesar's calendar reform from 45 BCE. Since the Daphnephoria are otherwise attested for as early as the sixth century BCE, if not before,

Albert Schachter has posited Proklos's description as reflective of (at least) one reform of the festival in the fourth century BCE. To this we ought to add ongoing adaptations and modifications over time. Traces from the Classical period are undeniable in Proklos, while other details of the passage can only be understood as later additions.[55]

Such a reading is supported by other sources, notably Pindar, whose oeuvre includes several Maiden Songs. *Ode 94b* honors a *daphnephoros* by the name of Agasikles, whose family played an eminent role in Theban politics. His father was the famous boiotarch Pagondas, who had led the Theban cavalry in the battle of the Delion in 424 BCE (chapter 5). Pagondas's father Aiolidas is praised in the song as head of an "all-renowned house" (lines 8–9). On the basis of these prosopographical observations, scholars traditionally view *Ode 94b* as a late work of Pindar's, dating from shortly before his death, c. 443 BCE.[56] Despite the fragmentary nature of the text, it is clear that the laurel-bearer and his sister were dressed in a special garb, including a gleaming robe, headgear with garlands, and sandals (lines 6. 11–12. 70). Walking next to her father, Agasikles's sister was leading the way for the *daphnephoros*; unlike in Proklos's account, the leader of the procession is accompanied by his daughter. Otherwise the constellation was similar. Headed by the father of the *daphnephoros* and the laurel-bearer himself, the procession comprised a series of cohorts of boys and girls who carried laurel branches and chanted songs in honor of Apollo.

The Daphnephoria have been studied in considerable detail. Among the prevailing interpretations, we find the notion of a centrifugal procession: with their *pompē*, the Thebans staked their claims over the *chōra* throughout the Teneric Plain north of the city. Much as with the tour of the Molpoi, it is striking to see how the route paid tribute to sacred landmarks in the countryside. Departing from an unknown spot, the procession left the city via the Elektran Gate and the Temple of Herakles. From there it headed toward one of the oldest sanctuaries, the nearby precinct of Apollo Ismenios—this was the site where Kadmos had slaughtered the dragon, before he founded the city (chapter 2). Subsequently, the party proceeded to the Galaxion, a location presumably on the western edge of the Theban *chōra*. Neither the site nor its religious context have been determined with certainty. Plutarch, likewise, had no knowledge of its location, stating merely that those who had once lived in its vicinity sensed the presence of the god "from the copious and abundant flow of milk" (*Mor.* 409a; Pind., frag. 104b Race). Cow milk could be a hint. Most likely, the Galaxion referenced Kadmos's cow track to Thebes in one way or another, providing the story with a real site that vouched for its validity.

Another interpretation is also possible, one that aligns the venture to the Galaxion with the astronomical adornments of the olive log: its decoration with globes, spheres, and bands that represented the sun and stars, the planets, and the moon, as well as the cycle of the year. We do not know when the Greek term for the Milky Way (*ho Galaxias kaloumenos kyklos*) came in use. If this was the case before the Galaxion had disappeared from the Theban countryside, presumably toward the end of the fourth century BCE, then the procession would have referenced the cosmic order in one way or the other, through its religious symbolism or reverence for a precinct that was associated with it, or both. Similar to the citation of the zodiacal wheel in Phlious (chapter 1), evocation of the Milky Way might have implied a subtle convergence of the cosmic order and the epichoric horizon. But there is no way for us to be certain about this.[57]

Another reading of the Daphnephoria focuses on features of the ritual that remind us of a rite of passage. The *daphnephoros*'s dress apparently imitated the coiffure and clothing of a girl: his loose hair and robe to his feet suggest as much. Corresponding rites from other cities supplement the idea that the young boy, masquerading as girl, was part of a transition ritual from childhood to maturity. We turn to evidence from elsewhere further below. The temple of Herakles, which lay along the procession route, was in any case closely associated with the training of youths at Thebes. If the interpretation of a rite of passage is correct, then the *daphnephoros* most likely represented the cohorts of boys and girls who, on the brink of adulthood, participated in the cult as part of their initiation into one of the most vital cults of the polis. A festival cycle of eight years implies that the subsequent age cohorts must have been ranked in one way or another. Maybe the choirs included younger youths who were still remote from puberty. Pindar and Proklos capture different stages in time in the long history of the Daphnephoria; most likely, their accounts were a blueprint that matched with and was informed by other performances of boys and girls that were staged frequently in the polis (e.g., singing and dancing, among others). For one age cohort, that of youths on the verge of maturity, the performance overlapped with a rite of passage. Be that as it may, the daphnephoric procession was clearly geared toward the display of youthly valor. Led by the laurel-bearer and his family, the youths experienced the countryside in a concrete manner, touring through its territory, embracing their responsibilities for the land of the polis.[58]

Local *nomima* prevailed throughout. Most eminently, the songs that were performed were epichoric in nature. In Pindar's case, we note that Ode 94 was commissioned for the particular occasion of Agasikles's *daphnephoria*. It was composed to celebrate the fame of an esteemed house at Thebes, that of Aiolidas and his descendants. Moreover, the usage of religious paraphernalia was locally charged. A comparison with similar processions in nearby cities—for instance, the one that was held in conjunction with the Daidala at Plataia—suggests as much. At Plataia, the *daidalē*, the young male leader of the procession, was dressed as a bride. In Thebes, the *daphnephoros* imitated the looks of a young female. The difference was due to the worship of a different deity in each case: Apollo in Thebes and Hera in Plataia. The rituals also had other structural similarities that allow us to address them together, yet the commonalities were subject to formidable idiosyncrasy. The cult object that was carried in the procession at Plataia was a log of oak wood. In Thebes, it was a branch of olive wood. This *kōpō*, essentially some kind of maypole, was wrapped at the bottom with a saffron-yellow cloth. The color is usually interpreted as a symbol of elite distinction because of its resource-intensive extraction from the thin, grass-shaped petals of the saffron plant (in Greek, *krokos*). Although species from the ancient Near East were notoriously rich in scent and color, saffron also flourished in the climate of central Boiotia and was harvested as local produce. According to Hesiod, the epichoric nymphs Telesto and Enyo, both of whom were worshipped in Thebes, were clad in saffron-yellow robes (*Theogony* 358). Pindar declares that Herakles, upon his birth in Thebes, was "laid in saffron-swathing bands" (*Nem.* 1.37). It is difficult to assert with certainty that the saffron in use came from local produce, but the association with and affinity for the use of *krokos*-dyed garments in a ritual context appears to be a local characteristic of Thebes.[59] Thebes and Plataia were only fifteen kilometers apart; evidently, they were united under the same umbrella of translocal *hiera*. The epichoric context of ritual practice, however, set them far apart.

Our final example takes us to Hermione in the Peloponnese. We have already noted the fame of the city's local production of *porphyra*, a red-purple dye the inhabitants harvested from predatory sea snails. Given the modest size of the city, Pausanias recounts a relatively high number of cult sites, Demeter sanctuaries in particular (chapter 3). The Temple of Demeter Chthonia, Demeter of the Earth, stood out. Every summer, the Hermionians led a captivating procession there. At the head of the *pompē* marched the priests and all public officeholders of the year, followed by echelons of men and women. The procession thus resembled the citizen body. In Pausanias's day, the celebrants also included cohorts of children who wore a special white dress for the occasion. Their wreaths were woven from a flower called *cosmosandalon* that grew in the area around Hermione; it appears to have been a local plant—so much so that Pausanias, judging from its size and color, could only conjecture its botany: he believed it belonged to the iris family. After the procession came a group of men who guarded an untamed, frisky cow that was led into the temple. Once the animal was inside, the doors were shut and the cow's throat cut by one of four elderly women who had awaited the animal with sharp sickles. After the first animal was slaughtered, the doors were reopened and a second cow was led in, and then two more. The act of the kill was rigidly prescribed: the sacrifice had to be carried out so that all four cows fell on the same side as the first animal that was slaughtered (2.35.4–8).

As usual, it is difficult to establish chronological certainty. Pausanias states that the Temple of Demeter Chthonia was among the oldest of the city. The festival displays similarities with other procession rituals during the late Archaic and Classical periods. At some point, the Hermionians made the effort to attract participants from throughout the Peloponnese, as is attested to in two *theōrodokoi* inscriptions from the third century BCE.[60] The inclusion of children most likely occurred later; Pausanias explains that this was a recent development, something that happened only in his own days. The *cosmosandalon*, typical to the region, seems to have grown there across the strands of time.[61]

The old age of the festival is independently confirmed by the lyric poetry of Lasos of Hermione from the last quarter of the sixth century BCE. Lasos enjoyed some stardom beyond his home town. He participated in choral contests in Athens; presumably, he introduced dithyrambic competitions there around 508. Moreover, he was remembered for his innovations in auletic technique, choral arrangements, and the creation of new sounds, all of which took the genre of dithyrambic song to a new level. His works are lost, with the exception of one fragment, the opening lines of a *Hymn to Demeter* that was composed for performance during the festival for Chthonia: "I sing of Demeter and Kore, wife of Klymenos, raising a sweet-toned hymn."[62] The fragment survives because of a linguistic peculiarity: the hymn was remembered for its asigmatism: that is, the song made no use of the letter *s*. Unfortunately, such curiosity teaches us nothing about contents. Given Lasos's qualities as a songwriter, along with the local pride the Hermionians would have felt for their poet, it is not unreasonable to assume that the performance of his pieces put the festival community into a state of excitement.[63] Aelian (*On Animals* 11.4) also portrays the procession to Demeter Chthonia as a time-honored rite. Referencing a certain Aristokles (Prauscello 2013, 85), he preserves part of the prayer that was said on the occasion of the festival. In it, the Hermionians urged the goddess to "show us your favor and grant that every farm (*klaros*) in Hermione may thrive exceedingly."

The inhabitants of these *klaroi* lived in a storied world. The local topography inspired their religious imagination. For instance, near the Temple of Chthonia were three places which the Hermionians called that of Klymenos, a local hero, that of Pluto, ruler of the underworld, and the Acherousian lake. According to Pausanias, all were surrounded by fences of stones, while in the place of Klymenos there was also a chasm in the earth. Through this, the Hermionians said, Herakles had brought up the hellhound Kerberos (2.35.10). For the Temple of Demeter Chthonia, Michael Jameson (2004, 181) has suggested the site of the Taxiarchos Church in modern Hermione as the most likely location. Of the other places, none has been identified with certainty. The topography is further complicated by the fact that the settlement of Hermione was moved in the second or first centuries BCE from the tip of a headland between two well-protected harbors to a new site about one kilometer further west to the lower slopes of Mt. Pron.

Pausanias's account puts the gorge of Klymenos, the site of Pluto, and the Acherousian lake, or swamp, beyond the sanctuary of Chthonia. All three were explicitly associated with the underworld; the Acheron, stream of pain, was considered since Homer (*Od.* 10.513) as one of the rivers that connected the world of the living to that of the dead. If the temple precinct of Demeter Chthonia was situated on the fringes of Hermione's territory, as it most likely was in Classical times, those dangerous places were relegated to realms outside the orderly world of the polis. Even there, precautionary measures were taken to contain their destructive force: they were surrounded by stone walls. The festival for Demeter Chthonia was then celebrated in an environment that reminded everyone of the delicate balance between communal well-being and the ubiquitous threat of disaster. We observed the same balance in our earlier discussion of various anxieties that were felt in the marginal lands of the city. In light of such potential jeopardy, it is likely no coincidence that the procession included the entire community, its priests, magistrates, and the full citizen body, including women. Consecrating the solidarity between the people and their fertility goddess, the Hermionians sought to settle their divine relations and please the gods. They didn't need much help with how this was done. The ritual dynamics came from within, and they precipitated a broad array of local cult expressions: spells of prayer and song, and the application of a peculiar sacrificial practice, all of which were enshrined in a topography of local meaning.

We have now surveyed the conduct of epichoric worship in three different places, at Miletus, in Thebes, and Hermione. The respective procession rites were performed by different constituent groups: a privileged group of cult experts, cohorts of youths, and the citizen body. What united these group constellations was that they all subscribed to the common theme of place. In each case, the procession through the countryside covered the manageable realm of the polis (or portions thereof), with the ritual party traversing to the fringe zones of the *chōra*, articulating its ownership of, and attachment to, the territory. In François de Polignac's sense, those processions were political demonstrations. They asserted the claim of territorial ownership. But they were also much more. We have seen how each procession rite was informed by the spiritual topography of the land. In turn, the local inspired idiosyncrasies in cults that enabled the city to foster a strong identity of place.

Ephebic Religion and the Sublime of the Local

In a brief note that is often overlooked amid the gruesome narrative in which it is couched, Thucydides states that when a band of Thracian mercenaries raided the town of Mykalessos in Eastern Boiotia in 413 BCE, they massacred everyone, including those who had sought refuge in the *didaskaleion paidōn*, the boys' school (7.29.5). The *didaskaleion* was "the largest in town," says Thucydides. If this is true, rather than dramatic hyperbole to denounce the cruelty of the Thracians, then there were other *didaskaleia* in town. By the time of the Peloponnesian War, Mykalessos, a small polis with a small population, maintained two or three buildings that were used in the training and education of local youths.[64]

The question of the nature of education, in Mykalessos and elsewhere, is of a different caliber. The issue has long been obfuscated by the sole concentration on the one training institution that is attested best in our sources, the so-called ephebate at Athens, that is, the public program by which the Athenians sought to familiarize the next generation of citizens with the public life of their city. The history of the Athenian *ephēbeia* is traditionally regarded as one marked by two stages of development: a period of shy beginnings in the Classical period, with few scattered pieces of literary and documentary evidence available, when the *ephēbeia* appears to have been a loose training program for members of the higher echelon; and a rigid, formalized organization, brought to life and governed by a major reform bill after the Battle of Chaironeia. Both phases sail under separate scholarly paradigms. The *ephēbeia* of the later period is typically seen as a public program that was rooted in the political culture of the Hellenistic World and its characteristic interplay between local city-states, on the one hand, and ruling courts and dynasties with a decidedly global outlook, on the other. In this vein, the institution appears as a vital expression of Hellenistic culture, its civic values and social ideologies. The assessment is largely preconditioned by the body of evidence. Apart from a brief section in the Aristotelian *Constitution of the Athenians* (42), the history of the Hellenistic ephebate is shaped by an ever-increasing number of ephebic inscriptions that shed light on the extent, administration, and delivery of the program—the training routine as well as the achievement of individual ephebic classes. The near ubiquitous habit of setting up ephebic inscriptions in the agora of the city, with examples ranging "from Marseilles to Babylon and from the Ukraine to North Africa," highlights the communal authority at play.[65]

In the pre-Hellenistic period, such evidence is notoriously absent. Without ephebic inscriptions that catalogue cohorts, disciplines, and training sessions (the earliest example comes from Athens, dating from 334/3 BCE), the prevailing paradigm in the approach to forerunners of the Hellenistic institution is that of a rite of passage. It is commonplace to see the purpose of late Archaic and Classical Greek polis education in sporadic and unorganized teachings of communal base skills, social practices, and collective forms of behavior: for example, the performance of song and dance, feasting, hunting and martial arts, religious ceremonies, and sacrifice. This type of education also included acts of deliberate transgression and temporary marginalization from the community, which had their origins in puberty rites and are paralleled by practices of initiation in many premodern societies: for instance, the ritual of self-castigation, notoriously attested for the training of Spartan and Cretan "herds" of youths, so-called *agelai*; ritualized stealth and stealing, also in conjunction with tests of courage, such as the notorious bull-lifting contests; or transgender masquerade through female coiffure and clothing, a reversal ritual that temporarily suspended the governing norms of the community.[66] So, while the Hellenistic *ephēbeia* is seen as a tight, state-sponsored institution, its Classical predecessors are typically subsumed under the labels of either elite training or the practice of communal base skills, or both. The contrast between both forms of the ephebate has therefore been described as resulting in a "proleptic narrative" (Too 2002, 8), indicating that if we speak of the *ephēbeia* of the fifth and early fourth centuries, the term only anticipates what was yet to come. It wasn't the real ephebate just yet.

We are not mistaken to think of subsequent phases in the history of the Greek *ephēbeia*. All the while, more recent renderings alert us not overstate the case. In particular, we shouldn't discount the earlier period as a preview of the real thing. First, the two-step development from occasional elite training and associated rites of passage to a state-sponsored program, each one targeting divergent societal goals, discounts the complexity of what was at different times and in different places included in the education of the youths. It also undervalues the dynamic with which both the contents and context of instruction evolved. We have already seen how, by the time of the Peloponnesian War, the ephebes participated in patrols of the countryside and the defense of the territory in case of emergency. At Argos, the training of young *logades* points in the same direction, while the Hellenistic ephebic program in Megara had similar forerunners in the fifth and fourth centuries BCE. The historical roots of such military engagement are now also better understood, thanks to the work of Lynn Kozak (2013), who has restored a literary link between Homer's poetry and the traces of an ephebic ethos in Greek tragedy. We are therefore well advised to emphasize the long duration of military engagement from the late Archaic to the early Hellenistic Age. Innovations in the training of the youths, sometimes supplemented by political reforms, added new facets to the picture, but this does not undermine the observation that the instruction of *ephēboi* had been on the agenda of the polis since the sixth century BCE at the latest.[67]

Thematic segregation has further obfuscated the picture. For heuristic purposes, scholarship tends to segregate military training and assignments in war from cultural techniques, such as expertise in song and dance. Yet other areas of education are again treated separately from these, such as athletic training, learning about polis traditions, and acquaintance with the local way of life and what this entailed: for instance, in the preparation of foodstuffs, appropriate attire, and basic artisanal knowledge (the harvest cycle, skinning animals, whittling arrows, and so on). While these rubrics are usually treated individually both in research and handbooks, we should imagine them as playing out in conjunction with each other, with close overlap, simultaneity, and cross-fertilization. To those who participated in it, the Classical ephebate was anything but a proleptic exercise. It shaped the public life in the polis, the experience of youths and of citizens alike.

Ephebic activities were carried out in a variety of places. Some of these were earmarked for communal interaction, e.g., the agora, theatre, stadium, or the *didaskaleion*, although the latter in most cases would have been a mundane building. Other exercises commenced in the meadows, fields, woodlands, on farmsteads in the countryside (for instance, for horseback maneuvers), and so on. This is not to say that the polis necessarily wielded tight control over each activity, let alone in a heavy-handed, monopolized manner. The instruction was overseen by different groups at different times: by elites such as Pagondas's family when they practiced songs with the youths; by clans, phratries, or "herds"—the Molpoi in Miletus used the seat of their ordinance in the instruction of the city's *neoi*, while the Spartan *paidonomos* ("boy-herder") oversaw the *agelai* in mess halls; and by the community itself, when it trained the next generation of hoplite citizens.[68]

Given the huge variety of polis structures across Aegean Greece, it should come as no surprise to us that the organization of youth training was subject to local variation. Yet there was also a common denominator, because the city had a firm, self-evident interest in the perpetuation of its customs and communal sensibilities from one generation to the next. With this interest in mind, the instruction—no matter how segmented and compartmentalized, and no matter by whom it was delivered—was designed to shape and tighten the bonds between the youths and the community. In turn, participation in various educational exercises that revolved around the polis—in dance and ritual as much as in field patrols—allowed the youths to experience their local world. They learned about their polis's place in time and space. Effectively, as they absorbed this type of knowledge, they safeguarded its value and validity over time.[69]

The crown witness for such an assertion comes from an inscribed stele that was once erected at the Sanctuary of Ares in Acharnai in northern Attica. It was discovered by Louis Robert in 1932, who detected it under a pile of manure. Local farmers had hidden it there. The stele contains the so-called ephebic oath from Athens, the fullest example of a citizen oath from Classical Greece. The inscription documenting the oath dates to the middle of the fourth century BCE, but scholars believe it is of considerably earlier origins. In conjunction with other evidence, also from vase scenes that depict the swearing ceremony, it is possible to place the oath in the first half of the fifth century BCE.[70] The text reminds the ephebes of two duties in particular: first, their obligations as hoplites who will not desert "the men beside them" (R&O 88, lines 7–8), a rule that was critical when it came to keeping up the phalanx in line. The second duty was more civic in nature, as the ephebes swore to obey the laws of their city (lines 11–12). The combination of both elements speaks to the heart of the concept of citizenship. The training of the youths—that is, the education of future citizens—aimed at turning these men into brave civilians and courageous soldiers. Toward the end of the oath, the twofold pledge culminates in the forceful call for divine witnesses who place the ephebic promise under the authority of the gods: "Witnesses: the Gods Aglauros, Hestia, Enyo, Enyalios, Ares and Athena Areia, Zeus, Thallo, Auxo, Hegemone, Herakles, and the boundaries of my fatherland, wheat, barley, vines, olives, figs" (lines 16–20).

It is intriguing to see how the *chōra* and its agrarian produce figure as deified witnesses here, referencing the link between the young men who swore the oath and the land they pledge to protect. This alone both magnified and enhanced the bond with the local horizon. As we learn from countless ephebic inscriptions, the ties between the ephebes and the land later evolved into regular excursions to the borderlands and liminal sanctuaries. En route, the ephebes learned about the intricacies of the *chōra*, its topography and geography, its major roads and lines of communication, and its areas of agricultural activity. But there was more at stake than practical knowledge. We have already noted how such field trips added to the formation of a mentality of territory (chapter 2). Recalling the testimony of wheat, barley, olives, and other agrarian goods, the ephebic oath elevated the local produce, assigning to it a spirited quality. Much like the sacred nature of caves and groves, the agrarian land, too, figures as a place with a spirited aura: the veneration of gods and goddesses "in the fields" or "in the marshes" exudes a deep rootedness of the divine in the agricultural landscape. The sacred aura clearly inspired the ephebes as much as it instilled in them the obligation to safeguard the land, observe its conditions, and perform their duties in deference to the holy covenant the polis had with the powers in place.[71]

Note the prominence of warrior deities—Enyo, Enyalios, Ares, and Athena Areia—along with deified figures that ensured the well-being of the community and its prosperity: Thallo ("Sprouting"), Auxo ("Growth"), Hegemone ("Leadership"), and Hestia, the personified "Common Hearth" and metaphorical center of the polis around which its members gathered to frolic and feast. Herakles, with whom the line-up segues from guarantors of prosperity to the field fruits themselves, has been an inspiration to Greek youths of all times; we already mentioned his importance for the youths at Thebes in the course of the daphnephoric festival. The youths at Thespiai, too, adored Herakles both for his courage and high levels of testosterone. At Athens, the ephebes offered wine to the demigod before they cut off their youthful locks at the Apaturia festival.[72]

This leaves us with the local heroine Aglauros, who is mentioned first— somewhat curiously so. In some sources, she is referenced as Agraulos—that is, "Of the Fields" which hints at the idea of earthboundness. The role of Aglauros has not gone unnoticed. Indeed, she was singled out as a special goddess of the ephebes, a "Sondergöttin der Epheben" (Merkelbach 1972). Her corresponding shrine, the Aglaureion, has been identified as the home of what scholars call an ephebic religion. The site was located on the eastern edge of the Acropolis, at a spot that was opposite to, and hence most remote from, the entrance to the Acropolis via the Propylaia. The precinct—basically a cave in the rock—resembled that of a hide-out. The ephebes assembled there for the celebration of the Aglauria festival. They also took an oath at the shrine before they ventured into the countryside or faced battle.[73]

By the later fourth century BCE, Philochoros (*BNJ* 328 F 105 and 106) reported the legendary tradition according to which Aglauros, a glowing young patriot, rose to fame over the heroic act of saving the polis all by herself. An oracular verdict in a distant past had declared that the city's fortune depended on whether any young Athenian would be willing to kill himself, or herself, in order to protect the city. Aglauros was the one, throwing herself off the Acropolis. She thus provided not only inspiration to adolescent Athenians but rose to "the role model par excellence for the teenaged ephebes" (Bayliss 2013, 17). In another legendary tradition summarized by Pausanias, Aglauros, along with her sister, had received from Athena the earthborn child Erichthonios, who was placed in a basket; Athena "forbade them to pry curiously into what was entrusted to their charge" (1.18.2). When the sisters disobeyed—they were too nosy not to open the basket, although they were told otherwise—they were stricken with panic and madness, throwing themselves off the steepest cliff of the Acropolis. Scholars have attempted to reconcile these accounts on the grounds of Aglauros's ultimate fate: in both cases she dies by plunging off the Acropolis. All the while, the latter version appears to paint a childish, silly picture of Aglauros, which is why it was found irreconcilable with the heroic portrait in Philochoros's story. According to Christiane Sourvinou-Inwood, the version of the "foolish girl who disobeyed Athena" (2011, 48) had no meaning for the ephebes.

It is doubtful whether the separation of two legendary strands, each one with its own trajectory of meaning, holds true. We have observed earlier that the isolation of mythical variants, with one being identified as the "true" version, while the other is deemed to be marginal or local, or both, is counterintuitive to the fabric of legendary traditions as such. Note the common threads that steer both narratives. Both versions of Aglauros were of Erechtheid descent: the smart one, the daughter of Aktaios, autochthonous king of Athens; her foolish counterpart, the daughter of Kekrops. Both died in the same place on the cliffs of the Acropolis, in the same way. And both were emotionally tied to their homeland. This latter aspect has not always been fully appreciated. While the foolish Aglauros is dismissed as an ill-bred child, her role was actually more complex, critical to the advancement of early Athens. Aglauros was handed over the earthborn hero Erichthonios; in some traditions she became his nurse.[74] Despite her young age, she was thus entrusted with the future of all Athenians—a precious gift for an adolescent to bear, and a burden that required commitment to the cause. The task wasn't so different after all from the one posed before the courageous Aglauros, who went on to save her country through self-sacrifice. Modern approaches to the two separate faces of Aglauros are sophisticated and instructive at the same time, but it is hard to imagine that the casual Athenian citizen would have dissected these roles and functions from each other and assigned them to one Aglauros or another. As we have seen, the social ideology behind the training of ephebes was also inspired by notions of temporary transgression and role reversals, both associated with the ritualized transition from boyhood to adult citizen. Aglauros beautifully related to this ideology: the future of the polis was placed in her hands; in both stories she was the protector of the earthbornness of all Athenians. When the ephebes celebrated her festival in the cave on the edge of the Acropolis, their own role as defenders of the fate must have been equally invoked. The idea was instilled in them while they were youths. As adult citizens, they were the ones who put it in action.[75]

The legendary tales of Aglauros, and the ephebic oath in general, teach us how the youths of the city were trained to become courageous agents of locality. The observation is, of course, not confined to Athens. In a document from Hellenistic Dreros on Crete we find a similar array of earthbound witness deities, culminating in "Earth, Heaven, heroes, heroines, and fountains and rivers." Once again, the land is a spirited place to which the people are tied.[76] As was noted by Nigel Kennell (2006, vii–xv), probably the best connoisseur of the diverse body of sources, most if not all Greek cities had education and training programs in place in the Classical period. From everything we have learned in this section, it is safe to conclude that, among other training purposes, these programs subscribed to an earthbound agenda in one way or the other.

The new discovery of a bronze inscription from Arkadia disperses all remaining doubts about the early beginnings of ephebic instruction and its embeddedness in local cult. Discussion of the inscription commenced only recently, with two separate works (Heinrichs 2015; Carbon and Clackson 2016). The difficult language, opaque grammar, and convoluted arrangement of the text—there are several corrections and erasures—along with blurs from multiple layers of corrosion pose tremendous challenges to our understanding. What complicates the matter further is the inscription's obscure history of discovery. According to Johannes Heinrichs (2015, 3), the bronze plaque was held in private ownership before it surfaced around 2010 on the London and Munich art markets. It is unclear where the document went from there and where it is kept today. The text consists of twenty-three lines that were written on a tablet of max. 44 cm width and c. 32.5 cm height. At the bottom, there is an empty space measuring about 10 cm. On linguistic and paleographic grounds, the text can be dated to the decades on either side of 500 BCE. Its dialect has been found appropriate by the leading specialists for Arkadia at that time.[77]

Beyond these introductory remarks, there are substantial differences in the way the editors constitute their text. On a very basic level, Jan-Mathieu Carbon and James Clackson assert that none of the twenty-three lines are complete, since letters have been lost at the beginning and end throughout (2016, 122). In Heinrichs's reading, the opening section starts with an uncertain number of letters, but he restores these to a complete sentence; he suggests that the restoration is the actual beginning of the inscription. The topographical information provided, according to Heinrichs, attests to the prominence of the Parrhasia mountain range, from Mt. Lykaion in the North to Lykosoura in the South. He is confident to identify the Sanctuary of Zeus Lykaios as its place of origin. Accordingly, he sees the document as pertaining to the cult there. Carbon and Clackson's text shows a concern with ritual practice in a plethora of Arkadian places rather than one or two. Given the variety of festivals that are referenced, Carbon and Clackson do not posit a specific polis or sanctuary as the inscription's point of origin and focus.

It is beyond our scope here to engage in an in-depth discussion of the text. The critical passage for us concerns a section where both editions established a fairly similar reading, which is remarkable in itself. Line 6, according to Carbon and Clackson, reads

]ατᾶι κορϝον ενϝοτοῖ ϝετει εξαγεν ασπιδα ακοντιον φοινικῖς ξιφος κ[

They translate as follows: "] for [. . .] a boy, in the ninth year, carries out: a shield, a small javelin, red cloak(s), a sword, . . . [." Heinrichs takes εξαγεν for εξαγελ(οι) and understands the last κ[in the line as κορυς. Effectively, he translates "For Kata<i?> b]atas a boy/youth, every ninth year. Mess(engers/ages from inside) out: (round) shield, javelin, purple/red (military) tunic, sword, h|elmet."

The appearance of the youth (κορϝος = *kouros*) is curious. The inscription appears otherwise concerned with festivals and sacrifices for which it provides itemized lists of sacrificial meats and other offerings, their prices, quantity, and quality as they were required for each festival. Reference to the youth is the only mention of a person. This alone suggests that his role was conspicuous. The military nature of his engagement is visible from his association with fighting equipment; whether the *kouros* was called out by certain messengers (Heinrichs) or he himself brought forth the armor (Carbon and Clackson) doesn't make much difference here. The way in which the prescription is phrased sets the boy apart from the rest of the document. He is the only one to carry material objects—a full set of hoplite armor; other objects mentioned include less martial items: sacrificial animals (sheep, cows, piglets, rams, bulls), plants (fennel), wineskins, aromatics, and honeycombs. Also, the long cycle of a ninth year (i.e., every eight years) betrays the importance that was assigned to the ceremony. We have already encountered a similar cycle in our discussion of the Daphnephoria at Thebes. Pausanias speaks of the same cycle for the performance of a cult on Mt. Lykaion.[78] Taken together, these observations suggest that the "arms and the boy" scene (Carbon and

Clackson) was highly charged. Presumably it was part of a (procession?) ritual to enlist certain youths into the military squads of their local citizen body. Like the *daphnephoros*, the *kouros* of our inscription would have represented a larger cohort of youths who underwent an associated rite of initiation, either at the beginning or end of their ephebic training.[79]

Entrenchment of the training in ritual and sacrifice is further supported by its connection with the cult of Demeter and Despoina in Lykosoura, if this connection is indeed the case. Heinrichs (2015, 38–41) believes that the inscription commences with reference to the "Eleusiniai" in line 1, goddesses of the land and its cultivation (we note that these Eleusiniai are absent from Carbon and Clackson's edition). Pausanias provides a detailed description of their sanctuary at Lykosoura, a city that he considered "the oldest of all cities the land and the islands have produced" (8.38.1). Before the temple of Despoina stood the altar to Demeter and two more to Despoina and the Great Mother, where the sacrifices were made. The actual cult statues of Demeter and Despoina, including the throne on which they sat, the footstool, and all drapery, were carved out of one block. The remarkable thing here was that the stone was not imported from elsewhere but came from the soil itself. It was dug up from within the precinct at the behest of a dream oracle: the goddess herself had revealed where the rock for her future cult statue was to be found (8.37.3). Her *agalma* was tied—literally—to the sanctuary site. We have already noted the importance of such boundedness through quarries and the stones they provide in our discussion of the Sikyonian treasure houses at Delphi and Olympia. The mysteries themselves followed a secret script—so much so that Pausanias refused to reveal the real name of Despoina to the uninitiated (8.37.9). Nearby were a sacred grove and a sanctuary to Pan, which once had an oracle cult where the god spoke through the lips of a local nymph.

Our inscription blends into this gallery. Pausanias declares that there was an inscribed tablet that informed visitors to the temple of Demeter about its mysteries (8.37.2). It is too much to see a relation between Pausanias's tablet and the newly discovered *pinax*, but the issue raises the basic question about the inscription's initial purpose. Heinrichs asserts that the text was not for public display but for internal use, a brief manual of the priesthood, as it were, because of its multiple spelling errors, erasures, and the general lack of a representative character (2015, 3). Indeed, the list is so compartmentalized, with so much local diversity, that it must have been advisable to have some sort of documentary evidence to recall the details. The short sequence of rites, recurring in multiple configurations and over different years and cycles, is remarkable. For instance, Carbon and Clackson's text mentions the river god

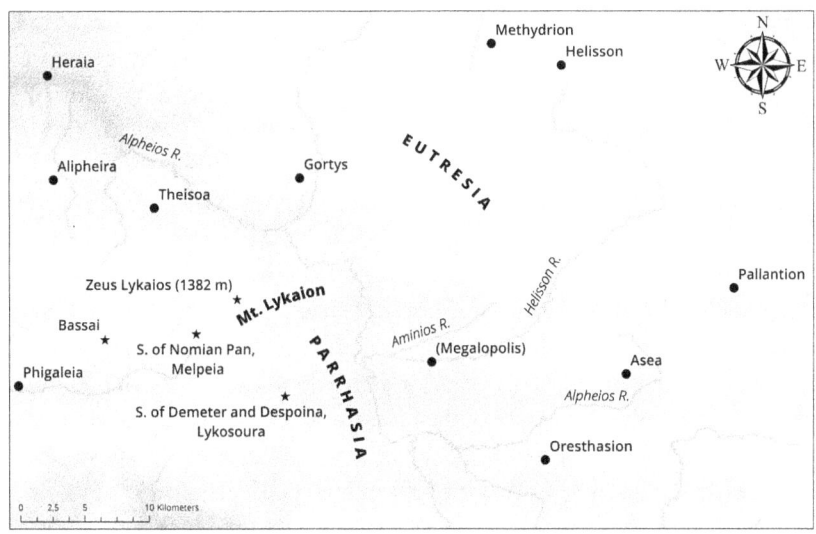

FIGURE 4.3. Map detailing the geography of the new cult law from Arkadia.

Alpheios on three occasions. But the offerings to him were different in each case (lines 1 f., 4, 12). In other cases, the text relates names of sites, games, and/or festivals that were previously unknown, each with its own sacrificial prescription: in Carbon and Clackson, we find up to sixteen toponyms and/or cult names that populate a crowded inscription. The text is, in this sense, a hyper-summation of locality (fig. 4.3). No matter what the actual catchment area of the inscription was, we are left with the impression of a rich diversity of prescriptions that each governed ritual practice in one place but were void in another.[80]

The new Arkadian *pinax* testifies to the diversification of local cult practice in Arkadia and in the Parrhasia in particular, where the spring of the Alpheios originated. Given the secluded terrain, the tapestry of local encoding there was most likely even more complex than in other regions in the Peloponnese and on the Greek mainland. The region's isolated pockets of land fostered a distinctly local ambience. As Odysseus connected to the land through orchards and wine (chapter 2), the mountain folks of Lykosoura did so through oak and walnut trees. They venerated their own local vegetation goddesses, and in doing so, they adhered to a special ritual script. Curiously enough, pomegranates, which were usually offered to Demeter in prayer for fertile land, were not permitted in the ritual at Lykosoura, although it wasn't clear to Pausanias why (8.37.7). Idiosyncrasies such as these filled place with meaning. They inspired a sense of belonging and communal fate, both of which commenced in relation to the land. As religious traditions were passed on from one generation to the next, the instruction of youths in the small local communities of Arkadia played a landmark role in providing continuity over time. The boy was a key agent of locality; his training was determined by, and geared toward, the reconciliation with the gods in place.

We have seen in this chapter how the local constituted a sphere of religious conduct in its own right. To be sure, the Panhellenic gallery of a joint pantheon, a web of shared religious narratives and associated cults and rituals, provided the backdrop to the exercise of Greek religion. But there was no universal signifier: no common prayer or common song, no single sacrificial protocol that united the Greeks in their daily religious conduct. In quotidian practice, an omnipresent force of the local was at play. We characterized this force as one that was not simply locally confined, but fused with idiosyncrasy and meaning. Place itself provided rich moments of adaption in ritual and cult: the legendary traditions that clustered around the physical features of the land; the divine spirits, nymphs, and demons that roamed through it; its natural produce, which shaped ritual practices such as prayer and sacrifice. Nothing of this was accidental. The training of the youths and their subsequent initiation into the local religious system speaks volumes to the cognition and consciousness with which the Greek city emphasized its character as a community of fate that was bound in time and place.

5
Big Politics, through the Local Lens

In *The Malice of Herodotus*, Plutarch adduces the Theban historian Aristophanes as one of his crown witnesses. Few fragments of Aristophanes's work survive, although some pieces assembled under the names of other authors in the latest edition of Boiotian local histories may well derive from Aristophanes. Despite their low number, Aristophanes's fragments offer exciting glimpses into the local discourse environment in Thebes in the later fifth century BCE. In one of the texts, Aristophanes relates how the Thebans handled the allegation of their medism in the Persian Wars, allegations raised so prominently in Herodotus's *Histories*. Aristophanes asserts that Herodotus "demanded money from the Thebans, but he received none, and when he tried to speak and argue with the youths, he was barred by the archons." The way in which this is pitched evokes the image of attempted bribery: Aristophanes claimed that Herodotus disseminated an unfavorable image of the Thebans because they were unwilling to pay him. They actually went as far as to prevent him from talking to, let alone instructing, the youths in the city.[1]

The passage has naturally caught the critical eye of scholarship, also because of Plutarch's blunt declaration at the beginning of the treatise defending the reputation of his Boiotian ancestors (*De malign. Her.* 1). Plutarch the patriot is at work.[2] Yet the constellation is not improbable. Herodotus had visited Thebes when he saw the notorious Kadmeian *grammata* in the Temple of Apollo Ismenios (5.59; see also 1.52; 1.92). During his stay, he might well have delivered a reading, and of course he would have engaged in conversations with many people in many contexts. It is therefore not impossible that he got into an argument with the archons at one point; Aristophanes, who was a younger contemporary of Herodotus, may have been among the youths in question and have known of the incident from personal experience.[3] Be that as it may, on a minimal interpretation, the fragment indicates three things: that the Persian Wars were a touchy topic in Thebes; that the ruling elites, represented here by the archons, were dismayed by the versions others told about them; and that the Thebans made an attempt to shape and, effectively, to cultivate their own assessment of the war, which in turn they sought to instill in the future generation of citizens. When the Thebans conversed about the Persian invasion, they had a different war in mind than the visitors who came to their city, and many of their fellow Hellenes, for that matter. In the shadow of the Kadmeia, the history of the Persian Wars had its own encoding.

Local encodings of the past were precious to the city-state at all times, because of their overarching importance for the community's core values and self-beliefs. For instance, in the first half of the sixth century BCE, Kleisthenes of Sikyon was said to have put an end to rhapsodic recitals of the Homeric poems since Argos and the Argives played such a prominent role in them; a role that certainly overshadowed that of Sikyon. There was also a tragic choral performance in Sikyon in honor of Adrastos, former ruler over the city, yet of Argive heritage, which Kleisthenes wanted to abolish. To the elites of Sikyon, singing the praises of others appeared to be the wrong message.[4] In nearby Megara, a local parody of the Homeric *Catalogue of Ships* ridiculed the section that claimed that Salamis had been an Athenian possession of old (*Il.* 2.557). According to the Megarian version, the case was turned on its head: some of the core contingents of the Athenians came from Megara—at least this was what the Megarians claimed.[5]

The desire to foster a local discourse environment and position the community in the wide web of Hellenic traditions was particularly pertinent in conversations about mythical origins. We have already noted how legendary tales of descent consolidated prevailing identities of place. Myths of primordial beginnings were both universal and local at the same time: they related to the overarching narrative of Hellenic traditions, and they added local visibility to the storied universe. In mythology, too, the epichoric quality of local traditions didn't end with confinement and a limited radius of persuasiveness. Rather, the local drew on the place as such, its physicality, topography, flora, and fauna, all of which inspired narratives of attachment and meaning. The local itself was therefore a powerful agent in Greek mythology. It provided an interface, in Henri Lefebvre's sense, between space and place (chapter 1).

According to Pausanias, the people of Troizen were among the most unscrupulous in crafting such interfaces; in fact, they were "glorifiers of their own country like no others" (2.30.5). The Greek word for "own country" that is used here, *ta enchōria*, captures both the charge of place and its agency in traditions of belonging. Support for Pausanias's verdict came from the writings of an unknown local historian, presumably an educated member of the city's elite—someone well-versed to speak of epichoric traditions. As we have seen earlier, such traditions were valuable commodities in Pausanias's days, since they linked the local horizon to a world that had grown infinitely larger. In the second century CE, the local elites of Troizen had their own reasons to circulate past traditions that corroborated their social status at home and attracted the attention of people in high places elsewhere. At the same time, their local histories resonated with a cultural heritage that was firmly rooted in the strands of place and time. The anonymous local historian propelled a foundation legend that tied Troizen to land and sea alike. He claimed that a certain Oros was their mythical king, from whom Saron, eponymous hero of the Saronic Gulf, descended. Oros himself was said to be "the first born in the land." He was virtually autochthonous, whereas Saron appeared as the prime mover in the Saronic Gulf.[6]

The mindset attested to in the literary sources is supported by site research. Through the examination of viewsheds in the countryside, recent scholarship has posited a particular visual awareness among the Troizenians. From mountain to coast, their *chōra* was spread out before them. Agriculture, industries, fisheries, and movements of ships all were in full view of the city, instilling a sense of discreteness and entirety.[7] Limited to the pockets along a coastal strip and encircled by multiple regional contestants—Epidauros, Aigina, Hermione—the people of Troizen fostered a special relation with their land, one that was expressed in embodied legends of primordial ownership of the *chōra* and claims for ancestral presence in the gulf region. Pausanias, on the other hand, thought that Oros had not even been a Greek but was of Egyptian origins. It would be eye-opening to know if he had shared his opinion about Oros's foreignness with his local informants at Troizen and, even more so, what their response was.[8]

We thus see that the faux pas committed by Herodotus in Thebes speaks to a broader theme: the claim of the polis to wield authority over the interpretation of its history. Yet the incident also distinguishes itself from mythopoietic conversations, in that it sparked controversy over the most recent past rather than a distant heroic age; many of the families who had fought and suffered losses in the Persian Wars were still around in Thebes. This immediacy of the constellation also provoked a direct and unmistakable response. Authentic or not, the episode plays on the idea that Herodotus had interfered with very basic political world views in Thebes and that such interference was not welcomed.

Incidentally, we detect the same constellation in the writings of the sophist-philosopher Favorinus, a younger contemporary of Plutarch. In his *Corinthian*

Oration, he asserted that Herodotus, upon his visit, brought many "stories (*logoi*) of Corinth" with him. It is unclear what their nature was and where they were performed, and yet, when Herodotus expected to receive some kind of remuneration for his *logoi*—there is no word of a request for bribes—the Corinthians refused on the grounds that they "did not deem it fitting to do business in renown." Only then, in response to the refusal to pay him, did Herodotus devise bad stories about the Corinthians: a prime example being their dubious role in the battle of Salamis.⁹

There are even more perplexities than those with the Theban incident. Favorinus states that the slander about Corinthian fickleness at Salamis was invented by Herodotus as payback because of the failure to receive payment for his *logoi*. Plutarch, too, criticizes Herodotus for unfairness vis-à-vis the Corinthians (*De malign. Her.* 39). But both he and Favorinus pass over in silence Herodotus's own remark that the negative tradition about Corinth was ultimately of Athenian provenance (8.94.3). Authenticity is again not the point. Jessica Priestley (2014) has explored the ways in which Herodotus's *Histories*, from the later fourth century BCE, became both a cultural commodity and a battleground on which cities articulated rich and varied responses to the role in history assigned to them by Herodotus. The point here is that the historical discourses that followed were as diverse, charged, and multi-tiered as conversations over remote mythical genealogies. If the heroic age was a widely connected web of stories that required communal positioning, so too, were conversations about interstate affairs in the immediate past. In their assessment of those affairs, polis societies operated in an auto-referential and sociocentric fashion: auto-referential because their historical traditions clustered around themselves first and foremost, with citizens and ancestors serving as main actors in history and as, almost exclusively, individuals of interest; and sociocentric because their views relied on readings and knowledge systems that were innately inward-looking. They were conceived of, and sanctioned by, the community itself.

We have already learned how cities took measures to foster a regime of truth in the future generation of citizens. If a small town like Mykalessos maintained several *didaskaleia* (chapter 4), cities like Thebes had many more places to cultivate collective convictions and amplify their meaning. In the present chapter we delve into local discourses that emanated from communicative arenas such as these—for instance, from *didaskaleia*, *agorai*, the street, and other locations, in Thebes and elsewhere. The purpose is to see the big picture of Greece through the lens of the local: to narrate Greek history through the prism of countless epichoric worlds. Such an approach is fraught with challenges. More often than not our sources are mute. The quest for local discourses resembles the exploration of dark matter: their existence is clear, yet they become visible only through their interplay with other, more tangible elements. One such element is the creative output of local histories, composed by authors who wrote about the local world of their polis. As we will see, the genre of local historiography, what it does and where its place is in the community, is often misunderstood. Both a mirror of the prioritization of the epichoric horizon and an outlet of corresponding world-views, local historiography is a crown witness of Hellenic localism. We turn to this particular trait of the genre in the first section. The second section weighs in on the discussion of how local the local discourse of the polis actually was. What were the roles of news circulation and formalized modes of communication—for instance, the *proxenia*? Did the omnipresence of news from elsewhere macerate the local reading of the world? In the last section, we immerse ourselves the world of local discourses as such. Disclosing divergent narratives of the Persian Wars as they prevailed in different cities, we shall learn how each of them told their own history, each one imparting meaning, relevance, and truth to those who shared it.

Putting the Local in Local Historiography

Few themes in classical studies suffer as much from preconceived ideas as the topic of local historiography. The orthodox picture was recently summarized by Rosalind Thomas, who observed that the notion of local history writing evokes "images of tiny, footling, or parochial studies which might be of interest perhaps only to the equivalent of a minor local history society" (2014a, 145). Belittling attitudes toward the genre are omnipresent. Emanating from a patriotic desire to acclaim the heroic past of their hometown, the works of the local historians of ancient Greece are typically regarded as intellectually low-key, bogus narrations of the past. Sketching out the past in a dry, year-by-year format and with little thematic coherence, local histories lacked finesse in both skill and style. In this sense, they were a negative counterfoil to the critical inquiries of Herodotus and Thucydides. And compared to the towering invention of universal history by protagonists such as Ephoros and Polybios, polis histories of Phigaleia, Argos, or Thebes appear to have been inspired by, and in turn to have catered to, precisely the sort of "minor local history society" that leaves them with little relevance to ancient audiences and modern scholars alike.

The endurance of the orthodox view owes much to the fact that it goes back to the great pioneer and leading authority in the field, Felix Jacoby (1876–1959). His scholarship has lost nothing of its fascination over time, leaving us with a legacy that is both awe-inspiring and inescapable.[10] Of the 853 authors in his original collection, *Die Fragmente der Griechischen Historiker*, more than half were considered by Jacoby as local or regional historians, whose works include, among others, *Makedonika, Thessalika, Ambrakika, Boiotika*, as well as *Thebaika, Orchomenika*, and *Thespika*; further, *Megarika, Argolika*, and *Sikyonika, Eliaka, Lakonika*, and *Arkadika*; *Attika* and the Atthis—that is the writings of the Atthidographers; in the Aegean, for example, *Naxiaka, Lesbika*, and *Thasiaka*; the local histories of many cities in Asia Minor, among them *Ephesiaka, Milesiaka, Magnetika*; and finally, a high volume of histories of cultural realms beyond the Aegean Sea (*Persika, Indika*). The latter indicate that it is not always easy to draw the line between local histories and works with a somewhat different scope, for instance, in the field of historical geography or ethnography. We should be cautious not to overstretch the idea of a set literary genre, with one narrative template. The high volume of local histories, their wide geographic dissemination, and the long period of time during which they were produced (Jacoby's authors span from the fifth century BCE well into the Roman Imperial Age) suggest that writing history through the lens of place was a ubiquitous practice. Judging from sheer quantity, local history writing was not only an extremely productive exercise but also a very common way to encounter the past.[11]

How this encounter played out, and what local historiography exactly entailed, are more difficult to judge. Jacoby asserted that local history was a form of literature that was "independent of, but connected with, great historiography" (1949, 68). In response to the rising prominence of Herodotus's *Histories*, many cities in the later fifth and fourth centuries BCE made it their goal to provide accounts of their history. At first, the task was absorbed by foreigners. Hellanikos of Lesbos wrote an *Atthis*, an Athenian local history from 683 BCE to the end of the Peloponnesian War, which is the oldest datable example.[12] Soon enough, local historiography became the domain of citizens, with series of local histories often following one another in one and the same city; as each author tried to outdo his predecessors, this also opened the door to all sorts of hyperbole. Because of occasional reference in the sources to the literary output as *hōrographiai*, or local chronicles (from *hōros*, "year"), Jacoby conjectured that many local histories followed the ordering principle of sequential stories or year-by-year accounts, often extrapolated from documentary records such as lists of eponymous officials of the polis, laws, treaties, and festival calendars. This view a priori defined a conceptual rift between local history and "great historiography," with its inherent discursive quality. In turn, the idea of a rift was endorsed by authors from the other side of the great divide. Thucydides had commented, in his typical authoritarian voice, that Hellanikos in his

Atthis had not given much space to some of the most eminent moments in the history of Athens; his treatment was superficial, his chronology flawed (1.97). Scholarship is often quick to piece these verdicts together: the idea of an unsystematic compilation of diverse pieces of evidence and their distillation into chronicles of little analytical skill and less intellectual stride. The uncritical repetition of this view in textbooks paved the way toward the overall conviction that local historiography merits little recognition. In all fairness, however, Jacoby himself had never drawn this summary conclusion.[13]

Scholars have identified various problems that relate to the typical picture, and there has been progress over the past decades. Attempts at a profound revision remain, however, few in number. This is not the place for a full-fledged reassessment either, including discussion of the notorious question of Athenian local histories and their relation to the overall phenomenon.[14] Some aspects of local historiography are, however, too important for our endeavor to be passed over in silence. The first is Jacoby's label *horography* and the narrative form it posits. To begin with, we ought to note that the word *horography* is confusingly close to Ptolemy's *chorography*, the study of place and distance (chapter 1).[15] Jacoby declared, in a succinct manner, that *horography* was a term used in antiquity, yet a brief search of the *Thesaurus Linguae Graecae* shows its usage to be extremely rare. The attested references boil down to less than a handful, and none of them stems from a Classical or Hellenistic background. This paucity alone urges us to caution with how we use the term.[16] As we shall see shortly, judging from the writings of the so-called horographers, the idea of literary annual chronicles does not receive much support from the fragments themselves. The widespread verdict that the surviving texts "generally share a simple style" (Lateiner 2013, 3304) does not live up to the evidence. Jacoby noticed this too, which is why he differentiated horography from bare chronicles and annual records, thus making room for two separate strands of horography, as it were: one more narrative, the other more chronicle-like, hence, *chronography*. In this vein of inquiry, subsequent scholars refined the idea of the chronicle, which was linked to an increasing interest among writers from the later fifth century BCE in scientific tabulation, cataloguing, and the composition of archival lists. Such a reading of the chronicle is very inspiring; it bridges the gap to other intellectual traditions at the time. But we should bear in mind that, effectively, it relegates the chronicle to a subfield amid the overall stratum of local historiography, rather than explaining the nature of the latter as such. Horography is left hollow in such an approach, while the semantics of the chronicle linger on.[17]

The problem is not dissimilar to that of Roman historiography and its "annalistic" tradition, although the term *annales*, "yearbooks," is found far more frequently in the Latin sources than *hōroi* in the Greek. Much like horography, Roman history writing in the Republican period has been considered a genre that was underdeveloped in form and style. Building off annual accounts (e.g., priestly lists and tables of magistrates), the so-called annalistic tradition was believed to follow a template that was at the mercy of its sources and exhausted itself in the uncritical recollection of the evidence. Only recently have scholars drawn attention to the fact that the surviving fragments of Rome's earliest historians do not match up with such a scenario. With writings as lively and, at times, discursive as those of, for instance, Q. Fabius Pictor, the term *annalistic* does no justice to the genre. If anything, the annalistic scheme as it resonates in Livy was owed to the desire to put the institutions of the republic, its annual officeholders in particular, at the center of a narrative that was energized by, and in turn gave interpretative force to, the long duration of the Roman state. It has been argued, therefore, that the term *annalistic* should not be used as a passe-partout for early Roman historiography but be reserved for the few literary subsets to whose form it applies.[18]

Horography follows a similar trajectory. We have seen how horography finds its most essential expression in one subset of local historiography: the chronicle. Beyond this, when the local historians of Greece integrated *hōroi* into their writings, they would have found this a convenient strategy to enhance the claim for authenticity and the authority both of themselves as historians and of their subject matter. The inherently local nature of time reckoning (chapter 4) supported this quest for authenticity and authority. As a synonym for local historiography in general, however, the term *horography* is of dubious value.[19]

The second problem with Jacoby's view that affects our discussion is the nexus between the local historians and Herodotus. Jacoby was presumably right to believe that Herodotus had few written historical narratives at his disposal when he composed his *Histories*; there were no "little Herodotoi" before the Father of History, as he famously put it (1949, 100). Yet, the tables were not bare either. For instance, a few decades before Herodotus, Akousilaos of Argos (*BNJ* 2) had recounted the genealogies of the legendary great houses of Argos. His work concluded with a summary of the events surrounding the Trojan War, which appeared to be an apt end of the Heroic Age. The overall tenor of the narrative honored his native Argos by highlighting its connections with various regions of the Greek world, but the way in which the city and its cults were represented leaves no doubt that the local cosmos of the Argolid was the true theme of the work. Dionysios of Halikarnassos included Akousilaos in his discussion of early Greek historians and said that these writers drew their material mostly from local traditions that had been passed down from generation to generation (*On Thuc.* 7). As was stated by the latest editor of the fragments in *BNJ*, David Toye, there is reason to suggest that Akousilaos employed "certain practices which Herodotus perfected," including source criticism, the rationalization of myth, and narrative flashbacks. So although Akousilaos was no "little Herodotus," when Herodotus visited Argos, he almost certainly learned about his writings, approaches, and narrative techniques.[20]

Since he stresses the origins of many of his sources, it is amply clear that Herodotus gave local traditions a pivotal role in his investigative analysis (Luraghi 2001a). To be sure, the interaction with local informants and traditions was appropriated to Herodotus's overall goal of implementing a greater, universal scheme: that is, the recollection of marvelous deeds of Greeks and barbarians, and an explanation of why they went to war (*Proem*). One of the obvious weaknesses of the traditional view of local historiography and its relation to Herodotus is that it overemphasizes the immediate force this universal scheme had on Greek audiences near and far and, in turn, that it reduces the local discourse to the desire to respond to the authoritative voice of Herodotus. We have already noted the need of city-states in later periods, from the early Hellenistic period in particular, to find their place in the narrative world of Aegean Greece as Herodotus had crafted it. Did such a magnetic force emanate already from Herodotus's inquiries during his traveling years, in the 450s and early 440s BCE? Once the earliest manuscripts of the *Histories* circulated in the later fifth and early fourth centuries, should we assume that the text burdened the citizenries of, for instance, Argos or Thebes with an identity crisis? If Herodotus visited Thebes shortly after the Battle of Koroneia in 447 BCE (see below), it would have been almost natural for the leading elites to have a dismissive attitude toward him. Herodotus, a man in his late thirties at the time, would have pitched his inquiries so that his conversation partners were able to tell "their" story. In the later book version of the *Histories*, this story would become the statement of an implicit informant or the explicit claim of *legousin*—"they say." But during his short stay in the city itself, there is little reason to suggest that Herodotus's visit threw the Thebans into such a crisis of meaning that they launched their own branch of local history-writing in response. They didn't like the stories he told, but the incident most likely ended there.

It is tempting to turn the traditional view on the relation between local histories and Herodotus on its head: with lively conversations between Herodotus and his informants under way, Herodotus's principle method of relating their story (but not necessarily subscribing to it: 7.152) made room for those views to enter—and this meant, to influence—his narrative. For example, in the famous description of a banquet for Persian nobles in Thebes on the eve of the Battle of Plataia, Herodotus says that his account of the dinner conversations relied fully on what he had learned from an Orchomenian oligarch named Thersander (9.16). As we note further below, the circumstances of the dinner were a matter of disagreement not only among various Boiotian cities but also within Thebes itself. So, in the passage in question, the *Histories* followed one local version among many. Herodotus was as much influenced by local historical traditions as local history writing was a reaction to Herodotus.[21] For most of the Classical period, then, it is misleading to consider the relationship between both types of historiography, local and "great," as one that deems the former an inept attempt to catch up with the latter. The idea of a sequential relation undervalues the ways in which both were intertwined. To the Thebans, Megarians, and Argives of the fourth century BCE, the ways in which their local historians told the stories of their communities might have easily appeared as greater, and in any case more meaningful, than the writings of Herodotus or Thucydides.

We have now arrived at a point where we can assess Greek local historiography within the same lively frame of reference that gave rise to it: the world of countless communities whose everyday concerns related to the place they occupied. It is worthwhile to explore how this epichoric trait provided structure, meaning, and authority to the interpretation of the past. Few scholars have taken seriously the capacity of the epichoric backdrop to energize historical conversations.[22] In her examination of Greek time concepts, Katherine Clarke demonstrated how the notion of time in local historiography was critical "in articulating a memorable, . . . high-status past" (2008, 7). Rather than seeing debates about the mythical past as automatically geared toward a romantic embellishment of foundation stories, Clarke illuminates the conditions that allowed for such romanticism in the first place—if this is the right category after all. In their attempt to research the beginnings of their polis, the local historians shouldered the task of establishing a chronological and in most cases also a spatial grid that provided orientation. Drawing a roadmap through time and space, local history enabled communities to navigate through the multiple layers of the past, from the remote *ktisis* period to more recent times and the present day. City history, Clarke concludes, played a decisive role in shaping polis mentalities. Producing images of continuity of time and place, in small and coherent communities, local historiography was both a forceful articulation and a reflection of polis identity.[23]

There are countless examples to illustrate how local historians conversed about the mythical foundations of their hometowns and how these conversations were inspired by claims over polis lands and contested fringes. We already noted how the people of Troizen fostered a *ktisis* legend that tied them to *ta enchōria*. Praxion of Megara (fourth century BCE) related that Athena Skiras, whom the Athenians said was of Eleusinian (hence, Athenian) provenance, had her name from Skiron, a small site along the road from Athens and Megara and in the territory of the latter. There was potential for all sorts of confusion of Skiron, the place, with Skiros, mythical king of Salamis, and Skiron the rogue bandit from Isthmia who tortured people along the Skironian Way to Corinth. The web of legends is impossible to disentangle, but Praxion's local history makes it clear that the Megarians saw Skiron in a particular light: he was one of their earliest kings (see Paus. 1.39.6; Plut., *Thes.* 10), firmly rooted on the Megarian side of the border; and so was the cultural capital that emanated from his legend.[24] In a similar vein, Proxenos of Chalkis, a slightly younger author, related a variant of the foundation legend of his city in his *Chalkidika* that emancipated the Chalkidians from the traditions told by others (*BNJ* 425 F 2, comm.).

The land was an active agent in those narratives. Place served as a backdrop to the narrative, which reverberated in, and was inspired by, features of the polis territory. As an intellectual exercise, local history engaged in spatial narratives whose focus and veracity were determined by the epichoric horizon. Take the case of Dieuchidas of Megara (*BNJ* 485, fourth century BCE) who, in his *Megarika*, dwelled on the physical features of the Megarian countryside, charging the place with historical meaning (F 3 and 8). Given the Megarid's particular location—a local world to the Megarians, yet a crowded highway for everybody else—, such a levy of the land appeared all the more critical. Indeed, it seems to have been a main character trait of the *Megarika* to articulate a special sense of territoriality, one that promoted the city's important role as a facilitator of movement between the Peloponnese and Central Greece.[25] Armenidas of Thebes (*BNJ* 378, late fifth century BCE), whose dialect reveals the local audience at which his history was directed, spoke variously about Theban places: the Kadmeia had a different name in the olden days, "Island of the Blest" (F 5). There was also a site called Seven Pyres, which had a rich narrative pedigree (F 6). Armenidas's younger contemporary Aristophanes explained to his readers the importance of the spring Tilphossa, a site at the western edge of the territory of Haliartos and hence beyond the Theban *chōra*, yet closely intertwined with the legendary cycle of *The Seven Against Thebes*.[26]

The strong link between narrative and place gives us a hint about a more general trait of local historiography—that is, how it extended beyond naïve nostalgia. Local history writing was not a self-surrender to the intellectual finesse of great historiography; on the contrary, it appears to be an authentic expression of Greek polis communities. This quality of the local lens becomes even more obvious when we consider that place isn't reduced to topography. As we have noted earlier, the main signifier of place is its charge with multiple types of meaning (chapter 1). The past of the community and its interaction with the gods are two important indicators, but we have also established that it is advisable to extend the notion of meaning to the broad array of custom and culture, one that embraces the full breadth of human agency. The local historians showed an eager sense to include precisely such local customs, or *nomima*. Amphion of Thespiai (early third century BCE) said that "serious (*meta spoudēs*) dancing by boys took place on Mt. Helikon." The way in which he evidences this (he cites an inscription that explains some of the details) suggests that he commented in depth on the performance, why it mattered, and how it was "serious."[27] In Argos, people followed a distinct mourning ritual, which included the wearing of a particular garment, as Sokrates of Argos (late fourth century) related in his writings: it was white, washed without detergents in pure water only.[28] For Phigaleia, home of star athlete Arrachion (chapter 3), the local historian Harmodios (early third century) related that the ritual practices of public feasting and dancing were subject to a unique script: in accordance with custom (*nomou charin*), cheese and light barley-cake was served in bronze baskets, locally known as *mazonomoi* ("barley-cake-servers"). "They were accustomed in all their meals, and especially among those called *mazones* ("barley-eaters") . . . to pour out more soup for those of the young men who have a more manly appetite and set before them barley-cakes and wheaten loaves. Such a young man was judged to be noble and manly; for among the Phigaleians eating a lot was admired and much talked of" (*BNJ* 319 F 1). Harmodios's *Nomima of the Phigaleians* might have emphasized aspects of drinking and conviviality, although such an angle could have been due to the referencing authority of his work, Athenaios, instead of reflecting Harmodios's privileged interest in this subject. But the more general point is clear: local perspectives on the polis always combined both its history and custom and culture, including, at times, idiosyncrasies in food consumption.[29]

Seeing that the local history was riddled with communal reasoning of all kinds, it comes as no surprise that the assessment of politics was also blended into the mix. Disagreement was both profound and far-reaching. Examples are as varied and manifold as they are for the foundation period. A few references will suffice for our purposes here, all stemming from authors of the fourth century BCE. Hereas of Megara betrays that the Megarians had a very different understanding of the events that led to the loss of their control over the island Salamis than the Athenians did. Daimachos of Plataia, whose hometown was sucked into this controversy due to its close proximity, also related this event. It is unclear if, and if so how, he contradicted the Megarian version, but he certainly refuted the Athenian narrative. Aristotle of Chalkis elaborated on the history of his city in the protracted wars with its neighbor Eretria. Among other pieces of evidence, his analysis included the discussion of a column monument erected in Chalkis, probably in the sixth century BCE, and a local song that was sung in his own times. Both verified his account vis-à-vis those of others.[30] Sokrates of Argos, who has already been introduced, offered a detailed account of the war with Sparta in the early fifth century, including the heroic stand of the Argive women led by the female poet, Telesilla, against the Spartan army (*BNJ* 310 F 6). In Sokrates's history, the narrative of the event was intertwined with references to various sites in the Argive countryside and cultural traditions at the local level, including a festival during which "they gird the women in manly shirts and cloaks and the men in robes and veils of women" and reference to "a law ordering married women having a beard to sleep with their husbands." As so often, it is difficult to discern Sokrates's fragment from its referencing source (Plut. *Mor.* 245c–f), yet the gist of the story is clear. Herodotus also knew of the war between Argos and Sparta and the atrocities committed by king Kleomenes, but his account is written mostly from the Spartan perspective (6.76–83). It doesn't take us much to decide which of the two accounts, that of Sokrates or that of Herodotus, mattered more to the Argives.[31]

Our last example takes us back to Aristophanes. Jacoby's testimonies suggest that his work was entitled *Theban Chronicles* (*BNJ* 379 T 2a/b). We have already seen how the Greek term for chronicle here, *hōros*, was reflective of a narrative strategy that aimed at authority and the claim for authenticity. At the same time, the creation of deep time allowed Aristophanes to put the past into a coherent perspective. Such a technique had strong structuring capacity; again, in Katherine Clarke's words, it "made time for the past" (2008). Aristophanes's work itself was a full-fledged analysis of Theban political history, with a focus on its Boiotian dimension. Fragment 4 discussed events after 457 BCE, when Athenian forces temporarily occupied several Boiotian towns but were driven out by a rebel gang of so-called Orchomenizers after the Battle of Koroneia in 447 (below). In fragment 6, Aristophanes takes his quarrels with Herodotus from fragment 5 to disagreement *in re*: While Herodotus claimed that the Theban commander at Thermopylai was named Leontiades, Aristophanes, drawing on public records in Thebes, said he was Anaxandros. Herodotus, so goes the obvious accusation, didn't get the names right. Scholars have been puzzled over the discrepancy, although the latest editor of Aristophanes in *BNJ*, Albert Schachter, is probably right to observe that we shall never know which, if either, version is true. Veracity is in any case not the point. No matter what Herodotus said about Thermopylai, the Thebans had their own understanding of the campaign. And unlike Herodotus's view—that of an outsider—their version was sanctioned from within. When Aristophanes wrote about his fellow citizens and their ancestors, he not only had access to material evidence to back up his findings, but was himself fully immersed in the local discourse that gave rise to the version he related. Most eminently, this included familiarity and everyday interaction with the main protagonists of polis politics—if the roles of magistrate and historian weren't altogether identical. It has been pointed out by scholars that his general at Thermopylai, Anaxandros, was most likely the grandfather of the Theban commander who aided the Milesians in their revolt of 411 BCE (Thuc. 8.100.3). If the family tree is correct, and the breakdown of generations holds true, then this younger Anaxandros was a contemporary of Aristophanes.[32] Likewise, Hereas of Megara, who told a decidedly Megarian version about the loss of Salamis to Athens (see above), appears to have acted as a *theōros* of his city, whereas his son was awarded the honor of *proxenos* of Delphi. Hence, the family belonged to the highest echelon of Megarian society.[33]

What made Aristophanes's work, and local historiography in general, so convincing, then, was its sociocentric voice, a voice that carried a distinct authority. Scholars have demonstrated how Herodotus's narration is interspersed with enunciative interventions that shape the discourse. Their form and intensity vary throughout: for example, their impact on the audience was particularly strong where he speaks in the first person and situates his information in time and space. Given Herodotus's universal audience, such an "enunciative shift-in" (Claude Calame) was both an entertaining and effective way to assert narrative authority.[34] The local historians operated in a different narrative environment. The fragmentary nature of their writings makes it difficult to trace corresponding narrator/speaker utterances, and the vast geographical and chronological stretch of the material makes it hazardous to subsume a plethora of author shift-ins under one. But the general point is clear. Local authors crafted their texts from diverse pieces of evidence, yet from a fairly homogeneous environment. As writers of history, they were embedded in a local discourse that was propelled by the polis, directed toward the polis, and expressed through commemorative practices that were part and parcel of polis procedures—the keeping of archival lists, festivals, monuments, and so on—all of which lend a pronounced voice to their texts. Local history thus drew on a type of knowingness and complicity that were profoundly different from those of an outsider. This inward-looking perspective allowed the community to find itself in, and connect with, the narrative in a unique way. Extending our earlier assertion that the text was linked to the people and place, local historiography appeared to be what Daniel Tober (2017) has called the "autobiography of society": inspiring authors to capture the cultural memory of their city, this type of autobiography privileged and endorsed both the agency of citizens and their views of the past. In turn, this narrative encounter with the past was validated by the same collective of agents, the body of citizens, who could claim mastery of local ways of expertise and knowing barred to the outsider. We shall return to the mechanics of autobiographical encoding below, when we recreate the discourse environment in Thebes in the post-Persian War period. For now, it suffices to note that Aristophanes's voice was, in all likelihood, more convincing, meaningful, and, effectively, true to the Thebans than anything a great historian had to say.

Global News and Networks, Locally Mediated

Before we turn to concrete examples of local discourse worlds, we ought to revisit briefly the topic of news and the polis. Greek city-states, we have argued throughout this study, were susceptible to a peculiar form of parochialism. How did such prioritization of the local hold up against the rich influx of news, both official and casual information? An answer to this question is not only of immediate importance to our assessment of the local point of view. It also relates back to the more general topic of Hellenic connectivity. The issue of circulating news is critical. As we saw in chapter 1, among the defining traits of a network society is that the high-powered flow of information leads participants to adjust their views according to the mechanics of the network. Merged by a multitude of horizontal ties, time and space shrink into a small, connected world where they inspire the rise of a global mindset. Did the Hellenic web of news exchanges have a comparable effect? As cities maintained institutionalized ties of exchange with poleis and *ethnē* near and far, did this impugn perceptions of the local self? In short, how local was the local discourse?

News traveled quickly, and it spread through various, sometimes unexpected channels. If we believe Plutarch (*Nik.* 30; cf. *Mor.* 509a–c), news about the outcome of the Sicilian expedition first reached Athens in 413 BCE when a stranger (*xenos*) walked into a barbershop in the Piraeus. He chatted away about the defeat, assuming that the Athenians were aware of what had happened. From there, word spread like wildfire, before the couriers from the Athenian fleet arrived.[35] Our messenger didn't necessarily come directly from Sicily. Most likely he would have learned about the Athenian defeat in a nearby shore along the Corinthian Gulf, from where he would have brought the news to Athens. Be that as it may, along the Central Greek corridor, news disseminated swiftly. There was no need for the far-flung network of messengers admired so much by Herodotus in Persia—"nothing mortal moves faster than these" (8.98). Distances were short and travel routes well established, although we should add that there were no long-distance roads for wheeled traffic, and many paths followed river gorges; hence, they were impassible during winter rains. These hinderances notwithstanding, the journey from one city to the next often took a mere hour or two on horseback. Short distances and easy travel led to considerable mobility among all echelons of society, which further enabled the distribution of news. The flow of information was swift on all accounts.[36]

This density of exchange should not automatically lead us to assume a high degree of informedness. News, understood conventionally as new information about recent developments, is measured against the broad picture of background information, that is, the societal knowledge about more generic conditions and constellations. The distinction is important. In one of the few studies on news and society in the Greek world, Sian Lewis (1996) reminded us that, in the absence of an organized system of gathering and disseminating news, there was indeed a plethora of official and unofficial sources that contributed to the flow of information between city-states. On the one hand, this flow provided communities with a robust background knowledge that allowed them to determine their place in the Greek world. It is this kind of circulating information that created the nuts and bolts of the common ties among the Hellenes, their joint customs, genealogies and foundation legends, traditions and beliefs, and so forth, all of which emanated from and were, in turn, endorsed by dense networks of communication. On the other hand, the polyphony of voices led to a persistent mixing and blending, a type of static that complicated the issue of transmission of news with the task of discerning it from hearsay, gossip, and rumor. Receiving and processing news from outside—the local news of others, so to speak—was never a straightforward process, nor was this process in sync between cities. Despite the heavy news traffic, with broadcasts volatile, contingent, or contradictory, there was ample room for miscommunication, uninformedness, and sheer ignorance.

Studies in media communication disentangle the dynamics at play. Highlighting the role of mediation—that is, the social embedding of news in context, translation, interpretation, and representation—the critical paradigm in media studies has advanced the idea that mediation of news is not opposed to communication but constitutive of it. Indeed, John Durham Peters, in his classic *Speaking Into the Air* (1999), has demonstrated that communication is mediation first and foremost, and that communication as such is essentially comprised of all sorts of demeanors that are commonly subsumed under the label of miscommunication: gaps, noises, errors, dropped signals, and so on. More recently, and in open dialogue with the social media revolution under way, the cultural encoding of news has been found to be even more generative of meaning than the actual content that is transmitted; whereas the decoding of this meaning is seen as subject to circumstances that are highly contingent, variable, and again culturally specific. In its most progressive scholarly reading, the process of decoding is considered the one pivotal moment of communication. In this view, the reception and interpretation of news are seen as subject to appropriation by the recipient audience and to the translation into its idiosyncratic discourse environment. In other words, news about others is never about others, but about the local discourse into which it is translated.[37]

Two implications stand out for the study of Classical Greece. The first is that, despite the heavy news traffic, in order for circulating news messages to mean something to the polis, they had to be mediated and decoded, with all variation from static and partiality, and with corresponding degrees of appropriation. For news to be communicable, it had to be translated into the local discourse. As we will see shortly, such translation was subject to all sorts of social dynamics that invited the polis to assert its own interpretative authority.[38] Second, in the specific news environment of Greece, the process of mediation was highly dependent on individual actors and agents, members of the local community who served as relay stations for the transmission of news. Mediation therefore became a complicated process, as it entailed interpretative entities within the community that were categorically separate and often in competition with one another (individuals, groups or factions, the body of citizens), creating a kaleidoscope of oppositions, boundaries, and divisions. At the same time, they were all part of the same local discourse.

The key institution in the processes of exchange and mediation of news was the *proxenia*, although we ought to note quickly that it was not designed to establish a regular news channel between any two or more poleis.[39] We have already seen how guest-friends, *proxenoi*, allowed cities to organize their relations with others; discussion of the corresponding networks weighs in heavily on conversations about connectivity and exchange across the Greek Mediterranean (chapter 1). Here, too, we are well advised to acknowledge that recent studies in the *proxenia* in the Classical and early Hellenistic period suggest a more mundane picture, alerting us that proxenic ties often extended over distances that were much less extensive than Mediterranean-wide network charts wish to insinuate. A vast number of *proxenia* grants were issued over short distances, covering the realm of regions or microregions: for example, Aigina maintained a *proxenos* in Plataia; Tanagra, in Eretria; Chalkis, in Oropos (and vice versa); the cities of Western Lokris, on the opposite shores of the Corinthian Gulf; and so forth.[40]

Due to the diversity of services it entailed, the *proxenia* helped to streamline the movement of goods and ideas. A *proxenos* acted as an anchorperson for visiting citizens from the polis that granted him his honorific status. For instance, he offered hospitality and lodging to visitors, arranged for embassies and delegations to relate to the political authorities, or for individuals to negotiate legal terms and strike economic deals. There is a long scholarly dispute over whether the grant of *proxenia* was motivated by the ethics of social distinction or the exercise of real economic privileges. Most likely, it was both. What is more, throughout their engagements, *proxenoi* vouched both for the identity of the visitors and their trustworthiness: they guaranteed that the visitors' agenda was credible and put forth in honesty. By implication, as key mediators in the exchange with others, guest-friends lent authenticity to visitors and the news they carried with them.[41]

Involvement in the mediating process underlines the ambiguous position in which many guest-friends found themselves. On the one hand, their privileged role in the transmission of news assigned an authenticating quality to the *proxenos*; he was both a news feeder and guarantor of news at the same time. On the other hand, such vouching for the agenda of foreigners was inherently precarious. At times, it required difficult splits between home and away: between agendas, loyalties, and interests. In Plato's *Laws* (642b), the granting city of a *proxenos* is labeled as his second *patria*, or hometown. What is meant here as distinction also captures a dilemma. It is easy to see how intimate association with another city made actors potentially vulnerable. What was generally true for agents of the polis in the outside world—commanders in the field, ambassadors, heralds—was especially true for *proxenoi* in particular. Athenian forensic speech offers flashy examples of how this vulnerability was used, or abused, to vilify guest-friends in the arena of politics.[42] In the absence of diplomatic protection and immunity, the honorific status of *proxenos* called for sure instincts. William Mack has argued that the anatomy of the institution was shaped not so much, let alone exclusively, by formalistic aspects as by an implicit code of conduct. This conduct followed a logic of appropriateness, requiring guest-friends to perform various functions according to local judgment. Adherence to expectations at home rather than legal compulsion, observes Mack, underwrote the obligations that *proxenoi* had and how they met those obligations in practice (2015, 22–24).

It is intriguing to see how the notion of appropriateness shifts the focus from connectivity to the local horizon. To be sure, acting as the official friend of another city came with certain perks—for instance, the right to own property and do business in the granting city, often coupled with tax exemption (*ateleia*). Another perk was the honorific status itself. As cities chose carefully upon whom the honor of *proxenia* was bestowed, holders of a proxeny enjoyed high social prestige; the people of another city had found them notable and worthy of their consideration. These privileges were one thing, the grass route of the polis another. At home, the far-flung privileges of a *proxenos* and corresponding capitals were subject to a different dynamic. It was there that the guest-friend of others was exposed to the pressures of his fellow citizens, where the appropriateness of proxenic conduct was measured according to the local attitudes, sentiments, and moods of the community. In other words, there was "another side of the stone," as Alex McAuley (forthcoming) has labeled it metaphorically, with reference to the hundreds of proxeny decrees that were chiseled in stone *stelai* and erected across the *agorai* of the Greek Mediterranean. This other side was the local context of the *proxenia*, the grounding of the institution and its actors in their everyday environment.

At home, the perks were quickly outweighed by perils. We have already noted in passing how the political discourse in Athens was susceptible to charges directed against individual *proxenoi*. In Pindar's poetry, the proxenic family of the Kleonymidai at Thebes is praised for showing no "loud-voiced arrogance," implying that the display of the same was not only potentially harmful to the concord of the citizens but also to those who showed it.[43] On Thasos, in the early fourth century BCE, a party of at least thirty-four citizens was exiled, including the local Athenian *proxenos*, because they were thought to have taken a stance against the community. We can only conjecture the complexity of events leading up to the expulsion.[44]

Roughly a century earlier, the case of Euthykles of Lokroi Epizephyrioi offers a glimpse at the danger zone in which mediators between inside and outside operated. A pentathletic victor at Olympia in 488 BCE, Euthykles was adored by his fellow citizens for the fame he brought to his hometown. Among other honors, he received a statue that was set up in the agora (chapter 3). According to Kallimachos (frags. 84 and 85 Pfeiffer), the Lokrians chose him as ambassador to go on an unspecified diplomatic mission abroad. In the city of his destination, he was gifted two mules and a cart. Upon his return, the present gave rise to all sorts of suspicion. The Lokrians saw it as a sign of bribery. They condemned Euthykles and threw him into prison, where he died. They even mutilated his statue. Next, a famine befell the city. Puzzled over what to do, the Lokrians sent to Delphi and received the oracle. "When you will hold in honor the one without honor, then you will plough your fields again." The message was understood, and an altar to the former champion was built. Euthykles's restored statue was henceforth honored "like that of Zeus."[45]

Leslie Kurke's discussion of the incident (1993, 152) has brought to light the conflict between two economies of kudos, that of praise from his fellow citizens versus the material prize from away (the cart, beasts of burden). While the former was subject to the will of the people of Lokroi, hence, dirigible and, if need be, revocable, the award from away was beyond local control. As such, the commodity from elsewhere, Kurke explains, was disruptive to the dynamics of kudos at home. Arguably, Euthykles was not a *proxenos* but an envoy; he was the local counterpart in the network of Lokroi's external relations. Nonetheless, he was fully immersed in the mechanics of reciprocity that were so characteristic of the *proxenia*. Such immersion created yet another conflict. His fame as an athlete brought Euthykles significant recognition. Presumably, this is why the Lokrians chose him for the embassy in the first place. We can picture Euthykles, the super athlete, socializing with his hosts, feasting with them in their halls, and, upon his departure, receiving gifts. For an athlete, rubbing shoulders with elites and gift-exchanges were obvious; they were part and parcel of a ritualized form of communication. On a diplomatic mission, however, such behavior was easily deemed to be incompatible with the code of conduct expected at home. Since Euthykles was sent on a political mission, his actions were subject to a different discourse. The conflict between opposite economies of kudos was magnified by a conflation and, effectively, a confusion of roles, which further fueled the suspicion of bribery. The people—all of them (*pantes*)—felt that Euthykles had betrayed them. "Choking with indignation against the rich (*aphneioi*)," the obvious explanation of the gift was that it was received "on the condition to harm the fatherland (*patris*)."[46]

Euthykles of Lokroi perfectly embodies the idea of Hellenic connectivity: a Greek from southern Italy who excelled in Olympia; an ambassador who served as official agent in his city's lively networks. At the end of the day, however, Euthykles was subjected to local sentiments of appropriateness. While his renown away generally enhanced his social status at home, there remained the danger of pushing the dialectics of global fame and local exploits too far. His case reveals how material assets potentially wielded a disruptive force over the local logic of praise. It demonstrates, furthermore, how the role of mediators was complicated by different arenas of agency. In the lived experience of the polis, those economies and agencies were in constant conversation with one another; they existed side-by-side, with the omnipresent potential for collision, or confusion. Rather than assessing the situation carefully and striking a delicate balance between various roles and economies of appreciation, the Lokrians made a vigorous statement. They asserted their full authority over the believed perpetrator: the agenda of his diplomatic mission fell flat, the man was thrown into prison, his actions were deemed to be harmful to the city. If and when push came to shove, there was only one supreme economy of kudos, and this economy was subject to the judgment of the local.

Returning to our initial question about global news flow and local discourses, we arrive at an ambiguous conclusion. In general terms, media studies urge us to caution as we gauge notions and degrees of informedness, especially in cultures of heavy news traffic. As we have seen, news is always the result of mediation: as information travels from one community to another, it is exposed to all sorts of encodings and translations. In the culture-specific variant of Mediterranean Greece, such encodings played out in a rather peculiar way. Visitors to the city might have carried with them news and/or differing points of view; the very nature of Greek political culture made it clear to everyone that there were countless stories out there. But this did not necessarily undermine local readings. Much as in the case of Herodotus's visit to Thebes, the arrival of an outside voice hardly altered prevailing views in the community; if anything, it seems to have provoked a counter-reaction, a robust reassertion of how the polis saw the world and its place in it. Such impenetrability was also true for the most obvious network of news exchanges, that of the *proxenoi*. Frequent references to the difficulties and dangers that *proxenoi* and other news agents experienced in their hometowns leave us wondering about the vertical depth of the Greek network mentality and the force it wielded over the local cosmos. Everything was entangled, but the discourse environment of the polis was also a firm bastion of local appropriateness and interpretive authority.

Three Persian Wars

As we have seen in the previous chapters, the local is a domain that informs how people think about the world. Referring to the materiality of place—its structures, monuments, and topographical distinctions—Maurice Halbwachs has described this physical dimension of place as the *cadre materiel* where social memories dwell and, by extension, local regimes of truth are negotiated. In ancient Greece, this inherent quality of place was magnified by its intimate association with a high-powered group of people, the *politai* or citizens, however defined in the political organization of the polis. The citizens were both the agents and assessors of communal affairs. At the juncture of past and present, they were the bearers of the polis's collective memory and its keepers in the future. This strong pull toward the inner core of citizen-society makes it notoriously difficult to strike the narrative balance between Greek polis histories and Greek history in general.

Nothing speaks more clearly to this challenge than the Persian Wars. It has long been recognized that the events on the battlefield were subject to political fragmentation. Also, profound differences in the ways the Persian Wars was subsequently remembered have been noted by many. But the verdict of atomization alone hardly accounts for the full force of commemorative localism in ancient Greece, nor does it spell out the consequences for our understanding of Greek political culture.

The basic configuration is well known, so a quick survey suffices. On the eve of the Persian invasion, the Greek cities were neither unanimous in their response to the impending threat nor united. Each polis formulated a stance based on a complicated set of local determinants and individual needs rather than a universal goal. Victory on the battlefields was sweet, but it didn't settle existing discordances. In Simonides's *Plataia Elegy*, composed in 478 or 477 BCE, less than two years after the hostilities, the achievement of averting "from Hellas the day of servitude" (frag. eleg. 11 W^2 26) is portrayed as a decidedly Spartan accomplishment. In the opening lines, the poem highlights the epic quality of the Battle of Plataia, the gravity of which is equated with that of the Trojan War. As the text unfolds, this universal quality of the battle is intertwined with Spartan claims for leadership. The elegy assigns the Spartans not only an elevated position among the Greeks, but it intermingles the fate of both, Spartans and Greeks, in an indissoluble manner.[47]

Such a rendering of Plataia, and of the Persian War in general, resonated poorly with others. When the allies dedicated a victory monument to Apollo at Delphi, the initial inscription, again written in the interest of showcasing Spartan accomplishments first and foremost, had to be removed and replaced with something more consensual.[48] The subsequent compromise, chiseled in the lower sections of the interlaced snakes of the famous Serpent Column, commences with these plain words: "The following fought the war" (M&L 27), followed by a list of thirty-one allies headed by Sparta, Athens, and Corinth. As the list moves on, the hierarchy most likely reflected the contributions (manpower or cash, or both) made by each community. A similar engraved offering was dedicated at Olympia (Paus. 5.23, listing twenty-seven allies). Neither monument quantified the contributions to the war, nor did any of the cities receive explicit praise for anything. Also, no reference to individual battles or to the (fluctuating) membership of the Hellenic alliance was made, obviously to avoid quarrels over who joined when; we note that the alliance as such isn't mentioned in the text either. The Serpent Column is typically understood as a dedication that attests to the collective spirit of the Hellenes; it has been labeled "the victory monument of all victory monuments" (Cartledge 2013). Yet its symbolic language and inscription also communicate the idea of fragmentation: the stark condensation and brevity of the text, both the result of quarrels over the very basic war narrative, are unmistakable reminders of the political and memorial fragmentation among the Greeks.[49]

Each city had its own way to converse about and commemorate what had happened. To be sure, there was a common dedication on the battlefield outside of Plataia, a sanctuary in honor of Zeus Eleutherios, which was erected from collective funds of the alliance. The pentameter inscription on its altar survives in the *Anthologia Graeca*; Plutarch's partial citation of the inscription deviates from the *Anthologia* only slightly. The text boasts that "the Hellenes with the mighty force of their hands . . . expelled the Persians" and "for the liberated Greece built the Altar of Zeus Eleutherios."[50] Unlike their dedication at Delphi, at the one near Plataia, the allies wanted to emphasize the notion of a concerted, or Panhellenic, action—despite the fact that the dedicands hardly represented "the Hellenes" as a whole in any grounded sense. In light of such sublime praise of togetherness, we might not be surprised to see that many of the allies also dedicated individual victory monuments in close vicinity to the altar, which allowed them to inscribe their names into the topography of the battlefield. The Spartans erected three tombs on site (one for their fallen priests, one for the Spartan warriors, one for the helots); the Athenians and Tegeans each erected one; the Megarians and Phliasians created a joint mound in which their dead were buried (Hdt. 9.85). The Plataians, too, built a tumulus with several grave stelai, to which they led an annual procession in honor of the dead. The ritual was also designed to celebrate "the men who had died for the freedom of the Hellenes," yet the heroic deeds of their ancestors were remembered and the commemorative practices performed in a genuinely local festival. Including age cohorts of young men (*neaniskoi*) as well as a local magistrate, whose dress code and ceremonial function were typically local, the festival epitomized the cultural traditions nourished by the citizens of Plataia.[51]

Each city commemorated its involvement in the Persian Wars at a different moment in the course of its festival calendar (see chapter 4). In Plataia, celebrations took place on 16 Alalkomenios (late October, November). In Athens, the Battle of Plataia was remembered on 3 Boëdromion (September or early October); in Sparta, as part of an annual Epitaphios in honor of Pausanias. In Megara, celebrations were held on an unknown date and continued for several centuries.[52]

We detect here the same inherent tension between local and universal commemorative practices that we have encountered earlier. Bernd Steinbock argued that the city-states of the Classical period engaged in "perpetual 'memory wars'" (2013, 87). Memorializing military achievements through monumental dedications, thanks offerings, or devotions of spoils, both in local sanctuaries and in Panhellenic shrines, city-states eagerly created material memory markers of their achievements in war. In both spheres, and before divergent audiences, these dedications filled the religious space of the sanctuary with a particular type of meaning. As much as this meaning was energized by pride and distinction, it was also fueled by persistent competition with others—hence Steinbock's "memory wars." When we attempt to unravel this sentiment, we ought to bear in mind that its expressions were usually surrounded by ritual practices and, hence, supported by a depth of emotion (see below). It is easy to see, for instance, how commemorative festivals shaped narratives that were both charged and self-evident at the same time. From the memorial turn, we learn how corresponding views of the past forged strong ties to the present, how those ties wielded an impact over the lived environment, and how they governed the assessment of the world writ large. From this perspective, then, in their historical encounter with the Persian War, no two cities had the same Persian War in mind. The differences were not only those of perspective. Demarcated by Halbwachs's *cadre materiel*, they were deeply rooted in place.[53]

The examples of Aigina and Argos, neighbors across the Saronic Gulf, illustrate the case. We don't know when or how the Aiginetans celebrated their participation in the Persian Wars, but we would not be mistaken to think that the celebration, itself most likely the epitome of a broader ritual discourse, was a forceful show of self-confidence and pride. Their island's location in the heart of the Saronic Gulf put the Aiginetans on a distinct trajectory. Proximity to Athens, the claims of which for hegemony over the bay area were too conspicuous to be ignored, was always a challenge. Aigina responded to this by establishing itself as a commercial nexus in the Saronic Gulf and across the pathways to Central Greece and the Peloponnese. Among the earliest poleis that circulated coins from c. 580 BCE, Aigina's weight standards gained significant prominence in the regional economy of the gulf, which further expanded its commanding position there.[54] Soon enough, the influx of wealth from outside allowed the local elites, the famous Aiakids, to overcome the social and political constraints of a genuine city-state. Geoffrey de Ste. Croix (2004) reminded us that the Aiakids were not necessarily a mercantile aristocracy in the strict sense of the word. Like any other class oligarchy in Greece, they drew revenue from large-scale landed property that added to the wealth accumulated from trade. All the while, the combination of both strands of income, with changing proportions over time, made Aigina a special case. Indeed, the island polis became what was labeled an "outlier" of the usual polis and *chōra* relation (Figueira 2016, 39), which highlights the Aiginetan *Sonderweg*. Guarantors of Aigina's way of life, the authority of the Aiakids wasn't challenged on the island for a very long time. In the 480s BCE, a certain Nikodromos plotted to hand over the island to Athens. The details of the unsuccessful attempt are obscure. According to Herodotus, seven hundred people were exiled (if we trust that number), and the rule of the Aiakids was secured.[55]

When Xerxes's campaign train hit Central Greece, this was not only a threat but also an opportunity for the Aiakids to rise to the occasion. The Aiginetans rank sixth on the Serpent Column, so their contribution was considerable. Herodotus claims that the burial mound on the battlefield of Plataia was built only about ten years after the event by their *proxenos* at Plataia, a certain Kleades (9.85.3); Aigina's hoplite contingent at Plataia was five hundred strong. There was a rush to erect tombs on the battlefield immediately after the campaign, as the lack of a monument might have suggested "shameful absence from the battle" (Hdt. 9.85.3). Such a race for visual presence at Plataia made it not only desirable for the Aiginetans to act, but necessary, if they really hadn't already done so. Indeed, if Herodotus's inquiry about the tomb was correct, then it is difficult to see why the Aiginetans missed out on setting up their monument in the first round of dedications.

The Aiakids immersed themselves in the narrative of success. We have already learned about some of their governing self-beliefs (chapter 3). The descendants of Zeus and Aigina, a river nymph, the Aiakids were living proof of Aiginetan autochthony: at the behest of Aiakos, Zeus had metamorphosed the island people from ants (see Hellanikos *BNJ* 323a F 27). To the ruling elites, victory over Persia was a powerful tool of self-aggrandizement. In the odes commissioned from Pindar for their young athletes, the Aiakids are hailed "for their shining excellence" (*Nem.* 7.59; variously dated). In *Isthmian* 5.46–50, their guardianship over the city is complemented, rather than disputed, by reference to the Aiginetan sailors who "upheld the city of Ajax" (47–49) in the Battle of Salamis—clearly a local response to traditions that credited the Athenians only with the successful outcome of the campaign. The same goes for *Isthmian* 8, which repeatedly echoes Aiginetan contributions to the liberation from "giant grieves" (7) and the removal of "the stone of Tantalus, . . . a task beyond daring set for Greece" (10–11). Composed in 478 BCE, the ode heralded the sentiments of the elites, who were eager to showcase their role in the defeat of the menace. We sense here how this outlier elite led the public discourse. In the words of Anne Pippin Burnett, "The story-tellers of Aigina began very early to patch together a mythic cloak, a combination of borrowed Aiakid traditions with basic local legend, which should lend a distinguishing identity to the island lords" (2005, 17). Success in the Persian Wars added to this "cloak." For the Aiakids, it provided a unique opportunity to promote their self-esteem, something that validated the social order of their local world.

Some ten nautical miles from Aigina to the west, on the shores of the Saronic Gulf in the territory of Argos, the Persian Wars played little if any role in the local discourse. The Argives had not supported the Greek alliance, but they had not supported the Persian cause either. This neutral stance gave rise to narratives of suspicion; Herodotus said these were free-floating "among Hellas" (7.150.1). In the less scurvy version, some Greeks (mostly Athenians, as Herodotus assures us, disclosing the names of his sources) conjectured that Xerxes had sent a messenger to Argos prior to this invasion. If the Argives held aloof from the upcoming conflict, they would be rewarded richly in the aftermath of the event (7.150). Another account, reported two chapters later, explicitly claimed that the Argives were responsible for the Persian invasion. In light of their recent desperate plight in the war against Sparta, they allegedly had invited the Persians to Greece to improve their situation in the Peloponnese (7.152).

The Argives had their own understanding of what had happened. Curiously enough, their point of view is also related by Herodotus. A few years before the Persian Wars, in about 494, they suffered a defeat by Sparta in the Battle of Sepeia that was smashing and traumatic. Nearly six thousand men fell, some of them burned alive by the Spartans in a sacred grove (Hdt. 6.75–81). With the largest portion of their citizen body dead, the Argives sent messengers to Delphi shortly before 480 BCE to seek oracular advice in case they were drawn into the vortex of war with Persia. By the time the Hellenic Alliance asked for their assistance, on the eve of Thermopylai, they had already pondered their response, which was sanctioned by Apollo. Despite Delphi's warnings, they were willing to join the Hellenes on two conditions: that they obtained a truce with Sparta, and that the Spartans shared the supreme command in war with them. Both conditions were fueled by Argos's vital desire to safeguard its integrity as an independent polis in the aftermath of Sepeia. Herodotus's high number of fallen citizens at Sepeia might be suspicious, but the overall picture appears clear. The battle threw Argos into an existential crisis, years before the Persians arrived on the horizon. At the time when the Hellenes sought their support against Xerxes, the Argives had already hit rock-bottom. From their perspective, the situation called for a choice between the lesser of two evils, Sparta and Persia. Given the Sepeia experience, the former must have appeared more dangerous than the latter. The Spartans, for their part, were coldhearted about the requested truce, although they eventually conceded to offer the Argives a corresponding arrangement. But the demand for a shared command was of a different caliber. When the Argives were denied the request, their negotiations with the Hellenes fell flat; hence, the path to Argive neutrality.[56]

With at least three versions of how Argive neutrality came into being available to him, Herodotus took the incident as an opportunity to explain his approach toward divergent source traditions. Indeed, the Argive affair provided room for one of Herodotus's great historiographical digressions. Herodotus famously remarked that he was unable to authenticate any one of these versions: "My business is to report what people say but I am by no means bound to believe it" (7.152.3). The quest for authenticity is futile; we are well advised to follow Herodotus's verdict. To the Argives, and this is what concerns us here, their own version was the one that mattered.

In the midst of a global crisis, they based their judgment on local authenticity. The councilors who received the representatives of the Hellenic Alliance were in all likelihood similar, if not the identical, to the group of citizens who had sent to the Pythia for oracular advice before. One generation later, their sons told the story to Herodotus on his visit to the city. To the Argives, their history was thus validated by individuals who were both the lead actors of events and the keepers of subsequent memories. The reasoning, too, was thoroughly local. In light of Sepeia, the Argives followed the simple but obvious logic "to give their sons a fair chance of growing up during enough peace" (7.149).

It was remarked in scholarship that Argos did extremely well in the post–Persian Wars period. Successively, Argos took hold of the towns of the surrounding countryside, including two active members of the former Hellenic Alliance, Mycenae and Tiryns, thus restoring the legacy of its heroic past. With the Argolid gradually uniting under the control of the Larissa, the gain of Kleonai, about twenty kilometers north, also brought the presidency over the Nemean Games. In the 460s BCE, an alliance with Athens was struck and, c. 451/50, peace with Sparta. The external consolidation was complemented by a vibrant cultural scene: the local school of sculptors reached its maximum influence with the works of Phidias and Polykleitos (mid-fifth century), both students of Ageladas of Argos. From 472 BCE, champions from Argos appear for the first time in the victory lists from Olympia.[57] In the realm of public administration, the city witnessed the rise of a distinct political organization, a democracy that worked on the basis of two councils, a *bola* and "the 80," which gave Argos a unique organizational outlook.[58] Little is known about Argive self-views during those decades of boom, but it is intriguing to see how unperturbed the city was by the Persian Wars. Argos was on its own curve of reasoning, one that was determined by the cataclysm of 494 BCE—and by a thoughtful response to the problems this had brought to the city.

Moving north from Argos across the Isthmus, we find that the people of Megara had a rather extraordinary perception of the Persian Wars. In a recent volume that looks at Greek history through the local lens of Megara (Beck and Smith 2018), the various contributions recreate the discourse environment of the city. Exploring "what it means to be from Megara," the authors trace the governing tenets and themes that shaped the Megarians' assessment of the world. From the Megarian perspective, a different picture of the Persian Wars surfaces. The city found itself in a grim situation after Thermopylai. Fear of an invasion of their territory was real (see Hdt. 8.71.1; 9.14). Insistence on a military strategy that would offer the Megarians protection from the enemy, fueled by the fear of annihilation, documents a decidedly local reading of the conflict. Between Alkathoos and Karia, the city's two acropoleis, the people of Megara developed their own stance regarding Xerxes's invasion.[59]

The surviving pieces of the Megarian tradition give us a hunch about how this stance was memorialized in retrospect. In his examination of the two Persian War poems of the Theognidean corpus (757–64, 773–82), David Yates (2018) restores a war narrative that is Megarian not simply because it cites the mythology, topography, and history of the city. Rather, it betrays a specific way of understanding the events on the battlefield. Yates identifies two main themes, both atypical of the way Greek cities saw and remembered their roles in the Persian Wars: that is, fear and discord. To be sure, heroic memories of their three thousand soldiers on the battlefield of Plataia were part of the story; Megara ranked seventh on the Serpent Column. The fallen soldiers were brought home and buried within the city (Paus. 1.43.2–3), where they were honored with sacrifices as heroes; we have already noted that the corresponding polis festival was celebrated well into the common era.[60] Yet the war also reminded the Megarians of the overall vulnerability of "this city of ours" (782), as the singer implores his audience toward the end of the second poem, now widely associated with the tense period between the battles of Thermopylai and Plataia. Seeing that the poem was added to the Theognidean corpus, we would assert that it had formidable purchase at Megara in the decades after the war. It captures both the mood at the time of Xerxes's invasion and the way this mood was henceforth remembered.[61]

In the opening line, Apollo is evoked as past benefactor of the city. His association with Alkathous, mythical founding father of Megara, makes it obvious that the god is called upon "to keep now away the arrogant army of the Persians from this city" (Thgn. 675–76), not from Hellas overall. Illustrious hecatombs are promised in return. Protection from the enemy will allow the

Megarians "to take pleasure in the lyre and lovely abundance, in the dances and sounds of paians around your altar" (678–79). Then comes the critical verdict. "For I am truly afraid when I see the stupidity and destructive discord (*stasis laophthoros*) of the Greeks" (680–81). The opposition is one of stark contrast, engrained in two possible futures of Megara: either the city will enjoy delightful celebrations next spring, or it will lie in ruins. Apollo alone might graciously decide their fate, the poem concludes by means of a ring composition, praising his role as protector of Megara in the final line.[62]

The frame of reference evinces a clear focus on the city, its urban topography (Apollo's altar, the dance ground), local cultural traditions (song, dance), and the countryside ("lovely abundance," *scil.*, of agricultural produce). The war put all of these in jeopardy.[63] Social and political realities had always exposed the Megarians to the aspirations of others. We have already noted that the loss of Salamis in the early sixth century BCE left deep, if not traumatic, marks on Megarian self-perceptions. With this came a special sense of territoriality, availing itself of the city's intermediary position between the Peloponnese and the rest of peninsular Greece (see above). The Persian Wars were a powerful—and painful—reminder of the volatile constellation into which they were placed. In fact, pushing the Megarians to the brink of invasion and, consequently, ruinous defeat must have magnified the sentiment of fear—a deep rooted angst that the Megarians were once again too powerless to sway the outcome of a war in their favor, while the Hellenes were too caught up in discord to resolve their misery. At Megara, then, the voice of valor and Panhellenic veneration was intermingled with local concerns, concerns that were in themselves informed by a long-lasting history of exposure and impotence. No matter how proud they were of their hoplite contingents, the Persian Wars taught the Megarians a lesson in fear and anxiety, one that was deeply entrenched in the local discourse over time.[64]

Yet Another Persian War

In August 479 BCE, Megara's most gruesome fears came true. The campaign at Plataia turned into a cataclysmic experience. When the battle was over and the Megarian troops departed from the plain, the Thebans caught sight of them. Charging them on horseback, they fell upon the defenseless Megarians. In the stampede that followed, the Thebans cut down six hundred men. Many more were wounded and barely managed to escape to the lower slopes of Mt. Kithairon, where the cavalry of the enemy was ineffective (Hdt. 9.69). Two chapters earlier, in 9.67, Herodotus leaves no doubt about the Theban motives behind these atrocities. While most Hellenes who fought in the Persian camp did so in a lukewarm manner, the Thebans "were keen to fight and not play the coward." The way in which this is voiced, combined with the glaring depiction of the Megarian massacre a few lines later, supports our initial impression that Herodotus presented Thebes in an unfavorable light. At the beginning of this chapter, we learned that this anti-Theban stance related somehow back to Herodotus's visit to the city. It is now time to revisit the issue and see what Herodotus actually said about the medism of Thebes. From there, we proceed to establish how the Thebans saw the affair. Our attempt to understand their point of view is supported by a surprisingly broad base of sources. Our tracing of the local discourse at Thebes therefore bears in many ways an exemplary character.

First, Herodotus. His account became formative for all other ancient traditions on the medism of Thebes. Incidentally, he also was the one who introduced the term "siding with the Mede" (*mēdizein*) into Greek literature, where it became so fatefully entangled with the city of Thebes.[65] The motif runs through several sections of the *Histories*. To orient ourselves, a brief recollection is in order.

In book 7, which relates the campaign at Thermopylai, Herodotus writes that a Theban contingent of four hundred men served under Leonidas's command. The reason for the inclusion of troops from Thebes was to test their loyalties, since "the Thebans were strongly suspected of Persian sympathies." For although the Thebans sent a detachment, "their sympathies nonetheless lay with the enemy" (7.205). A few chapters later (7.222), the Thebans are labeled as hostages of Leonidas, present at Thermopylai against their will. Consequently, once the Greek forces were overpowered, the Thebans "approached the enemy with outstretched hands, crying out that in their zeal for the Persian interest they had been among the first to give earth and water to the king, and had no share in the responsibility for the injury done him, because they had come to Thermopylai against their will" (7.233).

Herodotus returns to the motive of Theban ingratiation in the opening sections of book 9 (9.2), when the Thebans press Mardonios to make Boiotia his base camp for the attack on Athens and offer secret advice on how to subjugate all of Hellas. After describing a thriving banquet at Thebes hosted by a certain Attaginos to celebrate the alliance between the Theban aristocracy and the Persian nobility (9.16), the theme next resumes during the Battle of Plataia, when the Thebans are said to have "fought so hard that three hundred of their best and bravest men were killed." Meanwhile, the Boiotian cavalry "did good service to the [Persian] fugitives, . . . acting as a screen between their friends and the pursuing Greeks" (9.67–68). Although the battle is lost, the Theban cavalry, under the command of Asopodoros, son of Timandros, delivers the aforementioned blow to scattered units of Megarians and also Phliasians (9.69). Finally, once the Greeks have buried their dead, they turn to Thebes to besiege the city, issuing a "demand for the surrender of the traitors" (9.87). After twenty days of resistance, the Thebans agree to the terms of surrender. One of the leading figures, Attaginos, makes a cowardly escape, while others "expected to get a chance to defend themselves and hoped, in that case, to secure acquittal by bribery" (9.88). But, contrary to their expectations, Pausanias escorted the Thebans to Corinth and had them executed, presumably following a trial held before representatives of the Hellenic League.

It is a truism to note that the passages assembled here constitute a narrative rather than a historical checklist. This aspect does not always receive full attention. Narrative and event are not mutually exclusive of one another; both are inextricably entwined, and attempts to disentangle one from the other, and hence to present the "facts" independently from the narrative, are futile. Hayden White (1987) has famously argued that the primary carrier of historical writing and historical knowledge in general is the linguistic form in which both are clothed. This view has clearly become the new benchmark, although it ought not undermine the existence of basic epistemological differences in the approach to our sources: that is, whether our examination is driven by discourse analysis or the attempt to trace historical outlines, in Ranke's time-honored words, *wie es eigentlich gewesen ist*—always bearing in mind that Ranke's realness is a phantom.

Herodotus's story on the medism of Thebes is a perfect example. His account is usually taken at face value on the role of Thebes in the Persian Wars: Thebes medized, and these are the facts. All the while, Herodotus's account is charged with personal opinions that clearly discount the authenticity of his narrative. For instance, the picturesque banquet at Attaginos's house (9.15.4–16.5) is clearly a stereotypical depiction of a Greek symposium scene, with little historical veracity to it. Both the setting and the speeches betray a moralizing agenda, mingled with philosophical notions on fate and the brevity of life. It would be high-handed to declare the banquet not historical, but it is safe to assert that the detailing of the story, as on so many other occasions, was Herodotus's invention.[66]

To Herodotus's audience, on the other hand, the banquet was a reality. Originating from a learned display of inquiry and charged with highly individualistic sentiments and beliefs, Herodotus's work became the authoritative voice on the history of the Persian Wars. From the fourth century BCE, it fostered a narrative that was both widespread and widely accepted throughout the Greek world. For historians after him, the *Histories* marked the inevitable point of reference, and they almost certainly shaped widespread beliefs about the Persian Wars era. In this sense, the *Histories* offer exciting glimpses on how, for instance, the role of Thebes during the campaigns of 480 and 479 BCE was perceived by many Greeks. It should be noted, then, that the *Histories* shed as much light on popular constructions of history in Classical Greece as they do on the understanding of actual campaigns.

There is no doubt that the Herodotean narrative was harmful to Thebes. Although the account was at times contradictory in itself, the *Histories* presented a cut-and-dried image of Theban medism: driven by a general sense of pro-Persian sentiments and hatred for Athens, the Thebans were "staunch medizers and eager participants in the war" (9.40). On the battlefield, this was revealed in an almost overambitious zeal to do as much harm to the forces of the Hellenic League as possible; hence the strike against scattered Greek forces after the Persian defeat at Plataia. No matter how complicated the chain of events "really" was—we return to this below—Herodotus's tradition on the campaigns from Thermopylai to Plataia presented a thorny legacy for the Thebans.[67]

What was the emic perspective? Pindar's poetry, itself a unique body of evidence, offers a glimpse at the situation in Thebes in the early months after the surrender to the Hellenic League. In *Isthmian* 8, Pindar celebrates the victory of Kleandros of Aigina in the boy's pankration in the Games at Nemea. The ode does not seem to have been composed much later than 477 BCE—in the following year at the latest. Since Pindar, the Theban, praised Aigina, although both cities had recently fought against each other at Plataia, the poet justifies his composition with reference to their common namesake nymphs, born as twin daughters of Asopos.[68]

The ode reflects a mingled feeling of sorrow for the role of Thebes in the Persian Wars and of joy at the liberation of Greece. It states, "from above our heads some god has turned aside that stone of Tantalus, a weight Hellas could never dare. Now the terror (*deima*) has gone by" (lines 9–12). The ode then continues to praise the healing force of freedom (*eleutheria*), which straightens the "crooked way of life" (lines 14–15). The apologetic tenor illustrates redemption after a period of "terror," which seems to refer to the past threat of Persian domination. But the passage is ambiguous; it allows for Aiginetan or Theban connections, or both. With references to "great sorrows" (line 6) and "pain" (line 7), "ills" (line 7) and "toil" (line 8), the ode almost certainly mirrors the grief of the Aiginetans, who had lost so many men in the Persian Wars. At the same time, it airs a sense of disaffection with Theban politics in recent years. As such, the poem alludes to a certain degree of apprehension, maybe even a state of disarray at Thebes.[69]

It is easy to see how the Thebans, in the year following the punishment of the ringleaders of medism, would have been distressed about what had happened. Some of the most ardent advocates for medism were killed or executed; others had chosen exile; yet others, members of the ruling oligarchic elite, would have continued to participate in the governance of the city. So, by the time of the ode, the Thebans must have felt uncertain about how to deal with their troubled past; the substance of how the legacy of medism would shape their discourse in the future was yet unclear. Both the immediate consequences (the execution of a few men notwithstanding) and the long-term implications were open to negotiation. Pindar's poem tells us that the Theban assessment of the Persian War had only just begun.[70]

More explicit responses came a generation later. We have already seen how the Theban historian Aristophanes, in all likelihood a younger contemporary of Herodotus, voiced a different point of view: Herodotus, he argued, disseminated an unfavorable image of the Thebans because they were unwilling to pay him (F 5); specifically, Herodotus didn't even get the name of the Theban commander at Thermopylai right (F 6). Herodotus might have been a crook to the Thebans, but hazy allegations of bribery and the wrong name of a general were hardly strong enough arguments to alleviate the legacy of medism.

Later evidence indicates that the discourse was indeed more complex. Thucydides reveals some of the guiding motives. In his work, the topic is embedded in the recollection of hostile relations between Thebes, Athens, and Plataia in the first years of the Peloponnesian War. Again, a brief review of the narrative is in order. Beginning in 2.2, Thucydides recounts the Theban attack on Plataia in times of peace. After the Thebans entered the city, the boiotarchs assembled the Plataians in the agora, demanding that they break their alliance with Athens and inviting the Plataians "to resume their traditional place in the common *patria* of all Boiotians" (2.2.4). When the Plataians learn that the Theban force was only some three hundred strong, they turn against the intruders and slaughter the majority of them (2.3-4). With Athenian support, the Plataians withstand a series of Theban attacks (2.5-6), but when the Thebans gain support from Peloponnesian forces the following year (2.71), the tides turn against Plataia. In an attempt to avert impending raids on their land, the Plataians appeal to the Spartans, arguing that the attack was unjust and conducted in a manner unworthy of them as well as their fathers. We have already discussed the semantic charge of the Plataian appeal, which resonates with deep sentiments of epichoric attachment (see chapter 4). The Spartan regent, Pausanias, the Plataians claim, had restored their autonomy in return for their services in the Persian Wars, a grant that was accompanied by sacrifices and public oaths. The Plataian plea falls on deaf ears, and fighting ensues between both parties, in the course of which the Spartans turn to siegecraft (2.72–78). In 427, Plataia surrenders (3.52), and a trial before five Spartan judges is staged in the agora to inquire whether the Plataians had rendered any good services to the Spartans and their allies in the present war. The Plataians respond that they had helped the Spartans against both the Persians and the helots (3.54). When the Spartans dismiss this reference, the Plataians are left with no choice but to surrender (3.59).

At this point, the Thebans request permission to speak (3.60): "After we [the Thebans] had settled the rest of Boiotia and had occupied Plataia and other places of which we got possession by driving out a mixed population, the Plataians disdained to submit to our leadership, . . . and separating themselves from the Boiotians and breaking away from the customs of our fathers went over to the Athenians." (3.61) Next the Thebans address the subject of medism, a charge that was put on the table by the Plataians earlier (3.54.3; 3.56.4). "Consider the circumstances under which we . . . acted as we did. In those days our city was not governed by an oligarchy which granted equal justice (*oligarchia isonomos*) nor yet a democracy; affairs were in the hands of a small group of men, the form which is most opposed to law and the best regulated polity, most allied to a tyranny" (3.62.3). Once the Persians had departed and Thebes "returned to a lawful government" (3.62.5), its policy couldn't have been more different. For "when the Athenians attacked Hellas and endeavored to subjugate our country, . . . did we not fight and conquer at Koroneia and liberate Boiotia, and do we not now actively contribute to the liberation of the rest" (3.62.5)? This opens a set of charges directed at the Athenians, who, as the Thebans reiterate, were "endeavoring to enslave Hellas" (3.63.3). The Plataians were partners in this crime, deliberately so and by free choice. "Of our unwilling medism and your willful atticizing, this, then, is our explanation." (3.64) Wrapping up their case, the Thebans stress again their most immediate charge against the Plataians, which was their slaughtering of the Thebans who had entered their city in 431 (3.66). In doing so, the Plataians killed a particular group of men—the very men whose fathers died at Koroneia when Boiotia was brought over to the Spartan camp (3.67). The account ends with the condemnation of the Plataians and the destruction of their city (3.68).

The Plataian Debate, along with that concerning Mytilene (3.37–50), is a key moment in this section of Thucydides's work. Thucydides deals with these debates in great detail and with much careful reflection. Above all, the arguments put forth by the various parties reveal some of the guiding principles that led them to the contemplation of, or commitment to, atrocities so characteristic of the Peloponnesian War. Also, the debate presents stereotypical examples of another key theme in this section of the work: that is, the examination of the effect of the war on the smaller states of Hellas. The prominence of the Plataian Debate in particular lies in its interconnection with the outbreak of the hostilities of the Peloponnesian War, a topic Thucydides is greatly concerned with, especially in juxtaposition to how this outbreak related to the deeper causes and motivations that made war, in Thucydides's mind, inevitable (1.23.5–6).[71]

As for the Theban speech and its reference to medism, scholars usually focus on the strategy of exculpation as employed by the Thebans. In what might be labeled a disclaimer, they state that their city "was not governed by an oligarchy which granted equal justice to all nor yet a democracy" (3.62.3). The terminology of the passage has naturally received much attention, as has the question of how justified the call for an isonomous oligarchy or democracy was at the time of the Persian Wars.[72] By pointing to the rule of a small junta, the Thebans claim that their community of citizens cannot be held responsible for crimes that were committed by those in power. To highlight this and effectively portray themselves as hostages of Attaginos' regime, they stress the profound change in attitude that occurred once that clique was removed from power. As soon as the rule of law returned (3.62.5), the Thebans acted in accordance with all other Greek states that sought to defend their liberty and freedom. Hence, the Thebans did not debunk the charge of medism. Rather, they denied responsibility for it. Note how Herodotus, who painted Attaginos' rule in picturesque colors, dwelling on extravagant banquets and moralizing speeches, is supplanted here by the Thebans. In Thucydides, the Thebans fully adopt the Attaginos motif; however, it is given a different spin. While the Thebans in Thucydides strictly dissociate themselves from Attaginos—the implicit prerequisite for opposition to unlawful government and the rule of law—in Herodotus, they concede that their medism was something that was performed "in accord with the community, rather than by individuals" (9.87.2). In Thucydides, then, the Thebans deny communal responsibility, a bold rejection of Herodotus's assertion of collective action.

But the Theban explanation goes further. The freedom rhetoric suggests this much. In the middle section of their speech, following their denial of accountability, they juxtapose their medism and Plataia's collaboration with Athens, effectively labeled as atticism (3.64.5). In doing so, they depict their own medism once again as something that was forced upon them, whereas the stance of the Plataians is denounced as willful policy. Although the parallel between medism and atticism was not entirely accurate, the Thebans endorse this point and pursue it further, charging it with overtones of betrayal.[73]

Atticism was not treason to the cause and customs of the Hellenes, but it certainly betrayed the loyalties of the Plataians vis-à-vis their fellow Boiotians. Treason on Plataia's part is an ongoing theme in the Theban speech. Indeed, Plataian betrayal of Boiotia is so notorious that it can be traced back to the arrival of the Boiotians in what later became their home region: Again, in the words of the Thebans (3.61.2), "for after we had settled the rest of Boiotia and had occupied Plataia and other places of which we got possession by driving out a mixed population, the Plataians disdained to submit to our leadership, as had been agreed upon first, and separating themselves from the rest of the Boiotians and breaking away from the traditions of our fathers went over to the Athenians." This reference to the era before the original settlement of Boiotia has been dismissed as carrying little meaning, since the affair itself is so hazy.[74] Yet haziness is not the point. For the parties who were assembled in the agora of Plataia to witness the Theban speech, the heroic war against the aboriginal tribes who inhabited the region prior to the arrival of the Boiotians may well have been a shadowy event, yet it was considered a historical reality. All the same, it was commonly accepted that Thebes had played a prominent role in the defeat of those peoples and had established the foundations of a new Boiotian homeland.[75] With allusions to moral categories such as the ancestral traditions (*patria*: 3.61.2) of all Boiotians, reference to the origin of their settlement corroborates the allegation that the Plataians acted in violation of sanctioned, time-honored principles. Their actions fell short of nothing but betrayal.[76]

This was even more reprehensible, since Plataia joined Athens in its wrongdoings. Again, the invoked parallel between Persia's attempt to subjugate Hellas and Athens's "endeavour to enslave Greece" (3.63.3) wasn't really correct—the goals of Athens and Persia were perceived as different by the Greeks. Yet the Thebans endorse this idea energetically. In both cases, the attempt to restrict the freedom of the Greeks was met with fierce resistance. Just as the Persians were ultimately defeated in an almost epic battle that "averted slavery" (Simonides, above), the Thebans claimed that the Athenians were beaten and Boiotia effectively liberated from the yoke of foreign domination at Koroneia (3.62.5). Only a few sections later, this claim is repeated in a modified form when the Thebans state that the battle of Koroneia had liberated the Boiotians and brought them over to the Spartan camp (3.67.3). Koroneia is thus presented as a defining moment in the more recent history of Greece. Its participants are glorified as Boiotian liberation heroes. Indeed, when the Thebans summarize their grudges against Plataia, they make the slaughtering of the men whose fathers died at Koroneia the most immediate charge, which once again highlights the prominence attributed to the event.[77]

In book 4, the same theme occurs in a speech delivered by a certain Pagondas, son of Aiolidas, who addresses the troops of the Boiotian League before the battle at Delion in 427 BCE. It is customary with Boiotians, Pagondas proclaims, that "when a foreign army comes against you to ward it off" (4.92.3). In their dealings with the Athenians, "who are trying to enslave not only their neighbours but those far away" (4), such valour is even more rewarded. The best proof of this is to be found in the battle at Koroneia, "when we defeated them and won for Boiotia great security which lasts to this day" (6). As such, Koroneia is indicative of the noble spirit that impels his countrymen "always to fight for the liberty of their own land" (7). In sum, Pagondas's speech spotlights the collective force Koroneia held for the Boiotians. Cast in heroic terms of valour and victory, his speech presents the campaign as foundational; the battle is said to have altered the way of life in Boiotia. The way in which this is dramatized fosters the conclusion that Thucydides here picked up on a prominent theme, one that was widely discussed in Boiotia and beyond. Incidentally, from Xenophon's *Memorabilia* (3.5.4) it is obvious that the Athenians, too, assigned significance to the Battle of Koroneia: the disaster of Tolmides and his men there is presented as turning-point in their *archē*. Also, an elegiac poem discovered in the Kerameikos in Athens appears to have been composed for the Athenians who fell during the campaign. In it, the defeat is explained with the apparition of a demigod on the side of the Boiotians, which, by implication, seems to have diminished the responsibility of the Athenian commander and his men.[78] Be that as it may: To the Thebans, Koroneia was a consensual, self-evident point of reference. Put in the mouth of an esteemed member of the local elite, evocation of the battle was something that Thucydides's audience would have found both believable and convincing when a Theban commander exhorted his troops, especially in a campaign against Athens.[79]

In Thucydides's history, then, the Theban response to the charge of medism brings about a complex, tripartite narrative of justification. Embarking from the attempt to dissociate themselves from the corrupt leadership at the time of the Persian War, the Thebans claim that once they returned to lawfulness, they time and again fought for the good cause of their allies as well as the freedom of their fellow Boiotians. When the Athenians violated this freedom and sought to enslave all of Boiotia, they defeated them in the Battle of Koroneia, which restored liberty and brought lasting security to all.

The prominence of Koroneia in local and regional discourses in Boiotia deserves further attention. The battle marked a key moment in the generation after the Persian Wars. By 447 BCE, a group of exiles that later sources labeled "Orchomenizers" seized Orchomenos and Chaironeia. The term implies that the rebels were not necessarily from Orchomenos but rather "sided with the Orchomenians" or "behaved like them." Their leader, Sparton, apparently came from Thebes. His band was joined not only by like-minded Boiotians but also by oligarchs from Euboia and Lokris. It is thus best to see the Orchomenizers as a group of rebels from various places in Central Greece who sided with a faction that was based in Orchomenos.[80]

The common goal of the Orchomenizers was to drive out the pro-Athenian factions from Boiotia that had been put in place a decade earlier as a result of the Battle of Oinophyta (457 BCE). The obscure nature of Boiotian affairs in the 450s makes it difficult for us to assess whether the Athenians had actually employed a policy that favored the rise of democratic regimes or if they simply relied on oligarchic factions that supported their cause. Either way, the rebels were determined to challenge Athens's hegemony in Central Greece. The outbreak of the so-called Sacred War in 449, along with new upheavals in the Delian League in 447, connected the affairs in Boiotia to the big picture of power politics in Aegean Greece. The situation was precarious, and the Athenians were aware of this. In an attempt to confine the uprising to western Boiotia, they sent out a thousand hoplites plus allied contingents under Tolmides, probably in the spring of 447, to check on Orchomenos and its satellite Chaironeia. They quickly captured the latter and enslaved its population, but Orchomenos was too difficult to tackle with a force of this size.[81] So the main contingent, minus the garrison left at Chaironeia, fell back toward Haliartos to wait for reinforcements from Thebes. But the Orchomenizers moved quickly, and the Athenians were unprepared for their strike. Somewhere between modern Aghios Georgios, Solinari, and Alalkomenes, in the narrow corridor that runs along the banks of Lake Kopais, Tolmides and his forces were ambushed and killed.[82]

The fighting revamped the strategic picture in Central Greece. Whatever garrisons were stationed in the region were now cut off from their supplies from Athens; hence, they were easy prey for the enemy. Within weeks, oligarchic revolutions in Euboia and Megara forced the Athenians to withdraw their contingents. In Boiotia, an agreement was reached with the Athenians, who, in return for evacuating the region, were given back their prisoners.[83] Yet the rebels did not leave it at that. With one city after another defecting from Athens, the way was cleared for local aristocracies to initiate a new project of federal integration. Victory over Athens no doubt instilled in the Boiotians the sense that, united, they were a hard match for any invader.[84] Inspired by their success on the battlefield and based on sentiments of ethnic togetherness, the local elites of Boiotia assembled to found a new *koinon*. The constitution of the league is well attested in the *Hellenika* from Oxyrhynchos

(19 Chambers), whose author highlights the spirit of proportional representation and shared executive power. The tremendous success of the emerging "Boiotian superstate" (Cartledge 2000) is often attributed to the refined workings of its constitution. But when the league rose to power in the 440s, its initial success was not due to thoughtful integration alone. The new Boiotian Confederacy benefited from the fruitful cooperation between the local Boiotian elites who promoted the league through their social, political, and economic networks. The Battle of Koroneia both facilitated and energized this new sense of cooperation. It most surely invigorated the conversation between local oligarchic elites, many of whom had participated in the uprising against Athens. Within less than a year after the foundation of the Boiotian League, the Athenians were pressured to agree to the so-called Thirty Years Peace, which obligated them to forfeit their possessions in the Peloponnese, including the harbours in the Megarid. The impact of Koroneia and the newly established Boiotian League on Greek affairs in the mid-fifth century BCE can thus hardly be overstated.[85]

Thucydides's account of the Battle of Koroneia is notoriously short, which follows the narratological principles of the *pentekontaetia* section (1.89–117) in which the affair is couched.[86] At the same time, as we have seen, Thucydides references Koroneia three times in two different Theban speeches (3.62.5; 3.67.3; 4.102.6). It is reasonable at this point to assert that the frequent references to Koroneia betray the traces of a highly charged Theban and Boiotian discourse. Near the site of the battle, in front of the "richly-built" (Bacchyl. F 15 Campbell) Temple of Athena Itonia, the Boiotian cities set up a trophy that commemorated their victory. The trophy stood there for at least two generations after the battle; it might have been in place much longer. Erected along the main road through central Boiotia and in close vicinity to one of the region's most esteemed sanctuaries, it served as a forceful reminder of the victory to travelers and visitors to the temple alike.[87] The Itonion will have inspired a lively intersignification (chapter 1) with the victory trophy, since Athena was venerated at Koroneia as patron deity of warriors. In some traditions, she provides the Boiotians with the necessary weapons in their fight for freedom.[88] Various items of pottery associated with the cult show Athena in warlike guise. The most prominent of these, a black-figure *lekanis* from the mid-sixth century BCE, portrays an illustrious procession of men to the temple (fig. 5.1). The participants carry wreaths and wine jugs, gesturing with their swords; some are leading sacrificial animals. The parade is headed by a flute player, which adds to the overall atmosphere of frolicking and rejoicing. Presumably, the men journey to the sanctuary after victory in battle. Between the altar and the pillar, which represents a temple, Athena is shown next to a

FIGURE 5.1. Black-figure bowl of Boiotian provenance with sacrificial procession, commonly associated with Athena Itonia; c. 550 BCE. To the left of Athena, probably a crow (*korōnē*) identifies the site. British Museum, Object ID 1879,1004.1 © Trustees of the British Museum.

snake. The goddess is depicted in belligerent attire, with helmet, shield, and spear held high.[89]

As early as the sixth century BCE, a festival was held at the Sanctuary of Athenian Itonia that commemorated the settlement of the Boiotians. Its transregional importance is attested to by Alkaios (F 325 Campbell) and Bacchylides (F 15 Campbell) who reference musical performances in connection with the festival. Most likely, the celebrations were complemented by parades of hoplites and horsemen.[90] After 447 BCE, the new Boiotian League presumably would have continued with this practice. It is attractive, then, to imagine how the battle trophy, along the road to the nearby sanctuary, buttressed the tradition of Sparton, Theban leadership, and the Orchomenizing rebel gang. These details are, however, lost beyond recovery.

This does not mean, however, that it is impossible to illuminate the milieu in which the tradition was evoked. At Thebes, as elsewhere, communal festivals provided the stage for the evocation of such traditions. Recent scholarship emphasizes the salient nature of historical discourses at polis festivals; it has become a commonplace to see those festivals as collective practices that conveyed a high currency of local meaning (Beck and Wiemer 2009). Their impact on communal self-perceptions was not only that festivals suspended, in Émile Durkheim's sense, the quotidian life of the community, but that they regulated public behavior in ritual, including sacrifices, processions, feasts, and prayers.[91] Comprising the entire citizen body as well as the future generation of *politai*—the ephebes, who usually participated in cohorts of their own—the historical commemoration at polis festivals was shaped by an exceptional "depth of emotion,"[92] inviting citizens to embrace the experience of continuity in time and space.

We have already seen how the vector of continuity ran through the Theban Daphnephoria (chapter 4). The festival was deeply anchored in Theban images of the past. According to Proklos (fifth century CE), it was held to commemorate the deeds and achievements of the first Boiotian war leader, a certain Polematas, who was said to have instituted the festival in response to an apparition in a dream during the war against the Pelasgians. In his sleep, a young girl appeared and offered him a panoply with which he would prevail over the enemy if he performed a daphnephoric rite in honor of Apollo. By the fifth century BCE, at the latest, the war against the Pelasgians was considered a decisive moment in the settlement of Boiotia. As we have noted earlier, Thucydides attests that both their migration and habitation were highly charged topics among the Boiotians that served as robust points of reference in the political discourse of the fifth century (3.61.2, cited above). In conjunction with the procession to Thebes's most eminent places of memory, the Daphnephoria thus promoted a narrative of primordial unity that stretched back to the times of the initial settlement. In doing so, the festival strove to connect present claims, in particular Theban leadership, with the ethnic origins of the Boiotian people.[93]

Pindar's odes attest that the narrative of festival celebrations was rich in overtones of the recent past. *Isthmian* 1 praises a certain Herodotus of Thebes, who won the chariot race before 458 BCE.[94] His family belonged to the highest Theban echelon. Herodotus's father was no other than Asopodoros, leader of the Theban cavalry, who directed the massacre against the Megarians in the Battle of Plataia. Asopodoros, a man of "famous fortune" (line 33), is introduced in the poem as having suffered a shipwreck and come ashore at Orchomenos (lines 34–38). If the Hellenistic grammarian Didymos is correct, this piece of information could be understood metaphorically as Asopodoros having been exiled from Thebes at some point. By the time of his son's victory, "the fortune of his house embarked him on the fair weather of the old days" (39–40). Indeed, the poem boldly declares that "whosoever wins bright renown, either at the games or in war, receives the highest gain in the choicest praises of citizens and of strangers" (50–51), which parallels the achievements of son and father in the chariot race and cavalry fighting. Pindar's praise suggests that Asopodoros's house continued to flourish at Thebes after the Persian Wars. His role as a prominent medizer might have led to temporary exile, possibly in the aftermath of Plataia. By the 460s, however, things had cooled off, and Asopodoros had returned to Thebes, where he was a respected war hero. Pindar's praise illustrates that the Thebans did not stigmatize Asopodoros. On the contrary, they venerated his deeds in war. In all likelihood, *Isthmian* 1 mirrors his more or less unbroken prestige at Thebes. Following his return from exile in the 460s, at the very latest, the charge of medism did little or next to nothing to bring disrepute to Asopodoros.[95]

Maiden-Ode 94b, originally published as *P. Oxy.* 659 in 1904, praises another famous house at Thebes, that of the daphnephoros Agasikles. The text is very fragmentary, but clearly epichoric, in contrast to the more Panhellenic victory odes. Its agency is deeply entrenched in the festival framework of the local Daphnephoria (chapter 4).[96] Agasikles's family is otherwise mentioned in the literary sources. He was the son of no other than Pagondas, whom we encountered earlier as boiotarch in the battle at Delion, exhorting his fellow Boiotians to be faithful to their noble spirit and defend the freedom of their country. Pagondas and his son Agasikles were descendants of the house of Aiolidas, who was elsewhere praised in Pindar's odes.[97] *Ode 94b* sets out to praise the "immortal glory" (line 4) of Thebes, thanks to "the all-renowned house of Aiolidas and of his son Pagondas" (8–10). The text then continues to glorify Agasikles and his family (lines 38–49):

> As Agasikles' honest witness, / I have come to the dance, / and for his noble ancestors, / for their guest-friendship. For / then and still today they are venerated / by their fellowmen / for their celebrated victories with /swift-footed horses, / for which on the banks of famous Onchestos, / and at the acclaimed temple of Itonia / they adorned their hair with garlands, / and at Pisa . . .

According to Pindar, Aiolidas's house was among the most prestigious in Thebes. For three generations, its members were held in the highest esteem. In fact, extolling Agasikles and his parents, Pindar says that they were held in esteem "for the *proxenia* of their fellowmen," which recognizes their high social status in Boiotia and maybe adjacent territories.[98] Since Pagondas by 427 BCE was already advanced in his career (the role as leading boiotarch at Delion would make him around fifty years of age), his father Aiolidas would have flourished toward the end of the 450s. By the time of the composition of the *daphnephorikon*, Pagondas was already old enough to participate alongside his father in the military campaign recognized in the poem. As Pindar's death dates to c. 442 to 440, it is best to view the ode as one of Pindar's very latest works, dating around 445. At that time, Pagondas would have been in his early thirties; and his father, Aiolidas, about 50. Agasikles, the boy laurel-bearer, might easily have been around twelve years of age in the mid-440s, which fits with his assigned role as a young ephebe.

With the date of the ode in place, it is tempting to fix the occasion of the "celebrated victories with swift-footed horses" (lines 44–45). The passage is sometimes taken as a reference to victories in horse racing, an aristocratic pastime that fits well with the social standing of Aiolidas and his house.[99] In light of the poem's epichoric context, such an interpretation is not compelling, nor does it preclude another reading. For Koroneia, hippic agones are not attested to independently in the Archaic and early Classical periods, although we noted how the Boiotians performed military parades there. Nearby, the sanctuary of Poseidon at Onchestos, on a low ridge separating the Basin of Lake Kopais from the Theban *chōra*, in the fifth century served as a regional amphictyony for the veneration of pan-Boiotian cults. We might speculate about the existence of horse races at Onchestos at the time, but there is no independent evidence.[100] With these uncertainties in mind, another reading is possible. Note that the passage is ambiguous, stating that the victories in question were commemorated in Onchestos, the sanctuary of Athena Itonia, and at Pisa—that is, Olympia (lines 46–49). In other words, the poem does not claim that competitions were held at those sanctuaries, but that victories were celebrated there. Like Onchestos, the precinct of Athena Itonia was considered the major regional sanctuary. Its implicit role as parade ground for the forces of the Boiotian League has already been mentioned above. In later periods, the sanctuary hosted the Pan-Boiotian games.[101] The notion of "fellowmen" (*amphiktyoneis*, line 43), with its strong echo of tribal bonds, emphasizes the Boiotian dimension of the achievements brought about by the house of Aiolidas, while reference to their elevated role as *proxenoi* fixes on their political standing in Thebes and beyond. Finally, reference to Olympia suggests that Aiolidas's and Pagondas's victories were proclaimed before a wider audience, possibly by means of a victory monument and other dedications.

As in Asopodoros's case (*Isthmian* 1), praise for the achievements brought about by Aiolidas and his house might have been a mingled reflection of victory both in agonistic contest and on the battlefield. The ambiguous tone of the ode, along with its epichoric setting, suggest that the poem reflects combined success at the games and in war. If praise of "celebrated victories with swift-footed horses" in *Ode 94b* extolled the parents of Agasikles by alluding to military prowess, it seems obvious at this point that the only occasions upon which such fame could have been won was at the Battle of Koroneia and the succeeding raids of the Orchomenizers against Athenian strongholds in Boiotia, Lokris, Euboia, and Megara. These events predated the *daphnephorikon* by only two years or so.

It has been suggested that another ode, *Pythian* 8 in honor of Aristomenes of Aigina (446 BCE), also offers a reflection of the Battle of Koroneia, although the reference there is made in a more encrypted manner: Porphyrion, king of the Attic deme of Athmonon and identified with the leader of the giants, is struck dead by the bow of Apollo. If the identification of Porphyrion and Apollo as Athenian and Theban wildcards is correct, then *Phythian* 8 further supports the idea that Pindar had fully picked up on the theme of victory over Athens. The frame of reference would have been the same as that of Agasikles's *daphnephorikon*.[102] Such a context fully explains the "immortal glory" that shone on Thebes in *Ode 94b* (line 4): although the Orchomenizers had recruited rebel contingents from all over Boiotia and beyond, the Thebans persistently claimed leadership (partial or, as time elapsed, full), both in the maneuver itself and in the Boiotian League that was established following the uprising. The later sections of *94b*, although severely damaged, recount the "hateful and unrelenting strife" that had arisen in Boiotia, "yet he (they?) cherished the faithful ways of justice" (lines 63–65). This juxtaposition of strife and, by implication, disunity on the one hand and the commitment to lawfulness on the other, might also refer to the turmoil in Boiotian affairs in the decade prior to Koroneia, when the citizens were divided between pro-Athenian factions and those who supported a more traditional course of alignment with Sparta. We are thus led to think that their grievances were resolved through the foundation of the new Boiotian League, which was built on the "faithful way of justice."[103]

In conclusion, both Thucydides and Pindar attest to the eminent role the Battle of Koroneia played in the local discourse at Thebes. Victory on the battlefield allowed the Theban elites not only to promote their newly discovered prosperity, but to present Koroneia to support their claims for leadership among the fellow Boiotians. We detect here the same lively interplay of interests and identities between the city of Thebes and the rest of the *ethnos* that is so characteristic of affairs in Boiotia. By default, though, the Koroneia narrative must have played out differently in different corners of the region. It is futile to suggest one authoritative account, engrained with one trajectory of meaning. Despite the regional frame of reference, local variation remained visible. In Thespiai, for instance, the local discourse was hardly susceptible to glorifying views of Koroneia. At some point after the Persian Wars, Thespiai opened its citizen registers to enroll new *politai*, mostly from Athens, to compensate for the blood toll of Thermopylai and Plataia (Hdt. 8.75.1). After the Battle of Koroneia, the Thespians took on the role of mediators between Athens and Thebes. By the time of the Peloponnesian War, they too were branded by the Thebans as atticizers, with consequences similar to those faced by the Plataians. We sense that, despite many regional communalities, the discourse in Thespiai was deeply different from that in Thebes.[104]

The Koroneia narrative itself can be understood only in the wider context of local responses to the Persian Wars. It is well known that here, too, Thespiai and Thebes parted ways as early as the Battle of Thermopylai. Their respective decisions in favor of and against the Hellenic Alliance sent both on divergent military trajectories, and they steered their future assessment of the Persian Wars in oppositional directions. The Thespians were careful not to be lumped in with the camp of Boiotian medizers.[105] The Thebans, on the other hand, had to work through the legacy of medism. As we have followed them in this endeavor, it is exciting to see how they managed. After a period of perplexity, if not apprehension, they were eager to dissociate themselves from the actions of Attaginos and his group. In all likelihood, affairs in Thebes and on the battlefield itself were so intricate that there was enough room for such dissociation. Plutarch, so well known for his rebuttal of the Herodotean picture, claimed that the four hundred Thebans at Thermopylai were actually true patriots who had fought independently of Attaginos's regime, volunteering for the Greek cause. A few lines earlier, he explained that, in the early stages of the Persian invasion, five hundred Thebans, led by a certain Mnamias, took part in the allied expedition to Tempe in Thessaly to establish a first line of defense. Both notes stem from *The Malice of Herodotus* (31 and 32)—as we have seen, Plutarch relies strongly in this treatise on the local Boiotian historian, Aristophanes.

Scholars have been puzzled about what to make of Plutarch. While some simply reject the notion of a Theban Tempe contingent, others suggest a struggle within Thebes between pro- and anti-Persian factions in which Attaginos, ultimately, gained the upper hand. If this was the case, then the Theban platoon at Thermopylai might indeed have consisted of men who opposed their home regime and fought against Persia on their own account.[106] A third possibility would have been that the Thebans, as Xerxes trekked south, simply changed their minds: geopolitical exposure on the corridor into Central Greece made them particularly vulnerable to Persian attack; hence, the attempt to reconcile. Despite all scholarly attempts to gauge these variants, appreciate subtleties of reason and causality, and, effectively, restore an authentic picture, we should be frank to concede that this simply cannot be done. There are too many vagaries.

It is questionable, yet worthwhile to wonder, just how reprehensible the Theban course of action was at the very moment the decision was made to medize. Notions of "siding" or "working with the Mede" were well established since the later sixth century BCE. Referencing prevailing power relations with Persia in Asia Minor, there is little to suggest that medism bore the traits of deception, let alone moral betrayal of the Greek cause. Due to the freedom ideology of the Hellenic Alliance, the meaning of the term changed quickly and profoundly after Plataia, when medism became a key entry in the Greek vocabulary of cultural othering. Steamrolled by the new semantics, the Thebans soon became the most notorious medizers. Once *mēdizein* had obtained the quality of an inflammatory accusation, the room for narrative encounters with nuance and complexity dwindled. In response to universal stigma, the Thebans soon deployed their own narrative, or better, a new narrative perspective, one that was geared toward a sententious slogan: they fostered their own freedom narrative.[107] The great advantage of that narrative—the fight for the freedom of all Hellenes on the battlefield near Koroneia—allowed the Thebans to embrace and immerse themselves in the prevailing Hellenic discourse of the day—that is, the omnipresent, self-evident, and unchallengeable call for freedom. They were the new champions of *eleutheria*. In Thebes, then, the assessment of the world adhered to a global theme at the time, brought about and packaged in deeply local sentiments.

6

Toward a Local History of Ancient Greece

In *Idyll* 7, Theokritos recounts how a poet named Simichidas travels with his friends to a harvest festival for Demeter in the countryside, somewhere on the island of Kos. Along the way, the illustrious party crosses paths with Lykidas, a Cretan goatherd known far and wide as the best piper. They chat. Each of them performs a song. Then they part ways. The poem ends with Simichidas taking in the ambience at their final destination in the *chōra*:

> [We] laid ourselves down on deep couches of sweet rush and newly cut vine leaves. Many a poplar and elm murmured above our heads: trickling down from a cave of the nymphs, a sacred spring plashed nearby; on the shady branches the dusky cicadas worked hard at their song; far off in the dense brambles the tree frog kept up its crooning; linnets and finches sang; doves were cooing; and humming bees were flying around the spring. Everywhere was the smell of rich harvest, the smell of gathered fruits. Pears rolled plentiful at our feet and apples by our side, and the branches weighed down with sloes were bent to the ground. Wine jars were opened that had been sealed for four years. Nymphs of Castalia who dwell on Mt. Parnassos, could it have been a bowl like this that old Chiron provided for Herakles in Pholos' rocky cave? (135–50, trans. Hopkinson).

Following Simichidas's footsteps on Kos—sometimes literally so—scholars have attempted to trace his route through the country and locate the festival site. Their findings suggest that the poem displays "a topographical realism unique in Greek pastoral" (Zanker 1980, 373). On the whole, however, Theokritos's translation of the countryside into poetic space follows the provisions of a literary trope. Highly artificial and light-hearted at the same time, it captures a *locus amoenus* that is idealized for its tranquility. Inquiries into the onomatopoeic tone of Theokritos's language have revealed how the sound of song endorses the image of the mind. The cool, rushing water is represented in the Greek text in the sound of accumulated liquid *lambdas* and the swift meter. Many imitative *taus* bring the melodic sound of cicadas to life, whereas the shade and overall pleasance are understood in the buzzing of the bees. Bucolic as all this is, it evokes a concrete soundscape, one that invites the audience to embrace the realness of the moment.[1]

Theokritos flourished in the first half of the third century BCE, at a time when the Greeks experienced another dramatic expansion of their world, in the Mediterranean and beyond. We noted how, from the late fourth century BCE, corresponding conversations about the fainting force of globality also resonated with the challenge of rethinking the local, a process that was so characteristic of the early Hellenistic period (chapter 1). All the while, the cultural roots of Theokritos's fetishization of place are obvious. Linkages to the land through nymphs and demigods have been axiomatic to our quest for the ontological quality of the local. Indeed, Herakles's encounter with the centaur Pholos, descended from a tree nymph and a local *daimōn*, was not only a firmly localized episode, but one that was experienceable and in this sense real to hunting parties of boys and men who followed Herakles's traces in the western Peloponnese (chapter 4). We also learned about the excitement of place, noting how this generates a particular type of cultural meaning that is itself representative of place (chapter 3). In the closing lines of *Idyll* 7, Simichidas pleads, "May I plant my great winnowing shovel in [Demeter's] heap of grain once more" (155–56). The formulation has been found to be an allusion to the close of Odysseus' *nostos*: in *Od.* 11.119–137, Teiresias advises Odysseus to "plant" his oar in a place where people would mistake it for a winnowing shovel.[2] As we have seen, sentiments of belonging, articulated with reference to the land and derived from cultivation practices undertaken by those who call it home, were a hallmark in the long-lasting development of Hellenic identities of place (chapter 2). In sum, Theokritos's pastoral highlights the culminating point of Greek perceptions of the local since the Archaic period as much as it marks the arrival of a new literary genre.

The exploration of the local world of ancient Greece, always inherent in the study of historical topography and geography, has undergone a transformation in recent decades that is nothing but breathtaking. Hans-Joachim Gehrke, in a book that became programmatic to many, had famously advocated for a perspectivation of Greek history "beyond Athens and Sparta" (1986). To Gehrke, the political fragmentation of Aegean Greece implied not only a historical, but a historiographical challenge. In his words, Greek history marks a "hidden and often also real chaos. The 'multisubjectivity' of political units makes it impossible to offer an integral account, one that fully appreciates and recognizes this aspect in particular" (12). Gehrke tackled the problem by grouping city-states into rubrics with a similar demographic, economic, and political outlook. This allowed him, consequently, to establish various typologies that characterized both the world of "Third Greece" and, with it, of Greek civilization overall.

Around the same time, Robin Osborne (1987) proposed a shift in perspective from the urban environment of the polis to the countryside. The typical activities of polis societies, Osborne argued, were founded upon the production of the country. A more rural-centric view thus appeared both more desirable and necessary. Indeed, in Osborne's narrative, the new angle of the countryside revealed its all-pervading influence on every aspect of Hellenic culture. Both approaches became tremendously influential. While Osborne's focus on the *chōra* inspired a great many field-survey projects, Gehrke's verdict of multisubjectivity galvanized countless local and regional histories—typically written from literary sources and findings from survey work—that diversified the grand narrative of ancient Greece.[3]

It is somewhat ironic that the next chapter in the conceptual advancement came with the network turn. The shift in perspective to relational models of networks and interconnected accounts of what is now called the "Mediterranean mélange" (van Dommelen 2017, 628) has made the new quest for the local inevitable. Granted, in some of the earlier contributions to the emerging network turn, including Ian Morris's influential article on Mediterraneanization (2005; cf. chapter 1), the arrival of these models generated quite some euphoria over the ways in which they superseded what was then considered a siloed, cellular, and reductionist approach to Greek culture.[4] There is, however, a growing complementary understanding, one that sees the local both as a realization of universal processes and as an ontological force that relates people to the local domain. Arjun Appadurai's verdict of "globalization from below," which we encountered much earlier in this book, adumbrated such a dynamic. At this point, it has become clear how strong the magnetic pull of the epichoric horizon was. Universal conversations were always subject to the local world. The ancient Greek "local 2.0" is neither reductionist nor geared toward silofication, but itself a feature of vibrant connectivity.

The narratological challenge remains. It weighs heavily. Postcolonial theory exacerbates the problem; or, better: it allows for a sharper diagnosis. Explicating the need for a new model of decentered history in postcolonial times, Natalie Zemon Davis formulates the issue as follows: How do we hold onto "the subjects of decentered social and cultural history, often local and full of concrete detail, and still address the perspectives of global history" (2011,

188)? In other words: How do we reconcile, analytically and narratologically, local/global interventions, with multiple layers of intermediacy in-between, knowing that every local lifeworld injects its own essence into the nature of things? The high-powered localism that we have encountered throughout this book urges us all the more to push for decentrality.

Similar to epichoric variants of mythical traditions or expressions of local distinction in scripts, dialects, and material culture, the local horizon is easily understood as a divergence from the Panhellenic frame. Our quest for the local, on the other hand, has brought to the fore a specific epichoric quality, one that cannot be reduced to the notion of divergence or variant. As we have seen, the Greek local had specific traits: it was a rich source of knowledge and meaning, informing social practices and sensory cognitions; a home to suprahuman and divine beings who inhabited the land along with the people; a self-referencing bastion of reasoning; a compass that helped communities to navigate through changing circumstances; and a place where the breadth of the Hellenic experience melted into the tangible, quotidian horizon. The epichoric perspective is not a variant of Greek history. Rather, Classical Greek history *is* epichoric history.

In the previous chapters we have explored the local as a quantity in its own right so that its signature becomes visible in conversations that are concerned with networks and connectivity. While the study of glocal cross-fertilizations makes great efforts to theorize globalization and the global, the meaning of the local—what it is and why it matters—too often has been taken for granted. The local might appear as a realization of global processes, but most eminently it is a spatial and cultural force that is intimately entangled with and complements the universal. The next step in the endeavor is to craft a narrative that fully impersonates this epichoric trait and its entanglement with Greek culture.

How would we envision such a history, and how would it echo multi-subjectivity in a meaningful manner? The epichoric turn, while building on a wealth of local data, entails more than the recollection of local histories and cultural processes. According to Zemon Davis, the decentering historian does not tell the story "only from the vantage point of a single part of the world or of powerful elites, but rather widens his or her scope, socially and geographically, and introduces plural voices into the account" (2011, 190). The endeavor is relational. To be sure, narratives of less privileged agents require the history of their more powerful counterparts also. But even while describing all the parties, "the decentering historian may let the subalterns and their practices and beliefs carry the narrative. Through resistance, collaboration, craft, improvisation, or good luck, they can influence outcomes and their own destiny" (190).

The local/global binary suffers from similar imbalances between places with lesser and higher fame scores. As we have seen throughout, the local horizon is typically considered subject to a taxonomy of relevance that marginalizes it, especially when juxtaposed with universal constellations. Another point of view is possible. For instance, in the arena of political history, our approach to the universal theme of the Persian War has made use precisely of the principle of a plurality of perspectives. In doing so, we detected a rich tapestry of reactions at the grassroots level that shaped the course of big politics. Vice versa, we saw how events on the battlefield resonated back in the local sphere. The decentered approach left us with a picture quite different from power narratives about Athens and Sparta. An occasion to rise to and henceforth an affair of pride to the Aiginetans; a recrudescence of deeply rooted societal fear to the Megarians; a complicated decision at the time that transmorphed into a crushing legacy to the Thebans; or something that didn't really matter much at all to the Argives in light of their earlier and more cataclysmic plights: the local stance takes stock of another Persian War, one in which the big picture translates into lifeworlds that each had their own experience and understanding of what had happened.[5] We note that the shift in perspective from global to local (and back) advances readings in both arenas. For instance, the full implications of the "forgotten" Battle of Koroneia (chapter 5), an event that deeply altered the political constellation in core Greece and the Aegean, become visible only through the study of the local discourse in Thebes. Rather than moving in one direction from local to global or global to local, the historical analysis needs to "begin from both ends at the same time" (Osterhammel 2009, 43).

The first quality of a local history of Greece is its alertness to the big picture *and* to the polyphony of voices that carry the script—local and regional, large and small, powerful and less so. Interstate power, conventionally understood, is not a helpful device to structure the narrative to begin with. This is not to say that Athens and Sparta would be foolishly removed from the account. Rather, their agency needs to relate to questions of place and scale, top-down and bottom-up in Osterhammel's sense, to reverberate with the complexity of affairs. With this comes another challenge. Local perspectivation requires choices not only of sites and mediations between them, but of decisions in the distribution of themes—which theme is best accounted for through which local, which local is suited best to thicken the plot, and so on. None of these choices is harmless or innocent. Translations of place into text are generally a precarious exercise, because they produce, implicitly so, layers of meaning and interpretation that wield authority over how we conceive of a place. The expounding of universal themes through the local lens magnifies this risk of accumulating preconceptions.

The possible antidote—the second trait of the envisioned narrative—is to make deciphering the local discourse world central to both the analysis and the story. Disclosure of why individual cities arrived at a certain decision and how they got there sounds like a Thucydidean exercise, but it cuts deeper. As we have seen throughout, the local discourse environment of the city adhered to a grammar of resilience and autoreferentiality. Often immune to patterns of reasoning from outside, the lifeworld of the local drew on the long-lasting force of self-evidence from within: in the conduct of religion, in notions of attachment to the land, in sensory cognitions and excitements of place, and in the assessment of history and politics, including the canvas of local experience and conviction before which each city determined its course of action. In such a narrative, stepping out of the shadow of generalization, the local reveals its own guiding quality.

And then there is the third and presumably most demanding trait of the narrative: that is, its need to unravel the inherent, intricate, and intense entanglement of local and global processes. As much as the local lifeworld was real to its actors and, hence, foundational to communal practice and reasoning, the notion of the city as a self-enclosed entity precludes a significant part of the picture. In light of omnipresent connectivity and integrated processes, the image of the "closed city," in the words of Kostas Vlassopoulos, is a blueprint, a model that should not be "confuse[d] . . . with the reality of Greek history" (2019, 55). While emblematic of the way in which polis societies saw themselves, the networks between and across cities were too tight, too vibrant to segregate the local from the global. With neither realm set or static, the corresponding systems of meaning and orientation precipitated ever-new configurations and cross-fertilizations, malleable, adaptable, and volatile. One of the great challenges to the writing of a "histoire croisée" that is alert to this is to trace fast-paced change and reconcile its trajectory with the long continuity of time and place. The stance of the historian itself is moving with many academic turns as well as the great tidal waves of scholarship. Add to this the sheer volume of local place and ways of interrelatedness in Classical Greece, and the task is tantalizing.[6]

Simichidas beckons us to pause. Like him, we desire to embrace a delightful local, rich in sensation, satisfied with self-evidence. Yet Simichidas's epichoric tranquility, this study reminds us, is relational, too. A state and place of being with qualities foundational to the human experience, it flourishes in response to the pressing and often perplexing demands of globality.

Acknowledgments

This book was written under the umbrella of *The Parochial Polis Research Network*, an international collaborative project at McGill University that was in place from 2015 to 2018. The network was funded by the Anneliese Maier Research Prize awarded to me by the Alexander von Humboldt-Foundation in Germany and by the endowed chair I held at McGill, the John MacNaughton Chair of Classics. *The Parochial Polis* hosted a number of workshops and symposia at home and away, many of which received co-sponsoring grants from other sources, including the Social Sciences and Humanities Research Council of Canada, the European Cultural Center at Delphi, the Australian Government Research Fund, the Swiss National Research Foundation, the National Research Council of Argentina, the Waterloo Institute for Hellenistic Studies, and the Cluster of Excellence "Religion and Politics" at the University of Münster. The following edited volumes emanate from these collaborations:

Hans Beck and Philip J. Smith, eds. 2018. *Megarian Moments: The Local World of an Ancient Greek City-State. Teiresias Supplements Online*, vol. 1.
Hans Beck and Fabienne Marchand, eds. 2020. *The Dancing Floor of Ares: Local Conflict and Regional Violence in Central Greece. Ancient History Bulletin*, Supplement Series.
Sheila Ager and Hans Beck, eds. *Localism in the Hellenistic World* (in preparation).
Hans Beck and Julia Kindt, eds. *The Local Horizon of Ancient Greek Religion* (in preparation).

The Anneliese Maier Research Prize facilitated exciting global conversations about the local, led by scholars from different academic traditions and diverse backgrounds. At McGill, many graduate students joined in the discussion and developed their own projects on Greek localism. The ways in which scholars and students connected with the agenda not only fueled a lively exchange of insights and ideas, but also provided a source of inspiration throughout. It tells me that there is more at stake than an academic query.

As this book took shape, many offered advice and shared their expert knowledge. I am deeply grateful to Sheila Ager, Darin Barney, John Bintliff, Jordan Christopher, Rolando del Maestro, Peter Funke, Chandra Giroux, Katherine Grandjean, Pam Hall, Kathleen Holden, Karl-J. Hölkeskamp, Naomi Kaloudis, Julia Kindt, Achim Lichtenberger, Heather Loube, Susan Lupack, Irad Malkin, Fabienne Marchand, Nicholas May, Alex McAuley, Jeremy McInerney, Nancy Pedri, Marcel Piérart, Irene Polinskaya, Ruben Post, Albert Schachter, Sebastian Scharff, Darian Totten, Connor Trainor, Salvatore Tufano, Faith Wallis, Georgios Zachos, and Pamela Zinn. Geographical maps were drawn by Christian Fron with the aid of ArcGIS. At the Press, Susan Bielstein and James Toftness steered the manuscript through the production process in a seamless manner. They also solicited peer reviews from scholars whose expertise and advice was most welcome and appreciated as the final changes to the manuscript were made.

The attentive reader will notice, I believe, how this book is inspired also by broader conversations in the human sciences in Canada. As we begin an exciting new chapter in Münster, our family has been truly fortunate to call Montreal home for so many years.

Notes

Chapter One

1. Cf. Calame 1996/2011, 261 ("*une subtile dialectique entre le local et le global*"). On traveling heroes, see Lane Fox 2008. On economic entanglement, see Manning 2018.
2. See the various contributions to McInerney 2014c. Landmarks in the debate include Hall 1997 (notion of "discursively constructed ethnic identity," 2); Malkin 2011, 15–20; Wallace-Hadrill 2008, 3–37; cf. also Mitchell and Greatrex 2000 for how knotted the debate has become.
3. Carter, Donald, and Squires 1993; Hague and Jenkins 2005.
4. Garland 2014; cf. Montiglio 2005; Mackil 2004.
5. Go to polis.stanford.edu (last accessed October 19, 2018); Ober 2015, 21–44.
6. Cf. Osterhammel and Petersson 2005, esp. 8–10; Castells 2004 and 2006.
7. The standard text is Malkin, Constantakopoulou and Panagopoulou 2011, 1–11; on earlier periods, see Tartaron 2013; Broodbank 2013. On Roman globalization, see Hingley 2005; Pitts and Versluys 2015.
8. Cf. Morris 2005.
9. See the discussions in Malkin 2011, 14 and Hodos 2017a, 5–7 which build on Roland Robertson's word-creation; cf. also Hodos 2015.
10. Appadurai 1996 and 2002; Hodos 2010, 16.
11. Cf. also the volume by Concannon and Mazurek 2016.
12. W. H. Race, on frag. 169a: "What exactly Pindar means by *nomos* ("law," "custom") remains disputed." Cf. Humphreys 1987; Kurke 1999, 86–88; Asheri, Lloyd, and Corcella 2007, 436–37. Pindar's lines are also cited, in part, in Plato, *Gorg.* 484b.
13. Foucault's foundational text, "Truth and Power," is reprinted in Rabinov 1984, 51–75.
14. In Plato's *Krito* (52–54) we detect a similar reasoning: Socrates's argument there rests on the observation that one cannot live happily in accordance with the customs (*nomoi*) of others.
15. See chapter 3 for details.
16. Pind. frag. 106 Race; Antiphanes, frag. 233 *PCG* (Athen., *Deipn.* 1.27d); Eupolis, frag. 245–47 *PCG*.
17. Berggren and Jones 2000; cf. Cosgrove 2004, which discusses the long-lasting and convoluted legacies of Ptolemy's distinction.
18. Edition: Allen 1969; cf. W. Furley, in *BNP*, s.v. "Contest of Homer and Hesiod"; Bassino 2019 (commentary).

19. Simplicius (sixth cent. CE), in his *Physics* (467. 26) cites Archytas's views on space: D-K, 47A24.

20. Corinth and Megara: 1280b14–16; cf. also *Pol.* 1260b40–43: "The state (*politeia*) is essentially a form of community (*koinōnia*), and it must at any rate have a common locality (*tou topou koinōnein*). A single city (*polis*) occupies a single site (*topos*) and the single city belongs to its citizens in common (*politai koinōnoi*)." For further discussion, see Morison 2002 and Algra 2014 (emphasis on Aristotle's *Physics*).

21. Whitby 1984; Kleinman 2011.

22. Wright et al. 1990; Alcock 1991; Casselmann et al. 2004; Casselmann 2010. See also the ongoing Western Argolid Regional Project (westernargolid.org), under the rubric "Nemea, Phlius, and the Phliasian Plain."

23. Wine: Antiphanes, in Athen., *Deipn.* 1.27d; cf. also Paus. 2.13.6. The famous Agiorgitiko grape is labeled after the earlier name of modern Nemea, Hagios Georgios. When the name change of the village was initiated in the early twentieth century, Nemea appeared a more appealing choice than Phlious, although Phlious's ancient settlement was much closer to Hagios Georgios than ancient Nemea.

24. Cf. Piérart 2004, 613–14.

25. Diod. Sic. 15.69.1 says that Phlious defected from Sparta after the Battle of Leuktra; cf. Stylianou 1998, 459–61. On Xenophon's account, see Dillery 1995, 131; Buxton 2017.

26. *Pol.* 1327a, 1330a–b; see also 1318b on the natural environment of agricultural democracies.

27. Cf. Wright et al. 1990, 588; Urban and Fuchs 2005.

28. Survey archaeology has brought to light a shift in the settlement history of the Phliasia over time. The Bronze Age habitation, with its rich tholos tombs, was located to the west of the Asopos, while the classical polis was in the east, on the opposite end of the valley. It would be interesting to know how the fifth-century inhabitants saw their Mycenaean ruins.

29. Casselmann et al. 2004, 39–41. William Leake saw the remains of the site on his travels in the early nineteenth century (1830, 3:345–46); it is gone today.

30. Cf. Alcock 1991, 431. The "Pausanias problem" is discussed by Pretzler 2007. I express my views more comprehensively in Beck, forthcoming.

31. For pellets and wheel as zodiacal symbols, see Richer 1994; Evans 1999, 284–95.

32. Citation from Hawes 2017, 7. A similar entanglement of universal tradition and local variant shines through Pausanias's description of Pelops's chariot (2.14.10), which the locals claimed was dedicated on the roof of a local temple.

33. Harrison 1927, 396–415; Richer 1994, 98–101, 107 (recovery of an entire Phlious zodiac); Cole 2004, 74–79 (on the interplay of universal and local centrality). Boutsikas and Ruggles (2011) discuss a fascinating cross-reference between Artemis Orthia in Sparta and specific asterisms (the Pleiades and Orion).

34. Alcock 1991, 462–63.

35. We note that the radius of Phliasian proxeny ties was small. Of the attested cases (six samples, Hellenistic), none of the Phliasian *proxenoi* lived more than 100 km away. The one case of a *proxenos* residing at Phlious (Xen., *Hell.* 7.2.16) evidences ties to Pellene (50 km). Data retrieved online from proxenies.csad.ox.ac.uk. See the discussion of the proxeny below.

36. *LSAG*, 150, n. 1.

37. Cf. Gagarin 2005; Gagarin and Cohen 2005; Perlman 2018.

38. Fine 2010 advocates for such an approach; for local orthodoxies, see Hodos 2010, 14; van Dommelen 2017; Whitmarsh 2010 (discussion below). The brief guide to conversations about

local history among scholars in the field of English history by Hey 1996, although already somewhat dated, documents how much more work is needed.

39. Stollberg-Rilinger 2013, 37 (my translation of the German citation).

40. The term *intersignification* was coined by Roller 2013; cf. also Russell 2016.

41. Cf. de Polignac 1984/1995; Hölscher 1999; Hölkeskamp 2004; Scott 2013.

42. Governance of sublocal space: for example, according to Plutarch (*Sol.* 23; the authenticity of the measure need not concern us here), Solon specified that an Athenian might collect up to 12 *choes* (c. 38 L) of water a day from a neighbor if a public well was more than 4 *stadia* (c. 800 m) away, and on his own property no water had been found within about 18 m of ground level—an impressive piece of neighborhood legislation! Local subspaces: Hansen and Nielsen (2004, 1343–44) have compiled all attested cases of civic subdivisions in the Archaic and Classical Greek city, based on the data assembled in their inventory. Megara: Robu and Bîrzescu 2016; Beck and Smith 2018; Corinth: Dubbini 2016. The latest contribution to the ongoing conceptual debate is Grote 2016.

43. Halieis: McAllister 2005; Ault 2005. Olynth: Cahill 2002. Athens: Lohmann 1993.

44. See the discussion in Schmitz 2004, 52–60.

45. Schmitz 2004, 54.

46. Hippocrates, *Diseases* 1.30, on melancholy.

47. Hofer's medical dissertation on nostalgia (1688), which contains the earliest attested usage of the term, was reprinted in *Bulletin of the Institute of the History of Medicine* 2 (1934): 376–91 (English trans., C. Kiser Anspach). Most recently, see Clewell 2013 on this rich and varied phenomenon.

48. For more information, go to https://www.nobelprize.org/prizes/medicine/2014/summary; cf. Abbott 2014.

49. Hall 2013, 74–107; Hall 2017. For a similar approach to Canada's west coast, the buzzing island world of the Salish Sea between the mainland and Vancouver Island, cf. Harrington and Stevenson 2005.

50. *epichōrios, topikos*: Ambaglio 2001. On Bendis, cf. Planeaux 2000; Wijma 2014. *IG* II² 1283 (from 240/39 BCE) states that the Thracians had obtained the right to possess land in Athens at some point in the past.

51. The complicated relation between *astoi* and *politai* is discussed by Cohen (2000, 49–78), who argues forcefully for a sharp differentiation.

52. On this, see *The Old Oligarch* 2.8: "The Hellenes in general tend to keep to their own dialect [*phōnē*], way of life [*diaitē*], and fashion [*schēma*], whereas the Athenians mix theirs from all the Greeks and barbarians."

53. See the various wealth quantifications by Ober (2015, 71–100). Shipley (2018, 183–98) provides a useful synopsis of the rural survey data in the Peloponnese (late Classical and early Hellenistic periods). See also the data collections from intensive survey projects by Bintliff et al. 2017 (Thespai) and Fachard 2012 (Eretria). The programmatic text on integrated wealth distributions between city and countryside by Zimmermann (2015) is foundational for the Hellenistic period.

54. Locavores: Filson and Adekunle 2017. Translocal scales: Herod 2008; Greiner and Sakdapolrak 2013; Brickell and Datta 2016.

55. Bintliff 2006, with much bibliography; McHugh 2017, 99–131 (Argolid). See also Casson 1994, 512–13 for further calculations.

56. Hansen and Nielsen 2004a, 70–73; cf. Ober 2015, 22–32, 87.

57. The mechanics of *koina* in their regional context are fairly well understood: cf. Mackil 2013; Beck and Funke 2015b. On amphiktyonies, see Funke 2013. For regionalism (and globalization), see de Angelis 2013.

58. Lohmann 1993 (discussion above); Osborne 1985; Whitehead 1986; Fachard 2016; see also the fascinating case study on Acharnai in Kellogg 2013. For a different "reality of deme life," cf. Cohen 2000, 112–30, who posits a lack of residential and societal coherence for many Athenian demes. But Pindar says otherwise: see *Nem.* 2.15–24 (on Acharnai).

59. See also Soja 1989, 118–37, whose "spatialized ontology" has become a landmark contribution on the road toward the spatial turn.

60. Cf. Perlman 2000 and now the superb work by Rutherford 2013. Incidentally, Rutherford issues a disclaimer on the network approach to his topic, which he finds somewhat "too abstract or schematic" (9) to capture the political, religious, and social dynamic at play.

61. Malkin 2011, 20.

62. Mack 2015, 148.

63. On the calculation of fame scores, cf. Ober 2015, 35–36 (measured by columns of text in the CPC Inventory).

64. Corinth: works carried out by the American School in Athens; cf. Pettegrew 2016; Bonnier 2014. Eretria, Oropos, and Tanagra: see Fachard 2012 and 2017; see also the Mazi Archaeological Project in Northwestern Attica. Argolid: the Western Argolid Regional Project (above note 22). In the Kephissos Valley, the Deutsches Archäologisches Institut currently runs an extensive field project.

65. On Athenian figures and how to approach the evidence, see Hansen 2006; Akrigg 2011. Hansen suggests there were about 50,000–60,000 adult male citizens in the fifth century BCE, amounting to perhaps 250,000 inhabitants (?). For Syracuse (urban population of c. 50,000?), see Fischer-Hansen, Nielsen, and Ampolo 2004, 225–26. Ruschenbusch 1984 calculated a grand total of 3.6 million inhabitants of Aegean Greece in the Classical period, to which compare Ober 2015, 21–23: 2.2 million in core Greece and 4.8 million in the Greek-speaking world, c. 450 BCE. We thus shouldn't be too far off estimating an Athenian share of about 10 percent of the population of core Greece.

Chapter Two

1. Participation in the funeral contest for Amphidamas at Chalkis and the subsequent reward of a tripod for the song he had composed put Hesiod most likely in a different social bracket than that of a poor farmer. Reference to long-distance trade is confined to one passage in *Works and Days* only (618–94); cf. Edwards 2004, 48–51; Strauss Clay 2009. On the poetic theme of Hesiod's reluctance to travel, cf. Rosen 1990. Or was the comment about the trip to Euboia simply a joke? On Theognis, Nagy 1985 is still foundational. See also Yates 2018.

2. E. Bowie, "Phocylides," in *BNP*. See Itgenshorst 2014, 88, 208–10, and passim, who dismisses the idea of assigning the fragment to a Jewish-Egyptian author from the Imperial period (Korenjak and Rollinger 2001). Hall (2007, 74) conjectures that Phokylides has a "compact settlement" in mind that has expanded from an Iron Age nucleus, similar to the site portrayed on Achilles's shield in the *Iliad* (18.484–607). For political renderings of Phokylides, see Walter 2013, 518. For the polis and its *politai*, see also frags. 3, 5, and 12 Gentili/Prato. For Phokian cities, see Oulhen 2004; Sideris 2014 (Antikyra); Beck, forthcoming.

3. This scenario draws mostly on Deger-Jalkotzy and Lemos 2006; Dickinson 2006; Shelmerdine 2008. On new approaches to the redistributive nature of center-periphery relations, cf. the online forum "Redistribution in Aegean Palatial Societies," published in *American Journal of Archaeology* 115 (2011): 175–244 (multiple authors). Online at https://www.ajaonline.org/forum/905.

4. Cf. Shelmerdine 1981 and 1998; McDonald and Wilkie 1992; Thomas and Conant 1999, 32–59; Simpson 2017, 45–70; Nakassis 2013 (Pylos). See also the latest synthesis of the Pylos Regional Archaeological Project, Davis and Bennet 2017.

5. Thomas and Conant 1999, 41. The construction of several new cist tombs in the nearby cemetery of Lakkoules soon after 1075 speaks to this early continuity; cf. Spencer 1998, 167–69.

6. See the excavators' report in Rapp and Aschenbrenner 1978 = *Nichoria* 1:94–95; Thomas and Conant 1999, 44–45. Analysis of cattle bones: McDonald, Coulson, and Rosser 1983 = *Nichoria* 3:264–65, 323.

7. Lakonian sherds: cf. McDonald, Coulson, and Rosser 1983 = *Nichoria* 3:78–79. Absence of shellfish has been noted by Thomas and Conant 1999, 46. The excavators concluded that the lack of evidence was not due to a "lack of sophistication or care in recovery techniques" (McDonald, Coulson, and Rosser 1983 = *Nichoria* 3:324). In other words, this was not a problem of preservation so much as a real dearth of consumption.

8. Cf. Snodgrass 2000, 84–86; cf. also Coulson 1991.

9. Malkin 2011; cf. also Coldstream 1977/2003, 182–84; Hodos 2006 ("localized routes").

10. Cf. Sinn 1990; Morgan 1994.

11. Vegetation: L. Bürchner, "Ithake." *RE* 9.2 (1916) col. 2293–2303; Lienau 1989, 273–75; Horden and Purcell 2000, 2010. Vathy and Alalkomenai: cf. the excavation reports in *Praktika* 141 (1986): 234–40 and 145 (1990): 271–78.

12. Cf. Malkin 1998, 1–3, whose conceptual clarification of *nostos* is critical here.

13. Henderson 1997 introduces the orchard scene as "a final and significant retrospection and re-narration of the narrative," which is carried by the sign of the trees "as the staging of an exemplary model of cultural/narrative productivity" (87). See also Bittlestone's imaginative chapter "Laertes" (2005, 280–98); and Hall 2007, 238–39.

14. Cf. Deger-Jalkotzy and Lemos 2006, 154–57, 215–17; Dickinson 2006; Stein-Hölkeskamp 2015, 32–33.

15. Phokis: Fossey 1986; Luce 2011; Franchi 2016, 80–98, and 2017; Kalapodi: Sporn et al. 2016/2017; Lokris: Dominguez 2013, 405–10.

16. The site lies c. 700 m to the east from the Arkadiko bridge, near Aghios Ioannis. Evidence is on display in the Archaeological Museum in Nafplio. See Simpson and Dickinson 1979, 51; Antonaccio 1995, 28–29.

17. For instance, metallurgical activity at Nichoria involving tin, copper, and iron, despite the lack of local sources, does not inevitably attest to trade exchanges. Most of the metal work done at Nichoria involved, as demonstrated by metallurgists, the melting and reworking of bronze rather than the alloying of tin and copper (Shelmerdine 1998, 143). What at first glance appears as evidence of exchange was an exercise in recycling.

18. Cf. Hall 2007, 60–62, for an excellent summary discussion of the pastoralist paradigm.

19. Popham, Sackett, and Themelis 1979; Thomas and Conant 1999, 85–114; Dickinson 2006; Lemos 2007.

20. The old orthodoxy on Corinth—that the primary purpose of overseas foundations was to relieve population pressure (Salmon 1984, 95)—has lost much of its plausibility (see also the following note). On territory and missing hints at overpopulation, see Morgan 2003, 54–62; Stein-Hölkeskamp 2015, 101; Legon 2004, 465; Tartaron et al. 2006. For average territory size, cf. chapter 1.

21. Cf. de Angelis 2003 on the relatively well-attested case of Megara and Megara Hyblaia. Lelantine Plain/War: Hall 2007, 1–8. On the demographic dimension of overseas settlement and implausibility of the overpopulation verdict, see Scheidel 2003.

22. Edwards 2004, 127–58; Beck 2017 and 2019.

23. De Polignac 1995, 41–45, 64–65, 111–13; Billot 1997; Piérart 2006 (Argive Heraion); cf. also Graf 1996 on the ritual dynamics of *pompai* through the countryside; Mohr 2013 on the physicality of procession roads and their role in the state-formation process. Criticism of de Polignac's model was sparked by Hall 1995 over the question of how Argive the Argive Heraion was for much of the Archaic period (a prominent case for de Polignac's argument); see also Strøm 2009.

24. Cf. Hall 2002, 32–35; J. Tully, "Pelasgi," *EAH* (2013), 9:5126–127; McInerney 2014b.

25. Cf. Nielsen 2002, 69–72, with references, who also counters the argument by Rosivach 1987, 305–6, that *autochthon*, when applied to the Arkadians, meant "indigenous." Thucydides (1.2.3) stated that Arkadia never experienced any significant waves of migration.

26. Rosivach 1987; Loraux 1996/2000; Calame 2011; Roy 2014, 244–6. On Erichthonios, see Hdt. 8.55; and see Hom., *Il.* 2.547–548.

27. Cf. Laugrand and Oosten 2010, 136–37 (Inuit). For the Nisga'a, I am drawing on exchanges with Nicholas May, who has spent several years with the nation and conducted many interviews during that time. With regard to the Nass Valley, May reported that "[i]t was here that Raven released the Light after stealing it from the Chief of Heavens, and here that the trickster figure Txeemsim went about making the place more amenable to human thriving through his various acts. It is at the centre of Nisga'a cosmology, and its rhythms and particularities (for example, the best oolichan run on the entire coast) give the Nisga'a much of their identity. The valley is full of sacred places and supernatural beings, and it is perhaps the particular intensity of place they experience here that has instructed them on proper relationships with others that they carry with them when they leave the valley" (correspondence from October 29, 2015).

28. This is how *LSJ* references the word, s.v. *autochthōn*. See also Roy 2014, 241–43.

29. Arkas was thus a stereotypical culture hero; cf. Hall 1997, 53; Gehrke 1994, 255; Pretzler 2009. He figured prominently in the inscription that accompanied the dedication of the Arkadian League at Delphi, *FdD* III.1.3, lines 1-7.

30. Cf. Schachter 1985/2016; Vian 1963; Scheer 1993, 307–20; Kühr 2006 (cf. Ganter [née Kühr] 2014 for survey in English); Montiglio 2005, 73–74. Kadmos and the cow: McInerney 2010, 138–40.

31. Konon *BNJ* 26 F 1.37.5; Androtion *BNJ* 324 F 60b, with Sordi 1966, 18–20; cf. also Schol. Eur. *Phoin.* 670 (=Androtion F 60a); Diod. 19.53.4; Paus. 9.5.3. Sparton became a prominent name in Thebes and Boiotia in later periods.

32. Cf. Kühr 2006, 106–14, with further references.

33. Kühr 2006, 112–14; the dragon "earthborn": see Eur. *Phoin.* 931, 935.

34. Thuc. 2.36.1 (Perikles speaking). On communities of faith, cf. chapter 4.

35. Loraux 1996/2000; cf. also Loraux 1981/2006, 210–11 and passim.

36. Chapter 1. See Paus. 2.12.3–15.1; Frazer 1898, 2:76. The people of Plataia also appeared as autochthonous to Pausanias (9.1.1.)

37. Akousilaos *BNJ* 2 F 27 (with alternative versions of non-earthborn descent), picked up by Aisch. *Prometheus Bound* 566 (a mockery?). The narrative strands of autochthony and cultural/spatial continuity might have been equally entangled, as in Thebes. Cf. also Hall 1997, 53–56.

38. For discussion, cf. Hornblower 1991, 11–15; Montiglio 2005, 13–14.

39. Cf. Malkin 1994, 15–45; Meier 1998, 254–58; Hall 1997, 56–65 and passim.

40. Lelex: Paus. 3.1.1; Agis and Eurypon: Ephoros *BNJ* 70 F 118, with Malkin 1994, 110–11; McInerney 2014b. See also Roy 2014, 243, who suggests that autochthonous simply meant "local" here. Calame 1987 has offered a congenial reconciliation between Lelex and the myth of wandering Heraklids.

41. Paus. 7.2.3.

42. Much of this relates to the debate of ethnogenesis, in Classics and other disciplines. One of the most influential accounts on the (late) charge of Ionian and Dorian foundation myths is that of Ulf 1996.

43. *SEG* 23.297, after Roesch 1965, 61–63; cf. also Schachter 1981–1994, 3:106–8; Ager 1996, 69–70; Bonnechere 2003, 25.

44. Cf. Ager 1996, 70, who summarizes scholarly approaches.

45. Cf. Mackil 2017 (citations, 79).

46. See chapter 1. Kleisthenes: Anderson 2003; Raaflaub 2013. Material evidence: Lohmann 1993; Jones 2004; Lohmann and Mattern 2010.

47. Grote 2016, 47–65 (Sikyon) and 162–78 (Argos); Piérart 2004, 604.

48. Corinthian crossroads: Pettegrew 2016; the *phylai*: Grote 2016, 145–61; topography and spatial mentality: Dubbini 2016.

49. Among the most prominent wars that originated here, beyond the so-called Sacred Wars, was the Corinthian War, which started in 395 BCE in the muddled terrain of Phokis, Lokris, and Delphi. It is telling that even the ancient sources were uncertain about which Lokris was involved, and hence where exactly the war parties spilled first blood: Beck 2008, 23–28. Cf. Osborne 1987, 51 on the movement of seasonal flocks in the region; Daverio Rocchi 2011. Mc Inerney 2006, 47 comments pointedly that "grazing flocks do not pay much attention to whether they are chomping on grass on the east or west side of a line drawn on a map."

50. Cf. Meier 1990.

51. Thus the title of Ober 1985. Rubble camps: Oliver 2007, 153–58. Cf. Camp 1991; Daly 2015. Oinoe and Eleutherai: Fachard 2016 and 2017; see also the website of the Mazi Archaeological Project: www.maziplain.org.

52. [Arist.], *Ath. Pol.* 61.1; Ober 1985, 87–100, who places the office in the broader context of defense reforms in the *chōra*; cf. also Oliver 2007, 164–66.

53. *Peripoloi* and their *peripolarchos*: Thuc. 4.67.2–5; 8.92.2; see also Aischin. 2.165–67, who uses the terms *peripolos* and *ephēbos* interchangeably. See the intriguing case of the anonymous historian on Orthagoras of Sikyon, *BNJ* 105 F 2, who, albeit describing events of the seventh century BCE, seems to reflect the realities of the fourth century, when the history was written. See [Aristotle's] ephebic chapter, *Ath. Pol.* 42.1–5. The last collection of ephebic inscriptions is that of Reinmuth 1971. On various ephebic duties, cf. Burckhardt 2004; Oliver 2007, 175–76; Kozak 2013, with further references.

54. Cf. Ober 1985, 178–79; Oliver 2007, 138–89, passim.

55. Cf. Smith 2008, 89–92; Legon 1981, 21–41. On Aigosthena, see Freitag 2018.

56. Boiotian ephebes and Thespian chief dog handlers: *IThesp* 84, lines 26–28, with Post 2012, 128–35; Roesch 1965, 229–32; Chankowski 1993 and 2010, 158–65 (also 144–58 on Eretria); Robu 2014, 107–9 (Megarian ephebic catalogues).

57. Fachard 2012; McAuley 2018 (Megara). On borders in general: Daverio Rocchi 1988; cf. also Alcock 1993, 118–28 on the afterlife of this charged boundary concept in the Roman period.

58. See the various contributions in Alcock and Osborne 1994; Hägg 1996; Rosen and Sluiter 2006.

59. R&O 58 = *IG* II^3 1 292. For the Sacred Tract, which is first mentioned in Thuc. 1.139, cf. McInerney 2006, 50–53; Papazarkadas 2011, 244–59. The region continued to be a bone of contention in the fourth century: Androtion *BNJ* 324 F 30, and Philochoros *BNJ* 328 F 155. Both Athenians and Megarians had a watchtower on either side of the plain, the Athenians at Doskouri (Ober 1985, 175–78); the Megarians, the Loutropyrgos tower (Smith 2008, 73).

60. Alk. frag. 351 Campbell, with McInerney 2006, 47.

61. The so-called Dema wall in Attica is a notorious example; see Oliver 2007, 144 (contra Munn's view [1993, 47–57, 97–112] that the wall was built to withstand an actual Theban invasion from across the Thriasian Plain). See also Fachard 2016, who criticizes a static frontier model, with reference to the staggering of fortifications in frontier zones.

62. Cf. Burkert 1977/1985, 174–76, on nature deities; Brewster 1997; cf. also C. Weiss, "Fluvii," in *LIMC* 4.1 (1988): 139–48. Nymphs: Larson 2001.

63. Diod. 4.29.2–4, and Paus. 9.27.6–7; cf. also Herodoros *BNJ* 31 F 20 (seven nights); Apollod., *Bibl*. 2.4.10 (rationalizing, fifty nights); see Kühr 2011, 219–20. Cults of Herakles at Thespiai: Schachter 1981–1994, 2:31–36.

64. Paus. 1.40.1–2; Larson 2001, 146. Megara: Ager 2018; Solez 2018.

65. Calame 1990; Walker 1995; cf. chapter 4 for further discussion.

66. Hampl 1939. On the issue of wandering poleis, see chapter 1.

67. Cf. Hansen and Nielsen 2004, 70; see xii–xiii there for a full list of publications from The Copenhagen Polis Centre. Hampl's views have been critiqued by others before, including Habicht 1959 and Sakellariou 1989, 80–84. Cf. also Hall 2007, whose definition of polis builds on the paradigm of "communities of place."

68. Beck 2013, 4; Hansen 1998.

69. Athens: Blösel 2004, 193–99; Corinth and Argos: Whitby 1984; Sordi 2006; Thespiai: Tuplin 1986; Thebes after 335: Beck and Ganter 2015, 150–55; Gartland 2016.

70. The permanent loss of Salamis to Athens caused such grudges among the Megarians. The quarrels over the island persisted for a long time; see Legon 1981, 136–40; Beck 2018a, 34–42.

71. On Megalopolis, cf. Nielsen 2002 and 2015, 261–68 in the context of the Arkadian Confederacy; Mackil 2013, 72–73; Braunert and Petersen 1972; Hornblower 1990; Roy 2005. For the situation after the Battle of Mantineia, including the Theban intervention, see Beck 1997, 202–3, 220; Buckler 1989/2008, 224–25; Nielsen 2002, 414–18, noting that the synoikisized settlements in Mainalia and Parrhasia were not altogether abandoned.

72. On the tribal settlement pattern in Mainalia and Parrhasia, see Nielsen 2002, 271–308, with a full record of all attested cities and towns. For conditions in the plain of Megalopolis: Braunert and Petersen 1972; horse breeding: Osborne 1987, 53–54, from Strabo 8.8.1.

73. Roy 2007, 291 and Nielsen 2015, 264 remind us that we should be cautious about seeing the new foundation as a capital of the federal state.

74. The lyrics of Brothers in Arms (written and composed by Mark Knopfler) come to mind, in an inversion of the scene: "These mist-covered mountains are a home now for me. But my home is the lowlands, and always will be."

Chapter Three

1. Cf. Lesher 1992, 55–65 (*ad* frags. 2 and 3).

2. Following Xenophanes's assessment, Athenaios asserted that the development was a direct consequence of a lifestyle that ultimately "destroyed the city" (12.526c). At 12.525e he speaks of the lavish life in Ephesos.

3. Cf. Salmon 1984, 117, with Plin., *Nat*. 13.5. Athenaios (15.688–89 and 690) lists designers and brands, from a third-century BCE source. Sybaris: Timaios *FGrH* 56 F 50 (Athen. 12.519b–520c); Phylarchos *FGrH* 81 F 45 (Athen. 12.521b–e).

4. See Lesher 1992, 50–54.

5. Solon (frags. 4.5–10 West) dramatizes the ruin of the city by reference to the inability to behave properly at the banquet. On the *Theognidea*, see chapter 2 and Levine 1985 on the ideal symposium there; cf. also Yates 2018.

6. We do not know if the Persian conquest in 546 marked the point of Xenophanes's departure. One of the interpretative challenges his expat status poses is that we cannot be sure if discussions (e.g., of the symposium in frag. 1) built on personal experience in Kolophon or elsewhere.

7. Cf. also Beck 2018a, 17–18.

8. Morley 2015 is part of a collection that puts the study of smell in the ancient world on a new footing: see also Bradley 2015. Rudolph 2018 (same series) covers the topic of taste. See also Beck 2018b, 263–65 for a discussion of physiological and cultural encodings of sense and emotion.

9. Climatological, meteorological data can be retrieved from http://www.hnms.gr/hnms/english/index_html. If readers can lay their hands on it, Philippson 1948 is an invaluable source of historical climate data.

10. Kirk 1985, 176. For an intriguing case study in the Hesiodic corpus, see Bershadsky 2011, 17–22.

11. See Visser 1997, 78–146, for a comprehensive discussion and review of the literature; see also Kirk 1985, 168–240.

12. Sikyon: Lolos 2011, 38. Chaironeia and Orchomenos: Theophr. *Hist. pl.* 4.11.4–5; Paus. 9.41.7; Baumann 1982, 126. The local museum at Chaironeia has a perfume aryballos from the fifth century BCE on display. Karyai: Paus. 4.16.9 and 3.10.6–7, with Frazer 1898, 3:319–20; Calame, Collins, and Orion 2001, 150. Kos, prohibition to cut cedar wood in the sacred grove: *LSCG*, 150. In the Asklepieion in Sikyon, Pausanias (2.10.3; Frazer 1898, 3:65) saw the god holding the fruit of a cultivated pine (*pitus*).

13. Hippocrates, *Airs, Waters, Places* 1; cf. Haselberger 1999, 94–97 for intriguing observations on the interplay between the Hippocratic treatise, Aristotle, and Aristophanes in their respective assessment of wind, location, and communal well-being.

14. On Abydos and its rich natural resources, cf. E. Schwertheim, *DNP* s.v. Abydos (first published online 2006); Antiphon: Athen. 12.525b. On Aphrodite Pornē, see the next note.

15. Oysters: Marzano 2013, 173–95; Olson and Sens 2000. Aphrodite Pornē: Neanthes *BNJ* 84 F 9, with comm.; Burkert 1972/1983, 160 and 262.

16. Hastorf 2017, 42–54; Rudolph 2018; see also Crowther 2013, who inspires a holistic approach to food, stressing its formative impact on all human senses. The Netflix documentary series *Cooked*, by Michael Pollan, fully captures this.

17. See Filson and Adekunle 2017, with much bibliography.

18. Cf. Woolf 1998, 169–205 and passim; Pitts 2015.

19. Cf. Ober 1993.

20. Corinth: Koehler 1981; Maniatis et al. 1984. The imported amphorae are on display in the museum in Corinth. Tegea: *SEG* 11.423, with a correlating story in Arist., *Rhet.* 1365a and 1367b. The connection to Simon. *Epigr.* 41 Campbell is uncertain.

21. We note, not without irony, that some of Montreal's finest gourmet restaurants pride themselves in serving bread from Paris and fish from the Aegean, baked/caught the previous day, much to the delight of French and Greek monied elites in the city.

22. On imported wine and amphorae labels, cf. Lawall 2000; Boulay 2015. See also Lewis 2015 on the wide range of traded products on Athenian markets. Eel from Lake Kopais: Antiphanes, *Philothēbaios* (fourth century BCE), frag. 216 *PCG* (Athen. 14.622f–623a). See also the early

Hellenistic inscription from Akraiphnia containing a pricelist (*SEG* 32.450, with Lytle 2010). Along with tuna belly steaks, eel is listed as the most expensive item there. Sikyonian conger eel: Archestratos, frag. 19 Olson and Sens; Lolos 2011, 53–54. Agatharchides: *BNJ* 86 F 5 (Athen. 7.297d–e).

23. Olson and Sens 2000, xlvi–lv.

24. The Bintliff diameter endorses this picture of transport distance vs. cost efficiency (chapter 1). See Curtis 2015; Erdkamp 2015. According to Hansen 2006, almost every city relied on grain imports from distant places, yet the calculation is based on a substantially higher population figure than commonly assumed.

25. The passage comes from Athenaios 2.60b–c, who goes on (c–d) to cite Antiphanes (frag. 225 *PCG*) for a very similar saying. According to the speaker there, his dinner ingredients comprised whatever "the place (*topos*) affords us."

26. Plut., *de glor. Ath.* 6 = *Mor.* 349a endorses precisely this distinction: a common meal in Athens comprised barley, onions, and cheese. Eel, tender lettuces, kernels of garlic, and roast beef, on the other hand, were exceptional and noteworthy.

27. On cabbage, cf. Athenaios, *Deipn.* 9.369e–371a. Average annual rainfall and temperature levels: Athens 397mm/18.2°C, Megara 466mm/17.2°C (means of comparison: Sikyon 484mm/17.4°C, Thebes 545mm/17.0°C). Philippson 1948, 35–103 provides similar figures for the nineteenth century. His rainfall map (83) puts Megara in the transition zone from Athens to significantly wetter regions in Central Greece.

28. The classic text on this paragraph is Bourdieu 1984; cf. also Erdkamp 2012, 5; Corbeau and Poulain 2002, 69–70 and passim; Hastorf 2017, 219–72.

29. Dalby 1996, 111 and 174, on Hegesippos; Bober 1999, 109 and 346, n. 78.

30. Cf. Garlan 1988.

31. Marchand 2015. On the broader role of chefs, see Berthiaume 1982.

32. Iatrokles's book *On Bread Making* (of unknown date): Athenaios, *Deipn.* 14.646–647e; on Achaian *kreokakkabos*, see 9.384d (from a third-century BCE source). Thessalian *mattye*: Bober 1999, 112–113. Spartan black broth: e.g., Plut. *Lyk.* 12.6–7. Boiotian/Orchomenian geese: Aristoph., *Acharn.* 878. Boiotian *kollix*: Aristoph., *Acharn.* 872 = Athenaios, *Deipn.* 3.112f. Eretrian white bread: Athenaios, *Deipn.* 4.160a (from Sopater, third century BCE).

33. Hekataios *BNJ* 1 F 9; Harmodios *BNJ* 319 F 1.

34. The assignment of *Deipnon* to Philoxenos of Kythera is not entirely certain. Terpsion: Plat., *Phaid.* 59c; *Theait.* 142a–143c. On early cookbooks, cf. Olson and Sens 2000, xxviii–xliii; Nadeau 2015.

35. Olson and Sens 2000 provide the authoritative edition and commentary.

36. On the Theban *chōra*, cf. Buckler 1980, 4–14; Beck and Ganter 2015, 132–33; Farinetti 2011, 191–200.

37. On the topic of meat eating, see McInerney 2010 and 2014a; MacKinnon 2018.

38. Cf. also Vika 2011; Vika and Theodoropoulou 2012. For an update on the manuring debate, see Forbes 2012; McHugh 2017, 23–25.

39. Further stereotyping of Boiotian gluttony: Euboulos, frag. 52 Kassel-Austin; Plin., *Nat.* 27.145.

40. Hodos 2010, 3, drawing on Shanks 2001, 289. Cf. also Mattingly 2010 on the intersection of material culture and local/global identities; Nevett 2017.

41. Legon 1981, 87–88; Beck 2018a, 32–33.

42. The various sanctuaries of Demeter are mentioned by Paus. 2.34; see Jameson 2004, 178–83 for a catalog of sites. Connection to Argos by boat: cf. Ps.-Skylax 50–51.

43. Piérart 2004, 609–10; Jameson, Runnels, and van Andel 1994, 316–18; Pirenne-Delforge 1994, 186–87 (seashells in cult). Excavation reports from Argos: P. Aupert, *Bulletin de correspondance hellénique* 1974, 771–73; M. Sève, *Bulletin de correspondance hellénique Suppl.* 6, 295–321. On archaeological difficulties in tracing purple murex harvesting and dying, cf. Kardara 1961; Bruneau 1969 (Delos); see also Marzano 2013, 143–72, for later periods, and 151 on Hermione. Hamilton 1969, 96, referencing Alkiphron (3.10.4), has no doubt about the credibility of Plutarch's statement. Further parallels are found in the long-time preservation of honey.

44. Lolos 2011, 28–32; Trainor 2015, 19–39. I am grateful to Connor Trainor for further advice on Sikyonian clays (email communication, October 26, 2016).

45. Cf. G. Lippold, *RE* II 2.2 (1923), col. 2545–49, s.v. Sikyon (Kunststadt); Langlotz 1927, 1:30–53; Griffin 1982; Lolos 2011. According to Plut., *Arat.* 13, Apelles came to Sikyon "because he wanted the fame of having been associated with them."

46. Roller 1987. See also the online portal of the Canadian Institute in Greece, portal.cig-icg.gr, under "Tanagra Survey Project," for an updated bibliography.

47. Dillon 2012, 231. The most comprehensive discussion of the figures is in the museum catalog *Tanagra: Mythe et archéologie*, published by the Louvre in Paris, 2003.

48. *Tanagra: Mythe et archéologie*, 120–52.

49. Boutades: Plin., *Nat.* 36.151–52; see Griffin 1982, 100; Ziskowski 2016, 104 (quote) and passim.

50. Athens as place of origin: see Uhlenbrock 1990; Bell 1993.

51. Myrtis of Anthedon (late sixth century, Korinna's purported teacher) tells another intriguing story about the local women of Tanagra in her lyric poetry; see frag. 4 Campbell, from Plut., *Mor.* 300d–301a = *Greek Questions* #40.

52. See Haake 2018 on how to approach the Megarian school of philosophers.

53. Lys. 38.1–5; cf. Hypereides's speech *Against Athenogenes*, an Egyptian perfumer and permanent resident in Athens, who was accused of fraud in the sale of his business. "Dynasties of perfumers": Auberger 2010, 30.

54. See Theophr., *Hist. pl.* 4.10–11, for an extremely rich account. Cf. Post, forthcoming. The Hippocratic treatise *Ulcers* praises the healing quality of Orchomenian powder (17), most likely powdered ashes from the reeds of Lake Kopais.

55. Paus. 8.40.1–2; Philostr., *Gymn.* 21; Krumeich 1997, 202–3; Shear 2007, 109. Athletic hero cults: Bentz and Mann 2001. On the rugged topography, see Maher 2017, 295–99.

56. Xenophanes, frag. 2 Gerber. We note that none of the restored victory lists attest a winner from Kolophon in the pre-Hellenistic period: see Moretti 1957 (Olympia); Kostouros 2008 (Nemea); Farrington 2012 (Isthmia). For Delphi, J.-Y. Strasser announces the following forthcoming compilation: *Pythionikai: Recherches sur les vainqueurs aux Pythia de Delphes*. The earliest victor from Kolophon in the Mannheim database of ancient athletics (online at mafas.geschichte.uni-mannheim.de/athletes) dates from 320 BCE (Olympics).

57. Cf. Mann 2001, 30–39; Morgan 2010. In the horse race, the entire polis could be considered the winner; see Moretti 1957, no. 39 (Elis), and nos. 207 and 233 (Argos).

58. Exainetos: Moretti 1957, no. 346, from Diod. 13.82.7. See Buhmann 1972, 104–36 for a compilation of prizes in cash and kind; Pleket 2010.

59. Mann 2001, 33–35; Scott 2010, 159–62. Cf. also A. Chaniotis, *ThesCRA VII* (2012): 55–61.

60. Tellon: Paus. 6.10.9; *IvO* 147–48; Moretti 1957, no. 231.

61. Polydamas and Theagenes: Moretti 1957, nos. 201 and 348. Cf. Kurke 1991; Currie 2005, 120–57.

62. Moretti 1957, nos. 191, 214, 227; Currie 2002; Miller 2006, 162–63. On the broader phenomenon of colonies plugging into the pedigree of Panhellenic myth and heroic traditions, cf. Malkin 2005, 64 and passim.

63. Robert 1984, 38. "Less important contests": Remijsen 2011, 97; "local or regional appeal": van Nijf and Williamson 2016, 43.

64. See Schachter 1981–1994, 2.14–30.

65. Klee 1918 remains helpful on gymnasium games.

66. Nielsen 2016, 2018a, 2018b (Arkadia); cf. Ringwood 1927; Christesen 2007, 130–32, with ample evidence for victory lists of local games; Scharff, forthcoming.

67. Cf. van Nijf and Williamson 2016, 56. See also the case of Euthymenes (referenced below in note 77), who succeeded in competitions at Nemea, Megara, and his native Aigina. This appears to be a typical catchment area in pre-Hellenistic times.

68. Cf. Schachter 1981–1994: 1.122–23; Benchimol 2008.

69. Rhapsodic festivals: West 2010. Sophists at the Amphiaraia: *IOropos* 520, line 8. Tradition of rooster fights in Tanagra: Colum. 8.2.4 and 13; cf. Varr. *Rust.* 3.9.6; Plin., *Nat.* 10.48; A. Schachter, comm., *BNJ* 379 F 1a. Thessalian contests: Scharff 2016b (Thessalian triad: *taurothēria, aphippolampas, aphippodromē*); Graninger, forthcoming; Aston and Kerr 2018.

70. Cf. Moretti 1957, no. 29, who articulates a similar idea.

71. Elis: Paus. 4.24.2; *IvO* 217 (Hellenistic); Kroton: Mann 2001, 164–91.

72. Cf. Nicholson 2016.

73. Burnett 2005, 10.

74. "Supra-local background": D'Alessio 2009, 166–67.

75. Burnett 2005, 13–54. Gelzer 1985 argued that epinikian odes were performed at the sanctuary where victory was achieved, but the evidence, along with more general considerations, suggests otherwise: see Eckermann 2012. For example, in *Nem.* 4.24 Pindar addresses the assembled citizens of the polis.

76. Burnett 2005, 18.

77. Pind., *Nem.* 5, lines 41–46, with reference to the epichoric calendar of Aigina.

78. Cf. Polinskaya 2013, 126–96, on the topography.

79. Hence, Jacob Burckhardt's famous verdict of the *agonales Wesen* of the Hellenes. Cf. also Mann 2001, 22–24.

Chapter Four

1. This reading owes much to Gagné 2013, 394–438, who offers an ingenious interpretation of the *Oresteia* as an exemplary expression of ancestral fault in Classical literature.

2. Cf. Baehr 2008, 117–38, who provides helpful comments on the conceptual payload of the German translation of community of fate, "Schicksalsgemeinschaft," a term that is difficult due to its association with fascist ideology. Usage of the English word in conversations about globalization carries no such semantic legacy.

3. Cf. Baehr 2008 and 2016, with bibliography. See also Williams 2009, who discusses the concept at the juncture of citizenship and communal agency.

4. Parker 1983; cf. Matijević 2017 on the *lex sacra* from Selinus (see discussion below in this chapter). Note how Klytemnestra herself is branded a pollution to the community in line 1645, a "*miasma* of the land and its native gods (*theōn enchōriōn*)."

5. Gagné 2013, 344–93; cf. also Sommerstein 2011.

6. Cf. also Strauss Clay 2003 and 2009 (ample bibliography).

7. Cf. Kindt 2012, 123–25, with examples.

8. For example, see Scott 2010, who stresses that the catchment areas of Delphi and Olympia fluctuated greatly over time, which poses additional challenges to the Panhellenic view. Both sanctuaries' shifting roles as spaces of ritual practice make it difficult to label Delphi and Olympia, but this does not void their Panhellenic capacity altogether. Cf. Mitchell 2015, 50–56 for a nuanced approach.

9. Orchomenos over Koroneia: *SEG* 11.1208; Thebes over Hyettos: *SEG* 24.300, with Hansen 2004, 442–43; Tanagra: *SEG* 11.202 and 15.245. Cf. Beck 2014 for the regional dimension to these inscriptions.

10. Sybaris and the Serdaioi: M&L 10; Anaitoi and Metapioi: E&R 51; Elis and Heraia: M&L 17.

11. Cf. Raaflaub 2015, 434–35; and Beck 2016, who outline the small-scale foreign policy concept of city-states in the late Archaic period.

12. Cf. Scott 2010, 29–46.

13. Cf. Kindt 2012, 134–36 on epichoric encodings of the Altis at Olympia. Pausanias himself was forced to turn to his "expounders" (at Olympia: 5.10.7; 5.20.4). Pausanias occasionally speaks of an "expounder of local matters" (*tōn epichōriōn exēgētēs*): 1.13.8; 1.41.2; 7.6.5; 9.3.3; cf. Jones 2001, with further documentation.

14. Dörpfeld 1883; cf. also Lolos 2011, 57. The strengthening of mental ties between city and hinterland through the use of local building materials has been emphasized by Osborne 1987, 91.

15. Ismard 2015.

16. Cf. also Kindt 2015 on Greek personal religion.

17. Regional amphiktyonies: Funke 2013, with bibliography; Funke and Haake 2013. Kalapodi, the Homarion, and Messon are discussed in the respective contributions to Beck and Funke 2015b.

18. Sourvinou-Inwood 1990, 311–20. Cf. also Whitehead 1986, 176–222 on deme religion; Mikalson 2005, 133–59; see also Parker 1996, 328–42.

19. Sourvinou-Inwood 1990, 311–12.

20. Apollo: Schachter 1981–1994, 1:43–90. Orchomenos and Chaironeia: Schachter 1981–1994, 1:173–74 and 1:179–81. Thesmophoria at Eretria: Plut., *Mor.* 298b–c = *Quaest. Graec.* #31. See also Schachter 2000a for the development of divergent trajectories of religious conformity and diversity over time.

21. Cf. Hornblower 1991, 357–61; Polinskaya 2010 and 2012; Nottingham Oath Database, ID 1598 and 1576.

22. Polinskaya 2013, 36–43.

23. For Attica, Parker 1996 has masterfully unraveled the religious fabric of caves, mountain and hill shrines, and sanctuaries that were inspired by, and in turn geared toward, such a localization of the divine.

24. Cf., for instance, Ogden 2007, 9; Polinskaya 2013, 41–42; Garland 2014, 184.

25. Étienne and Knoepfler 1976, 178–81, 200–201. The quality of the local ore, and its impact on the economy, is debated; cf. Bintliff 1992.

26. Xenophon and his estate at Skillous: *Anab.* 5.3.7–13; Paus. 5.6.4–6; Diog. Laert. 2.52–53; cf. Anderson 1974, 165–66; Tuplin 1993, 183–85.

27. Location: Pritchett 1989, 67; Nielsen 2004, 546. Xenophon himself (*Anab.* 5.3.7–13) and Pausanias (5.6.4) place the site twenty stades south of Olympia (c. 3.5 kilometers), which makes the archaeological area of Kambuli north of Makrisia a strong candidate. See also Koiv 2013, 327.

28. Sinn 1978 and 1981; Luraghi 2008, 24, n. 34, and 157, n. 32.

29. Xen., *Anab.* 5.3.7-8. Archestratos (frag. 13 Olson and Sens) says the Selinus in Asia Minor was rich in gilthead.

30. Cf. Weiss 1984, 138-39, with references.

31. Pholos: Schmidt, *RE* 19.2 (1941) col. 517-22.

32. The funds that allowed Xenophon to get the ball rolling were delivered by a certain Megabyzos, treasurer at the Temple of Artemis in Ephesos, who had traveled to Olympia to attend the games (*Anab.* 5.3.6-7).

33. Badian 2004. It would be interesting to know who the vendor of the estate was.

34. Skillous is a small-scale community with a territory of unknown size; cf. Nielsen 2004 in Hansen and Nielsen 2004, 545-46.

35. Cf. Clarke 2008, 1-89.

36. Cf. Clarke 2008, 90-120.

37. The opening section of the inscription is broken off. See Jameson, Jordan, and Kotansky 1993, 27; Christesen 2005, 328; Theotikou 2013, 124-25; Matijević 2017, 15-16, 36-37; for in-depth discussion, see also Robertson 2010, 67-83.

38. Clarke 2008, 193-229; cf. also Möller 2002.

39. The data is drawn from Trümpy 1997; see also under "Jahresbeginn" there for more examples; cf. Hannah 2013, 355-57.

40. The local calendar on Delos was up to six months askew from the Athenian calendar; see Trümpy 1997, 10-38; Hannah 2013, 357-58.

41. Cf. Jones 2017, 85-87, 91-93 and passim.

42. Jones 2017, 51-52, 89-91, 146.

43. Cf. for example, Mikalson 1976 on the Athenian festival calendar.

44. Cf. also Scullion 1994, 75-119; Kearns 2011.

45. Demeter Malophoros in the Megarid: Bremmer 2012; Freitag 2018, 107. Selinus: de Polignac 1984/1995, 89-118 passim. On Corinth, see the various fascicles of *Corinth* XVIII, *The Sanctuary of Demeter and Kore*.

46. Lolos 2011, 16-17 on the difficulties of establishing the western border of the Sikyonia, near the Sythas river (Paus. 2.7.8); cf. also Larson 2001, 232-33.

47. The Pitsa panels are discussed in Kaltsas and Shapiro 2008, 225 (E. Stasinopoulou-Kakarouga; with bibliography).

48. Fontenrose 1988, 28-30 is concise; cf. also Mohr 2013, 59-64; and, most notably, the exhaustive study by Herda 2006. *SEG* 36.694 from Olbia (c. 525-500 BCE) sheds curious light on the connectivity of the sanctuary in the late Archaic period. See also Ehrhardt 1988, 139, 142-43, 199.

49. Cf. Herda 2006, 9 for a list of previous editions. Philtes: *Milet* 1.3.122, lines I 77.

50. Herda 2006, passim; Mohr 2013, 62-63.

51. On Chares and his initial statue group from c. 575 to 550 BCE, see Fontenrose 1988, 166; Herda 2006, 327-28. Worship of the nymphs on the hilltop is independently attested by the remains of a seated figure inscribed to the nymphs; see Ehrhardt 1993; Larson 2001, 201-2.

52. Offering to Phylios: Fontenrose 1988, 167-68; Herda 2006, 315-17.

53. Cf. Herda 2006, 326.

54. Herda's discussion of the Molpoi's role in Miletus (2006, 31-35) demonstrates this *Sonderstellung* of their board, which was closely interwoven with the organization of the local phylai and also the polis executive, yet distinct from the political organization.

55. Schachter 2000b/2016; cf. also Lehnus 1984. Iphikratic foot gear (Schachter 2000b/2016: 262, with n. 21) is a neat example of a universally recognizable design labeled after its illustrious creator, similar to Elvis sideburns or the Stresemann suit. Most likely, something about the daphnephoric shoe reminded Proklos or his source of the Iphikratic style.

56. *Pythian* 8, composed in or shortly after 446 BCE, attests Pindar's productivity at the time.

57. The earliest attestation of the Milky Way is found in Diod. 5.23.2. For a discussion of the route through the countryside, see Schachter 2000b/2016.

58. Cf. Calame 1977, 117-24, 190-94. In his brief reference to the festival, Paus. 9.10.4 suggests a close relation between the procession ritual and the veneration of Herakles in particular.

59. The collection of crocus plants for ceremonial purposes is depicted in the Santorini frescos and also attested in measured units in the Linear B record from Knossos and Pylos. Later Greek sources associated saffron with the Near East, but this does not preclude the idea of cultivation in the mainland. The crocus plant grows profusely in Greece today, in Boiotia and also further north. In Kozani, a high-quality organic and origin-certified saffron is grown and marketed under the local brand-label of Krokos Kozanis.

60. For the details, see Johnston 2012. *Theōrodokoi*: Perlman 2000, 157-66; Rutherford 2013, 57-58.

61. Frazer 1898, 2:296.

62. *PMG* 702.1-2, from Athen. 14.624e-f; Privitera 1965; Hall 1997, 101; Kowalzig 2007, 151.

63. Lasos's song *Centaurs* was equally asigmatic: *PMG* 704, from Athen. 10.455c; see Porter 2007.

64. Hansen (2004, 446) catalogues Mykalessos as a type 2 polis (i.e., 25-100 km^2). For Thucydides's narrative of the incident, see Hornblower 2008, 598-600, who sees traces of Thucydides's Thracian expertise here.

65. Quote, Kennell 2006, viii. Cf. Pélékidis 1962; Burckhardt 1996; Chankowski 2010; Kozak 2013.

66. Jeanmaire 1939 and Vidal-Naquet 1981 have become extremely influential here. On Sparta, cf. Meier 1998, 208-16 and passim.

67. Argive ephebes/*logades*: Thuc. 5.67.2, with Hornblower 2008, 177-78; Diod. 12.75.7; Plut., *Alk*. 15.3. Megara: McAuley 2018.

68. Cf. Hölscher 2007; Hedrick 2013. For a similar approach to the *didaskaleion* and what its purpose was in the public life of the Greek city, see Scholz 1998, 40-41, n. 116. Sparta: Xen., *Lak. Pol*. 2.2.10; Miletus: Kennell 2006, 81-83; Herda 2006, 92-98 and passim.

69. Cf. McAuley 2018, who provides a brilliant analysis of how the ephebes of Megara became vital keepers of local traditions over time.

70. Bayliss 2013, 14, with nn. 18-19; Nottingham Oath Database, ID 340 (mid-fourth century).

71. In the marshes and fields: *IG* II^2 1358. The collection of ephebic inscriptions from Athens by Reinmuth 1971, although now supplemented by countless new texts, offers a helpful first orientation, also on ephebic tours through the *chōra*. [Arist.], *Ath. Pol*. 42.3 highlights the idea of ephebic learning through venturing.

72. Cf. Siewert 1977; Bayliss 2013, 13-22; Scharff 2016a, 311-16 and passim. Thespiai: Apoll., *Bibl*. 2.4.10; Paus. 9.27.7; see Diod. 4.29.1-6, on Herakles's sexual encounter with the fifty daughters of Thespios, according to local tradition either in one night or in fifty consecutive nights. Apaturia: Mikalson 2005, 142.

73. Dem. 19.303. Scholars located the Aglaureion for the longest time on the north slope of the Acropolis, but an inscribed stele from "the shrine of Aglauros" (Dontas 1983, third century BCE) resolves the issue in favor of the east slope; see also Hurwit 1999, 172.

74. Sourvinou-Inwood 2011, 26–107 masterfully dissects the various strands.

75. For a similar take, cf. Parker 1987, 197; Bayliss 2013, 18–19. See also Osborne 1987, 147, who highlights the faithful relation between the ephebes and the land. Basso 1996 captures a similar intergenerational tie between people and the land among the Western Apache.

76. *ICret* I.IX.1, lines 31–35 from c. 220–180 BCE.

77. Heinrichs 2015, 7–9; Carbon and Clackson 2016, 140–43.

78. Paus. 8.2.6. Notorious traditions about human sacrifice on Mt. Lykaion, so prominent in Heinrichs's commentary, find no resonance in the text.

79. Heinrichs's suggestion of a full-fledged ephebate in the lands of rural Arkadia and the recruitment of elders misses the nature of the inscription.

80. See Carbon and Clackson 2016, 152–55 (Carbon) on the issue of catchment, proposing that "we are dealing with small local communities and sanctuary sites within this limited geographical range [i.e., central and southwestern Arkadia, H.B.], rather than a truly pan-Arkadian sweep" (153).—Curiously enough, lines 1 and 2 reference awards in local athletic competitions. For potential candidates, see the list of local Arkadian games compiled in Nielsen 2018b, 408–15.

Chapter Five

1. Citation: *BNJ* 379 F 5, from Plut., *De malign. Her.* 31–33 = *Mor.* 864d. On Aristophanes, cf. A. Schachter's Biographical Essay in *BNJ* 379; Fowler 2013, 637–38; Tufano 2019, 189–96 and 227–40 on the cited passage.

2. Cf. Priestley 2014, 42–44.

3. Aristophanes's lifespan: cf. Schachter, *BNJ* 379; Buck 1979, 129–30; Fowler 2013, 637 (early fourth century BCE). F 5 states that the archons barred Herodotus from speaking to the youths because of their "boorish and misologic mindset." To Fowler, this "may, but need not, suggest an anti-Theban stance" (638). If indeed from another Boiotian city than Thebes, Aristophanes would have had little room to disparage the boorish Theban character; the notorious stigma of rough people ("swine": Pind., *Ol.* 6.89–90; see above, chap. 3) applied to all Boiotians, not only to the Thebans. If the reference is not inspired by the topic of *De malign. Her.* itself, I take it as an expression of the anger of (young?) Aristophanes at the (old) polis authorities at the time. On Herodotus in Thebes, see Papazarkadas 2014a, 242–47.

4. Hdt. 5.67; Lolos 2011, 62–63.

5. Strabo 9.1.10; Freitag 2018, 100.

6. See *BNJ* 607 F 1, with biographical essay.

7. Viewsheds: McHugh 2017, 129; see also Frazer 1898: 2:273, who painted the picturesque image of a unique countryside.

8. Pretzler 2007, 32–34 discusses an intriguing incident of inversion on Pausanias's travels to Egypt, where the question of local and foreign origins of the so-called Statue of Memnon at Thebes inspired considerable debate.

9. Favorinus [Dio Chrysostom] 37.7, with Priestley 2014, 44. The vexing issue of Herodotus's account of the Battle of Salamis (8.94) is discussed by Bowie 2007, 182–83.

10. Cf. Fowler (2000, "Preface"), who describes Jacoby as "the undisputed master of Greek historiography of our time and all who work after him must labour merely in his shadow."

11. Jacoby's views were spelled out in countless commentaries of *FGrH* and, more systematically, in his *Atthis* (1949, 51–70, esp. 68–69).

12. *BNJ* 4 (F. Pownall).

13. Horography: Diod. 1.26.5 (*BNJ* 264 F 25, but the term does not stem from Hekataios of Abdera there); Dion. Hal., *Ant.* 7.1.6 (*BNJ* 251 F 9); Plut., *De malign. Her.* 36 = *Mor.* 869b; also 677d. See the discussion below.

14. In this sense, too, Jacoby's legacy is inescapable. In addition to the new edition of individual authors in *BNJ*, see Harding 2008. For more recent discussions of the Atthidographers, see Harding 2007; Clarke 2008; Fowler 2013, 447–93.

15. Chorography: Ptol., *Geog.* Praef. 1, with Malkin 2011, 13, and chapter 1; see also Polyb. 34.1.5; Walbank 1979, 572; Strab. 8.3.17.

16. To the examples in note 13 above, add Hesych. and [Zon.], under *hōrographoi*, *hōrographiai*. The term *hōroi* appears more frequently.

17. See also the critical interventions by Marincola 1999 and Harding 2007, esp. 185–86. For the chronicle, Möller 2001 and 2006 provide an all-new point of departure.

18. This view draws on my previous edition of the early Roman historians, *FRH* I^2 and II, co-edited with U. Walter. Cf. also Beck 2007 for a summary perspective.

19. Cf. Thomas 2014, 159, who explains that Jacoby, in his later career, appears to have departed from his early fascination with *horoi* and chronicles.

20. Cf. Fowler 2013, 623–29. Herodotus's intimate knowledge of Argive affairs makes a visit likely. Akousilaos might have been among the learned men (*logioi*) of whom Herodotus speaks in the opening paragraphs of his *Histories*.

21. Another fine example is Herodotus's reference to a man named Dithyrambos of Thespiai (7.227). Little is known about him; he was Thespiai's best fighter at Plataia. Kowalzig 2007, 338–39 argues that his name resonates with a broader stream of pro-Athenian convictions at Thespiai. If correct, then this stream entered "great historiography" through Herodotus.

22. Noteworthy exceptions include Fornara 1983, 1–46, esp. 16–23; Orsi 1994; Schepens 2001; Clarke 2005 and 2008; Thomas 2014b; Tober 2017.

23. Clarke 2008, 7–27, 177–93 and passim.

24. On Praxion's account (*BNJ* 484 F 1, with comm. P. Liddel), see the detailed discussion by Ager 2018; cf. also Neils 1987, 143–48.

25. "What was local for Megara was a highway for others" (Ager 2018, 47). Cf. also Tober 2018, who explains the lively sense of territoriality in Megarian local traditions.

26. Armenidas: *BNJ* 378; Fowler 2013, 639–40; Tufano 2019, 131–88. Aristophanes: *BNJ* 379 F 4; and Schachter 1990/2016. See also Aristophanes F 9 on the Argyneion, which apparently was a place charged with local and regional meaning in Boiotia.

27. *BNJ* 387 F 1. The musical festival was so renowned that it attracted participants from elsewhere, including a *chorēgos* from Sikyon and a rock-star *aulētēs*, Anakos of Phigaleia.

28. *BNJ* 310 F 3. The passage derives either from Sokrates's *Argolika* or his *On Holy Things* (*in Argos?*), as initially suggested by Jacoby.

29. Judging from the two other remaining fragments of Harmodios (F 2–3), it appears that the city nourished a convivial culture of heavy drinking.

30. Hereas of Megara *BNJ* 486 F 4, with comm. P. Liddel; Ager 2018; Tober 2018. Daimachos *BNJ* 65 F 7; Tufano 2019, 315–98. Aristotle *BNJ* 423 F 5, with comm. S. Sprawski.

31. In Herodotus 6.84.1, the Argive version on Kleomenes's end is referenced. Also, 77.2 cites the oracle that was given to the Argives beforehand. On the local reception in Argos, see Franchi 2012.

32. Comm. on *BNJ* 379 F 6; Buck 1974; Chaniotis 1988, 193.

33. The epigraphic evidence is compiled in *BNJ* 486, biographical essay (P. Liddel); cf. also Tober 2018, 190–93.

34. Calame 1995, 75–96: "embroyage énonciatif"; cf. also Calame 1987; Luraghi 2001a, 141 and n. 11.

35. See Gottesmann 2014, 57–61, who offers an intriguing reading of barbershops as places for the exchange of gossip and shoptalk; cf. also Matuszewski (2019, 63–69 and passim) on informal realms of conversation in fourth-century Athens.

36. Cf. Purcell 1990.

37. Encoding/decoding: Hall 1980. For the elaboration of the ritualized view of communication that sees civic rituals surrounding communication as more generative of meaning than the content that is transmitted in a message, cf. Carey 2009.

38. In similar vein, cf. Lewis 1996, 156.

39. On official heralds (*kērykes*, sing. *kēryx*), see H. Beck, *BNP*, s.v. *keryx*; Lewis 1996, 51–74.

40. The material is easily traceable via http://proxenies.csad.ox.ac.uk/, which supplements Mack 2015. For the Lokrian radius, see Daverio Rocchi 2019. Boiotia: Fossey 2014, 3–22. See also below on the regional proxenies of the Theban Aiolidai and the Kleonymidai of Aigina.

41. F. Gschnitzer's landmark lemma "Proxenos" (*RE* Suppl. 13 [1973]: 629–730) continues to inform the debate. Gerolymatos 1986 notoriously presented *proxenoi* as spy agents, which didn't receive much support in subsequent scholarship.

42. Examples are discussed by Lewis 1996, 9–24 and passim; cf. also Mack 2015, 115–22.

43. Pind., *Isthm.* 4, lines 8–10. Incidentally, the passage states that the Kleonymidai served as "*proxenoi* of their neighbors" (*amphiktionōn*), which couches proxenic ties in the context of relations between neighboring communities. The same radius of proxenic neighborhood ties applies to the Theban Aiolidai; see further below.

44. *IG* II² 33, lines 6–7 (385 BCE); Mack 2015, 116.

45. Onomaos *ap.* Euseb., *Praep. evang.* 5.34.15–16; Moretti 1957, no. 180.

46. Kallimachos, frag. 85 Pfeiffer, lines 5–9; cf. Barigazzi 1976.

47. P. Oxy. 3965 = Sim. frag. eleg. 11 W²; cf. West 1993; Schachter 1998/2016; Boedeker and Sider 2001.

48. Thuc. 1.132.2; [Dem.] 59.96–97; cf. Beck 2009, 64–65.

49. Cf. Jung 2006, 225–97 and passim; Vannicelli 2007 (Thermopylai); Marincola 2007; Cartledge 2013, 122–57. The dedications of giant bronze statues at Olympia and Isthmia (Hdt. 9.81.1) were most likely adorned with equally "mute" inscriptions.

50. Plut., *Arist.* 19.7; *Anth. Graec.* 6.50 (complete inscription). The related festival of the Eleutheria was established only later.

51. Plut., *Arist.* 21.1–6; Beck 2009, 61–68; Kalliontzis 2014, 342–46.

52. Plataia: Plut., *Arist.* 21.3; Athens: Plut., *Mor.* 349f; Sparta: *IG* V1 18 and 660; Paus. 3.14.1; Megara, below note 60.

53. Steinbock 2013, 84–94.

54. See Figueira 2004, 622 for context and references.

55. Hdt. 6.88–91, with Figueira 1993, 113–49, who disentangles the Herodotean narrative. Cf. the various contributions to Powell and Meidani 2016.

56. Sepeia: Bearzot 2006, 106–14; Robinson 2011, 6–9.

57. Kleonai: Piérart 2004, 610–11; treaties with Athens and Sparta: Thuc. 1.102.4; *StV* 144; Olympia: Moretti 1957, no. 222; Ageladas: R. Neudecker, *BNP*, s.v.

58. Argive democracy: Leppin 1999; Bearzot and Landucci 2006; Robinson 2011, 10–21.

59. See also Legon 1981, 157–73, for a narrative history of Megara in the Persian War.

60. Cf. Reeves 2018, 173–75 on the Persian War monument in Megara visited by Pausanias (1.43.2–3). Its inscription (*SEG* 13.312), restored around 300 CE, honored "those who died in the Persian War and are buried here as heroes" (lines 1–2).

61. Cf. Yates 2018, 143–45, for a discussion of the date, authorship, and relation to the corpus.

62. The earlier Persian War poem (757–64) addresses the topic of fear in its final line. Yates's ingenious interpretation (2018, 141) deserves reference in full: "On the surface, the poet intends to purge the revelers of any negative thoughts of the war, but in fact achieves the opposite by bringing the threat very much to mind just as the poem closes. No longer is danger presented in general terms, as it was in the opening lines. Rather, the poet now defines the threat quite specifically. . . . Outside the exhortation of the poet, the Megarians are terrified, and the audience is not allowed to forget it."

63. The altar might have been the stone on the Alkathoos where Apollo had famously laid down his gilded lyre to help with the city foundation (Paus. 1.42.2). If so, this was clearly a hypercharged place in the urban topography. See Frazer 1898, 1:530; Yates 2018, 159, n. 77.

64. Megara's vexed history of access to its harbors on the Corinthian and Saronic Gulfs is paradigmatic of a deep sense of uncertainty and often impotence. Whenever it suited greater powers around them, they seized Megara's harbor places: see Freitag 2018.

65. Cf. Graf 1984, 11–55. On Herodotus's medizing Thebans, see Steinbock 2013, 115–18.

66. In similar vein, see, for example, Hdt 1.96–101 (Deiokes), 3.80–82 (constitutional debate), 7.46 (Xerxes's reflections); cf. Flower and Marincola 2002, 126–33.

67. Steinbock 2013, 113–15 has demonstrated how the historical memorialization was crafted, endorsed, and kept alive mostly by Athens—an effective strategy to shape images of self and other.

68. Carey 1981, 184; Burnett 2005, 113.

69. See Carey 1981, 184–85, 188–190; Demand 1982, 29; Burnett 2005, 107–18. A recently discovered funerary epigram for citizens who had vigorously fought for the existence of their patria may well date from one of the concluding battles of the Persian War: see Papazarkadas 2014b, 223–33.

70. See also *Isthm.* 4 with Schachter 1981–1994, 2:18, who detects the desire for a new beginning in Thebes at the time of the ode, c. 474 BCE.

71. Hornblower 1991, 420–41, 444–66; cf. Macleod 1983, 103–22.

72. Cf. Hornblower 1991, 456–57. For a discussion, see below.

73. The term is introduced by Thucydides in 3.62.2, where it is stated that "the only reason the Plataians did not medize was because the Athenians did not, and that, moreover, on the same principle, when the Athenians afterwards assailed all Hellas, they were the only Boiotians who atticized." The charge resembles what Herodotus says about the Phokians: they only abstained from medism because the neigboring Thessalians did medize (8.30.1). Hornblower 1991, 455 is right to stress that the term "to side with the Athenians," although technically a neologism in the literary tradition, appears to have been in ordinary use (contra Macleod 1983, 116). Note the parallel in 4.133.1, which denounces the atticism of Thespiai. See also below on the notion of "Orchomenizers."

74. Hornblower 1991, 455.

75. Thucydides himself offers only an abridged narrative on Boiotian migration and habitation (1.12.1–4), yet he, too, emphasizes the role of Kadmeians/Thebans.

76. This also reverberates in Thuc. 3.65.2, when the intention of reinstating Plataia's traditional place in Boiotia is ascribed to "some of your [Plataia's] best citizens, men of substance from the best families."

77. See Thuc. 3.67.3. The young men who entered Plataia in 431 are identified as the sons of those who fought at Koroneia. Either they grew up without their fathers, or their fathers, war heroes of the past, now lamented the death of their sons. The chiasm put Koroneia at the hinge between the generations.

78. Cf. Bowra 1938; Pritchett 1979, 89–90; *SEG* 10.410; 21.123; 23.41 = *IG* I³ 1163. Arrington 2012 offers a full reexamination that assigns the epigram to the Battle of Delion.

79. Cf. Larson 2007, 185–86, whose pointed observations fully endorse this interpretation.

80. Sources for the battle: Thuc. 1.113.1; Diod. 12.6; cf. Paus. 1.27.5; Plut., *Per.* 18.2. The term *Orchomenizers* appears only in Steph. Byz., s.v. Chaironeia. Under the same entry, Stephanus cites Aristophanes *BNJ* 379, who will have dealt with the issue in greater detail. Sparton: Plut., *Ages.* 19.2; Buck 1979, 150. Lokrian and Euboian exiles are mentioned in Thucydides. It is notoriously difficult to sketch the outline of events in 447 and 446. The sequence presented here follows Buck 1979, 150–52; Demand 1982, 31–40; Gehrke 1986, 168.

81. Date: *ATL* 174 and 178, n. 65; capture of Chaironia: Buck 1979, 152.

82. The precise location is unknown. Plutarch (*Ages.* 19.2; see also below) says it was near the Temple of Athena Itonia, which complements Paus. 1.27.5, who claims that the Athenians were on their way to Haliartos. See also the discussion of the terrain by Buckler 1996/2008, 60–62, on the topography of the second Battle at Koroneia, 395 BCE.

83. Revolutions in Euboia and Megara: Thuc. 1.114, with Hornblower 1991, 184–86; evacuation of Boiotia: Thuc. 1.113.3. Buck 1979, 153, infers a long list of details of the agreement between Athens and Boiotia from later actions, but much of this is conjectural. The contemporary Athenian decree (*IG* I² 36), honoring some men from Thespiai, relates to the turnover in one way or another: Gomme 1956, 339.

84. The idea is also present in Xen., *Mem.* 3.5.4, where the younger Perikles states that "the Theban disposition toward the Athenians has been strengthened [by Koroneia], so that the Boiotians who formerly would not dare to stand against the Athenians . . . even in their own land, now threaten to invade Attica by themselves."

85. The causality between Koroneia and the foundation of the new league has been pointed out by many (e.g., Larson 2007, 187; Hornblower 1995, 674, who detects a general momentousness after the battle in Boiotia). On the new *koinon*, see Demand 1982, 35–40; Beck 1997, 88–96; Mackil 2013 and 2014; Beck and Ganter 2015. Thirty Years Peace: Thuc. 1.115.1 (*StV* 156).

86. The guiding literary principle is selectivity, resulting from the desire to chart the growth of Athenian power; cf. Hornblower 1991, 133–34; Rood 1998, 225–48, esp. 246.

87. Plut., *Ages.* 19.2 (on the year 395).

88. Ps.-Apollodoros 2.4.11.

89. Schachter 1981–1994, 1:119–20 and 1994/2016, 181; Kowalzig 2007, 360–64; Kaltsas and Shapiro 2008, 106–7; Paleothodoros 2016 (discussion of the Boiotian *lekanis* and its dissemination abroad).

90. Cf. Benchimol 2008; Larson 2007, 133–36, 161–62. See also Tufano 2019, 134–38, who traces the longue durée of parades near Koroneia from early times to the Hellenistic Pamboiotia.

91. My interpretation of the social function of those and related rituals builds on Burkert 1977/1985 and 1987, whose reading owes much to Émile Durkheim. Durkheim extended the concept of suspension of everyday life to the notion of collective euphoria ("effervescence"), which empowers festival participants with the experience of belonging together and, hence, living through the basic foundations of their identity as a group. Historians and sociologists have developed this further; cf., for instance, Assmann 1997, whose definition of festivals as "*Urform*

des kulturellen Gedächtnisses" (archetypes of cultural memory) builds on the celebration's capacity to transcend everyday societal communications.

92. The term was introduced in German ("*Emotionstiefe historischer Erfahrung*") in Beck 2009, 75–78; cf. also Beck and Wiemer 2009, 10; Ganter 2013 and 2019 (Boiotia). The concept draws strongly on Angelos Chaniotis's work on the importance of the emotion paradigm for the study of rituals: Chaniotis 2006 and 2008; Chaniotis, Kaltsas, and Mylonopoulos 2017.

93. Proklos: *Chrestomathia* 25, with Schachter 2000b/2016, 261–70 (above, chapter 4). For Thucydides on the Pelasgians, cf. Larson 2007, 52–66; McInerney 2014b. The earliest account that elaborates on them is Ephoros *BNJ* 70 F 119 = Strab. 9.2.2–5, in which the Thebans go through multiple cycles of exile and return; see Kühr 2006, 267–68.

94. The ode presents Thebans and Spartans as allied through the mythical figures Iolaos and Castor (lines 17, 28–31). Their cooperation was terminated when Athens took control over Boiotia in the Battle of Oinophyta in 457, which provides the terminus ante quem.

95. The interpretation, naturally, is debated, as is the actual identification of Asopodoros. Scholars have been divided on both questions since antiquity: see the grammarian Didymos's notes, *Schol. Isth.* 1.52 a–b. Cf. Demand 1982, 28–29 and Sevieri 1999, who both lean toward the interpretation offered here. A similar view was already promoted by Wilamowitz-Moellendorff 1922, 330–31.

96. Cf. Kurke 2007, whose study of the ode delineates a characteristically Theban chorality.

97. Cf. *Parth.* 1 = 94a. Pagondas has a lengthy *RE* entry: T. Lenschau, *RE* 18.2 (1942): 2313–15, s.v. (1); cf. Wilamowitz-Moellendorff 1922, 434. The family's fame also reverberates in an unpublished inscription from Thebes from the late fifth century; see *Teiresias Epigraphica* 2017–2018, E471.03 = Papazarkadas 2018.

98. Ode 94b, lines 41–43; Mackil 2013, 193; Kurke 2007, 90; Schachter 2000b/2016, 258–59.

99. See, for example, Larson 2007, 133–34; Schachter 1981–1994, 2:219–20. Kurke 2007, 90–91 also suggests athletic victories, but not without noticing the emphasis that is put on Boiotia. If this reading is correct, we note that the regional contests of Onchestos and Koroneia are mentioned before the Olympic crown.

100. Schachter 1981–1994, 2:207–21, citing Pind., *Isth.* 1.52–54 as evidence. The case is inconclusive.

101. Schachter 1981–1994, 1:117–27.

102. Cf. lines 10–20, where Porphyrion is overthrown. A Boiotian audience might have been compelled to draw an analogy with current affairs: cf. Lefkowitz 1977; Burton 1962, 175–77; Burnett 2005, 225–38.

103. In similar vein, see Schachter 2000b/2016, 260. Beyond its commitment to the principle of proportional representation, the new Boiotian League managed to contain traditional rivalries between Thebes and Orchomenos: each of them were awarded the same weight in the league's administration (two out of nine shares in 447), which might have been viewed as both "faithful" and "just."

104. Cf. Schachter 1996. Polygnotos of Thasos, famous for his murals in Athens and elsewhere, also visited Thespiai and painted works in the public sphere: Plin., *Nat.* 35.40. Were these historical paintings, similar to his works in the Stoa Poikile on the Athenian agora?

105. *SEG* 31.358, with Beck 2014, 38–41.

106. The debate was recently summarized by Steinbock 2013, 103–5, with ample reference to previous scholarship.

107. Giroux 2020, detects similar traces of a Theban freedom-narrative in Diodorus's recollection (4.10.2–4) of a mythical war between Thebans and Orchomenians.

Chapter Six

1. *Idyll* 7: cf. Hunter 1996, 20–28; Rosenmeyer 1969, 145–67 (both also on the use of sound). Porter 2010, 18–21 and passim fleshes out the experience through euphonist theory. I am thankful to Naomi Kaloudis for discussing the issue of euphonism with me, including the text under scrutiny here (email correspondence from April 18, 2018).

2. Hunter 1996, 23. The Greek word for "to plant" is *pēgnumi* in both cases.

3. Cf. also the plea for epichoric history by Figueira 1993, 1, which was formulated to engender in the reader an appreciation of Aiginetan local history. Brock and Hodkinson 2000 sought to counterbalance celebrations of democratic Athens; the focus there was on the variety of political organization. Research on Greek *ethnos* and federal states followed a similar trajectory: cf. Beck and Funke 2015b, with a survey of the history of scholarship.

4. Cf. Malkin 2011, 12–13.

5. In a similar vein, cf. Yates 2019, whose book came out too late for me to take it into full consideration.

6. Vlassopoulos's concept builds strongly on his seminal work from 2007. "Histoire croisée": Werner and Zimmermann 2006. On academic turns, see chapter 1. Bang 2016 observes shifting economies of interest in, and concern with, the idea of universalism in the human sciences.

References

Abbreviations

ATL	B. D. Meritt, H. T. Wade-Gery, and M. F. McGregor, *The Athenian Tribute Lists*. Vol. 3. Princeton, NJ, 1950.
BCD	A. S. Walker. *The BCD Collection: Coins of Peloponnesos*. Zurich, 2006.
BNJ	*Brill's New Jacoby*.
BNP	*Brill's New Pauly*.
CAH	*The Cambridge Ancient History*. 2nd ed.
D-K	H. Diels and W. Kranz. *Die Fragmente der Vorsokratiker*. 6th ed. Berlin, 1951–1952.
DNP	*Der Neue Pauly*.
EAH	*Encyclopedia of Ancient History*.
E&R	H. van Effenterre and F. Ruze, *Nomima: Recueil d'inscriptions politiques et juridiques de l'archaïsme grec*. 2 vols. Paris, 1994.
FdD	*Les fouilles de Delphes*.
FGrH	*Die Fragmente der griechischen Historiker*.
FRH	H. Beck and U. Walter. *Die Frühen Römischen Historiker*. 2 vols. Darmstadt, 2004 and 2005.
ICret	*Inscriptiones Creticae*.
IG	*Inscriptiones Graecae*.
I.Oropos	*Oi epigraphes tou Oropou [The Inscriptions of Oropos]*.
IThesp	*Les inscriptions de Thespies*.
IvO	*Die Inschriften von Olympia*.
LIMC	*Lexicon Iconographicum Mythologiae Classicae*.
LSAG	L. A. Jeffery, *The Local Scripts of Archaic Greece*. Oxford, 1961.
LSCG	F. Sokolowski, *Lois sacrées des cités grecques*. Paris, 1969.
LSJ	*Greek-English Lexicon*, compiled by H. G. Liddell and R. Scott, with a revised supplement by H. S. Jones.
M&L	R. Meiggs and D. M. Lewis, *A Selection of Greek Historical Inscriptions to the End of the Fifth Century*. Rev. ed. Oxford, 1988.

PCG	*Poetae Comici Graeci.*
PMG	*Poetae Melici Graeci.*
RE	*Realencyclopädie der classischen Altertumswissenschaft.*
R&O	P. J. Rhodes and R. Osborne, *Greek Historical Inscriptions, 404–323 BC.* Oxford, 2003.
SEG	*Supplementum Epigraphicum Graecum.*
StV	H. Bengtson and R. Werner. *Die Staatsverträge des Altertums.* Vol 2. 2nd ed. Munich, 1975.
ThesCRA	*Thesaurus Cultus et Rituum Antiquorum.*

Referenced Literature

Abbott, A. 2014. "Brains of Norway." *Nature. International Weekly Journal of Science* 514:154–57.

Ager, S. L. 1996. *Interstate Arbitrations in the Greek World, 337 to 90 B.C.* Berkeley.

———. 2018. "Mythic Highways of the Megarid." In Beck and Smith 2018, 47–75.

———, and H. Beck, eds. Forthcoming. *Localism in the Hellenistic World.*

———, and R. A. Faber, eds. 2013. *Belonging and Isolation in the Hellenistic World.* Toronto.

Akrigg, B. 2011. "Demography and Classical Athens." In *Demography and the Graeco-Roman World: New Insights and Approaches*, ed. C. Holleran and A. Pudsey, 37–59. Cambridge.

Alcock, S. E. 1991. "Urban Survey and the Polis of Phlius." *Hesperia* 60:421–63.

———. 1993. *Graecia Capta: The Landscapes of Roman Greece.* Cambridge.

———, and R. Osborne, eds. 1994. *Placing the Gods: Sanctuaries and Sacred Space in Ancient Greece.* Oxford.

———, and R. Osborne, eds. 2007. *Classical Archaeology.* Oxford.

Algra, K. 2014. "Aristotle's Conception of Place and Its Reception in the Hellenistic World." In *Space in Hellenistic Philosophy: Critical Studies in Ancient Physics*, ed. G. Ranocchia, C. Helmig, and C. Horn, 11–52. Berlin.

Allen, T. W. 1969. *Homeri Opera.* Vol. 5. Oxford.

Ambaglio, D. 2001. "Epichorios: Un termine tecnico storiografico?" In *Atti del Congresso Storiografia locale e storiografia universale*, 7–21. Como.

Anderson, G. 2003. *The Athenian Experiment: Building an Imagined Political Community in Ancient Attica, 508–490 B.C.* Ann Arbor.

Anderson, J. K. 1974. *Xenophon.* Bristol.

Anderson, B. (1983) 2016. *Imagined Communities: Reflections on the Origin and Spread of Nationalism.* London.

Antonaccio, C. M. 1995. *An Archaeology of Ancestors: Tomb Cult and Hero Cult in Early Greece.* London.

Appadurai, A. 1996. *Modernity at Large: Cultural Dimensions of Globalization.* Minneapolis.

———, ed. 2002. *Globalization.* London.

Arrington, N. T. 2012. "The Form(s) and Date(s) of a Classical War Monument: Re-evaluating *IG* I³ 1163 and the Case for Delion." *Zeitschrift für Papyrologie und Epigraphik* 181:61–75.

Asheri, D., A. Lloyd, and A. Corcella. 2007. *A Commentary on Herodotus, Books I–IV.* Ed. O. Murray and A. Moreno. Oxford.

Assmann, J. 1997. *Das kulturelle Gedächtnis: Schrift, Erinnerung und politische Identität in frühen Hochkulturen.* 2nd ed. Munich.

Aston, E., and J. Kerr. 2018. "Battlefield and Racetrack: The Role of Horses in Thessalian Society." *Historia* 67:2–35.

Auberger, J. 2010. *Manger en Grèce classique: La nourriture, ses plaisirs et ses contraintes.* Québec.

Ault, B. A. 2005. *The Excavations at Ancient Halieis. Vol. 2. The Houses: The Organization and Use of Domestic Space.* Bloomington.

Badian, E. 2004. "Xenophon the Athenian." In *Xenophon and His World*, C. Tuplin, ed., 33–54. Stuttgart.

Baehr, P. 2008. *Caesarism, Charisma, and Fate: Historical Sources and Modern Resonances in the Work of Max Weber.* New York.

———. 2016. "Community of Fate." *The Blackwell Encyclopedia of Sociology.* Ed. G. Ritzer. Malden, MA.

Bang, P. 2016. "'*Zum ewigen Frieden*': Cosmopolitanism, Comparison, and Empire." In Lavan, Payne, and Weisweiler 2016, 231–38.

Barabási, A.-L. 2002. *Linked: The New Science of Networks.* New York.

Barigazzi, A. 1976. "L'aition callimacheo di Euticle di Locri." *Prometheus* 2:145–50.

Bassino, P. 2019. *The "Certamen Homeri et Hesiodi": A Commentary.* Berlin.

Basso, K. H. 1996. *Wisdom Sits in Places: Landscape and Language among the Western Apache.* Albuquerque.

Baumann, H. 1982. *Greek Wild Flowers.* London.

Bayliss, A. J. 2013. "Oath and Citizenship." In *Oath and State in Ancient Greece*, by A. H. Sommerstein and A. J. Bayliss, 9–32. Berlin.

Bearzot, C. 2006. "Argo nel V secolo: Ambizioni egemoniche, crisi interne, condizionamenti esterni." In Bearzot and Landucci 2006, 105–46.

Bearzot, C., and F. Landucci, eds. 2006. *Argo: Una democrazia diversa.* Milano.

Beck, H. 1997. *Polis und Koinon: Untersuchungen zur Geschichte und Struktur der griechischen Bundesstaaten im 4. Jh. v. Chr.* Stuttgart.

———. 2007. "The Early Roman Tradition." In *A Companion to Greek and Roman Historiography*, ed. J. Marincola, 1:259–66. 2 vols. Malden, MA.

———. 2008. "Prologue: Power Politics in Fourth-Century Greece." In Buckler and Beck 2008, 1–30.

———. 2009. "Ephebie—Ritual—Geschichte: Polisfest und historische Erinnerung im klassischen Griechenland." In Beck and Wiemer 2009, 55–82.

———, ed. 2013. *A Companion to Ancient Greek Government.* Malden, MA.

———. 2014. "Ethnic Identity and Integration in Boiotia: The Evidence of the Inscriptions (6th and 5th centuries BCE)." In Papazarkadas 2014b, 19–44.

———. 2016. "Between Demarcation and Integration: The Context of Foreign Policy in Classical Greece." In *The Transformation of Foreign Policy: Drawing and Managing Boundaries from Antiquity to the Present*, ed. G. Hellmann, A. Fahrmeir, and M. Več, 75–104. Oxford.

———. 2017. "Dem Lokalen auf der Spur. Einige Vorbemerkungen zur *Parochial Polis*." In *Von Magna Graecia nach Asia Minor*, ed. H. Beck, B. Eckhardt, C. Michels, and S. Richter, 35–54. Wiesbaden.

———. 2018a. "'If I am from Megara—so what?' Introduction to the Local Discourse Environment of an Ancient Greek City-State." In Beck and Smith 2018, 1–31.

———. 2018b. "Of Fragments and Feelings: Roman Funeral Oratory Revisited." In *Reading Republican Oratory. Reconstructions, Contexts, Receptions*, ed. C. Grey et al., 263–80. Oxford.

———. 2019. "The Aiolians—a Phanthom *Ethnos*?" In Beck, Buraselis, and McAuley 2019, 365–84.

———. Forthcoming. "Living on a Rock: The Cities of Ancient Phokis and the Importance of Place." In *Ancient Phokis: Papers from an International Symposium in the German Archaeological Institute, Athens*, ed. K. Sporn and E. Laufer.

———, K. Buraselis, and A. McAuley, eds. 2019. *Ethnos and Koinon*. Stuttgart.

———, and P. Funke. 2015a. "An Introduction to Federalism in Greek Antiquity." In Beck and Funke 2015b, 1–29.

———, and P. Funke, eds. 2015b. *Federalism in Greek Antiquity*. Cambridge.

———, and A. Ganter. 2015. "Boiotia and the Boiotian League." In Beck and Funke 2015b, 132–57.

———, and P. J. Smith, eds. 2018. *Megarian Moments: The Local World of an Ancient Greek City-State*. Teiresias Supplements Online, vol. 1.

———, and H.-U. Wiemer, eds. 2009. *Feiern und Erinnern: Geschichtsbilder im Spiegel antiker Feste*. Berlin.

Bell, M. 1993. "Tanagras and the Idea of Type." *Harvard University Art Museums Bulletin* 1:39–53.

Benchimol, E. 2008. "L'hoplite, le char et le javelot: Un defile militaire à l'Itônion de Coronée à l'époque archaïque?" *Ktema* 33:421–32.

Bentz, M., and C. Mann. 2001. "Zur Heroisierung von Athleten." In *Konstruktionen von Wirklichkeit: Bilder im Griechenland des 5. und 4. Jahrhunderts v.Chr.*, ed. R. von den Hoff and S. Schmidt, 225–40. Stuttgart.

Berggren, J. L., and A. Jones. 2000. *Ptolemy's "Geography": An Annotated Translation of the Theoretical Chapters*. Princeton, NJ.

Berman, D. W. 2010. "The Landscape and Language of Korinna." *Greek, Roman, and Byzantine Studies* 50:41–62.

Bershadsky, N. 2011. "A Picnic, a Tomb, and a Crow. Hesiod's Cult in the *Works and Days*." *Classical Philology* 106:1–45.

Berthiaume, G. 1982. *Les rôles du Mágeiros: Étude sur la boucherie, la cuisine et le sacrifice dans la Grèce ancienne*. Leiden.

Billot, M.-F. 1997. "Recherches archéologiques récentes à l'Héraion d'Argos." In *Héra. Images, espaces, cultes*, ed. J. de la Genière, 11–56. Naples.

Bintliff, J. L. 1992. "The Boeotia Project 1991: Survey of the City of Hyettos." *University of Durham and University of Newcastle upon Tyne Archaeological Reports*, 23–28.

———. 2002. "Going to the Market in Antiquity." In *Zu Wasser und zu Land*. E. Olshausen and H. Sonnabend, eds., 209–50. Stuttgart.

———. 2006. "City-Country Relationships in the 'Normal Polis.'" In Rosen and Sluiter 2006, 13–32.

———, E. Farinetti, B. Slapšak, and A. Snodgrass. 2017. *Boeotia Project*. Vol. 2. *The City of Thespiai: Survey at a Complex Urban Site*. Cambridge.

Bittlestone, R. 2005. *Odysseus Unbound: The Search for Homer's Ithaca*. Cambridge.

Blösel, W. 2004. *Themistokles bei Herodot: Spiegel Athens im fünften Jahrhundert*. Stuttgart.

Bober, Ph. P. 1999. *Art, Culture, and Cuisine: Ancient and Medieval Gastronomy*. Chicago.

Boedeker, D., and D. Sider, eds. 2001. *The New Simonides: Contexts of Praise and Desire*. Oxford.

Bonnechere, P. 2003. *Trophonios de Lébadée: Cultures et mythes d'une cite béotienne au miroir de la mentalité antique*. Leiden.

Bonnier, A. 2014. *Harbours and Hinterlands: Landscape, Site Patterns and Coast-Hinterland Interconnections by the Corinthian Gulf, c. 600–300 BC*. Oxford.

Boulay, T. 2015. "Wine Appreciation in Ancient Greece." In Wilkins and Nadeau 2015, 273–82.

Bourdieu, P. 1984. *Distinction: A Social Critic of the Judgment of Taste*. Cambridge, MA.

Boutsikas, E., and C. Ruggles. 2011. "Temples, Stars, and Ritual Landscapes: The Potential for Archaeoastronomy in Ancient Greece." *American Journal of Archaeology* 115:55–68.
Bowie, A. M., ed. 2007. *Herodotus, Histories: Book VIII*. Cambridge.
Bowra, C. M. 1938. "The Epigram of the Fallen of Coronea." *Classical Quarterly* 32:80–88.
———. 1957. *The Greek Experience*. London.
Bradley, M., ed. 2015. *Smell and the Ancient Senses*. New York.
Braunert, H., and T. Petersen. 1972. "Megalopolis. Anspruch und Wirklichkeit." *Chiron* 2:57–90.
Bremmer, J. 2010. "Manteis, Magic, Mysteries, and Mythography: Messy Margins of Polis Religion?" *Kernos* 23:13–25.
———. 2012. "Demeter in Megara." In *Demeter, Isis, Vesta, and Cybele*, ed. A. Mastrocinque and C. G. Scibona, 31–33. Stuttgart.
———, ed. 1987. *Interpretations of Greek Mythology*. London.
Brewster, H. 1997. *The River Gods of Greece: Myths and Mountain Waters in the Hellenic World*. London.
Brickell, K., and A. Datta, eds. 2016. *Translocal Geographies: Spaces, Places, Connections*. London.
Bridges, E., E. Hall, and P. J. Rhodes, eds. 2007. *Cultural Responses to the Persian Wars: Antiquity to the Third Millenium*. Oxford.
Brock, R., and S. Hodkinson, eds. 2000. *Alternatives to Athens: Varieties of Political Organization and Community in Ancient Greece*. Oxford.
Broodbank, C. 2013. *The Making of the Middle Sea: A History of the Mediterranean from the Beginning to the Emergence of the Classical World*. Oxford.
Bruneau, P. 1969. "Documents sur l'industrie délienne de la pourpre." *Bulletin de correspondance hellénique* 93:759–91.
Buck, R. J. 1974. "Boiotiarchs at Thermophylae." *Classical Philology* 69:47–48.
———. 1979. *A History of Boeotia*. Edmonton.
Buckler, J. 1980. *The Theban Hegemony, 371–362 BC*. Cambridge, MA.
———. (1989) 2008. "Pammenes, the Persians, and the Sacred War." In Buckler and Beck 2008, 224–32.
———. (1996) 2008. "The Battle of Coronea and Its Historiographical Legacy." In Buckler and Beck 2008, 59–70.
———, and H. Beck. 2008. *Central Greece and the Politics of Power in the Fourth Century BCE*. Cambridge.
Buhmann, H. 1972. *Der Sieg in Olympia und in anderen panhellenischen Spielen*. Munich.
Burckhardt, L. A. 1996. *Bürger und Soldaten: Aspekte der politischen und militärischen Rolle athenischer Bürger im Kriegswesen des 4. Jahrhunderts v. Chr*. Stuttgart.
———. 2004. "Die attische Ephebie in hellenistischer Zeit." In *Das hellenistische Gymnasion*, ed. D. Kah and P. Scholz, 193–206. Berlin.
Burkert, W. (1972) 1983. *Homo Necans: The Anthropology of Ancient Greek Sacrificial Ritual and Myth*. Berkeley.
———. (1977) 1985. *Greek Religion: Archaic and Classical*. Oxford.
———. 1987. *Ancient Mystery Cults*. Cambridge, MA.
Burnett, A. P. 2005. *Pindar's Songs for Young Athletes of Aigina*. Oxford.
Burton, R. W. B. 1962. *Pindar's Pythian Odes: Essays in Interpretation*. London.
Buxton, R. 2017. "Modeling Hegemony Through Stasis: Xenophon on Sparta at Thebes and Phlius." *Illinois Classical Studies* 42:21–40.
Cahill, N. 2002. *Household and City Organization at Olynthus*. New Haven.

Calame, C. 1977. *Les Chœurs de jeunes filles en Grèce archaïque*. 2 vols. Rome.

———. 1987. "Spartan Genealogies: The Mythological Representation of a Spatial Organization." In Bremmer 1987, 153–86.

———. 1990. *Thésée et l'imaginaire athénien: Légende et culte en Grèce classique*. Lausanne.

———. 1995. *The Craft of Poetic Speech in Ancient Greece* (English trans. of the French original, 1986). Ithaca, NY, and London.

———. (1996) 2011. *Mythe et histoire dans l'Antiquité grecque: La création symbolique d'une colonie*. 2nd ed. Paris.

———, D. Collins, and J. Orion. 2001. *Choruses of Young Women in Ancient Greece: Their Morphology, Religious Role, and Social Functions* (new and revised English trans. of Calame 1977, vol. 1). Lanham, MD.

Camp, J. McK. 1991. "Notes on the Towers and Borders of Classical Boiotia." *American Journal of Archaeology* 95:193–202.

Carbon, J.-M., and J. Clackson. 2016. "Arms and the Boy: On the New Festival Calendar from Arkadia." *Kernos* 29:119–58.

Carey, C. 1981. *A Commentary on Five Odes of Pindar*. Salem.

Carey, J. W. 2009. "A Cultural Approach to Communication." In *Communication as Culture: Essays on Media and Society*, by J. W. Carey, 11–28. Rev. ed. New York.

Carter, E., J. Donald, and J. Squires, eds. 1993. *Space and Place: Theories of Identity and Location*. London.

Cartledge, P. 2000. "Boiotian Swine F(or)ever? The Boiotian Superstate in 395 BC." In *Polis and Politcs: Studies in Ancient Greek History*, ed. P. Flensted-Jensen, T. H. Nielsen, and L. Rubinstein, 397–420. Copenhagen.

———. 2013. *After Thermopylae: The Oath of Plataea and the End of the Graeco-Persian Wars*. Oxford.

Casselmann, C., M. Fuchs, D. Ittameier, et al. 2004. "Interdisziplinäre landschaftsarchäologische Forschungen im Becken von Phlious, 1998–2002." *Archäologischer Anzeiger* 1–57.

———. 2010. *Spuren des Menschen: Erkennen von Strukturen archäologischer Fundstreuungen*. Bonn.

Casson, L. 1994. "Mediterranean Communications." *CAH*. Vol. 6. *The Fourth Century B.C.*, 512–26. Cambridge.

Castells, M., ed. 2004. *The Network Society: A Cross-Cultural Perspective*. Northampton, MA.

———, M. Fernández-Ardèvol, J. Linchuan Qiu, et al. 2006. *Mobile Communication and Society: A Global Perspective*. Cambridge, MA.

Chaniotis, A. 1988. *Historie und Historiker in den griechischen Inschriften: Epigraphische Beiträge zur griechischen Historiographie*. Stuttgart.

———. 2006. "Rituals between Norms and Emotions: Rituals as Shared Experience and Memory." In *Rituals and Communication in the Graeco-Roman World*, ed. E. Stavrianopoulou, 211–38. Liège.

———. 2008. "Konkurrenz und Profilierung von Kultgemeinden im Fest." In *Festrituale in der römischen Kaiserzeit*, ed. J. Rüpke, 67–87. Tübingen.

———, ed. 2012. *Unveiling Emotions. Sources and Methods for the Study of Emotions in the Greek World*. Stuttgart.

———, N. Kaltsas, and I. Mylonopoulos, eds. 2017. *A World of Emotions: Ancient Greece, 700 BC–200 AD*. New York.

Chankowski, A. S. 1993. "Date et circonstances de l'institution de l'éphébie à Érétrie." *Dialogues d'histoire ancienne* 19:17–44.

———. 2010. *L'éphébie hellénistique*. Paris.
Chin, T. T. 2016. "What Is Imperial Cosmopolitanism? Revisiting *Kosmopolitēs* and *Mundanus*." In Lavan, Payne, and Weisweiler 2016, 129–52.
Christesen, P. 2005. "Imagining Olympia: Hippias of Elis and the First Olympic Victor List." In *A Tall Order: Writing the Social History of the Ancient World*, ed. Z. Várhelyi and J.-J. Aubert, 319–56. Munich.
———. 2007. *Olympic Victor Lists and Ancient Greek History*. Cambridge.
Clarke, K. 2005. "Parochial Tales in a Global Empire: Creating and Recreating the World of the Itinerant Historian." In *La cultura storica nei primi due secoli dell'imperio Romano*, ed. L. Troiani and G. Zecchini, 111–28. Rome.
———. 2008. *Making Time for the Past: Local History and the Polis*. Oxford.
Clewell, T., ed. 2013. *Modernism and Nostalgia: Bodies, Locations, Aesthetics*. New York.
Cohen, E. E. 2000. *The Athenian Nation*. Princeton, NJ.
Coldstream, J. N. (1977) 2003. *Geometric Greece, 900–700 BC*. London.
Cole, S. G. 2004. *Landscape, Gender, and Ritual Space: The Greek Experience*. Los Angeles.
Concannon, C., and L. A. Mazurek, eds. 2016. *Across the Corrupting Sea: Post-Braudelian Approaches to the Ancient Eastern Mediterranean*. London.
Corbeau, J.-P., and J. P. Poulain 2002. *Penser l'alimentation: Entre imaginaire et rationalité*. Toulouse.
Cosgrove, D. 2004. "Landscape and Landschaft." *German Historical Institute Bulletin* 35:57–71.
Coulson, W. 1991. "The Protogeometric from Polis Reconsidered." *Annual of the British School at Athens* 86:42–64.
Crowther, G. 2013. *Eating Culture: An Anthropological Guide to Food*. Toronto.
Crumley, C. L., T. Lennartsson, and A. Westin, eds. 2017. *Issues and Concepts in Historical Ecology: The Past and Future of Landscapes and Regions*. Cambridge.
Currie, B. 2002. "Euthymos of Locri: A Case-Study in Heroization in the Classical Period." *Journal of Hellenic Studies* 122:22–44.
———. 2005. *Pindar and the Cult of Heroes*. Oxford.
Curtis 2015. "Storage and Transport." In Wilkins and Nadeau 2015, 173–82.
Cutroni Tusa, A. 2010. "La monetazione di Selinunte." In *Selinunte*, ed. S. Tusa, 157–65. Rome.
D'Alessio, G. B. 2009. "Defining Local Identity in Greek Lyric Poetry." In *Wandering Poets in Ancient Greek Culture. Travel, Locality, and Pan-Hellenism*, ed. R. Hunter and I. Rutherford, 137–67. Cambridge.
Dalby, A. 1996. *Siren Feasts: A History of Food and Gastronomy in Greece*. London.
Daly, K. F. 2015. "On Where and When to Find Athenian Forts." In *Cities called Athens*, ed. K. F. Daly and L. A. Riccardi, 23–60. Lanham, MD.
Daverio Rocchi, G. 1988. *Frontiera e confini nella Grecia antica*. Rome.
———. 2011. *Frontiere del Parnasso: Identità etnica e dinamiche locali nella Focide antica*. Alessandria.
———. 2019. "Lokrian Federal and Local Proxenies in Interstate Relations: A Case Study." In Beck, Buraselis, and McAuley 2019, 21–37.
Davidson, J. N. 1997. *Courtesans and Fishcakes: Consuming Passions of Classical Athens*. Chicago.
Davis, J. L., and J. Bennet, eds. 2017. *The Pylos Regional Archaeological Project: A Retrospective*. Princeton, NJ.
de Angelis, F. 2003. *Megara Hyblaia and Selinous: The Development of Two Greek City-States in Archaic Sicily*. Oxford.

———, ed. 2013. *Regionalism and Globalism in Antiquity: Exploring Their Limits.* Oxford.
de Garine, Igor. 1979. "Anthropology of Food." *Social Science Information* 18:895–901.
de Polignac, F. (1984) 1995. *Cults, Territory, and the Origins of the Greek City-State.* Chicago.
de Ste. Croix, G. E. M. 2004. "But What about Aigina?" In *G.E.M. de Ste. Croix: Athenian Democratic Origins and Other Essays*, ed. D. Harvey and R. Parker, 371–411. Oxford.
Deger-Jalkotzy, S., and I. Lemos, eds. 2006. *Ancient Greece: From the Mycenaean Palaces to the Age of Homer.* Edinburgh.
Demand, N. H. 1982. *Thebes in the Fifth Century: Heracles Resurgent.* London.
Dickinson, O. 2006. *The Aegean from Bronze Age to Iron Age: Continuity and Change between the Twelfth and Eighth Centuries BC.* London.
Dietler, M. 2010. *Archaeologies of Colonialism: Consumption, Entanglement, and Violence in Ancient Mediterranean France.* Berkeley.
Dillery, J. 1995. *Xenophon and the History of His Times.* London.
Dillon, S. 2012. "Hellenistic Tanagra Figurines." In *A Companion to Women in the Ancient World*, ed. S. L. James and S. Dillon, 231–34. Malden, MA.
Domínguez Monedero, A. J. 2013. "Early Settlement and Configuration of the Archaic Poleis." In *Topography and History of Ancient Epicnemidian Locris*, ed. J. Pascual and M.-F. Papakonstantinou, 405–44. Leiden.
Dontas, D. S. 1983. "The True Aglaurion." *Hesperia* 52:48–63.
Dörpfeld, W. 1883. "Über das Schatzhaus der Sikyonier in Olympia." *Mitteilungen des Deutschen Archäologischen Instituts (Athen. Abt.)* 8:67–70.
Dubbini, R. 2016. "The Organization of Public Spaces in the Emergent Polis: The Example of Archaic Corinth." In *Raum-Ordnung. Raum und soziopolitische Ordnungen im Altertum*, ed. S. Schmidt-Hofner, C. Ambos, and P. Eich, 47–70. Heidelberg.
Durham Peters, J. 1999. *Speaking Into the Air: A History of the Idea of Communication.* Chicago.
Eckerman, C. C. 2012. "Was Epinician Poetry Performed at Panhellenic Sanctuaries?" *Greek, Roman, and Byzantine Studies* 52:338–60.
Edwards, A. T. 2004. *Hesiod's Ascra.* Berkeley.
Ehrhardt, N. 1988. *Milet und seine Kolonien.* Frankfurt am Main.
———. 1993. "Zwei archaische Statuen mit Nymphen-Weihungen aus Milet." *Epigraphica Anatolica* 21:3–8.
Eidinow, E. 2015. "Ancient Greek Religion. Embedded . . . and Embodied." In Taylor and Vlassopoulos 2015, 54–79.
Erdkamp, P. 2015. "Supplying Cities." In Wilkins and Nadeau 2015, 183–92.
———, ed. 2012. *A Cultural History of Food in Antiquity.* Malden, MA.
Étienne, R., and D. Knoepfler. 1976. *Hyettos de Béotie et la chronologie des archontes fédéraux entre 250 et 171 avant J.-C.* Paris.
Evans, J. 1999. "The Material Culture of Greek Astronomy." *Journal for the History of Astronomy* 30:237–306.
Fachard, S. 2012. *La défense du territoire: Étude de la chôra érétrienne et de ses fortifications.* Gollion.
———. 2016. "Modelling the Territories of Attic Demes: A Computational Approach." In *The Archaeology of Greece and Rome*, ed. J. Bintliff and K. Rutter, 192–222. Edinburgh.
———. 2017. "The Resources of the Borderlands: Control, Inequality, and Exchange on the Attic-Boeotian Borders." 63e *Entretiens sur l'Antiquité Classique, Fondation Hardt*, 19–73.
Farinetti, E. 2011. *Boeotian Landscapes: A GIS-Based Study for the Reconstruction and Interpretation of the Archaeological Datasets of Ancient Boeotia.* Leiden.

Farrington, A. 2012. *Isthmionikai: A Catalogue of Isthmian Victors*. Hildesheim.
Feld, S., and K. H. Basso, eds. 1996. *Senses of Place*. Santa Fe.
Figueira, T. J. 1993. *Excursions in Epichoric History: Aiginetan Essays*. Lanham, MD.
———. 2004. "The Saronic Gulf." In Hansen and Nielsen 2004b, 620–23.
———. 2016. "Aigina: Island as Paradigm and Counterparadigm." In Powell and Meidani 2016, 19–50.
———, and G. Nagy, eds. 1985. *Theognis of Megara: Poetry and the Polis*. Baltimore.
Filson, G. C. and B. Adekunle. 2017. *Eat Local, Taste Global: How Ethnocultural Food Reaches Our Table*. Waterloo, ON.
Fine, E. A. 2010. "The Sociology of the Local: Action and Its Publics." *Sociological Theory* 28:355–76.
Finley, M. I. 1973. *The Ancient Economy*. Berkeley.
Fischer-Hansen, T., T. H. Nielsen, and C. Ampolo. 2004. "Sikelia." In Hansen and Nielsen 2004, 172–248.
Florence, M. 2003. "Wild Neighbors: Perceptions of Megarian Ethnic Identity in Fifth-Century Athenian Comedy." *Syllecta Classica* 14:37–58.
Flower, M. A. and J. Marincola, eds. 2002. *Herodotus, Histories: Book IX*. Cambridge.
Fontenrose, J. 1968. "The Hero as Athlete." *California Studies in Classical Antiquity* 1:73–104.
———. 1988. *Didyma: Apollo's Oracle, Cult, and Companions*. Berkeley.
Forbes, H. 2012. "Lost Souls: Ethnographic Observations on Manuring Practices in a Mediterranean Community." In *Manure Matters: Historical, Archaeological, and Ethnographic Perspectives*, ed. R. Jones, 159–72. Ann Arbor, MI.
Fornara, C. W. 1983. *The Nature of History in Ancient Greece and Rome*. Berkeley.
Fossey, J. M. 1986. *The Ancient Topography of Eastern Phokis*. Amsterdam.
———. 2014. *Epigraphica Boeotica II: Further Studies on Boiotian Inscriptions*. Leiden.
Fowler, R. L. 2000. *Early Greek Mythography*. Vol. 1. *Text and Introduction*. Oxford.
———. 2013. *Early Greek Mythography*. Vol. 2. *Commentary*. Oxford.
Franchi, E. 2012. "Conflitto e memoria ad Argo arcaica: Le tradizioni cittadine intorno a Telesilla." In *Forme della memoria e dinamiche identitarie nell'antichità greco-romana*, ed. E. Franchi and G. Proietti, 207–27. Trento.
———. 2016. *Die Konflikte zwischen Thessalern und Phokern: Krieg und Identität in der griechischen Erinnerungskultur des 4. Jahrhunderts*. Munich.
———. 2017. "Genealogies and Politics: Phocus on the Road." *Klio* 99:1–25.
Frazer, J. G. 1898. *Pausanias' Description of Greece*. 6 vols. Cambridge.
Freitag, K. 2018. "With and Without You: Megara's Harbours." In Beck and Smith 2018, 97–127.
Funke, P. 2013. "Greek Amphiktyonies: An Experiment in Transregional Governance." In Beck 2013, 451–55.
———, and M. Haake, eds. 2013. *Greek Federal States and their Sanctuaries: Identity and Integration*. Stuttgart.
———, and N. Luraghi, eds. 2009. *The Politics of Ethnicity and the Crisis of the Peloponnesian League*. Washington, DC.
Gagarin, M. 2005. "The Unity of Greek Law." In Gagarin and Cohen 2005, 29–40.
———, and D. Cohen, eds. 2005. *The Cambridge Companion to Ancient Greek Law*. Cambridge.
Gagné, R. 2013. *Ancestral Fault in Ancient Greece*. Cambridge.
Ganter, A. 2013. "A Two-Sided Story of Integration: The Cultic Dimension of Boeotian Ethnogenesis." In Funke and Haake 2013, 85–105.

———. 2014. "Ethnicity and Local Myth." In McInerney, ed. 2014c: 228–240.

———. 2019. "Federalism Based on Emotions? Pamboiotian Festivals in Hellenistic and Roman Times." In Beck, Buraselis, and McAuley 2019, 78–93.

Garlan, Y. 1988. *Vin et amphores de Thasos*. Athens.

Garland, R. 2014. *Wandering Greeks: The Ancient Greek Diaspora from the Age of Homer to the Death of Alexander the Great*. Princeton, NJ.

Garnsey, P. 1999. *Food and Society in Classical Antiquity*. Cambridge.

Gartland, S.D. 2016. "New Boiotia? Exiles, Landscapes, and Kings." In *Boiotia in the Fourth Century BC*, ed. S. D. Gartland, 147–64. Philadelphia.

Geertz, C. (1983) 2000. *Local Knowledge: Further Essays in Interpretive Anthropology*. 3rd ed. New York.

Gehrke, H.-J. 1986. *Jenseits von Athen und Sparta: Das Dritte Griechenland und seine Staatenwelt*. Munich.

———. 1994. "Mythos, Politik, Geschichte: Antik und modern." *Saeculum* 45:239–64.

Gelzer, T. 1985. "*Mousa Authigenes*: Bemerkungen zu einem Typ Pindarischer und Bacchylideischer Epinikien." *Museum Helveticum* 42:95–120.

Gerolymatos, A. 1986. *Espionage and Treason: A Study of the Proxenia in Political and Military Intelligence Gathering in Classical Greece*. Leiden.

Giroux, C. 2020. "Mythologizing Conflict: Memory and the Minyae." In *The Dancing Floor of Ares: Local Conflict and Regional Violence in Central Greece*, ed. H. Beck and F. Marchand. *Ancient History Bulletin, Supplement Series*.

Goldhill, S. 2010. "What Is Local Identity? The Politics of Cultural Mapping." In Whitmarsh 2010, 17–45.

Gomme, A. W. 1956. *A Historical Commentary on Thucydides*. Vol. 1. Oxford.

Gottesmann, A. 2014. *Politics and the Street in Democratic Athens*. Cambridge.

Graf, D. F. 1984. "Medism: The Origin and Significance of the Term." *Journal of Hellenic Studies* 104:15–30.

Graf, F. 1996. "*Pompai* in Greece. Some Considerations about Space and Ritual in the Greek Polis." In Hägg 1996, 55–65.

Graninger, D. Forthcoming. "Rome, Macedonia, and the Lash in Hellenistic Larisa: Festival Perspectives." In Ager and Beck, forthcoming.

Greiner, C., and P. Sakdapolrak. 2013. "Translocality: Concepts, Applications, and Emerging Research Perspectives." *Geography Compass* 7:373–84.

Griffin, A. 1982. *Sikyon*. Oxford.

Grote, O. 2016. *Die griechischen Phylen. Funktion—Entstehung—Leistung*. Stuttgart.

Haake, M. 2018. "Megara and the Megarians: A City and its Philosophical School." In Beck and Smith 2018, 237–56.

Habicht, C. 1959. "Review of F. Gschnitzer, *Abhängige Orte im griechischen Altertum*." *Gnomon* 31:704–12.

Hägg, R., ed. 1996. *The Role of Religion in the Early Greek Polis*. Stockholm.

Hague, C., and P. Jenkins, eds. 2005. *Place Identity, Planning and Participation*. London and New York.

Hales, S., and T. Hodos, eds. 2010. *Material Culture and Social Identities in the Ancient World*. Cambridge.

Hall, J. M. 1995. "How Argive was the 'Argive' Heraion?" *American Journal of Archaeology* 99:577–613.

———. 1997. *Ethnic Identity in Greek Antiquity*. Cambridge.
———. 2002. *Hellenicity: Between Ethnicity and Culture*. Chicago.
———. 2007. *A History of the Archaic Greek World, ca. 1200–479 BCE*. Malden, MA.
Hall, P. 2013. *Recruiting the Visual: Knowing Our Common Place*. PhD diss. Memorial University, St. John's, NL.
———. 2017. *Towards an Encyclopedia of Local Knowledge: Excerpts from Chapters I and II*. St. John's, NL.
Hall, S. 1980. "Encoding, Decoding." In *Culture, Media, Language*, ed. S. Hall, D. Hobson, A. Lowe, et al., 128–38. London.
Hamilton, J. R. 1969. *Plutarch, Life of Alexander: A Commentary*. Oxford.
Hampl, F. 1939. "Poleis ohne Territorium." *Klio* 32:1–60.
Hannah, R. 2013. "Greek Government and the Organization of Time." In Beck 2013, 349–65.
Hansen, M. H., ed. 1998. *Polis and City-State: An Ancient Concept and Its Modern Equivalent*. Copenhagen.
———. 2004. "Boiotia." In Hansen and Nielsen 2004b, 431–61.
———. 2006. *The Shotgun Method: The Demography of the Ancient Greek City-State Culture*. London.
———, and T. H. Nielsen. 2004a. "Introduction." In Hansen and Nielsen 2004b.
———, and T. H. Nielsen, eds. 2004b. *An Inventory of Archaic and Classical Poleis*. Oxford.
Harding, P. 2007. "Local History and Atthidography." In *A Companion to Greek and Roman Historiography*, ed. J. Marincola, 1:180–88. 2 vols. Malden, MA.
———. 2008. *The Story of Athens: The Fragments of the Local Chronicles of Attika*. London.
Harrington, S., and J. Stevenson, eds. 2005. *Islands in the Salish Sea: A Community Atlas*. Surrey, UK.
Harrison, J. E. 1927. *Themis: A Study of the Social Origins of Greek Religion*. 2nd ed. Cambridge.
Harvey, D. (1979) 2006. "Space as a Keyword." In *David Harvey: A Critical Reader*, ed. N. Castree and D. Gregory, 270–94. Malden, MA.
Haselberger, L. 1999. "Geometrie der Winde, windige Geometrie: Städtebau nach Vitruv und Aristophanes." In *Stadt und Umland. Neue Ergebnisse der archäologischen Bau- und Siedlungsforschung*, ed. E.-L. Schwandner and K. Rheidt, 90–100. Mainz.
Hastorf, C. A. 2017. *The Social Archaeology of Food: Thinking About Eating from Prehistory to the Present*. Cambridge.
Hawes, G. 2017. "Introduction: Of Myths and Maps." In *Myths on the Map: The Storied Landscapes of Ancient Greece*, ed. G. Hawes, 1–13. Oxford.
Head, B. V. 1911. *Historia Numorum: A Manual of Greek Numismatics*. 2nd ed. Oxford.
Hedrick, C. W. 2013. "Spaces of Government: Civic Architecture and Memory." In Beck 2013, 385–99.
Heinrichs, J. 2015. "Military Integration in Late Archaic Arkadia: New Evidence from a Bronze Pinax (c. 500 BC) of the Lykaion." In *The Many Faces of War in the Ancient World*, ed. W. Heckel, S. Müller, and G. Wrightson, 1–89. Cambridge.
Henderson, J. 1997. "The Name of the Tree: Recounting Odyssey XXIV 340–42." *Journal of Hellenic Studies* 97:87–116.
Herda, A. 2006. *Der Apollon-Delphinios-Kult in Milet und die Neujahrsprozession nach Didyma: Ein neuer Kommentar der sog. Molpoi-Satzung*. Mainz.
Herod, A. 2008. "Scale: The Local and the Global." In *Key Concepts in Geography*, ed. S. Holloway et al., 217–35. 2nd ed. London.
Hey, D., ed. 1996. *The Oxford Companion to Family and Local History*. Oxford.

Hingley, R. 2005. *Globalizing Roman Culture: Unity, Diversity, and Empire.* London.
Hodos, T. 2006. *Local Responses to Colonization in the Iron Age Mediterranean.* London.
———. 2010. "Local and Global Perspectives in the Study of Social and Cultural Identities." In Hales and Hodos 2010, 3–31.
———. 2015. "Global, local, and in Between: Connectivity and the Mediterranean." In Pitts and Versluys 2015, 240–53.
———. 2017a. "Globalization: Some Basics." In Hodos, ed. 2017b, 3–11.
———, ed. 2017b. *The Routledge Handbook of Archaeology and Globalization.* London.
Hölkeskamp, K.-J. 2004. "The Polis and Its Spaces—the Politics of Spatiality: Tendencies in Recent Research." *Ordia Prima* 3:25–40.
———. 2015. "Performative Turn Meets Spatial Turn: Prozessionen und andere Rituale in der neueren Forschung." In *Raum und Performanz. Rituale in Residenzen von der Antike bis 1815*, ed. D. Boschung, K.-J. Hölkeskamp, and C. Sode, 15–74. Stuttgart.
Hölscher, T. 1999. *Öffentliche Räume in frühen griechischen Städten.* 2nd ed. Heidelberg.
———. 2007. "Urban Spaces and Central Places: The Greek World." In Alcock and Osborne 2007, 165–81.
Horden, P., and N. Purcell. 2000. *The Corrupting Sea: A Study of Mediterranean History.* Malden, MA.
Hornblower, S. 1990. "When Was Megalopolis founded?" *Annual of the British School at Athens* 85:71–77.
———. 1991. *A Commentary on Thucydides.* Vol. 1. *Books I–III.* Oxford.
———. 1995. *A Commentary on Thucydides.* Vol 2. *Books IV–V.24.* Oxford.
———. 2008. *A Commentary on Thucydides.* Vol 3. *Books V.25–VIII.109.* Oxford.
Humphreys, S. 1987. "Law, Custom and Culture in Herodotus." *Arethusa* 20:211–20.
Hunter, R. L. 1996. *Theocritus and the Archaeology of Greek Poetry.* Cambridge.
Hurwit, J. M. 1999. *The Athenian Acropolis: History, Mythology, and Archaeology, from Antiquity to the Present.* Cambridge.
Ismard, P. 2015. "'Playing with Scales' in the Classical City: The Case of the Marathonian Tetrapolis." In Taylor and Vlassopoulos 2015, 80–100.
Itgenshorst, T. 2014. *Denker und Gemeinschaft: Polis und politisches Denken im archaischen Griechenland.* Paderborn.
Jacoby, F. 1949. *Atthis: The Local Chronicles of Ancient Athens.* Oxford.
Jameson, M. H. 2004. "Mapping Greek Cults." In *Chora und Polis*, ed. F. Kolb, 147–183. Munich.
———, D. R. Jordan, and R. D. Kotansky. 1993. *A Lex Sacra from Selinous.* Durham, NC.
———, C. N. Runnels, and T. H. Van Andel, et al. 1994. *A Greek Countryside: The Southern Argolid from Prehistory to the Present Day.* Stanford, CA.
Jeanmaire, H. 1939. *Couroi et Courètes: Essai sur l'éducation spartiate et sur les rites d'adolescence dans l'Antiquité hellénique.* Lille.
Johnston, S. I. 2012. "Demeter in Hermione: Sacrifice and Ritual Polyvalence." *Arethusa* 45, 211–41.
Jones, A. 2017. *A Portable Cosmos: Revealing the Antikythera Mechanism, Scientific Wonder of the Ancient World.* Oxford.
Jones, C. P. 2001. "Pausanias and His Guides." In *Pausanias: Travel and Memory in Roman Greece*, ed. S. E. Alcock, J. F. Cherry, and J. Elsner, 33–39. Oxford.
Jones, N. F. 2004. *Rural Athens Under Democracy.* Philadelphia.

REFERENCES

Jung, M. 2006. *Marathon und Plataiai: Zwei Perserschlachten als lieux de mémoire im antiken Griechenland*. Göttingen.
Kalliontzis, Y. 2014. "Digging in Storerooms for Inscriptions: An Unpublished Casualty List from Plataia in the Museum of Thebes and the Memory of War in Boeotia." In Papazarkadas 2014a, 332–72.
Kaltsas, N., and A. Shapiro, eds. 2008. *Worshipping Women: Ritual and Reality in Classical Athens*. Athens.
Kardara, C. 1961. "Dyeing and Weaving Works at Isthmia." *American Journal of Archaeology* 56:261–66.
Kearns, E. 2011. "Chthonic Deities." *The Homer Encyclopedia* 1:166.
Kellogg, D. L. 2013. *Marathon Fighters and Men of Maple: Ancient Acharnai*. Oxford.
Kennell, N. 2006. *Ephebeia: A register of Greek Cities with Citizen Training Systems in the Hellenistic and Roman Periods*. Hildesheim.
Kindt, J. 2012. *Rethinking Greek Religion*. Cambridge.
———. 2015. "Personal Religion: A Productive Category for the Study of Ancient Greek Religion?" *Journal of Hellenic Studies* 135:35–50.
Kirk, G. S. 1985. *The Iliad: A Commentary*. Vol. 1. Cambridge.
Klee, T. 1918. *Zur Geschichte der gymnische Agone und griechischen Feste*. Leipzig.
Kleinman, B. 2011. "The Union of Corinth and Argos: Foreign Policy, Citizenship and Ethnicity." *Hirundo* 9:32–55.
Knapp, R., and J. D. Mac Isaac 2005. *Excavations at Nemea III: The Coins*. Berkeley.
Koehler, C. G. 1981. "Corinthian Developments in the Study of Trade in the Fifth Century." *Hesperia* 50:449–58.
Koiv, M. 2013. "Early History of Elis and Pisa: Invented or Evolving Traditions?" *Klio* 95: 15–68.
König, J., ed. 2010. *Greek Athletics*. Edinburgh.
Korenjak, M., and R. Rollinger, 2001. "Phokylides und der Fall Ninives." *Philologus* 145:195–202.
Kostouros, G. P. 2008. Νεμέων Ἄθλων Διήγησις, II: Νεμεᾶται· 286 Νεμεονίκες της Αρχαιότητας. Nemea.
Kowalzig, B. 2007. *Singing for the Gods: Performances of Myth and Ritual in Archaic and Classical Greece*. Oxford.
Kozak, L. 2013. "Greek Government and Education: Reexamining the Ephēbeia." In Beck 2013, 302–16.
Krumeich, R. 1997. *Bildnisse griechischer Herrscher und Staatsmänner im 5. Jh. v. Chr*. Munich.
Kühr, A. 2006. *Als Kadmos nach Boiotien kam: Polis und Ethnos im Spiegel thebanischer Gründungsmythen*. Stuttgart.
———. 2011. "Going West: Thespians in Sardinia." In *Ethne, identità e tradizioni: La "terza" Grecia e l'Occidente*, ed. L. Breglia, A. Moletti, and M. L. Napolitano, 219–35. Pisa.
Kurke, L. 1991. *The Traffic in Praise: Pindar and the Poetics of Social Economy*. Ithaca, NY.
———. 1993. "The Economy of Kudos." In *Cultural Poetics in Archaic Greece: Cult, Performance, Politics*, ed. C. Dougherty and L. Kurke, 131–63. Cambridge.
———. 1999. *Coins, Bodies, Games, and Gold: The Politics of Meaning in Archaic Greece*. Princeton, NJ.
———. 2007. "Visualizing the Choral: Epichoric Poetry, Ritual, and Elite Negotiation in Fifth-Century Thebes." In *Visualizing the Tragic: Drama, Myth, and Ritual in Greek Art and Literature*, ed. C. Kraus, S. Goldhill, H. P. Foley, et al., 63–104. Oxford.

———. 2012. "The Value of Chorality in Ancient Greece." In *The Construction of Value in the Ancient World*, ed. J. K. Papadopoulos and G. Urton, 218–35. Los Angeles.

Lambert, S. 2000. "Individual and Collective in the Funding of Sacrifices in Classical Athens: The Sacrificial Calendar of the Marathonian Tetrapolis." In *Feasting and Polis Institutions*, ed. F. van den Eijnde, J. Blok, and R. Strootman, 149–80. Leiden.

Lane Fox, R. 2008. *Travelling Heroes: Greeks and Their Myths in the Epic Age of Homer*. London.

Lang, F. 2007. "House—Community—Settlement: The New Concept of Living in Archaic Greece." In *Building communities: House, settlement and society in the Aegean and beyond*, ed. R. Westgate, J. Whitley, and N. Fisher, 184–93. Athens.

Langlotz, E. 1927. *Frühgriechische Bildhauerschulen*. 2 vols. Nuremberg.

Larson, J. 2001. *Greek Nymphs: Myth, Cult, Lore*. Oxford.

Larson, S. 2007. *Tales of Epic Ancestry: Boiotian Collective Identity in the Late Archaic and Early Classical Periods*. Stuttgart.

Lateiner, D. 2013. "Horography." *EAH* 6:3304–5.

Laugrand, F. B., and J. G. Oosten. 2010. *Inuit Shamanism and Christianity: Transitions and Transformations in the Twentieth Century*. Montreal.

Lavan, M., R. E. Payne, and J. Weisweiler, eds. 2016. *Cosmopolitanism and Empire: Universal Rulers, Local Elites, and Cultural Integration in the Ancient Near East and Mediterranean*. Oxford.

Lawall, M. L. 2000. "Graffiti, Wine Selling, and the Reuse of Amphoras in the Athenian Agora, ca. 430 to 400 B.C." *Hesperia* 69:3–90.

Leake, W. M. 1830. *Travels in the Morea*. 3 vols. Reprint 2004, Chicago.

Lefebvre, H. (1974) 1991. *The Production of Space*. Trans. D. Nicholson-Smith. Malden, MA.

Lefkowitz, M. R. 1977. "Pindar's *Pythian 8*." *Classical Journal* 72:209–21.

Legon, R. P. 1981. *Megara: The Political History of a City-State to 336 B.C.* Ithaca, NY.

———. 2004. "Megaris, Korinthia, Sikyonia." In Hansen and Nielsen 2004b, 462–71.

Lehnus, L. 1984. "Pindaro: Il dafneforico per Agasicle." *Bulletin of the Institute of Classical Studies* 31:61–92.

Lemos, I. S. 2007. "Recent Archaeological Work on Xeropolis, Lefkandi: A Preliminary Report." In *Oropos and Euboia in the Early Iron Age*, ed. A. Mazarakis-Ainian, 123–33. Volos.

Leppin, H. 1999. "Argos: Eine griechische Demokratie des 5. Jahrhunderts v. Chr." *Ktema* 24:297–312.

Lesher, J. H. 1992. *Xenophanes of Colophon, Fragments: A Text with Translation and Commentary*. Toronto.

Levine, D. B. 1985. "Symposium and the Polis." In Figueira and Nagy 1985, 176–96.

Lévi-Strauss, C. (1964) 1969. *Mythologiques*. Vol. 1. *Le cru et le cuit*. Paris.

Lewis, D. M. 2015. "Commodities in Classical Athens: The Evidence of Old Comedy." In *The Ancient Greek Economy. Markets, Households and City-States*, ed. E. M. Harris, D. M. Lewis, and M. Woolmer, 381–98. Cambridge.

Lewis, S. 1996. *News and Society in the Greek Polis*. Chapel Hill, NC.

Lienau, C. 1989. *Griechenland: Geographie eines Staates der europäischen Südperipherie*. Darmstadt.

Lohmann, H. 1993. ATENE: *Forschungen zur Siedlungs- und Wirtschaftsstruktur des klassischen Attika*. Cologne.

———, and T. Mattern, eds. 2010. *Attika—Archäologie einer zentralen Kulturlandschaft*. Wiesbaden.

Lolos, Y. 2011. *Land of Sikyon: Archaeology and History of a Greek City-State*. Princeton, NJ.
Loraux, N. (1981) 2006. *The Invention of Athens: The Funeral Oration in the Classical City*. New York.
———. (1996) 2000. *Born of the Earth: Myth and Politics in Athens*. Ithaca, NY.
Luce, J. M. 2011. "La Phocide à l'Âge du fer." In *The Dark Ages Revisited*, ed. A. Mazakaris Ainian, 349–74. Volos.
Lupi, M. 2018. "Citizenship and Civic Subdivisions: The Case of Sparta." In *Defining Citizenship in Archaic Greece*, ed. A. Duplouy and R. Brock, 161–78. Cambridge.
Luraghi, N. 2001a. "Local Knowledge in Herodotus' *Histories*." In Luraghi 2001b: 138–60.
———, 2008. *The Ancient Messenians. Constructions of Ethnicity and Memory*. Cambridge.
———, ed. 2001b. *The Historian's Craft in the Age of Herodotus*. Oxford.
Lytle, E. 2010. "Fish Lists in the Wilderness: The Social and Economic History of a Boiotian Price Decree." *Hesperia* 79:253–303.
Ma, J. 2000. "Fighting Poleis of the Hellenistic World." In *War and Violence in Ancient Greece*, ed. H. van Wees, 337–76. London.
Mack, W. 2015. *Proxeny and Polis: International Networks in the Ancient Greek World*. Oxford.
Mackil, E. 2004. "Wandering Cities: Alternatives to Catastrophe in the Greek Polis." *American Journal of Archaeology* 108:493–516.
———. 2013. *Creating a Common Polity: Religion, Economy, and Politics in the Making of the Greek Koinon*. Berkeley.
———. 2014. "Ethnos and Koinon." In McInerney 2014c: 270–84.
———. 2017. "Property Claims and State Formation in the Archaic Greek World." In *Ancient States and Infrastructural Power. Europe, Asia, and America*, ed. C. Ando and S. Richardson, 63–90. Philadelphia.
Macleod, C. W. 1983. "Thucydides' Plataean Debate." In *Collected Essays*, by C. W. Macleod, 103–22. Oxford.
Maher, M. P. 2017. *The Fortifications of Arkadian City States in the Classical and Hellenistic Periods*. Oxford.
Malkin, I. 1994. *Myth and Territory in the Spartan Mediterranean*. Cambridge.
———, 1998. *The Returns of Odysseus: Colonization and Ethnicity*. Berkeley.
———, 2011. *A Small Greek World: Networks in the Ancient Mediterranean*. Oxford.
———, ed. 2005. *Mediterranean Paradigms and Classical Antiquity* (= *Mediterranean Historical Review* 18). London.
———, C. Constantakopoulou, and K. Panagopoulou, eds. 2011. *Greek and Roman Networks in the Mediterranean*. New York.
Mallett, S. 2004. "Understanding Home: A Critical Review of the Literature." *Sociological Review* 52:62–89.
Maniatis, Y., R. E. Jones, I. K. Whitbread, et al. 1984. "Punic Amphoras Found at Corinth, Greece: An Investigation of Their Origin and Technology." *Journal of Field Archaeology* 11:207–22.
Mann, C. 2001. *Athlet und Polis im archaischen und frühklassischen Griechenland*. Göttingen.
———, S. Scharff, and S. Remijsen, eds. 2016. *Athletics in the Hellenistic World*. Stuttgart.
Manning, J. G. 2018. *The Open Sea: The Economic Life of the Ancient Mediterranean World from the Iron Age to the Rise of Rome*. Princeton, NJ.
Marchand, F. 2015. "The Associations of Tanagra: Epigraphic Practice and Regional Context." *Chiron* 45:239–66.
Marconi, C. 2006. *Temple Decoration and Cultural Identity in the Archaic Greek World: The Metopes of Selinus*. Cambridge.

Marincola, J. 1999. "Genre, Convention, and Innovation in Greco-Roman Historiography." In *The Limits of Historiography*, ed. C. Kraus, 281–324. Leiden.

———. 2007. "The Persian Wars in Fourth-Century Oratory and Historiography." In Bridges, Hall, and Rhodes 2007, 105–25.

Marzano, A. 2013. *Harvesting the Sea: The Exploitation of Marine Resources in the Roman Mediterranean*. Oxford.

Mason, S. 1995. "Acornutopia?" In *Food in Antiquity*, ed. J. Wilkins et al., 12–24. Exeter.

Matijević, K. 2017. *Die lex sacra von Selinunt: Totenmanipulation in der Archaik und Klassik*. Wiesbaden.

Mattingly, D. 2010. "Cultural Crossovers: Global and Local Identities in the Classical World." In Hales and Hodos 2010, 283–96.

Matuszewski, R. 2019. *Räume der Reputation: Zur bürgerlichen Kommunikation im Athen des 4. Jahrhunderts v. Chr*. Stuttgart.

McAllister, M. H. 2005. *The Excavations at Ancient Halieis*. Vol. 1. *The Fortifications and Adjacent Structures*. Bloomington.

McAuley, A. 2018. "From the Cradle: Reconstructing the *ephebeia* in Hellenistic Megara." In Beck and Smith 2018, 217–36.

McAuley, A. Forthcoming. "The Other Side of the Stone: Local Proxenia in the Euboian Gulf." In Ager and Beck, forthcoming.

McDonald, W. A., W. D. E. Coulson, and J. Rosser, eds. 1983. *Excavations at Nichoria in Southwest Greece*. Vol. 3. *Dark Age and Byzantine Occupation*. Minneapolis.

———, and N. Wilkie. 1992. *Excavations at Nichoria in Southwest Greece*. Vol. 2. *The Bronze Age Occupation*. Minneapolis.

McHugh, M. 2017. *The Ancient Greek Farmstead*. Oxford.

McInerney, J. 2006. "On the Border: Sacred Land and the Margins of the Community." In Rosen and Sluiter 2006, 33–60.

———. 2010. *The Cattle of the Sun: Cows and Culture in the World of the Ancient Greeks*. Princeton, NJ.

McInerney, J. 2014a. "Civilization, Gastronomy, and Meat Eating." In *The Oxford Handbook of Animals in Classical Thought and Life*, ed. G. L. Campbell, 248–68. Oxford.

———. 2014b. "Pelasgians and Leleges: Using the Past to Understand the Present." In *Valuing the Past in the Greco-Roman World*, ed. J. Ker and C. Pieper, 25–55. Leiden.

McInerney, J., ed. 2014c. *A Companion to Ethnicity in the Ancient Mediterranean*. Malden, Mass.

Meier, C. 1990. "Die Rolle des Krieges im klassischen Athen." *Historische Zeitschrift* 251:555–605.

Meier, M. 1998. *Aristokraten und Damoden*. Stuttgart.

Merkelbach, R. 1972. "Aglauros: Die Religion der Epheben." *Zeitschrift für Papyrologie und Epigraphik* 9:277–83.

Mikalson, J. D. 1976. *The Sacred and Civil Calendar of the Athenian Year*. Princeton, NJ.

———. 2005. *Ancient Greek Religion*. Oxford.

Miller, S. G. 2006. *Ancient Greek Athletics*. New Haven, CT.

Mitchell, L. 2015. "The Community of the Hellenes." In Beck and Funke 2015b, 49–65.

Mitchell, S., and G. Greatrex, eds. 2000. *Ethnicity and Culture in Late Antiquity*. London.

Mohr, M. 2013. *Die Heilige Straße—ein 'Weg der Mittte'? Soziale Gruppenbildung im Spannungsfeld der archaischen Polis*. Rahden, Westfalen.

Möller, A. 2001. "The Beginning of Chronography: Hellanicus' *Hiereiai*." In Luraghi 2001b: 241–62.

———. 2002. *Genealogien, Listen, Synchronismen: Studien zur griechischen Chronographie.* Habilitationsschrift Freiburg i.Br. (MS).

———. 2006. "Felix Jacoby and Ancient Greek Chronography." In *Aspetti dell'opera di Felix Jacoby*, ed. C. Ampolo, 259–75. Pisa.

Montiglio, S. 2005. *Wandering in Ancient Greek Culture.* Chicago.

Moretti, L. 1957. "Olympionikai, i vincitori negli antichi agoni olimpici." In *Memorie della Accademia Nazionale dei Lincei, Classe di Scienze Morali, Storiche e Filologiche* 8:53–198.

Morgan, C. 1994. "The Evolution of Sacral Landscape: Isthmia, Perachora, and the Early Corinthian State." In *Placing the Gods: Sanctuaries and Sacred Space in Ancient Greece*, ed. S. E. Alcock and R. Osborne, 105–42. New York.

———. 2003. *Early Greek States beyond the Polis.* London.

———. 2010. "Sanctuaries, the State and the Individual." In König 2010, 23–35.

Morison, B. 2002. *On Location: Aristotle's Concept of Place.* Oxford.

Morley, N. 2015. "Urban Smells and Roman Noses. " In Bradley 2015, 110–19.

Morris, I. 1998. "Archaeology and Archaic Greek History." In *Archaic Greece: New Approaches and New Evidence*, ed. N. Fisher and H. van Wees, 1–91. London.

———. 2005. "Mediterraneanization." In Malkin 2005, 30–55.

Munn, M. H. 1993. *The Defense of Attica: The Dema Wall and the Boeotian War of 378–375 B.C.* Berkeley.

Murray, O., and S. Price, eds. 1990. *The Greek City from Homer to Alexander.* Oxford.

Nadeau, R. 2015. "Cookery Books." In Wilkins and Nadeau 2015, 53–58.

Nafissi, M. 1991. *La nascità del kosmos: Studi sulla storia e la società di Sparta.* Naples.

Nagy, G. 1985. "Theognis and Megara: A Poet's Vision of his City." In Figueira and Nagy 1985, 22–81.

Nakassis, D. 2013. *Individuals and Society in Mycenaean Pylos.* Leiden.

Nevett, L. C., ed. 2017. *Theoretical Approaches to the Archaeology of Ancient Greece: Manipulating Material Culture.* Ann Arbor, MI.

Ngũgĩ wa Thiong'o. 2012. *Globalectics: Theory and the Politcs of Knowing.* New York.

Nicholson, N. 2016. *The Poetics of Victory in the Greek West: Epinician, Oral Tradition, and the Deinomenid Empire.* Oxford.

Niels, J. 1987. *The Youthful Deeds of Theseus.* Rome.

Nielsen, T. H. 2002. *Arkadia and Its Poleis in the Archaic and Classical Periods.* Göttingen.

———. 2004. "Arkadia." In Hansen and Nielsen 2004b, 505–46.

———. 2015. "The Arkadian Confederacy." In Beck and Funke 2015b: 250–68.

———. 2016. "Reflections of the Number of Athletic Festivals in Pre-Hellenistic Greece." In Mann, Scharff, and Remijsen 2016, 31–42.

———. 2018a. *Two Studies in the History of Ancient Greek Athletics.* Copenhagen.

———. 2018b. "Athletics in Late-Archaic and Classical Arkadia." In *Arkadien im Altertum. Geschichte und Kultur einer antiken Gebirgslandschaft*, ed. K. Tausend, 407–40. Graz.

Ober, J. 1985. *Fortress Attica: Defense of the Athenian Land Frontier, 404–322 B.C.* Leiden.

———. 1993. "The Polis as a Society: Aristotle, John Rawls and the Athenian Social Contract." In *The Ancient Greek City-State*, ed. M. H. Hansen, 129–60. Copenhagen.

———. 2015. *The Rise and Fall of Classical Greece.* Princeton, NJ.

Ogden, D., ed. 2007. *A Companion to Greek Religion.* Malden, MA.

Oliver, G. 2007. *War, Food and Politics in Early Hellenistic Athens.* Oxford.

Olson, S. D., and A. Sens. 2000. *Archestratos of Gela: Greek Culture and Cuisine in the Fourth Century BCE.* Oxford.

Orsi, D. P. 1994. "La storiografia locale." In *Lo spazio letterario della Grecia antica*, 3.1, ed. G. Cambiano, L. Canfora, and D. Lanza, 149–79. Rome.

Osborne, R. 1985. *Demos: The Discovery of Classical Attika*. Cambridge.

———. 1987. *Classical Landscape with Figures: The Ancient Greek City and Its Countryside*. London.

Osterhammel, J. 2009. "A 'Transnational' History of Society: Continuity or New Departure?" In *Comparative and Transnational History*, ed. H.-G. Haupt and J. Kocka, 39–51. New York.

———, and N. P. Petersson. 2005. *Globalization: A Short History*. Princeton, NJ.

Oulhen, J. 2004. "Phokis." In Hansen and Nielsen 2004b, 399–430.

Paleothodoros, D. 2016. "Boeotian Vases Abroad." *ηχαδιν* 2:267–86.

Papazarkadas, N. 2011. *Sacred and Public Land in Ancient Athens*. Oxford.

———. 2014a. "Two New Epigrams from Thebes." In Papazarkadas 2014b: 223–51.

———. 2018. "Pindaric Reverberations: An Unpublished Inscription from the Museum of Thebes." In *Munus Laetitiae: Studi miscellanei offerti a Maria Letizia Lazzarini*, ed. F. Camia, L. Del Monaco and M. Nocita, 19–32. Rome.

———, ed. 2014b. *The Epigraphy and History of Boeotia: New Finds, New Prospects*. Leiden.

Parker, R. 1983. *Miasma: Pollution and Purification in Early Greek Religion*. Oxford.

———. 1986. "Greek Religion." In *The Oxford History of the Classical World*, ed. J. Boardman, J. Griffin, and O. Murray, 254–74. Oxford.

———. 1987. "Myths of Early Athens." In Bremmer 1987, 187–214.

———. 1996. *Athenian Religion: A History*. Oxford.

Pélékidis, C. 1962. *Histoire de l'ephebie attique: des origines a 31 avant Jesus-Christ*. Paris.

Perlman, P. 2000. *City and Sanctuary in Ancient Greece: The "Theorodokia" in the Peloponnese*. Göttingen.

———, ed. 2018. *Ancient Greek Law in the 21st Century*. Austin.

Pettegrew, D. K. 2016. *The Isthmus of Corinth: Crossroads of the Mediterranean World*. Ann Arbor, MI.

Philippson, A. 1892. *Der Peloponnes: Versuch einer Landeskunde auf geologischer Grundlage*. Berlin.

———. 1948. *Das Klima Griechenlands*. Bonn.

Piérart, M. 2004. "Argos." In Hansen and Nielsen 2004b, 599–619.

———. 2006. "Argos de origins au synœcisme du VIIIe siècle avant J.-C." In Bearzot and Landucci 2006, 3–26.

Pirenne-Delforge, V. 1994. *L'Aphrodite grecque: Contributions à l'étude de ses cultes et de sa personnalité dans le panthéon archaïque et classique*. Athens and Liege.

Pitts, M. 2015. "The Archaeology of Food Consumption." In Wilkins and Nadeau 2015, 95–104.

Pitts, M., and M. J. Versluys, eds. 2015. *Globalisation and the Roman World: World History, Connectivity and Material Culture*. Cambridge.

Planeaux, C. 2000. "The Date of Bendis' Entry into Attica." *Classical Journal* 96:165–92.

Pleket, H. W. 2010. "Games, Prizes, Athletes and Ideology." In König 2010, 145–74.

Polinskaya, I. 2010. "Shared Sanctuaries and the Gods of Others: On the Meaning of 'Common' in Herodotus 8.144." In *Valuing Others in Greco-Roman Antiquity*, ed. R. Rosen and I. Sluiter, 43–70. Leiden.

———. 2012. "Calling Upon Gods as Witnesses in Ancient Greece." *Metis* 10:23–37.

———. 2013. *A Local History of Greek Polytheism: Gods, People and the Land of Aigina, 800–400 BCE*. Leiden.

Popham, M. R., L. H. Sackett, and P. G. Themelis. 1979. *Lefkandi 1: The Iron Age*. London.
Porter, J. I. 2007. "Lasus of Hermione, Pindar, and the Riddle of S." *Classical Quarterly* 57:1–21.
———. 2010. *The Origins of Aesthetic Thought in Ancient Greece: Matter, Sensation, and Experience*. Cambridge.
Post, R. 2012. *The Military Policy of the Hellenistic Boiotian League*. MA Diss. McGill University, Montreal.
———. Forthcoming. "Localism and Environmental History in the Hellenistic Kopaic Basin." In Ager and Beck, forthcoming.
Powell, A., and K. Meidani, eds. 2016. *"The Eyesore of Aigina": Anti-Athenian Attitudes across the Greek, Hellenistic and Roman Worlds*. Swansea.
Prauscello, L. 2013. "Demeter and Dionysos in the Sixth-Century Argolid: Lasos of Hermione, the Cult of Demeter Chthonia and the Origins of Dithyramb." In *Dithyramb in Context*, ed. B. Kowalzig and P. Wilson, 76–92. Oxford.
Pretzler, M. 2007. *Pausanias: Travel Writing in Ancient Greece*. London.
———. 2009. "Arcadia: Ethnicity and Politics in the Fifth and Fourth Centuries." In Funke and Luraghi 2009, 86–109.
Priestley, J. 2014. *Herodotus and Hellenistic Culture: Literary Studies in the Reception of the Histories*. Oxford.
Pritchett, W. K. 1979. *The Greek State at War*. Vol. 3. Berkeley.
———. 1989. *Studies in Ancient Greek Topography*, Part 6. Berkeley.
Privitera, G. A. 1965. *Laso di Ermione nella cultura ateniese e nella tradizione storiografica*. Rome.
Purcell, N. 1990. "Mobility and the Polis." In Murray and Price 1990, 29–58.
Raaflaub, K. 2013. "Archaic and Classical Greek Reflections on Politics and Government: From Description to Conceptualization, Analysis, and Theory." In Beck 2013, 73–92.
———. 2015. "Forerunners of Federal States: Collaboration and Integration through Alliance in Archaic and Classical Greece." In Beck and Funke 2015b: 434–51.
Rabinov, P., ed. 1984. *The Foucault Reader: Introduction to Foucault's Political Thought*. New York.
Rapp, G., and S. E. Aschenbrenner, eds. 1978. *Excavations at Nichoria in Southwest Greece*. Vol. 1. *Site, Environs, and Techniques*. Minneapolis.
Reeves, J. 2018. "Megarian Valour and Its Place in the Local Discourse at Megara." In Beck and Smith 2018, 167–82.
Reinmuth, O. W. 1971. *The Ephebic Inscriptions of the Fourth Century B.C.* Leiden.
Remijsen, S. 2011. "The So-Called 'Crown-Games': Terminology and Historical Context of the Ancient Categories for Agones." *Zeitschrift für Papyrologie und Epigraphik* 177:97–109.
Richer, J. 1994. *The Sacred Geography of the Ancient Greeks*. Albany.
Ringwood, J. C. 1927. *Agonistic Features of Local Greek Festivals*. Poughkeepsie, NY.
Robert, L. 1984. "Discours d'ouverture." In *Actes du VIIIe Congrès international d'épigraphie grecque et latine*, 35–45. Athens.
Robertson, N. 2010. *Religion and Reconciliation in Greek Cities: The Sacred Laws of Selinus and Cyrene*. Oxford.
Robinson, E. W. 2011. *Democracy beyond Athens: Popular Government in the Greek Classical Age*. Cambridge.
Robu, A. 2014. *Mégare et les établissements mégariens de Sicile, de la Propontide et du Pont-Euxin: Histoire et institutions*. Frankfurt.
———, and I. Bîrzescu, eds. 2016. *Mégarika: Nouvelles recherches sur Mégare, les cités de la Propontide et du Pont-Euxin*. Paris

Roesch, P. 1965. *Thespies et la confederation béotienne*. Paris.
Roller, D. W. 1987. "The Tanagra Survey Project 1985: The Site of Grimadha." *Annual of the British School at Athens* 82:213–32.
Roller, M. 2013. "On the Intersignification of Monuments in Augustan Rome." *American Journal of Philology* 134:119–31.
Rood, T. 1998. *Thucydides: Narrative and Explanation*. Oxford.
Rosen, R. M. 1990. "Poetry and Sailing in Hesiod's *Works and Days*." *Classical Antiquity* 9:99–113.
———, and I. Sluiter, eds. 2006. *City, Countryside, and the Spatial Organization of Value in Classical Antiquity*. Leiden.
Rosenmeyer, T. J. 1969. *The Green Cabinet: Theocritus and the European Pastoral Lyric*. Berkeley.
Rosivach, V. J. 1987. "Autochthony and the Athenians." *Classical Quarterly* 37:294–306.
Roy, J. 2005. "Synoikizing Megalopolis: The Scope of Synoikism and the Interests of Local Arkadian Communities." In *Ancient Arkadia*, ed. E. Østby, 261–71. Athens.
———. 2007. "The Urban Layout of Megalopolis in Its Civic and Confederate Context." In *Building Communities. House, Settlement, and Society in the Aegean and Beyond*, ed. R. Westgate, N. Fisher, and J. Whitley, 289–95. Exeter.
———. 2011. "On Seeming Backward: How the Arkadians Did It." In *Sociable Man*, ed. S. D. Lambert, 67–85. Swansea.
———. 2014. "Autochthony in Ancient Greece." In McInerney 2014c, 241–55.
Rudolph, K. C., ed. 2018. *Taste and the Ancient Senses*. New York.
Ruschenbusch, E. 1984. "Die Bevölkerungszahl Griechenlands im 5. und 4. Jh. v. Chr." *Zeitschrift für Papyrologie und Epigraphik* 56:55–57.
Russell, A. 2016. *The Politics of Public Space in Republican Rome*. Cambridge.
Rutherford, I. 2013. *State Pilgrims and Sacred Observers in Ancient Greece: A Study of Theōria and Theōroi*. Cambridge.
Sakellariou, M. B. 1989. *The Polis-State: Definition and Origin*. Athens.
Salmon, J. B. 1984. *Wealthy Corinth*. Oxford.
Schachter, A. 1981–1994. *Cults of Boiotia*. 4 vols. London.
———. 1996. "Reconstructing Thespiai." In *La Montagne des Muses*, ed. A. Hurst and A. Schachter, 99–126. Geneva.
———. (1985) 2016. "Kadmos and the Implications of the Tradition for Boiotian History." In Schachter 2016, 25–35.
———. (1990) 2016. "Tilphossa: The Site and Its Cults." In Schachter 2016, 372–80.
———. (1994) 2016. "Gods in the Service of the State: The Boiotian Experience." In Schachter 2016, 175–92.
———. (1998) 2016. "Simonides' elegy on Plataia: The Occasion of Its Performance." In Schachter 2016, 227–35.
———. 2000a. "Greek Deities: Local and Panhellenic Identities." In *Further Studies in the Ancient Greek Polis*, ed. P. Flensted-Jensen, 9–18. Stuttgart.
———. (2000b) 2016. "The Daphnephoria of Thebes." In Schachter 2016, 255–78.
———. (2003) 2016. "Tanagra. The Geographical and Historical Context: Part One." In Schachter 2016, 80–112.
———. 2016. *Boiotia in Antiquity: Selected Papers*. Cambridge.
Scharff, S. 2016a. *Eid und Außenpolitik: Studien zur religiösen Fundierung der Akzeptanz zwischenstaatlicher Vereinbarungen im vorrömischen Griechenland*. Stuttgart.

———. 2016b. "Das Pferd Aithon, die Skopaden und die *patris Thessalia*: Zur Selbstdarstellung hippischer Sieger aus Thessalien im Hellenismus." In Mann, Scharff, and Remijsen 2016, 209–30.

———. 2016c. "Improving the Public Image Through Athletics: Young Victors in Hellenistic Thebes." *CHS Research Bulletin* 5 (online publication).

———, ed. Forthcoming. *Beyond the Grand Four: The Local Games of Ancient Greece*. Teiresias Supplements Online, vol. 3.

Scheer, T. 1993. *Mythische Vorväter: Zur Bedeutung griechischer Heroenmythen im Selbstverständnis Kleinasiatischer Städte*. Munich.

Scheidel, W. 2003. "The Greek Demographic Expansion: Models and Comparisons." *Journal of Hellenic Studies* 123:120–40.

Schepens, G. 2001. "Ancient Greek City Histories: Self-Definition Through History Writing." In *The Greek City from Antiquity to the Present: Historical Reality, Ideological Construction, Literary Representation*, ed. K. Demoen, 3–25. Leuven.

Schlesier, R. 1991–1992. "Olympian versus Chthonian Religion." *Scripta Classical Israelica* 11:38–51.

Schmitt-Pantel, P. 1992. *La cité au banquet: Histoire des repas publics dans les cités grecques*. Rome.

Schmitz, W. 2004. *Nachbarschaft und Dorfgemeinschaft im archaischen und klassischen Griechenland*. Berlin.

Scholz, P. 1998. *Der Philosoph und die Politik: Die Ausbildung der philosophischen Lebensform und die Entwicklung des Verhältnisses von Philosophie und Politik im 4. und 3. Jahrhundert v.Chr.* Stuttgart.

Scott, M. 2010. *Delphi and Olympia: The Spatial Politics of Panhellenism in the Archaic and Classical Periods*. Cambridge.

———. 2013. *Space and Society in the Greek and Roman Worlds*. Cambridge.

Scullion, S. 1994. "Olympian and Chthonian." *Classical Antiquity* 13:75–119.

Sennett, R. 1996. *Flesh and Stone: The Body and the City in Western Civilization*. New York.

Sevieri, R. 1999. "Un eroe in cerca d'identità: Oreste in Pitica XI di Pindaro per Trasideo di Tebe." *Materiali e discussioni per l'analisi dei testi classici* 43:77–110.

Shanks, M. 2001. "Culture/Archaeology: The Dispersion of a Discipline and Its Objects." In *Archaeological Theory Today*, ed. I. Hodder, 284–305. Cambridge.

Shear, J. L. 2007. "Cultural Change, Space, and the Politics of Commemoration in Athens." In *Debating the Athenian Cultural Revolution*, ed. R. Osborne, 91–115. Cambridge.

Shelmerdine, C. W. 1981. "Nichoria in Context: A Major Town in the Pylos Kingdom." *American Journal of Archaeology* 85:319–25.

———. 1998. "The Ano Englianos Hilltop after the Palace"; "The Perfumed Oil Industry"; "Umme and Nichoria." In *Sandy Pylos: From Nestor to Navarino*, ed. J. L. Davis, 81–96, 101–9, 139–44, respectively. Austin.

———, ed. 2008. *The Cambridge Companion to the Aegean Bronze Age*. Cambridge.

Shipley, D. G. J. 2018. *The Early Hellenistic Peloponnese: Politics, Economies, and Networks 338–197 BC*. Cambridge.

Short, J. R. 2006. *Urban Theory: A Critical Assessment*. Basingstoke.

Sideris, A. 2014. *Antikyra: History and Archaeology*. Athens.

Siewert, P. 1977. "The Ephebic Oath in Fifth-Century Athens." *Journal of Hellenic Studies* 97:102–11.

Simpson, R. H., and O. Dickinson. 1979. *A Gazetter of Aegean Civilization in the Bronze Age, 1: The Mainland and Islands*. Göteborg.

———. 2017. *Mycenaean Messenia and the Kingdom of Pylos*. Philadelphia.

Sinn, U. 1978. "Das Heiligtum der Artemis Limnatis bei Kombothekra." *Mitteilungen des Deutschen Archäologischen Instituts (Athen. Abt.)* 93:45–82.

———. 1981. "Das Heiligtum der Artemis Limnatis bei Kombothekra." *Mitteilungen des Deutschen Archäologischen Instituts (Athen. Abt.)* 96:25–71.

———. 1990. "Das Heraion von Perachora: Eine sakrale Schutzzone in der korinthischen Peraia." *Mitteilungen des Deutschen Archäologischen Instituts (Athen. Abt.)* 105:53–116.

Smith, P. H. 2004. *The Body of the Artisan: Art and Experience in the Scientific Revolution*. Chicago.

Smith, P. J. 2008. *The Archaeology and Epigraphy of Hellenistic and Roman Megaris, Greece*. Oxford.

Smith, M. E., and J. Novic. 2012. "Neighborhoods and Districts in Ancient Mesoamerica." In *The Neighborhood as a Social and Spatial Unit in Mesoamerican Cities*, ed. M. C. Arnauld, L. Manzanilla, and M. E. Smith, 1–26. Tucson.

Snodgrass, A. (1971) 2000. *The Dark Age of Greece: An Archaeological Survey of the Eleventh to the Eighth Centuries BC*. London.

Soja, E. W. 1989. *Postmodern Geographies: The Reassertion of Space in Critical Social Theory*. London.

Solez, K. 2018. "Megarian Myths: Extrapolating the Narrative Traditions of Megara." In Beck and Smith 2018, 77–96.

Sommerstein, A. H. 2011. "Sophocles and the Guilt of Oedipus." *Estudios griegos e indoeuropeos* 21:103–17.

Sordi, M. 1966. "Mitologia e propaganda nella Beozia antica." *Atene e Roma* 2:15–24.

———. 2006. "Atene e l'unione fra Argo e Corinto." In Bearzot and Landucci 2006, 299–309.

Sourvinou-Inwood, C. 1990. "What Is Polis Religion?" In Murray and Price 1990, 295–322.

———. 2011. *Athenian Myths and Festivals: Aglauros, Erechtheus, Plynteria, Panathenaia, Dionysia* (posthumously edited and published by R. Parker). Oxford.

Spencer, N. 1998. "Nichoria: An Early Iron Age Village in Messenia." In *Sandy Pylos: From Nestor to Navarino*, ed. J. L. Davis, 167–70. Austin.

Sporn, K. et al. 2016/2017. "Forschungen zur Anlage, Ausdehnung und Infrastruktur des Heiligtums von Kalapodi. Die Kampagnen 2014–2016." *Mitteilungen des Deutschen Archäologischen Instituts (Athen. Abt.)* 131/132:193–278.

Stein-Hölkeskamp, E. 2015. *Das archaische Griechenland: Die Stadt und das Meer*. Munich.

Steinbock, B. 2013. *Social Memory in Athenian Public Discourse: Uses and Meanings of the Past*. Ann Arbor, MI.

Stollberg-Rilinger, B. 2013. *Rituale*. Frankfurt.

Strauss Clay, J. 2003. *Hesiod's Cosmos*. Cambridge.

———. 2009. "Works and Days: Tracing the Path to Arete." In *Brill's Companion to Hesiod*, ed. F. Montanari, C. Tsagalis, and A. Rengakos, 71–90. Leiden.

Strøm, I. 2009. "The Early Sanctuary of the Argive Heraion and Its External Relations: Conclusions." *Proceedings of the Danish Institute at Athens* 6:73–159.

Stylianou, P. J. 1998. *A Historical Commentary on Diodorus Siculus Book 15*. Oxford.

Tartaron, T. 2013. *Maritime Networks in the Mycenaean World*. Cambridge.

———, T. Gregory, D. Pullen, et al. 2006. "The Eastern Korinthia Archaeological Survey: Integrated Methods for a Dynamic Landscape." *Hesperia* 75:453–523.

Taylor, C., and K. Vlassopoulos, eds. 2015. *Communities and Networks in Ancient Greece*. Cambridge.

Theotikou, M. 2013. *Die ekecheiria zwischen Religion und Politik: Der sogenannte Gottesfriede als Instrument in den zwischenstaatlichen Beziehungen der griechischen Welt*. Münster.

Thomas, C. G., and C. Conant. 1999. *Citadel to City-State*. Bloomington.

Thomas, R. 2014a. "The Greek Polis and the Tradition of Polis History: Local History, Chronicles and the Patterning of the Past." In *Patterns of the Past: Epitedeumata in the Greek Tradition*, ed. A. Moreno and R. Thomas, 145–72. Oxford.

Thomas, R. 2014b. "Local History, Polis History, and the Politics of Place." In G. Parmegianni (ed), *Between Thucydides and Polybius: The Golden Age of Greek Historiography*. Washington, DC: 239-262.

Tober, D. 2017. "Greek Local Historiography and Its Audiences." *Classical Quarterly* 67:460–84.

———. 2018. "Megarians' Tears: Localism and Dislocation in the *Megarika*." In Beck and Smith 2018, 183–207.

Too, Y. L. 2002. "Introduction: Writing the History of Ancient Education." In *Education in Greek and Roman Antiquity*, ed. Y. L. Too, 1–22. Leiden.

Trainor, C. 2015. *The Ceramics Industry of Roman Sikyon: A Technological Study*. Uppsala.

Trümpy, C. 1997. *Untersuchungen zu den altgriechischen Monatsnamen und Monatsfolgen*. Heidelberg.

Tufano, S. 2019. *Boiotia from Within. The Beginning of Boiotian Historiography. Teiresias Supplements Online*, vol. 2.

Tuplin, C. 1986. "The Fate of Thespiae during the Theban Hegemony." *Athenaeum* 74:321–41.

———. 1993. *The Failings of Empire: A Reading of Xenophon, "Hellenica" 2.3.11–7.5.27*. Stuttgart.

Uhlenbrock, J. P. 1990. "The Hellenistic Terra Cottas of Athens and the Tanagra Style." In *The Coroplast's Art: Greek Terracottas of the Hellenistic World*, ed. J. P. Uhlenbrock, 48–53. New Rochelle, NY.

Ulf, C. 2009. "The Development of Greek *Ethnê* and Their Ethnicity." In Funke and Luraghi 2009, 215–49.

———, ed. 1996. *Wege zur Genese griechischer Identität: Die Bedeutung der früharchaischen Zeit*. Berlin.

Urban, B., and M. Fuchs. 2005. "Late Pleistocene Vegetation of the Basin of Phlious, NE Peloponnese, Greece." *Review of Palaeobotany and Palynology* 137:115–29.

van Dommelen, P. 2017. "Classical Connections and Mediterranean Practices: Exploring Connectivity and Local Interactions." In Hodos 2017b, 618–33.

van Nijf, O. M., and C. G. Williamson 2016. "Connecting the Greeks: Festival Networks in the Hellenistic World." In Mann, Scharff, and Remijsen 2016, 43–72.

Vannicelli, P. 2007. "To Each His Own: Simonides and Herodotus on Thermopylae." In *A Companion to Greek and Roman Historiography*, ed. J. Marincola, 1:315–21. Malden, MA.

Vernant, J.-P. 1974. "Le mythe prométhéen chez Hésiode." In *Mythe et société en Grèce ancienne*, ed. J.-P. Vernant, 178–94. Paris.

———. 1979. "À la table des hommes: Mythe de fondation du sacrifice chez Hésiode." In *La cuisine du sacrifice en pays grec*, ed. M. Detienne and J.-P. Vernant, 37–132. Paris.

Vian, F. 1963. *Les origines de Thèbes: Cadmos et les Spartes*. Paris.

Vidal-Naquet, P. 1981. *Le chasseur noir: Formes de pensées et formes de société dans le monde grec*. Paris.

Vika, E. 2011. "Diachronic Dietary Reconstructions in Ancient Thebes, Greece: Results from Stable Isotope Analyses." *Journal of Archaeological Science* 38:1157–63.

———, V. Aravantinos, and M. P. Richards. 2009. "Aristophanes and Stable Isotopes: A Taste for Freshwater Fish in Classical Thebes (Greece)?" *Antiquity* 83:1076–83.

———, and T. Theodoropoulou. 2012. "Re-investigating Fish Consumption in Greek Antiquity: Results from δ13C and δ15N Analysis from Fish Bone Collagen." *Journal of Archaeological Science* 39:1–20.

Visser, E. 1997. *Homers Katalog der Schiffe*. Stuttgart.

Vlassopoulos, K. 2007. *Unthinking the Greek Polis: Ancient Greek History beyond Eurocentrism*. Cambridge.

———. 2019. "Historicizing the Closed City." In *La cite interconnectée dans le monde gréco-romain*, ed. M. Dana and I. Savalli-Lestrade, 43–60. Bordeaux.

Walbank, F. W. 1979. *Polybius III: A Historical Commentary on Polybius*. Oxford.

Walker, H. J. 1995. *Theseus and Athens*. Oxford.

Wallace-Hadrill, A. 2008. *Rome's Cultural Revolution*. Cambridge.

Walter, U. 2013. "Epilogue: The Legacy of Greek Government—Something That Has 'Never Occurred Again'?" In Beck 2013, 512–24.

Weiss, C. 1984. *Griechische Flussgottheiten in vorhellenistischer Zeit. Ikonographie und Bedeutung*. Würzburg.

Werner, M., and B. Zimmermann. 2006. "Beyond Comparison: Histoire Croisée and the Challenge of Reflexivity." *History and Theory* 45:30–50.

West, M. L. 1993. "Simonides Redivivus." *Zeitschrift für Papyrologie und Epigraphik* 98:1–14.

———. 2010. "Rhapsodes at Festivals." *Zeitschrift für Papyrologie und Epigraphik* 173:1–13.

Whitby, M. 1984. "The Union of Corinth and Argos: A Reconsideration." *Historia* 33:295–308.

White, H. 1987. *The Content of the Form: Narrative Discourse and Historical Representation*. Baltimore.

Whitehead, D. 1986. *The Demes of Attica, 508/7 to ca. 250 BC: A Political and Social Study*. Princeton, NJ.

Whitmarsh, T., ed. 2010. *Local Knowledge and Microidentities in the Imperial Greek World*. Cambridge.

Wijma, S. M. 2014. *Embracing the Immigrant: The Participation of Metics in Athenian Polis Religion (5th–4th Century BC)*. Stuttgart.

Wilamowitz-Moellendorff, U. von. 1922. *Pindaros*. Berlin.

Wilkins, J., and R. Nadeau, eds. 2015. *A Companion to Food in the Ancient World*. Malden, MA.

Williams, M. S. 2009. "Citizenship as Agency within Communities of Shared Fate." In *Unsettled Legitimacy. Political Community, Power, and Authority in a Global Era*, ed. W. D. Coleman and S. F. Bernstein, 33–52. Vancouver, BC.

Woolf, G. 1998. *Becoming Roman: The Origins of Provincial Civilization in Gaul*. Cambridge.

Wright, J., J. Cherry, J. Davis, et al. 1990. "The Nemea Valley Archaeological Project: A Preliminary Report." *Hesperia* 59:579–659.

Yates, D. 2018. "'This City of Ours': Fear, Discord, and the Persian War at Megara." In Beck and Smith 2018, 139–65.

———. 2019. *States of Memory: The Polis, Panhellenism, and the Persian War*. Oxford.

Zanker, G. 1980. "Simichidas' Walk and the Locality of Bourina in Theocritus, Id. 7." *Classical Quarterly* 30:373–77.

Zemon Davis, N. 2011. "Decentering History: Local Stories and Cultural Crossings in a Global World." *History and Theory* 50:188–202.

Zimmermann, M. 2015. "Neue Perspektiven der Stadtforschung: städtische Physiognomien im Horizont der Mikroregion." In *Urbane Strukturen und bürgerliche Identität im Hellenismus*, ed. A. Matthaei and M. Zimmermann, 400–405. Heidelberg.

Ziskowski, A. 2016. "Networks of Influence: Reconsidering Braudel in Archaic Corinth." In Concannon and Mazurek 2016, 91–110.

Index

Abdera, 231
Abydos, 82–83, 92, 223
Achaia, 46, 49, 89–90, 129, 224
Acharnai, 153, 218
Acheloos River, 69
Acherousian Lake, 149
Achilles, 118, 119, 218
Adrastos, 162
Aetos, Mount, 46, 49
Agamemnon, 98, 121, 122
Agasikles, 145, 202, 204
Agatharchidas, 85
Ageladas, 187
Agesilaos, 13
Agis, 59, 60
Aglauros, 153, 154, 155, 156, 229
agriculture, 46–47, 73, 93, 124, 136, 137, 139, 163
Aiakids (Aiginetan clan), 184–86
Aiakos, 118–19, 185
Aigeidai (Theban/Spartan clan), 57
Aigina, 92, 97, 113, 117–19, 127, 163, 177, 184–86, 192, 204, 211, 226, 232, 236; Temple of Aphaia, 118–19
Aigion, 9
Aigosthena, 65, 221
Ainos, 92
Aiolidas, 145, 147, 197, 202–3, 232
Aitolia, 53
Ajax (the Great), 118, 185
Akarnania, 69
Akousilaos of Argos, 58, 168–69
Akragas, 108
Akraiphnia, 224
Aktaios, 155
Alalkomenes, 198
alcohol, 116, 143
Alexander (the Great), 40, 94, 98

Alexandria, 10, 102
Alkestis, 112
Alpheios River, 69, 73, 135, 136, 159
Amorgos, 105
Amphidamas, 218
amphiktyonies, 33, 38, 129–30, 203, 217, 227, 232
Amphissa, 63–64
Amymone, 70
Anaxandros, 173–74
Anderson, Greg, 62
Anthedon, 95, 225
Antikythera Mechanism, 138–39
Apelles of Kos, 99, 104, 225
Aphrodite, 80; Pontia and Limenia, 98; Pornē/ "the Prostitute", 82–83
Apollo, 57, 67, 130, 132, 141, 182, 186, 188–89, 201, 204, 233; Epikourios, 107; Hyakinthios, 53; Ismenios, 56, 144–45, 147, 161; Kyparissios, 81
Appadurai, Arjun, 7, 67, 209
Archestratos of Gela, 82, 83, 91–92
Archidamos, 131
Archytas, 11, 216
Ares 56, 153, 154
Arethusa, 69, 135
Argolid, 14, 23, 32, 39, 49, 70, 97–98, 168, 187, 217–18
Argos, 9, 11–17, 35–36, 45, 49, 58, 62, 72, 85, 97–98, 105, 107, 110, 113–14, 121–22, 151, 162, 168–73, 184–88, 220, 222, 224–25, 229, 231–32
Aristinas, 14
Aristokles, 148
Aristophanes (of Athens, comedian), 89, 90, 94, 223
Aristophanes (of Thebes, historian), 161, 171, 173–75, 193, 205, 230
Aristotle (of Chalkis), 173
Aristotle (philosopher), 11, 13, 19, 35, 65, 84, 96, 223

Arkadia, 13–14, 38, 53–55, 72–74, 80, 85, 88, 90, 106, 108, 112–13, 116, 156, 159–60, 220, 222, 226, 230
Arkadian League, 72, 74, 220
Armenidas of Thebes, 171
Arrachion, 107–8, 172
Artemis, 14, 139, 228; cult at Skillous, 133–34, 136; Limnatis, 134; Orthia, 216
Asia Minor, 91, 133–34, 166, 206, 228
Askra, 10, 50, 52
Asopodoros, 190, 201, 202, 235
Asopos River, 12, 69, 99, 192, 216
Assmann, Jan, 234
Astykles, 110
Athena, 55, 70, 155; Areia, 153–54; Itonia, 114, 199–200, 202–3, 234; Pallas, 47–48, 117; Skiras, 171
Athenogenes (Egyptian perfumer in Athens), 225
Athens, 9, 14, 18, 23, 29–30, 35, 36, 38–39, 53, 55, 57–62, 64–67, 69–72, 82, 86–90, 94–97, 103–4, 113, 138, 148–55, 162, 164–67, 171–75, 178–79, 182–86, 190–99, 204–5, 208, 211, 217–18, 221–25, 228, 229, 231–36; Acropolis, 154–55, 229; Propylaia, 154
athletics, 76, 81–82, 107, 111–13, 115, 117, 119–20, 133, 152, 225, 230
Atreus, 121–23
Attaginos, 190–91, 195
Aulis, 80
autochthony, 53–58, 60–61, 68, 185, 220
autonomy, *autonomia*, 2, 19, 43, 84, 193

Babylon, 101, 151
Bakchiads (Corinthian clan), 63
Barabási, Albert-László, xi, 4
Bassai, Sanctuary of Apollo Epikourios, 107
Bendis, 29
Bintliff, John, 32, 39
Bintliff diameter, 32, 35, 224
Black Sea, 4, 51
Blest, Island of the, 171
Boiotia, 9, 39, 41, 43, 49, 56, 59, 61, 65–66, 69, 85, 89, 93–95, 99, 102–3, 106, 113–14, 127, 129, 130, 133, 144, 147, 150, 161, 173, 190, 194–205, 221, 224, 229–35; Altar of Zeus, 61, 67
Boiotian League, 61, 66, 197–200, 203–4, 234, 235
Boutades of Sikyon, 99, 102
Bowra, Maurice, 79
Braudel, Fernand, 7
Bremmer, Jan, 129
Burckhardt, Jacob, 226
Byzantium, 88–89, 92

Cadiz, 85
Calame, Claude, 116, 174
calendar, 17, 19, 137–39, 144, 166, 183, 226, 228
Canada, 27, 53–54, 217
carnivores, 92, 94–95, 115, 224
Castells, Manuel, 5

Chaironea, 81, 130, 150, 197–98, 223, 227, 234
Chalkis, 43, 51–52, 92, 171, 173, 177, 218
Chaniotis, Angelos, 235
Chares, 142
China, 101
Chios, 85
chorography, 10, 167
Clarke, Katherine, 170, 173
climate, xii, 12, 13–14, 79, 80, 87, 122, 147, 223
coinage, coins, 15–16, 17, 19, 89, 110, 184
colonization, 4, 6, 41, 51
community of fate, 58, 122–24, 160, 226
Corinth, 9, 11–12, 14, 23, 35, 51, 62–63, 72, 76, 85, 102–3, 110, 138–40, 164, 171, 182, 191, 217, 219, 221–23, 228; Corinthian Gulf, 12, 46, 65, 98–99, 175, 178, 233; Isthmus of, 11, 39, 41; Potter's Quarter, 102
cosmopolitanism, 21, 40
Crete, 151, 156, 207
Cyclopes, Island of the, 9

Daimachos of Plataia, 172
dance, 81, 115, 116, 124, 132, 151, 152, 153, 189, 202
daphnephoria, 144–46, 157, 201–2
Davidson, James, 75
de Garine, Igor, 87
Delion, 145, 197, 202, 234
Delos, 17, 225, 228
Delphi, 17, 36, 55, 67, 107, 109–14, 120, 125–127, 132, 158, 174, 179, 182, 183, 186, 220–21, 225, 227; Oracle of Apollo, 67
demes, 23, 35, 62, 64, 67, 129, 130
Demeter, 15, 92, 97, 139, 147, 158, 159, 207, 208; and Kore, 97, 148; Chthonia/"of the Earth," 97, 147–49; liminal Demeter (of Hermione), 97; Malaphoros/"the Fruit-Bearer," 52, 140; Malophoros, 139; on the Pron, 97; Prostasia and Kore, 140; Thermasia, 97
demography, 39, 51
de Polignac, François, 52, 150, 220
de Ste. Croix, Geoffrey, 184
Diagoras of Rhodes, 113
Didyma, 141–43; Sanctuary of Apollo, 141–42
Dietler, Michael, 96
Dieuchidas of Megara, 171
Diogenes of Sinope, 40, 97
Dionysos, 89, 93, 139
Diphilos of Sinope, 88
Dirke River, 56, 93
dislocation, 72–73
Dörpfeld, Wilhelm, 127
Dreros, 156
Durham Peters, John, 176
Durkheim, Émile, 201, 234

Echekrates of Phlious, 17, 18
Egypt, 163, 225, 230

INDEX

Eleusis, 65, 171
Eleutherai, 36, 65, 221, 232
Elis, 114–15, 126–27, 136, 138, 225
Elvis sideburns, 229
emotions, 24, 48, 155, 184, 201, 223, 235
Enyo, 147, 153–54
ephebes, 65–71, 124, 151–56, 201, 229, 230
Ephesos, 76–77, 92, 134, 222, 228; Temple of Artemis, 133–34, 228
epichōrioi, 27, 29–31, 36, 110, 127
Epidauros, 36, 80–81, 163; Sanctuary to Askleipios, 81
epinikia, 115–18, 226
Eretria, 39, 51–52, 66–67, 89, 130, 173, 177, 217–18, 221, 224, 227
Erichthonios, 53–54, 155
Erineus, 59
Erymanthian boar, 135
Erythrai, 92
Erzgebirge, 28
Ethiopia, 119
Euboia, 43, 49, 52, 66, 92, 198, 204, 218, 234; Gulf of, 67; Straits of, 67
Eupompos of Sikyon, 99
Eurotas Valley, 43, 59–60
Euthykles of Lokroi Epizephyrioi, 109, 179, 180
Euthymenes, 118, 226
Euthymos of Lokroi Epizephyrioi, 110–11, 117
Exainetos of Akragas, 108

Fair Isle, 106
Farchard, Sylvain, 67
federalism, federal states, 38, 61, 65, 67, 72–74, 129, 198, 222, 236
festivals, 17, 19, 33, 36, 52, 81, 108, 116, 118, 130, 134–36, 137, 144–46, 148–49, 154, 156, 157, 159, 173, 174, 183–84, 188, 200–202, 207, 229, 231, 232
Finley, Moses, 86
fish, 9, 61, 82, 85, 88, 89, 91, 92, 94, 95, 98, 133–34, 223–24
flowers, 9, 80–81, 144, 147
food, 13, 27, 32, 42, 46, 47, 50, 73, 76, 80, 81, 82–95, 96, 123, 152, 172, 223. See also *sitos*
Foucault, Michel, 8
Frazer, James G., 16

Gaia, 17, 56, 58, 119–20, 123, 156
Galaxion, 145–46
games: Crown Games, 107, 111–15, 120; local games, 111–13, 226, 230. See also Olympic Games; Nemean Games
Garnsey, Peter, 83
Geertz, Clifford, 26
Gehrke, Hans-Joachim, 32, 208–9
globalization, xi–xiii, 1, 5–7, 10, 40, 122, 209, 210
glocal, glocalization, xi, 6, 210

Goldhill, Simon, 78
GPS, 3, 27, 32; brain GPS, 26

Halbwachs, Maurice, 181, 184
Haliartos, 80, 171, 234
Halieis, 23–24, 217
Hall, Pam, 27, 105
Hampl, Franz, 71, 72
Hansen, Mogens Herman, 218
Harmodios, 90, 172, 231
Harrison, Jane, 17
Harvey, David, 33
Hegesippos of Taras, 88
Hekataios (of Abdera), 231
Hekataios (of Miletus), 90
Hekate, 142, 143
Helikon, Mount, 172
Helission River, 73
Hellanikos of Lesbos, 166
Hellespont, 82
Hera, 46, 53, 97, 147
Heraia, 126
Herakles, 15–17, 59, 69–70, 93, 112, 117, 135, 145–49, 153, 154, 207–8, 229
Hereas of Megara, 172, 174
Hermes, 90; Kelados, 142
Hermione, 32, 36, 80, 97–98, 104–5, 147–49, 163, 225; Sanctuaries of Aphrodite, 98; Sanctuaries of Demeter, 97, 147–49
Herodotus (of Halikarnassos), 8, 51–60, 125, 161–70, 173–74, 176, 181, 185–95, 230, 231, 233
Herodotus (of Thebes, Isthmian champion), 201
Hesiod, 10, 24, 43, 52, 123, 124, 147, 218
Hillier, Bill, 31
histoire croisée, 20, 212, 236
Hodos, Tamar, 7
Hofer, Johannes, 25
Hölkeskamp, Karl-J., 20
home, 14, 23, 25, 29, 32, 47–48, 72–74, 81, 86, 128, 178, 179, 180, 208, 222; homesickness, 25, 81
Homer, 9–10, 48–49, 79, 149
Horden, Peregrine, 3
Husserl, Edmund, 34
Hyettos, 126, 133, 227

identity of place, 2–4, 7, 11, 18, 20, 22, 28, 30, 34, 96–97, 102, 104–5, 124, 150, 162, 208
intersignification, 21, 199, 217
Inuit, 53–54, 220
Iokaste, 122
Iolaos, 235
Ionia, 41, 60–61, 77, 88, 90, 92, 138, 221; Ionian Islands, 40; Ionian Sea, 46, 115
Iphikratic foot gear, 144, 229
Ismenian Hill (Thebes), 56
Ismenios (epithet). See *under* Apollo

Isthmia, 80, 107, 109, 114, 120, 171, 225, 232
Ithaka, 24–25, 46–49, 80

Jacoby, Felix, 165, 166, 167, 168, 173, 231

Kadmeia, 93, 162, 171
Kadmos, 55, 56, 57, 93, 145
Kaikines River, 110–11
Kalapodi, 129, 219, 227
Kalaureia, 129
Kallisto, 54
Kalydon, 80
Kamarina, 117
Karyai, 81, 223
Karystos, 89
Kazarma, 49
Kekrops, 155
Kephissos Valley, 39, 49, 80, 218
Kerberos, 149
Kindt, Julia, 126
Kithairon, Mount, 189
Kleandros of Aigina, 192
Kleisthenes (of Athens), 62
Kleisthenes (of Sikyon), 162
Kleitor, 73
Kleonai, 17, 110, 187
Kleonymidai (Theban clan), 179, 232
Klymenos, 148–49
Klytemnestra, 97, 121–22, 226
Knopfler, Mark, 222
Knossos, 229
knowledge, local, 6, 20, 26–28, 30, 92, 105; nomological, 8
koinon, 33, 61, 65, 198, 234. *See also* federalism, federal states
Kolophon, 75–78, 88, 107, 225
Kopais, Lake, 61, 85, 89, 92, 95, 106, 114, 198, 203, 223, 225
Korinna, 103, 225
Koroneia, 61, 63, 67, 95, 114, 126, 169, 173, 194–98, 203–6, 211, 227, 234–235; Sanctuary of Athena Itonia, 114
Koroneia, Battle of (447 BCE), 169, 173, 196–99, 204–5, 211, 234
Kos, 81, 99, 207, 223; Cult Site of Apollo Kyparissos, 81
Kreontidas, 119
Kroton, 112, 115, 226
ktisis, city-foundation, 55–57, 59–60, 73–74, 170, 171, 233
kudos, economy of, 108–9, 180–81
Kühr, Angela, 56
Kurke, Leslie, 107, 132, 180
Kynouria, 53, 55, 58
Kypselids (Corinthian clan), 63
Kyrene, 80

Kythera, 91, 224
Kyzikos, 83

Laertes, 48
Lakonia, 9, 46, 49, 57, 59, 219
Lampon, 118
Laphystion, Mount, 61
Lapithos, Mount, 134
Lasos of Hermione, 148, 229
Leake, William, 216
Lebadeia, 61, 63, 67
Lechaion, 72
Lefebvre, Henri, 33, 162
Lefkandi, 50
Lelantine Plain, 52, 219
Lelex, 59, 60, 220
Leonidas, 190
Leontiades, 173
Lerna, 70
Lesbos, 129, 166
Leuktra, 13, 216
Lévi-Strauss, Claude, 83
Libya, 15
Lilaia, 80
local discourse environment, 4, 34–35, 104, 161–62, 212
Lokris, 49, 111, 178, 198, 204, 219, 221
Lokroi Epizephyroi, 109–11, 117, 179–80
Loraux, Nicole, 58
Lotus-Eaters, 9
Lydia, 76, 88
Lykaion, Mount, 157, 230
Lykosoura, 74, 157–59
Lynkeus of Samos, 87, 88
Lysippos of Sikyon, 99

Ma, John, 64
Mack, William, 178
Mainalia, 73–74, 108, 112, 222
Malkin, Irad, 6, 46
Mallett, Shelley, 24
Mantineia, 14, 72–73, 222
Mantineia, Battle of (362 BCE), 72–73, 222
Marathon, 80, 129, 139; Marathonian Tetrapolis, 128–29, 139–40
Maroneia, 85
Marseilles, 151
Mazi Plain, 65
McAuley, Alex, 179
medism, 161, 190–97, 202, 205–6, 233
Mediterranean, 8, 36–37, 40, 50–51, 76, 83, 101, 105, 208
Mediterraneanization, 5–6, 209
Mediterranean triad, 13, 83–84. *See also* food
Megalopolis, 72–74, 222
Megara, Megarid, 10–11, 23, 51–52, 65–69, 89–91, 96–97, 99, 104–6, 112–13, 118, 138, 140, 152, 162,

INDEX 265

170–74, 183, 188–91, 198, 204, 217–26, 229–34;
Fountain House of Theagenes, 69; Sanctuary of
Demeter Malophoros, 139–40, 228
Megara Hyblaia, 219
Melia River, 93
Mende, 85
Messenia, 49
Messon, 129, 227
Methana, 32
microhistory, xii, 7
microregion, 7, 13, 39, 64, 66, 67, 135, 177
migration, 4, 52, 58–60, 138, 201, 220, 233
Miletus, 11, 43, 60, 92, 138, 141–43, 149, 152, 174, 228–29
Milky Way, 146, 229
Mnamias, 205
Molpoi ("crown-bearers" from Miletus), 141–45, 152, 228
Montreal, 223
Morley, Neville, 79
Morris, Ian, 39, 209
Moser, Edvard and May-Britt, 25
Mosul, 44
Mycenae, 44–45, 187
Mykalessos, 150, 164, 229
Myron, 99
Myrtis of Anthedon, 225
Mytilene, 194

Nass Valley (British Columbia), 54, 220
Nauplion, 70, 219
Neda River, 106
neighborhood, 20, 22–24, 30, 31, 64, 124, 126, 130, 134, 217, 232
Nemea, 12, 17, 107, 109–10, 113–14, 118, 120, 187, 192, 216, 225–26; Valley of, 12, 17
Nemean Games, 17, 107, 109–10, 113, 118, 120, 187, 192, 226. *See also under* games
Neriton, 80
Newfoundland, 27–28, 105, 106
Nichoria, 45–50, 219
Nikias of Megara, 96
Nikodromos, 185
Nineveh, 43–44, 51, 74
Nisaia, 139
Nisga'a, 54, 220
Ngũgĩ wa Thiong'o, xi, 26
nomos, 8–9, 215
nostalgy, *nostos*, 10, 24–25, 47–48, 111, 171, 208, 217, 219
nymphs, 69–70, 130, 131, 139–43, 147, 160, 192, 207, 208, 222, 228

O'Keefe, John, 25
Oanis River, 117
Ober, Josiah, xii, 2, 39, 68

Odysseus, 24–25, 46–48, 80, 111, 159, 208
Oedipus, 122–23
oikos, 23, 24, 47, 48, 124, 129, 136
Oinoe, 65, 221
Oinophyta, 198, 235
Olbia, 228
Olympia, 77, 107–14, 117, 119–20, 125–28, 132–38, 158, 179–80, 182, 187, 203, 225, 227–28, 232; Sanctuary of Zeus, 99
Olympic Games, 75, 107–9, 111, 113, 120, 137–38, 187, 228. *See also under* games
Olympos, Mount, 139
Olynthos, 23, 217
omphalos, navel, 15–17
Onchestos, 92, 129, 202, 203, 235; Sanctuary of Poseidon, 203
Onomastos of Smyrna, 114
Orchomenos, 81, 89, 106, 126, 130, 170, 173, 197–201, 204, 223–27, 233, 235
Oresthasion, 108
Oropos, 39, 67, 113, 177, 218
Orthagoras of Sikyon, 99, 221
Osborne, Robin, 209
Osterhammel, Jürgen, 211

Pagondas, 145, 152, 197, 202
Pamphilos, 99, 104
Panakton, 65
Panopeus, 50
Parker, Robert, 125, 227
Parnassos, Mount, 64, 207
Parrhasia, 74, 222
Parrhasia Mountains, 73, 80, 157, 159
Pausanias, 14–15, 27, 30, 58, 69, 74, 80, 99, 107, 110–11, 127, 135, 147–49, 155, 157–59, 162–63, 183, 191, 193, 216, 220, 223, 227, 230
Pelasgia, 53, 60, 201
Peleus, 118
Pelion, Mount, 79, 80
Pellene, 113, 140
Pelops, 216
Peparethos, 85
Perachora, 46; Sanctuary of Hera, 46
perfumes, 9, 75–77, 80
Perikles, 86, 234
Perinthos, 88, 90
Persia, 8, 57, 72, 76, 94, 98, 102, 137, 161–63, 170, 176, 181–97, 202, 205–6, 211, 223
Persian War, xii, 94, 137, 161–65, 175, 181–97, 202, 205, 211, 232, 233
Pherai, 49
Phidias, 187
Phigaleia, 90, 106–8, 165, 172, 231
Philippson, Alfred, 97
Philoxenos of Kythera, 91, 224
Phlious, 9, 12–18, 35, 41, 58, 110, 146, 183, 216

Phoinikia, 55
Phokis, 38–39, 41, 44, 49, 129, 218–19, 221, 233
Phokylides of Miletus, 11, 43–44, 74, 107, 218
Pholoë, Mount, 134–35
Pholos (centaur), 135, 207–8
phylai, 23, 62, 63, 221, 228
Pindar, 8–9, 95, 113, 116–18, 145–47, 179, 185, 192–93, 201–4, 215, 226, 229
Piraeus, 29, 36, 175
Pisatis, 69, 202
Pitsa panels, 140–41
Plataia, 94–95, 131, 132, 147, 170, 172, 177, 182–83, 185, 188–96, 201–2, 205–6, 220, 231, 233–34; Sanctuary of Zeus Eleutherios, 183
Plato (comic poet), 91
Plato (philosopher), 17, 29, 30, 36, 75, 178
Plutarch, 95, 98, 139, 145, 161–64, 175, 183, 205, 225
Pluto, 149
Polematas, 201
Polinskaya, Irene, 131
Poliochos, 86
Pollan, Michael, 223
Polybios, 95, 116, 165
Polydamas of Skotussa, 109
Polygnotos of Thasos, 235
Polykleitos, 187
polytheism, 124, 130, 131
Poros, 129
Porphyrion, 204
Poseidon, 59, 70, 203
pottery, 18, 19, 46, 49, 57, 96, 99, 102, 103, 133, 199
Pratinas, 14
Praxidamas, 119
Praxion of Megara, 171
prayer, 116, 124, 130, 132, 143, 148, 149, 159, 160, 201
processions (*pompai*), 21, 29, 52, 63, 124, 132, 139–50, 158, 183, 199–201, 220, 229
proxenia, proxenoi, 37, 39, 116, 165, 177–81, 202, 203, 216, 232
Proxenos of Chalkis, 171
Psaumis of Kamarina, 117
Ptolemy of Alexandria, 10, 167
Purcell, Nicholas, 3
purple dye, 97–98, 105, 147, 225
Pylos, 45–46, 99, 219, 229
Pyraia, 140
Pyrasos, 80
Pytheas, 118–19

quarries, 31, 158
Quebec, xiii

Race, William H., 215
Ranke, Leopold, 191
Räuchermännchen, 28
reeds, 61, 106, 225

regime of truth, 8–9, 78, 164
Rhamnous, 36
Rhegion, 110–11
Rhodes, 88, 113
Rider Painter, 57
Robert, Louis, 111, 153
Roman Empire, 84; historiograhy, 167–68
Roy, Jim, 90

St. John's, 28, 105
Salamis, 57, 89, 162, 164, 171–72, 174, 185, 189, 222, 230
Salish Sea, 217
Samos, 87
Santorini, 229
Sardis, 17
Saronic Gulf, 97, 163, 184, 186, 233
Schachter, Albert, 103, 145, 173
Scharff, Sebastian, 115
Schlesier, Renate, 139
Schmitt-Pantel, Pauline, 87
schools (artistic, philosophical), 19, 99, 102, 104, 187, 225
Scott, Michael, 113
seafood, 44, 45, 82–83, 85, 88, 90, 91, 92, 98, 134, 219
sedentariness, 50, 54, 59–60
Selinus, 52, 82, 134–35, 137–38, 140, 226, 228; Sanctuary of Demeter Malaphoros, 52
Selinus (rustic *daimon*), 135
Sennett, Richard, 21
sense of place, 25, 42, 43, 53, 60
senses, 25, 42, 75, 78, 80, 223
Sepeia, 186–87
Seven Pyres, 171
sex, 11, 69, 70, 82, 89, 118, 229
Shetland Islands, 106
Sicily, 9, 41, 43, 51–52, 135, 140, 175
Sikyon, 9, 12, 14–15, 62, 80, 85, 98–99, 102–6, 110, 127–28, 140, 162, 221–25, 231
Simichidas, 207–8, 212
Sinope, 88, 97
sitos, 85, 89, 91
Skillous, 133–36, 227–28
Skiron (bandit and site), 171; Skironian Way, 171
Skiros (mythical king of Salamis), 171
Skotussa, 109
Skourta Plain, 65
Skyros, 9
smell, 78–82, 94, 207, 223
Smith, Michael, 22
Smith, Pamela, 28, 97
Smyrna, 114
Socrates (philosopher), 18, 29–30, 91, 215
Sogenes, 117
Sokrates (of Argos), 172–73, 231
Solon, 77, 217, 223

songs, song culture, 115–18, 120, 143–46, 152. See also *epinikia*
Sourvinou-Inwood, Christiane, 128–30, 155
Sparta, 13, 38, 43, 46, 57–61, 72, 74, 89, 105, 131, 136, 139, 151–52, 173, 182–83, 186–87, 193–94, 196, 204, 208, 211, 216, 224, 229, 232, 235
Sparton, 198, 200, 220
spatial turn, 19, 20, 218
statues, 103, 108–10, 142, 158, 232
Steinbock, Bernd, 183–84, 233
stereotyping, cultural, 78, 82, 87, 90, 95, 224
Stresemann suit, 229
Strymon River, 92
sublocality, 22–23, 24, 31, 217
Susa, 98
Swiss Disease, 25, 47
Sybaris, 76, 126, 222, 227
Syracuse, 38–39, 57, 218
Sythas River, 228

Tanagra, 39, 67, 89, 99–106, 114, 126, 177, 218, 225–27
Taras, Tarentum, 11, 88, 102
taste, 7, 42, 48, 81–85, 87–90, 105, 106, 114, 117, 127, 223
Tegea, 73, 85, 112, 183, 223
Teiresias, 208
Telamon, 118
Telesilla, 173
Telesto, 147
Tellon of Oresthasion, 108–9, 112
Temesa, 111
Tenedos, 114
Teneric Plain, 92, 145
Terpsion, 91
territoriality, 30, 61, 63, 143, 171, 189, 231
Thasos, 88–91, 109, 115, 179, 235
Theagenes (of Megara), 69
Theagenes (of Thasos), 109, 115
Theaios of Argos, 113–14
Thebes, 9, 55–58, 72–73, 79, 92–95, 99, 103, 105, 106, 112–13, 115, 122–23, 126, 138, 144–49, 154, 157, 161–65, 169–75, 179–206, 211, 220, 222, 224, 227, 230, 232–33, 235; Elektran Gate, 145; Temple of Herakles, 145–56
Themistokles, 72
Theognetos, 127
Theognis of Megara, 10, 43, 77, 188
Theokritos, 207–8
theōrodokoi, *theōroi*, 36, 37, 108, 125, 148, 229
Thermopylai, 173–74, 186, 188, 190, 192–93, 205, 232

Thersander, 170
Theseus, 69
Thespiai, 69, 72, 112, 154, 172, 204–5, 217, 221–22, 229, 231, 233–34
Thessaly, 49, 59, 79–80, 89, 114, 118, 205, 224, 226, 233
Thetis, 118
Thisbe, 80
Thomas, Rosalind, 164
Thrace, 29–30, 92, 150, 217, 229
Thriasian Plain, 222
Thucydides, 51, 59, 65, 71, 86, 131, 150, 165–66, 170, 193–99, 204, 229, 233
Thyestes, 121, 122
Tilphossa, 171
Timandros, 190
time-space-continuum, 5, 132
Tiryns, 187
Tober, Daniel, 175
Tolmides, 197, 198
trigger mitts, 28, 105
Triphylia, 69
Troizen, 97, 162–63, 171
Troy, 46, 168, 182

Ukraine, 151

Vancouver, 217
vegetarianism, 95
Vernant, Jean-Pierre, 124
Vlassopoulos, Kostas, 136, 212, 236

Werner, Michael, 20
Western Apache, 230
White, Hayden, 191
wind, 12, 14, 31, 59, 80, 81, 106, 223, 247
wine, 9, 12, 13, 15, 31, 47, 48, 64, 69, 76, 85, 86, 89, 116, 134, 142, 143, 154, 157, 159, 199, 207, 216, 223

Xenophanes of Kolophon, 75–78, 107, 222, 223
Xenophon, 8, 11–15, 18, 96–97, 133–36, 140, 197, 227, 228
Xerxes, 185, 186, 188, 205

Yates, David, 188, 233

Zemon Davis, Natalie, 209
Zeus, 17, 48, 54, 59, 61, 67, 69, 118, 123, 153, 179, 185; Eleutherios, 183; Homarios, 129; Lykaios, 73, 157
Zimmermann, Bénédicte, 20
zodiac, 16–17, 146, 216

www.ingramcontent.com/pod-product-compliance
Lightning Source LLC
Chambersburg PA
CBHW051352290426
44108CB00015B/1986